CLEVELAND
The Best Kept Secret

CLEVELAND
The Best Kept Secret

GEORGE E. CONDON

Garden City, New York

DOUBLEDAY & COMPANY, INC.

1967

Grateful acknowledgment is made to the following for copyrighted material:

Farrar, Straus & Giroux, Inc.
Excerpts from *Briton Hadden,* by Noel F. Busch. Copyright 1949 by Noel F. Busch. Reprinted by permission.

Harcourt, Brace & World, Inc.
Excerpts from *The Autobiography of Lincoln Steffens,* copyright 1931, by Harcourt, Brace & World, Inc.; renewed, 1959, by Peter Steffens. Excerpts from *Lincoln Steffens Speaking,* copyright 1936 by Harcourt, Brace & World, Inc.; renewed, 1964, by Peter Steffens. Reprinted by permission of the publishers.

Harper & Row, Publishers
Excerpts from *Damned Old Crank: A Self-Portrait of E. W. Scripps,* edited by Charles R. McCabe (1951). Reprinted by permission of the publishers.

Dr. H. D. Piercy
Excerpts from *The Valley of God's Pleasure,* by Caroline B. Piercy. Reprinted by permission.

Simon and Schuster, Inc.
Excerpts from *Have Tux, Will Travel,* by Bob Hope. Copyright © 1954 by Curtis Publishing Company, copyright © 1954 by Bob and Dolores Hope Charitable Foundation. Reprinted by permission of Simon and Schuster, Inc., and Frederick Muller Ltd.

THIS BOOK IS DEDICATED TO . . .

Marjorie, Theresa, John, George,
Katherine, Mary, Susan—and, of course,
Mary O'Malley Condon, my mother.
A lovely, patient family.

CONTENTS

INTRODUCTION

Moses led his followers across the Pennsylvania state line and into the Promised Land on July 4, 1796, thereby giving fresh luster to a date already highly illuminated by historic significance. In this case, the wilderness leader was Moses Cleaveland and his followers were surveyors enlisted by the Connecticut Land Company to survey its newly acquired holdings in the Western Reserve—an area called New Connecticut, extending from Pennsylvania to the Cuyahoga River on the west.

General Cleaveland understandably was moved to record the historic arrival in his journal. His entry for that day said, in part:

". . . And after many difficulties perplexities and hardships were surmounted, and we were on the good and promised land, [we] felt that a just tribute of respect to the day ought to be paid. There were in all, including men, women and children, fifty in number. The men, under Captain Tinker ranged themselves on the beach, and fired a Federal salute of fifteen rounds, and then the sixteenth in honor of New Connecticut. We gave three cheers and christened the place Port Independence. Drank several toasts, viz:

"*1st*. The President of the United States.

"*2d*. The State of New Connecticut.

"*3d*. The Connecticut Land Company.

"*4th*. May the Port of Independence and the fifty sons and daughters who have entered it this day be successful and prosperous.

"*5th*. May these sons and daughters multiply in sixteen years sixteen times fifty.

"*6th*. May every person have his bowsprit trimmed and ready to enter every port that opens.

"Closed with three cheers. Drank several pails of grog, supped and retired in remarkable good order."

Looking back, this particular Fourth of July outing presents itself as a rather modest bash, considering all that Cleaveland and his followers had to celebrate. Not only did the day signify the twentieth anniversary of American independence, it also marked an important westward movement by the United States—an entrance into the richly fertile, forested Ohio country to extend the white man's domain some ninety miles further, as far away as the place where the Cuyahoga River meanders into Lake Erie. Here, where the latter-day Moses struck his surveying rods, a city named in his honor quickly gushed forth, but this spectacular achievement never qualified as a miracle. A number of wise men— George Washington, Benjamin Franklin, and a Moravian missionary named John Heckewelder, among them—had spoken favorably of this strategic site. It was more or less expected that one day a city would grow there. And it did.

The thing that nobody could predict accurately was what *kind* of city would spring out of the bulrushes along the Cuyahoga, and since it is now acknowledged to be one of the great cities of the world, it does appear to be high time for a close examination of this city called Cleveland, past and present. That's what this book is all about. It is, admittedly, a sympathetic scrutiny; one which has eyes for the people as much as the place, for how can you divorce one from the other? Wherever possible, I have tried to part the syntax to let some of their laughter slip through as a reminder that Cleveland is their creation. Historians who like to stifle the human side of humanity can accept this as a rebuke.

I have had much help; too much to separate and identify by source in its entirety. Still, I must acknowledge the many helpful contributions of my wife, Marjorie; the typing assistance and research help of my daughter, Theresa Ann Condon, and, in that same department, the invaluable work of Miss Madeline Grimoldi. And there are those old friends who spurred me into writing action when the instinct was strong to flee and take cover—Frank and Ginnie McCullough, Ronald and Katie Robbins. I thank them as I thank all who helped; indeed, as I thank all who, with bowsprits properly trimmed, choose to enter this port with me.

GEORGE E. CONDON

Cleveland, Ohio

CLEVELAND
The Best Kept Secret

I

The Muscovite's Delight

ANASTAS MIKOYAN, an Armenian who made good in politics by becoming President of the Union of Soviet Socialist Republics, once visited Cleveland, and it is said he was visibly moved by his first glimpse of the Lake Erie metropolis. Reporters who stood close to him as he looked at the downtown skyline swear that the old Communist's mustache twitched and his eyes were misty as he raised an arm in comradely approbation and said:

"Now you're talking! This is *my* kind of town!"

That may or may not be a completely accurate quotation because even the best encomiums have a way of losing something in the translation. But that, roughly, is what Mikoyan said, and it is obviously the way Mikoyan felt. And even if you subtract something for the fact that Armenians are highly emotional, this reaction is owed the proper appreciation that every hard-won compliment deserves, and more, some scholarly inquiry.

The fact is that Clevelanders themselves took Mr. Mikoyan's heavy flattery in stride. It was something they had come to expect because other earlier visitors from the U.S.S.R. upon visiting Cleveland for the first time had spoken out vigorously in approval of Ohio's largest city. The touring Communists almost unanimously have compared it with New York City and other effete communities to the east, entirely to the disadvantage of those cities.

It helps if you understand that Cleveland is—or was—one of the recommended stopping-off places in America for Russian tourists; a "must" attraction on the Intourist list of Places to See in the Imperialist West. There are some obvious factors which would make the city attractive to those visitors. It is a great industrial center and, plainly, the home of a lot of working men and women. It is also the home of Cyrus Eaton, one of the paradoxical celebrities of our time—the man who is perhaps the last survivor of the Age of Tycoons, a capitalist's capitalist, and, withal, the great and good friend of the Soviet Union.

However this puzzling mixture of identities resolves itself, there is no doubt that Cyrus Eaton commands great respect from the leaders of the

Communist world. It used to be that no Soviet representative visiting the United States would think about going home to face the Central Presidium without having paid a courtesy call on Eaton. Consequently, the traffic in Soviet delegations traveling in and out of Cleveland used to be very brisk until the United States Government, in a fit of pique over the action of the U.S.S.R. in limiting the travel of Americans, ruled Cleveland out-of-bounds for all Russians, except when granted special permission.

Until this regrettable breakdown in international relations occurred, Clevelanders had become accustomed to the sight of the visiting Russian firemen, and had found a uniform pattern of approval in the Russians' attitudes and reactions.

Most of the Reds came into the Best Location in the Nation (as the Cleveland electric utility extravagantly describes the city in its advertising literature) looking like second-rate imitations of Andrei Gromyko on one of his bad days at the United Nations; that is to say, with a dark, glowering, beetle-browed visage, more commonly associated in the United States with morning backache.

But Cleveland has some very strong medicine that wipes the scowl off the Russian countenance and puts a happy smile in its place every time. It's a building called the Terminal Tower. When the average Russian sees it for the first time he is in danger of losing control of his emotions. There is no question whatsoever that the Terminal Tower has a headier effect on a homesick Muscovite than a jug of vodka spiked with four-way cold tablets. It chases the vapors, establishes regularity, restores skin tone, and otherwise energizes the Russian onlooker. There have been Reds occasionally who have lost their composure entirely and reacted by giving their comrades violent bear hugs, the popular expression of Russian approval. That sort of enthusiasm is highly contagious, of course, and it isn't surprising that once in a while the Russians dropped to their haunches for a quick kazatsky, the traditional folk dance of their country, kicking out their legs with great agility and shouting unintelligible lyrics of an old Soviet hit ballad about a farm tractor.

People who are not familiar with Cleveland surely must be wondering about this point just what the Terminal Tower has to do with international politics. They will be wondering, at the very least, how a mere building possibly could arouse our usually phlegmatic adversaries in the world arena to a state of unhinged delight bordering on complete giddiness.

The answer, of course, is that the Terminal Tower is not an ordinary building. It is a very uncommon structure. They don't build buildings any more the way the Terminal Tower was built. It is not one of those straight up-and-down rectangular-shaped slabs, nor is it one of those glass wall buildings with the general conformation of a box of soap chips. The Terminal Tower is a classic structure of its type. It is built along the lines of a tiered wedding cake, complete with frosting and candles. It is Cleveland's most conspicuous landmark, a spire of neo-Gothic design which rises some fifty-two stories and some 708 feet high above the city. There was a time, indeed, when it was known as the tallest building in all the world outside of New York City.

Architects and other building fanciers will find such information about the Terminal Tower important—perhaps even fascinating. Still, the points cited are not the kind of attributes calculated to make a real dent in the Slavic mind. There has to be something more important about the Terminal Tower, and there is. The key to the building's fascination is that it bears a remarkable resemblance to the skyscraper tower of Moscow University in—where else?—Moscow, Russia, U.S.S.R.

The Russian counterpart of the Terminal Tower is only twelve feet higher, and there is no denying that the architecture and the general appearance of the two buildings bear a close similarity—so much so that every Russian who visits Cleveland immediately is smitten with an overpowering attack of homesickness. This is the reason for the strange and excited behavior of all the Soviet delegations upon their arrival in the city.

None of the Russians ever have come right out and said as much, but you get the inescapable impression, from the sly winks and nods and digging of elbows into each other's stomachs while toasting Cyrus Eaton's troika horses, that the Russians really and truly believe that they are the ones who invented the Terminal Tower.

Nothing could be farther from the truth, and every single Clevelander worth his salt (and all Clevelanders, incidentally, are rich in salt, but more about that later) resents the implied Soviet claim.

The established truth is that the Terminal Tower was invented by a pair of Americans, two brothers who made their homes, their reputations, and their fortunes in Cleveland. Their names were O. P. and M. J. Van Sweringen, and there is no room for shilly-shallying or beating around the bush when you talk about the Vans. They were a pair of genuine capitalists.

All Clevelanders are aware that the Van Sweringens were responsible for the design and construction of the city's leading landmark and, to a man, they resent any sly insinuations by the Russians to the contrary. The indignation runs especially high among members of the very exclusive Union Club. The Union Clubbers are morose enough just thinking about Cyrus Eaton, without being flicked by this added provocation. One of the things about Cyrus Eaton that makes his fellow Union Clubbers morose, apart from the fact that he is smarter and richer than they are, is his past insistence on entertaining some of his Soviet friends in the parlors of the club. Some of them feel that this was a very cheeky thing for him to do.

It would be a terrible mistake, however, to believe that the only things in Cleveland that the Russians like are the Terminal Tower and Cyrus Eaton. The appreciation of the foreign visitors runs deeper than that. Cleveland is a formidable city. It is a city with the biceps of industry and it has a rough-hewn manner that is indigenous to the Midwest of America. Cleveland also has some of the charm and grace of an old European city and, withal, it shows indisputable traces of its New England heritage as no other city west of the Alleghenies does.

The muzhik pulses pound when the Russians see the entire sweep of the industrial Cuyahoga River valley which twists and turns its way through the entire city, coming in from the southeast and ending at Lake Erie at a point which is virtually the geographical center of the city. This is the northern anchor of that area of incredibly heavy industrial production called the American Ruhr. The axis of the region extends from Lake Erie through Cleveland, Akron, Warren, Youngstown, and all the way to Pittsburgh.

Beauty does indeed rest in the eyes of the beholder, and there is a muscular, dynamic, sullen beauty in this industrial valley which is known to most Clevelanders simply as "the Flats." Margaret Bourke White, the distinguished photographer, fell in love with the Flats when she was a young student at Western Reserve University. She saw beauty, photographically speaking, where none had seen it before, and her classic pictures of the steel mills, the machinery, and the smoking stacks were an artistic revelation and even something of a revolution.

It must be said that Miss White had great material to work with when she took her cameras down into the Flats. There are few such concentrations of industrial might anywhere in the world, and the grouping is spectacular. Little wonder that the Russians respect Cleveland. They understand as few other peoples do the significance of the smoking, sprawling steel mills, the flame-topped towers of the gasoline catalytic cracking plants, the red hills of iron ore stacked along the banks, and the bulky freighters angling their way up and down the river, and, of course, the night-and-day caravans of thousands of laborers up and down the steep roads leading to and from the valley.

It is at night that the Flats show off at their very best—especially when the clouds hang heavy and low over the city, giving the open-hearth steel furnaces flaring below a sky-screen against which to project their flickering glare. It is a sight that never gets tiresome to people of the city because they know that when the underbelly of the clouds shines with rubious light at night, it is the healthy glow of industry that is reflected. Even apart from this unromantic interpretation there is the simple fact of beauty in being, a condition which needs no explanation.

There is no satisfactory way to describe a city or to convey its spirit in words. Facts and statistics, names and dates, prose and poesy all are well-intentioned bids to give flesh and breath to a chunk of real estate, but they hang lifelessly on the skeleton. If there is a way to give life to a city with words, those words must try to renew some of the lives that created the city. This is the route I chose to follow, ignoring all the commandments of the Chamber of Commerce, skirting around most of the treasured civic boasts, and searching out, as diligently as I could, the rare good men and the rogues alike, fast in the belief that where I found them, I would find Cleveland.

I cannot forget the words of a New Yorker who ventured as far west as Cleveland a few years ago. He looked at the vast sweep of the forested city, the soft gray-blue lake lapping at the foot of the high bluffs, the ubiquitous placement of beautiful residential neighborhoods and parks, and he blinked.

"This Cleveland," he said, pondering, "has to be the best kept secret in the United States."

What he meant to say, of course, was that it was a secret to other Americans. Not the Russians. That is one thing you have to say about those Russians—they are very quick to notice a good thing like Cleveland.

II

Cleave as in Cleaveland

CLEVELAND was founded by a man named Moses Cleaveland, and the similarity of names is more than just a coincidence. The city took its name from its founder, but somewhere along the way very early in the game the townspeople changed the spelling, summarily dropping an "a" from the name.

Literary societies and other study groups still like to argue over the significance of this name change, and some purists remain in something of a snit because of the variation. They say it reflects on the ability of Clevelanders to spell. The fact is, the "a" in Cleaveland was sort of a surplus letter anyway, and its elimination had no effect whatsoever in the pronunciation of the name. It was expendable, even if it was dropped—as the legend has it—by a newspaper editor who was short an "a" in his font of type. That is a rather unexciting explanation for the variation; one which does not compare at all with the story that the "a" was dropped deliberately by the independent-minded colonists by way of striking back at some of the snobs from the East who dropped in on their wilderness outpost from time to time. The New Englanders made it a point then, even as they do today, of dropping the letter "r" from words wherever they could. Clevelanders showed them that two could play at that game, not only in the cavalier way they changed the spelling of Cleaveland, but also in the summary treatment they gave the name of Aaron Olmstead, a stockholder in the real estate company that staked out the city. Several communities in the modern metropolitan area bear Olmstead's name—almost. They are Olmsted Falls, Olmsted Township, and North Olmsted. As in the case of Cleaveland, the "a" was dropped from Olmstead's name; given short shrift by clear-eyed, economy-minded, straight-thinking pioneers who saw no purpose in carrying letters that served no useful function.

It is not known that Moses Cleaveland himself ever protested the tampering with the spelling of his name, or even cared. Moses was not the sentimental kind of a city-founder. Once he had nailed down the site of Cleveland in 1796, surveyed its limits, and laid out its street plan, he hightailed it back to his comfortable Connecticut home, never more to return. Altogether, he spent no more than a month in the town named for him.

"While I was in New Connecticut," he later wrote, in a report of his adventure, "I laid out a town on the bank of Lake Erie which was called by my name, and I believe the child is now born that may live to see that place as large as Old Windham (Conn.)."

Cleaveland, as we know, was a conservative prophet. The latest population check shows that Cleveland has not only grown as large as Old Windham (now just Windham), it has even managed to pass that eastern metropolis. The latest available population count, that of 1960, showed Windham with 16,973 persons, compared with Cleveland's 876,050.

There is an organization of civic boosters today which is known as the Come-to-Cleveland Committee, and it has the devil's own time trying to explain why Moses took it on the lam the way he did. Some of them say, privately, it would have served the founding father right if more than the "a" had been dropped from his name.

One of the best analyses of Moses' defection points out that he was a Yale man, Class of 1777, and reasons that he naturally wanted to hustle back home in 1797 for the fun and games at the twentieth annual reunion of his class. There's absolutely no factual evidence supporting this theory, but it is rendered acceptable by the fantastic devotion of Yale men everywhere to class reunions.

Some historians say that founding Cleveland was the smartest thing that Cleaveland ever did in an otherwise humdrum career in which he served as a brigadier general of the Connecticut militia, a state representative, and a lawyer. If so, the second smartest thing that he ever did was to get himself named Moses Cleaveland.

The surname, in this case, is everything. The Moses part is inconsequential. The course of American history would not have been affected one whit if Moses had been named, instead, Titus, or Elijah, or even Charlie. If, on the other hand, his surname had been Abernathy, or Cadwallader, or Frothingham, the Forest City would have been right up a tree for a name.

The thing is, Cleveland had to be named Cleveland. No other name would serve. Under the physical and civic circumstances that prevail in Cleveland, any other name would have been unthinkable.

Consider the astonishing coincidence:

Moses Cleaveland was the second son of Aaron and Thankful Paine Cleaveland, descendants of an English family whose home seat was in Yorkshire. They had owned the surname since a time prior to the Norman conquest, and it is reasonable to assume that they took their family name from their large estate. The most prominent physical characteristic of the land was its numerous fissures which were called clefts, or cleves, by the Saxons. The landholders aptly were named Clefflands, Cleves, or Cleaveland.

Now everyone who has visited the city named Cleveland, Ohio, knows that one thing the city has, if nothing else, is cleavage. It is there for everybody to see. This is municipal décolletage with a vengeance. Cleveland is cleaved right down the middle by an eccentric river called the Cuyahoga. The Cuyahoga River valley is a fissure to end all fissures and its influence on the city cannot be underestimated. Without it, Cleveland would be nothing. But while the valley has contributed richly to the industrial and commercial strength of the community, it also has been a divisive force, splitting the town in twain. Cleveland should be regarded rightly as two separate entities with only tenuous cultural and commercial connections and virtually no diplomatic relations. These two entities are the East Side and the West Side.

For one reason or other, there really is no south side or north side. Lake Erie lies to the north of the city and except for a few hardy swimmers, a couple of men tending the Five Mile Crib (a water inlet which is only four miles out in the lake), and a handful of Coast Guardsmen, the population count on the north side is negligible. The people who live on the south side are numerous, but they won't call themselves South Siders. They count themselves either as East Siders or West Siders, depending on which side of the Cuyahoga they happen to be living on. Perhaps it is just as well that the situation should be thus simplified. It is complicated enough as it stands, especially having a dividing line like the Cuyahoga River.

An honest, sensible dividing line should be relatively straight so that everybody would know where he stands. This is not much to ask of a line, really. But if a city were to set out in a deliberate search for the world's worst dividing line, the Cuyahoga River would win hands down. Its very name suggests as much. Cuyahoga is an Indian word meaning "crooked," which it certainly is. I hope the news does not come as too much of a shock to certain business enterprises which have borrowed the picturesque word.

It would not be inaccurate to describe the Cuyahoga as a meandering river, but the description certainly would be inadequate. It is a river which twists and turns at ninety-degree angles; whose forward movement can be toward any given point on the compass at any given place, but which somehow, miraculously, manages to proceed from the south to north in a lurching, staggering, splay-footed way that has commanded the respect and attention of geologists, mariners, and plain, old-fashioned river rats everywhere.

There is no more interesting maritime sight anywhere than the sight of a six- or seven-hundred-foot-long ore boat making its way up and down the river. Rounding some bends, the prow will be touching the east bank while the stern is scraping the west bank. The crookedness of the river results in some strange situations wherein some East Siders actually find themselves living to the west of some West Siders, and vice versa. The all-important consideration for Clevelanders, however, is to determine which side of the river they are on. All other geographical issues are relatively unimportant.

The original plan laying out the town did not consider the river as the east-west dividing line because it contemplated a community which would be entirely on the east side of the river. The Indians still held title to the land west of the winding waters. The center of the city then, as now, was the Public Square, a ten-acre meadow.

Officially, Ontario Street, which runs through the center of Public Square, is the line that divides east from west, but it is not a realistic boundary and is honored as such only in name. Even City Hall knows this to be true because there is a question on the municipal civil service test which asks, slyly, on which side of the city, east or west, the tallest building in Cleveland may be found. Almost everybody falls in the trap by identifying the tallest building as the Terminal Tower and placing it on the east side. The answer is wrong. The building is west of Ontario Street, and, technically, is on the west side.

For all practical purposes, though—and hang the technicalities—everything east of the river constitutes the East Side. Everything west of the river can be considered the West Side. That is the realistic view taken by Clevelanders.

When two Clevelanders meet for the first time, they fence conversationally until the vital question of East or West is answered. Knowing which side of town a new acquaintance comes from makes a subtle difference. It is a starting point in the effort to understand one another. Which raises the point that, considering the divisive nature of the city and the civic ambivalence that prevails, East Siders and West Siders get along together rather well. There is hardly any outspoken acrimony any more. It was not always thus.

The East Siders are so deeply convinced that they have all the better of it that they pity West Siders more than they resent them. When the average East Sider looks at the average West Sider, a troubled look comes upon his face. It's approximately the same look that you see on the faces of members of the church congregation as the minister or priest reminds them of the underprivileged tribes along the Amazon and the need for renewed missionary efforts. It is a look that windows a troubled conscience.

Curiously enough, the West Siders don't consider themselves underprivileged at all. They have had their choice of both sides of the city and they have chosen. Many of them, not illogically, will tell you that they are the real winners in the civic game of choosing up sides even as they concede that the area across the river has the new freeways, the lush country clubs, the sophisticated night clubs, the fanciest restaurants, the richest suburbs, the most beautiful homes, the wealthiest families and virtually all of the major cultural assets of the city (including the home of the famous Cleveland Orchestra), the four major universities, the community college, the Cleveland Play House, the Art Museum, and a long list of other attractions.

"No question," admit West Siders, "the East Side is a nice place to visit, but we'd hate to live there."

The West Side, conversely, is not much for visiting, but it is a good place for day-to-day living.

It is this very charming simplicity that disarms most of the East Siders and leaves them spluttering for a reasonable reply. With the mighty concentration of wealth and culture that is to be found east of the river, of course, they have an overwhelming argument in their favor, but they never seem to use it. Ask an East Sider why he lives where he does, and he will use a stock answer that, however puerile, is very popular.

"People who live on the West Side," he will say, "drive into the sun in the morning. This is bad enough, but then when they are driving home after work, there is the very same sun shining right into their eyes again. Tch. Tch. Twice a day they have to drive into the sun! I don't know how they do it. It's a wonder they aren't all blind!

"East Siders, on the other hand, hardly ever find themselves driving into the sun, except maybe as a personal whim. Nosiree. The sun is at their backs in the morning and it's at their backs in the late afternoon. Man, that's the way to live! With the sun at your back!"

Otherwise sensible, rational people find themselves talking that way after they have lived in Cleveland for a while. It's an infectious sort of thing, this East Side-West Side argument, and it has been going on for a long time.

The Cuyahoga River has been dividing people as far back as historical research can reach—even into the times when the Indians held dominion over the rich forests and waters of the Western Reserve.

Previous to the arrival of the white man, the Iroquois Indians controlled the territory east of the Cuyahoga (or "Cayahoga"). The area west of the river belonged to the Hurons. The river was their boundary line, too, you see.

According to agreements concluded by Moses Cleaveland with the Indian leaders at conferences held near Buffalo, New York, and at Conneaut, en route to the site of the new colony at the mouth of the river, the colonization of the Connecticut Land Company would be confined to the east bank of the Cuyahoga. The Indians would retain control and ownership of the western lands across the river.

With this in mind, Moses must have been plunged into deep, brooding thought when, upon arriving at the mouth of the Cuyahoga, he and his men beheld a cabin snuggled comfortably against the hill on the west bank of the river.

The cabin of rough-hewn timbers was that of a fur trading outfit, the North-West Fur Company, allegedly an enterprise of the Astor family. The legend has it that the cabin had been built in the wilderness about 1785, give or take a year, when this was completely Indian country. The story of the Astor connection is unlikely, but popularly accepted nevertheless.

Finding the cabin there, in the heart of the wilderness, must have given the exploring party the same kind of anticlimactic sensation that a lunar expedition would feel as its rocket ship settled to the pock-marked surface of the moon—narrowly missing a busy delicatessen. The cabin, which came to be known as "The Astor House," was around Cleveland for a long time thereafter, but the crude, historic little hut was given cruel treatment. It was moved from place to place, and finally was torn down in 1922 in one of those typically American gestures of disdain for relics of the past. But West Siders never get tired of reminding the East Siders that the very first house to be built in the city was placed on their side of the river, and that the East Side is something of a Johnny-come-lately part of town.

History, reduced to its basics, is one big real estate transaction after another. Cleveland's founding is a splendid example.

The story begins with the formation of the Connecticut Land Company, a syndicate of forty-nine men of substance, which successfully negotiated with a state commission for the purchase of approximately three million acres of Connecticut-owned land in the Western Reserve of the Ohio country. The bargain was arrived at on September 2, 1795.

Even in a day when land literally was dirt cheap in the United States, this was a remarkably good deal for the Connecticut investors. The price their company paid for a territory ranging from the Pennsylvania state line on the east to the Cuyahoga River on the west averaged about forty cents an acre.

The names of the forty-nine land speculators are worth the listing for several reasons. One is that many of them have come down to this generation as significant names still in the modern community, giving proof that the ties that bind a New Englander to his investment are stronger than the toughest hemp. There is also something definitely revealing in any coupling of these names with Cleveland of today. The rolling thunder of all the Biblical names tells us of stern-visaged, severe Puritans; of frugal, hard-working, simple-living men. Out of such stock does not emerge a Paris or a Vienna.

The investors included Joseph Howland, Daniel L. Coit, Elias Morgan, Caleb Atwater, Daniel Holbrook, Joseph Williams, William Love, William Judd, Elisha Hyde, Uriah Tracey, James Johnston, Samuel Mather, Jr., Ephraim Kirby, Elijah Boardman, Uriel Holmes, Jr., Solomon Griswold, Oliver Phelps, Gideon Granger, Jr., William Hart, Henry Champion II, Asher Miller, Robert C. Johnson, Ephraim Root, Nehemiah Hubbard, Jr., Solomon Cowles, Asahel Hathaway, John Caldwell, Peleg Sanford, Timothy Burr, Luther Loomis, Ebenezer King, Jr., William Lyman, John Stoddard, David King, Moses Cleaveland, Samuel P. Lord, Roger Newberry, Enoch Perkins, Jonathan Brace, Ephraim Starr, Sylvanus Griswold, Joseb Stocking, Joshua Stow, Titus Street, James Bull, Aaron Olmstead, John Wyles, Pierpoint Edwards, and Samuel W. Johnson.

Selected from this group to be members of the board of directors were Moses Cleaveland of Canterbury, Oliver Phelps of Suffield, Henry Champion II of Colchester, Samuel W. Johnson, Ephraim Kirby, Samuel Mather, Jr., of Lynn, and Roger Newberry of West Windsor.

The vast tract of western land that had come under the proprietary control of the Connecticut Land Company was dubbed "New Connecticut," and there was serious talk that the company might just go into the state business for itself. Pending this happy development, the company would go on running the vast territory as a kind of absentee government with its capital in Hartford, Connecticut, a long way from the kinky Cuyahoga. After all, New England itself had experienced the rule of a far-off government for a long time up to the Revolutionary War and ostensibly understood all the intricacies of such an arrangement.

The first order of the day, of course, was to sell some of the real estate in Ohio and thus achieve two fundamental aims: A return on the investment and the colonization of the territory. It's precisely the same situation that faces any enterprising real estate developer today, except that there are few land companies now which have to cope with unfriendly Indians and unexplored wilderness.

To deal with the Indians, whatever claims the redskins may have held to the lands purchased by the Connecticut investors, and survey the three-million-acre empire so that it could be subdivided into lots, the Connecticut Land Company turned to Moses Cleaveland.

Cleaveland, already one of the investors and a director of the company, was named general agent of a company expedition which would open the Western Reserve to settlers. His chief assistants were Augustus Porter of Salisbury, principal surveyor and deputy superintendent; Seth Pease, astronomer and surveyor; Amos Spafford, John Milton Holley, Richard M. Stoddard, and Moses Warren, Jr., all surveyors. Joshua Stow was commissary and Theodore Shepard, physician.

Two married couples accompanied the party, Elijah and Anna Gun, and Job P. Stiles and his wife, Tabitha Cumi. The Guns would take charge of Stow's supply station at Conneaut, while Job and Tabitha would go on to a certain kind of immortality as the first husband and wife to live on the site of Cleveland, which is where they would spend the winter of 1796–97, tending the company's supply stores there.

Economists, politicians, geographers, and geologists all have their own explanations for the success of the Cleveland colony, and some of their reasons are rather well thought out, but my own theory is that the little settlement was imparted undying strength by the ordinary employees of Moses Cleaveland's expedition. There were thirty-seven of them, and their names sing of the virility of early America. The roll call has the rhythm and meter of great poetry, enough to make you tap your toes, and you can see their wonderful, weatherbeaten grizzled faces, if you try, grinning through the cold formality of the records that dismiss them simply as "Employees of the Company."

These employee-heroes who hacked through the forests and pushed through the thickets, carrying the frontier with them as they changed the map of the world, included:

Joseph Tinker, boatman; George Proudfoot, Samuel Forbes, Stephen Benton, Samuel Hungerford, Samuel Davenport, Amzi Atwater, Elisha Ayres, Norman Wilcox, George Gooding, Samuel Agnew, David Beard, Titus V. Munson, Charles Parker, Nathaniel Doan, James Halket, Olney F. Rice, Samuel Barnes, Daniel Shulay, Joseph M'Intyre, Francis Gray, Amos Sawtel, Amos Barber, William B. Hall, Asa Mason, Michael Coffin, Thomas Harris, Timothy Dunham, Shadrach Benham, Wareham Shepard, John Briant, Joseph Landon, Ezekiel Morly, Luke Hanchet, James Hamilton, John Lock, Stephen Burbank.

Moses Cleaveland himself must have been among the most interesting men of the expedition. He was forty-one years old and, by all accounts, a man who did not have any truck with the lighter, frivolous things in life. All his biographers agree in describing him as a stocky man, tending toward stoutness, but powerful in physique with the thick legs of the outdoors type and a swarthy complexion. One of his men, Amzi Atwater, recalled that Cleaveland "furnished himself with an Indian dress and afforded an excellent likeness of an Indian chief . . ."

There never has been any question but that Cleaveland was the strong man of the surveying party, and perhaps the strong man of the entire Connecticut Land Company. It was agreed before his group left for the western wilderness, at any rate, that he should establish a capital city for New Connecticut at the place where the Cuyahoga River joined Lake Erie, and that the capital city should bear the name of "Cleaveland." And, presumably to elevate his prestige and to implement his authority further, Connecticut made Cleaveland a general in the state militia in 1795, just prior to the expedition.

Before anything else, however, Cleaveland had the duty, in the delicate phraseology of the Connecticut businessmen, "to extinguish" the Indian claims to the vast area of land reaching to the Cuyahoga. Cleaveland was adequate to the challenge. He didn't merely extinguish the claims to the land held by the Indians over so many centuries; he doused, soaked, and inundated the claims with a torrent of fine words, a flood of whiskey, and a trickle of money. In New England bargaining circles, they still talk of Cleaveland's shrewd and economical handling of what could have been a rather sticky situation, and they speak his name with same respect accorded Peter Minuit by the Dutch for his Manhattan coup.

The deal took place with the arrival of Cleaveland's band at Buffalo Creek in New York State. There, waiting to talk over the crisis brought about by the impending westward movement of the white men, were representatives of the Six Nations of the Iroquois Confederation. The meetings began on June 21, 1796, and ended four days later.

Such accounts of the conference as are available indicate it was a pretty good party, not one of those stuffy affairs where everybody sits around the campfire grunting and staring into the flames. Moses and his men had been thoughtful enough to bring with them a plentiful supply of whiskey, and the Indians were thirsty. It was a busy four days. When the Indians weren't drinking or dickering with the white men, they insisted on doing ceremonial dances. And there probably was a certain amount of good-natured joshing over how swarthy Moses Cleaveland's complexion was, and how much he looked like an Indian himself, although the historians don't come right out and say as much. It's one of those things you instinctively read between the lines.

The deal finally was arranged, and, after another conference at Conneaut, the question of the ownership of three million choice acres of American land was settled in this wise: The Indian leaders relinquished their claims to all the lands from the Pennsylvania line to the Cuyahoga River, some seventy-five miles deep into the Ohio country, in return for five hundred pounds in New York currency, two beef cattle, and one hundred gallons of whiskey.

There must have been some ceremonial dancing in the streets back in Connecticut when Cleaveland sent back word of the bargain. This was the key arrangement, aside from its cheapness, upon which hinged the quick success of the Western Reserve real estate speculation. As is well known, real estate prospects have a way of getting skittish and offering incredible sales resistance when there is any kind of a cloud on the land title, or when there is a possibility that the housewarming may begin with a shower of flaming arrows.

The expedition now was free to move into the Ohio country and to undertake its major work, that of surveying the millions of acres in the land company's empire. It was a gigantic, exhausting, dangerous chore—so demanding that it was summer's end before Cleaveland and his assistants got around to discovering Cleveland. Even so, a funny thing happened to them on their way to the site.

While some members of the group continued with their surveying duties, Cleaveland and a select party moved westward by water. They rode in a large, open bateau which they kept close to the southern shore of Lake Erie as they searched for the mouth of the Cuyahoga River. Their vigil was rewarded when, suddenly, they came on a large, attractive river spilling into the lake.

The bateau careened in a sharp left turn and started up the river while the New Englanders sent their joyous cries ringing across the water and into the forest fastness. After a while, though, the river began to narrow, and the growing suspicion that they were birchbarking up the wrong creek finally became conviction. Cleaveland ordered the boat turned around, but not before he or some other imaginative member of the party had dubbed the waterway, the Chagrin River. It was a meaningful monicker; an appropriate name to memorialize the disappointment.

Some spoilsports among the historians say otherwise. They reject this account with the contention that the name of the Chagrin River—which is, incidentally, just east of Cleveland in Geauga County—really stemmed from an old Indian name, either Shagrin or Shaguin, meaning "clear water." In pushing such a preposterous theory, of course, they have succeeded in doing nothing more than muddying the water. The chances are, anyway, that if Cleaveland only had been less impulsive and had curbed his well-known weakness for naming every river that popped into view, he probably would have reserved the graphic name of the Chagrin River for the Cuyahoga River. To this very day, the polluted Cuyahoga is a source of deep chagrin to Clevelanders and to almost everyone else who sees it or sails upon it.

The founding party finally did arrive at the site of Cleveland in mid-September 1796, and debarked at what is today the foot of St. Clair Avenue on the east bank of the steep-sided river. And if the party paused in silent dismay at the sight that immediately greeted its eyes, that would have been entirely understandable. It was obvious that an awful lot of work would have to be done to make this place fit for human habitation.

This Cuyahoga Valley was not, from early descriptions, a cheerful, inviting retreat. Its river was no restful stream flowing through green-meadowed banks, but a river that was darkened by the shadows of the flanking hills, smelling of the bogs and swampland that prevailed to either side. There was the odor of decay and miasma that spelled out its own warning of the dreaded malaria. Shortly after their arrival, two members of the surveying party, John Holley and Titus Munson, caught a rattlesnake on the riverbank, boiled it, and ate it.

This was the untampered, untouched wilderness. High above the eastern bank of the river was the virgin forest of chestnut, oak, walnut, ash, and sugar maple trees that covered the land in thick assembly and tufted the heights. The view above contrasted with the gloom of the valley, and it was, all in all, a splendid outcropping of natural beauty, yet a formidable site for men in search of a foothold on the land.

And there was the river, which their knowing eyes told them was of incalculable value. It was broad and navigable upstream for a distance of at least five miles, however tortuous its watery trail to the south. Eventually it narrowed, but it was reasonably easy portage over the continental divide to a connection with the mighty Muskingum River that flowed to the Ohio, the major waterway linking the eastern states with the west and the south.

And, finally, there was Lake Erie itself; an inland sea broad and deep, ringed with natural riches; one of the world's great bodies of fresh water.

The junction of these two, the river and the lake, had to be the site of a city. The wise people of the time knew it from looking at a crude map. George Washington had said so. Benjamin Franklin had said so. And now Moses Cleaveland said so and contributed the conversational stopper.

He put Cleveland there. Right where it belonged.

It really is not the easiest job in the world, this founding of a city, and that fact alone sets Moses Cleaveland apart from the rank and file of humanity. He is even more deserving of respect for the dispatch and efficiency with which he went about his founding duties.

Approximately a month after the landing of the pioneer group, the town had been surveyed, its street plan fairly well established, and a couple of cabins built. The Cleaveland party then took its leave.

It may have been a new world's record for starting a new city in the midst of the wilderness, but Moses was a man with a mission; a Connecticut Yankee who moved simply and directly toward his established goals. In this instance, the goal was the creation of a community. No time was lost, obviously, in grandiose dreams. Cleaveland and his principal assistants—Augustus Porter, Seth Pease, and Amos Spafford—took note of the terrain and then, simply, tried to superimpose on the site a conventional New England town with its grid pattern of streets assembled in orderly, mathematic array about a traditional centerpiece of community land for use as a park, the grazing of cattle, or the assembly of the people. Cleveland's commons, or public square, was laid out as a ten-acre area into which would lead two principal thoroughfares, Superior Avenue (running east and west) and Ontario Street (north and south).

It was a conventional layout and one which certainly should have been expected to issue from its developers in the light of their background and their own community environment. But they were surprisingly progressive and farsighted in at least one respect, that being the generous measure of the streets they gave the embryo town. Superior Avenue, for example, was paced off at 132 feet in its width, dimensions of boulevard quality, while Ontario Street was planned to have a width of ninety feet.

The modern city has benefited tremendously by the liberality of those pioneer planners in the matter of street width, and the broad streets are among Cleveland's outstanding features to this day. There is no ready explanation why Cleaveland and his men should have departed from the path of probability, which would have meant narrow avenues, but a major city today is grateful that they did.

Another point of wonderment—even astonishment—is that in the matter of only three or four weeks, these men should have so definitely fixed the city's pattern of growth and development for the future. Good or bad, the plan was followed, and even as you look at the first primitive layout, called the "Original Plan of the Town and Village of Cleaveland, Ohio, October 1st, 1796," you can instantly recognize the outline of downtown Cleveland, Ohio, October 1st, 1967.

On October 20, Cleaveland and his men, the main part of their surveying-planning work completed, took their leave of the forest camp. Mr. and Mrs. Stiles and, briefly, Joseph Landon, stayed behind to watch over the supplies. Landon, as previously mentioned, soon took his leave, too, and was replaced by Edward Paine, who wandered in from the east.

This casual coming and going in the great western wilderness must be a subject of everlasting amazement to anyone who takes the time to consider the distances involved in traveling, say, from New York or New England to northeastern Ohio, not to mention the absence of roads and the lack of traveling facilities beyond the horse and wagon. But people did manage to make their way back and forth and one, apparently, never knew when some old friend from a faraway place would pop in for a little socializing, a bit of venison and, perhaps, a spot of Old Monongahela.

If Moses Cleaveland and his men seemed a trifle quick in the way they sped through the surveying and planning of the new town on the lake, it might be well to remember that they had spent a fairly rugged half-year living in and off the wilderness, and that they had done an incredibly large job of surveying in such a short time.

They were tired, no question, and they were homesick. Those were two very good reasons for hastening back to Connecticut, and an even larger reason was the warning of the calendar. There is no more admirable weather anywhere in all the world than October in Ohio, but November is a month of a different color and a different temper. November in Ohio is when the sky comes on gray and the clouds pile up. It is when the trees lose the last of the leaves that blazoned so brilliantly only weeks before, and the bare branches click in the chill winds that suddenly blow out of the northwest, putting whitecaps on the waters of Lake Erie. It is when the first snow flies and the ground underneath gets hard and crusty. It is when travelers had best be moving on.

There is no indication in the literature of the city that Moses Cleaveland felt any real pang in his parting with the forest site which would support the city bearing his name. There is nothing to say that he did any more than give a last sweeping look at the florid hardwood forest that covered the table land overlooking the river and the lake before he hunched his stocky shoulders and turned to the east, never to return.

Cleveland dutifully has recognized its obligation to this taciturn pioneer with a large bronze statue which occupies the center position in the southwest quadrant of the modern Public Square. It was erected July 23, 1888, by the Early Settlers Association. It has a polished granite base 7½ feet high which is surmounted by a statue of the general, 7¾ feet high and 1450 pounds heavy. He stands there in heroic posture, the Jacob's staff of the surveyor in his right hand and an old-fashioned compass clasped in the crook of his left elbow, while the roaring traffic of the city swirls about him and the soft, blue haze of the exhaust fumes settles gently on his broad shoulders.

There is an unanswered question here as to how far a city—any city— properly should extend itself in filial devotion to its founding father. Cleveland showed the soft streak in 1899 when two of its citizens, Mr. and Mrs. Elroy M. Avery, attempted a pilgrimage to the grave of Moses Cleaveland near Canterbury, Connecticut. Upon reaching the scene, they were given instructions by the bemused villagers which required them to leave the road, to cross a cornfield, and then to climb a rough stone wall before they reached the old burial ground. It was, plainly, a neglected graveyard. Weeds covered most of the lot, and many of the stone markers tilted in sad disarray. There was a path through the weeds and it twisted among memorial markers whose lettering was almost obliterated by the muddy covering of the years. One such slab, carefully scraped free of grime, revealed the inscription: "Gen. Moses Cleaveland. Died Nov. 16, 1806. Aged 52."

Nearby were graves of his parents and of "Esther, Relict of Moses Cleaveland, Esq. Died Jan. 17, 1840, aged 74."

The Averys reported this grievous graveyard situation to Cleveland civic officials upon their return home and there was a proper show of community dissatisfaction over the treatment of the founding father's bones. There also was querulous side comment over the failure of the tombstone chiseler to make some kind of passing reference to Moses Cleaveland's most memorable achievement in life. A lot of Clevelanders felt the city deserved a footnote mention, at the very least.

The Cleveland *Plain Dealer's* editorial columns demanded that the situation be righted, plunking the challenge at the entire community.

"What," demanded the *Plain Dealer,* "are you going to do about it?"

The Cleveland Chamber of Commerce replied by appointing a committee to study the problem, and in the resulting public fervor, funds were raised to purchase land between the burial ground and the highway, thereby providing an access route to the cemetery. Title to the land was given to the town.

Meanwhile, a suitable monument had been commissioned and built, and on November 16, 1906, dedication ceremonies were held in Canterbury. A delegation of Clevelanders attended. The Chamber of Commerce was represented by F. F. Prentiss, Munson Havens, Ambrose Swasey, Hubert B. Fuller, and Elroy M. Avery. Liberty E. Holden, owner of the *Plain Dealer,* represented the Western Reserve Historical Society.

The tablet on the bronze memorial placed in the cemetery reads:

"In this cemetery rest the remains of Moses Cleaveland, founder of the City of Cleveland. He was born in Canterbury, January 29, 1754, and died there Nov. 16, 1806. He was a lawyer, a soldier, a legislator and a leader of men. In grateful recognition of his services, this memorial is erected by the Cleveland Chamber of Commerce on November 16, 1906, the one hundredth anniversary of his death."

Moses, incidentally, was not the only member of his family to leave a mark in the western wilderness. Two of his brothers, Paine and Camden Cleaveland, ventured into the Ohio country also, and like Moses, they too founded a town—Liberty, Ohio, in Trumbull County. It is some sixty miles to the southeast of the mighty metropolis founded by their older brother. It is a tiny town still.

III

The Real Cleveland Indians

A BOSTONIAN chanced the hazards and discomforts of the Midwest with a visit to Cleveland a few years ago and he found the experience to be an eye-opener. His very first day in town, as he was making a preliminary scouting stroll down Euclid Avenue, he saw two Indians.

"There was no mistaking them," he says. "They looked just the way I always imagined Indians looked; just the way that James Fenimore Cooper, one of our eastern experts in this field, described them in his books. They were lean and swarthy and their coppery skin was stretched tight over their high cheekbones.

"They were, in fact, perfect Indians except for one or two minor details. That is to say, they did not wear the feathery headdress which I have always understood was more or less traditional with Indians, and they were not wearing moccasins. They had on regular business suits, two-button models with drape lapels, and—this really surprised me!—Hush Puppies."

Up to that time, he said, he had always supposed that the expression, "Cleveland Indians," was one of those amusing little baseball nicknames.

"Take the Boston Red Sox," he explained. "There's a name that is interesting and colorful, but it doesn't really indicate a thing about Boston. I've lived in Boston a long time and never have I seen a Bostonian wearing red socks. But those Clevelanders were *really* Indians! I mean they were the real thing!"

Of course they were. Indians are a solid part of the city's history and played a prominent role in the earliest days of the town. Then they gradually disappeared, either dying off or drifting westward with their dispossessed tribes. They were gone from the city for about 150 years, and then the United States Bureau of Indian Affairs in 1957 chose Cleveland as one of several metropolitan centers to participate in a noble experiment.

The government agency, rightly perturbed by the depressing fortunes of Indians who lived as wards of Uncle Sam on the reservations, persuaded some of them to try living and working as self-reliant citizens in cities like Cleveland. As a result, Indians have been returning in significant numbers over the past ten years to a city that had not known their kind in a century and a half. Cleveland now is home to several thousand Indians, representing forty-seven great American tribes, and it's almost like old times again. Almost.

Only time will tell if any of the modern Indians will contribute as generously to the anecdotal lore of the town as did the Indians who lived in the thick forests of northeastern Ohio and along the banks of the Cuyahoga when Moses Cleaveland's expedition arrived in 1796.

Those Cleveland Indians of 1796 were, man for man, a more interesting aggregation than the ones who play baseball under that name today. It is even possible, judging from the recent history of the American League, that they also were better ball players, but this is sheer conjecture.

There were some great names among them, notably Chief Seneca and John O'Mic.

The very first people to live in Cleveland, that cold winter of 1796–97, came to know the Indians and to admire them. There were only two cabins on the east bank of the Cuyahoga that winter, having been hastily put together by the men of the surveying party. One was for the use of the surveying party and the other was for Job Stiles and his good wife, Tabitha Cumi.

The surveyors returned to the East for the winter, but Job and Tabitha stayed on, as did a man named Joseph Landon, who shared their quarters for a while. Something shortly altered Landon's plan to winter in Cleveland with the Stiles couple; perhaps it was the wind whistling in off the icy stretches of Lake Erie, or maybe the Stiles snored. Historians never really got around to investigating the whys of the situation, but Landon left. However, if Job and Tabitha thought they were going to enjoy a little privacy, they learned otherwise very quickly. Edward Paine arrived from the East and took Landon's place in the cozy little log cabin. The site of the cabin, incidentally, is where West 6th Street and Superior Avenue meet in today's city.

It was a rough, tough winter for the three white pioneers. The Indians camped on the west side of the Cuyahoga knew of the hardships the new settlers were enduring, and they extended a helping hand bearing gifts of food. A special benefactor was a chief named Seneca.

Edward Paine, who later moved on to found the city named Painesville, writing of that first Cleveland winter, paid an extravagant tribute to Chief Seneca and the other Indians of the Cuyahoga Valley:

"That they are capable of disinterested benevolence and confer favors when none are expected, cannot be doubted by anyone acquainted with Seneca, or as his tribe called him, Stigwanish. This in English means 'Standing Stone.'

"In him there was the dignity of the Roman, the honesty of Aristides, and the benevolence of Penn."

Chief Seneca lived in Cleveland until 1809. He was a teetotaler, and this alone was enough to set him apart from all the other Indians of the day and to mark him as a special person. The old joke about the weakness of the redskins for firewater was no joke. It was a terrible weakness and a very real one; it helped to undo the Indian sovereignty over the continent and, in the specific case of Chief Seneca, it helped to bring about a personal tragedy.

Once Seneca had been among the leaders in the chug-a-lug competition, but he came home to his wigwam one time after a drunken spree and his wife presumably spoke reprovingly to him, as wives are wont to do, even today, when the old man rolls in at an ungodly hour absolutely crocked. Whatever transpired between the two, the chief became enraged and, according to Paine, "he aimed a blow at his wife with a tomahawk and split the head of his child which was on her back . . ."

After that tragic happening, Seneca abjured ardent spirits and preached the evils of drink. He made his home, later, in Seneca County, Ohio, named in his honor, but he died in Holmes County, Ohio, in 1816. And, ironically, this distinguished chief who had befriended the white man died a violent death at the hands of a white man. He was shot to death by a man named Jacob Ammond, who claimed self-defense, alleging that Chief Seneca had fired upon him first.

Despite the deleterious effects of firewater on the Indians, whiskey was a prized commodity in the pioneering scheme of things. In 1800, when Cleveland was little more than a clearing with three or four cabins, an enterprising pair, David Bryant and his son, Gilman, set up a still at the foot of Superior Lane (Avenue) on the bank of the Cuyahoga. The still, which they had hauled all the way from Virginia, had a capacity of two quarts of raw spirits a day. Thus, if one excludes the fur trading outpost which predated the town, Cleveland's first business enterprise was a booze factory, not—as some propagandists have tried to mislead us—a comb factory.

It is not reasonable to think the Bryants would have gone to all the work and risk of establishing their operation at this particular place in the wilderness simply to keep a few colonists supplied with spirits. They must have had their sights trained on a larger clientele, as indeed they did. The site met the most rigid qualifications for a successful saloon operation because the mouth of the Cuyahoga was a busy crossroads meeting place for the Indian tribes east and west. This was the jumping-off place to the happy hunting grounds to the south for the Senecas,

Ottawas, Delawares, and Chippewas. They would gather here as the year waned, park their canoes where the Cuyahoga empties into the lake, and then plunge inland where the game was thick. They would return in the early spring heavily laden with furs which they would sell at the small trading post.

The first order of business among the hunters after a successful winter in the woods was an old-fashioned binge with the white man's firewater, and there, not a tomahawk's throw away, stood the Bryants' still, steaming and bubbling and sending out the seductive smell of sour mash to be wafted by the springtime breezes deep into the forest glen. Little wonder that the Indians, in a burst of emotion, threw a big banquet to celebrate the opening of the distillery. Bryant the younger was guest of honor. His father, wiser in the ways of the wilderness world, apparently took a quick business trip so as to be away on the big night, sending his regrets in his R.S.V.P. The Indians, with undiminished enthusiasm, went all out to indicate their affection for Gilman Bryant by bringing forth as the *pièce de résistance* that indescribable forest delicacy, White Dog Soup—a dish which, understandably, was regarded as sacred among the Iroquois.

Young Mr. Bryant, unaccustomed to a fancy cuisine, blanched when he was served his portion. It seems that his hosts had singled him out in a special way by reserving for him the sacred right forepaw of the white dog, which still had a fair patch of partially singed hair on it.

Bryant protested that his hosts were overdoing the hospitality bit and pushed the sacred right forepaw back at them.

"I can't eat another bite," he said. "I'm full; I mean I really am stuffed."

"Why, you've hardly touched your food," replied the Indians. "You haven't got the appetite of a bird. Here, eat some sacred right forepaw and put some meat on your bones."

"No, thanks," said Gilman. "One more bite and I'll burst. You know what I mean, fellows?"

"How about," said one of the Indians, thoughtfully, "if we put the sacred right forepaw in a bowwow bag and you take it home with you to eat later, hey?"

Bryant gulped and protested he couldn't consider such a breach of etiquette, finally satisfying the Indians that he was serious in his refusal to eat the delicacy, whereupon one of them, presumably, lashed into it, while the guest of honor lurched off into the forest in search of some roots, herbs, and simples to soothe his frenzied nerve ends and still his flapping pyloric valve.

It is possible to understand better the heartfelt delight of the Indians over the arrival of the Bryants and the establishment of their distillery in the light of what had happened in Cleveland the previous year,

1799, when the only source of supply was Major Lorenzo Carter, Cleveland's first permanent settler and a pioneer who quickly asserted his leadership as the tiny new community grew.

Several hundred Chippewas and Ottawas came out of the forests that spring, disposed of their furs, and headed for Major Carter's cabin to pick up some syrup for their blowout. But before doing so, all the tribesmen yielded their tomahawks and other deadly weapons to their squaws with orders to hide them "so that, in the height of their frenzy, they need not harm each other."

"Then," writes an anonymous historian, "they sent to the major for whiskey from time to time as they wanted it; and in proportion as they became intoxicated, he weakened it with water.

"After a while, it resulted in the Indians becoming partially sober from drinking freely of diluted liquor. Perceiving the trick, they became much enraged. Nine of them came on to the major's swearing vengeance on him and family."

Then, as now, it is clear, drinking men were terribly thin-skinned about any tampering with their drinks. Major Carter was treading dangerous ground. And in view of the fact that the Indians had thoughtfully disarmed themselves so as not to harm anybody else after becoming drunk, it is not easy to appreciate Major Carter's trickery. The Indians certainly did not. Nine of them swept down on the major's cabin.

It was an unfair contest in terms of numbers—nine to one—but Major Carter did have certain advantages. He was sober, he had a strong defensive position, and he had a good stout poker.

As the Indians poured through the narrow doorway of his cabin, the major laid about him with the poker, crashing the weapon down on the tufted skulls with devastating results. At least four of the Indians were toppled and the other five took it on the run with the major in pursuit. They were fortunate enough to escape in their birchbark canoes, leaving the major the victor.

Relations between the Indians and the Cleveland pioneer were mended a short while later when a committee of squaws visited him to apologize, in effect, for the unseemly conduct of their braves. The major, in a magnanimous gesture, then went to the encampment of the tribe and in a powwow with the leaders settled the dispute.

There can be no doubt that Lorenzo Carter was one of the strong men of the early city, or that he was highly versatile. He not only operated Cleveland's first tavern-hotel, he also served as a kind of unofficial mayor, sheriff, police chief, magistrate, and bouncer. Carter Road, which runs from the river, near the mouth, up the hillside to West 3rd Street, is named in his honor, as is a large hotel, the Pick-Carter. He was, by all accounts, a strong-willed character, but still a good man to have on your side; a man born for the tough, crude time in which he lived. And somehow—probably through his penchant for quick, direct action—Carter came to own what amounted to an Indian sign over all the tribes in that part of the Western Reserve.

There is, inevitably, wonderment that some of the more impulsive Indians didn't bury a tomahawk in the hardheaded major's skull. The thought likely occurred to any number of the red warriors, but they withheld the attack, probably because of a strong legend that had arisen that Major Carter was invulnerable to bodily harm. The word that was passed along from one tepee to the next was that arrows and bullets merely glanced off the Carter person and only served to irritate him. It was, from the Indian standpoint, a rather discouraging legend, and they faced up to its message realistically. They wasted no time attempting the impossible.

One Indian, at least, was unimpressed by the myth that enveloped Cleveland's own Major Carter, but he was very young—only sixteen years old.

His name was John O'Mic.

With all the thousands of guitar players and folk singers bred in the United States in recent times, it is astonishing that no one of them has gotten around to composing a sad ballad about the Indian named O'Mic. His is a story that deserves the proper telling against the thrumming of a guitar, or maybe a whole nest of guitars.

As in all Cleveland stories, it is best to begin by establishing that he was a West Sider, and of course all West Siders claim him as their very own, which is as it should be. He lived on the Indian-owned side of the Cuyahoga, on the hillside slope that later became a famous Cleveland neighborhood with the picturesque name of "The Angle."

When you search into the origins of local names, such as this one, inevitably you are overwhelmed by the logic of the people of the community and their talent for descriptive speech. The Angle was called such because its border streets enclosed a neighborhood shaped—right! —like an isosceles triangle.

The Angle was a hillside settlement predominantly Irish in character—if it isn't extravagant to consider 100 per cent a predominant total—and there is something incredibly prophetic in the fact that the area's most famous name, prior to the arrival of the Irish, should have had the Gaelic ring of O'Mic.

O'Mic first aroused the awareness of the Cleveland colony when, at the reckless age of sixteen, he was apprehended by Mrs. Lorenzo Carter in the family garden as he was helping himself to some of the homegrown vegetables. The lady was, of course, the wife of Major Carter, the hotheaded one.

Mrs. Carter shrieked at the boy and flapped her apron in his direction, but he, like any normal, healthy, red-blooded juvenile delinquent, whipped out a knife—they had switchblades in those days?—and chased the poor woman around the yard, apparently just for kicks. But his funning was interrupted by the approach of a young man, and O'Mic scooted off into the forest primeval.

When Carter heard of the outrageous incident he made a series of short, bull-like rushes hither and yon that hinted at his contained fury. And before setting out in pursuit of the redskin rascal he crammed into his buckskin pocket a length of stout rope which he vowed he would use to hang O'Mic by the neck until he was dead. Carter had definite ideas on how to deal with youthful delinquents so as to teach them a lasting lesson.

Following the trail on the west side of the river with the relentless skill which had earned him fame as a tracker of game, the major finally did trace the boy to an Indian encampment. It is likely that Carter's fury had cooled as he followed the spoor because, with his quarry at hand, he allowed himself to be dissuaded from his plan to hang the boy by the father, O'Mic, senior.

The older O'Mic promised that the young miscreant would be confined to the west bank of the Cuyahoga from that time hence, and Carter was assured that he need not expect any further trouble from the boy ever again.

The major accepted the assurance and, rope in hand, returned to his own side of the river and Cleveland-town.

This should have been the happy ending, but it was not to be. Call it only the beginning because, as it turned out, John O'Mic *did* cross the river again to Cleveland, and his path did cross that of Major Carter again, bringing high excitement and an event of great moment to the colony.

On April 3, 1812, two white fur trappers named Buel and Gibbs were murdered in their sleep and their traps and pelts were stolen. The crime occurred near Sandusky City in Huron County, about sixty miles to the west of Cleveland.

Three Indians were arrested for the foul deed, and one of them was John O'Mic, now in his early twenties and grown up to a flabby manhood.

One of his two companions in crime escaped from his captors via the suicide route and the other was released because of his extreme youth. Only four years later, ironically, the same lad led two other Indians in the murder of another pair of white men and he was executed in Huron County.

At the time of the Buel-Gibbs murders, Huron County was within the jurisdiction of legal authorities in Cuyahoga County, and young

O'Mic therefore was returned to Cleveland, the town from which he had been banished. Even worse, from his standpoint, he was delivered into the custody of his old nemesis, Major Carter.

Cleveland in 1812 was a town of limited facilities, lacking even such everyday essentials as a jail and a courthouse. But this lack was swiftly circumvented by the resourceful Carter, who took O'Mic to his cabin and tied him to a rafter in the attic.

The term of imprisonment was brief, just long enough for justice to marshal its forces and for word to be spread through the forests and thickets of the impending excitement in Cleveland-town. A murder trial was just as thrilling to the frontiersmen as it is to today's suburbanites; perhaps more, considering the limited pleasures and *divertissements* of the wilderness.

Within weeks after the double murder, still in April, the trial was held in an open-air court under the shade of a large oak tree at the corner of Water and Superior streets. The largest crowd that ever had collected in the tiny town, drawn from all parts of the Ohio country, massed on the grassy edges of the "courtroom."

The dramatis personae featured William W. Irvin and Ethan Allen Brown as judges; Samuel S. Baldwin as sheriff; Alfred Kelley as prosecuting attorney, and Peter Hitchcock as counsel for the defense. John O'Mic was the central attraction, of course.

He was charged, specifically, with the murder of Daniel Buel, who, intoned the court, had been done in "with a certain Tomahawk, made of iron and Steele."

The trial moved along quickly in a no-nonsense manner, eschewing oratory and leaning heavily on simple recital of fact. The judgment, thus swiftly arrived at, was inevitable. John O'Mic was declared guilty of murder in the first degree and he was sentenced to be hanged by the neck until he was dead. The date set for the execution was two months hence, June 26.

O'Mic was returned to Major Carter's attic to await the fateful day, while the entire territory buzzed with the news of the exciting and historic occasion in the immediate offing. Pioneer families all throughout the Western Reserve and even some in Pennsylvania, it is said, began their preparations for the rugged trip to Cleveland. Some of them would need weeks to make the trek and there was much to be done.

But if the white men thought that the impending execution would unnerve the Indian prisoner, they soon came to know that he was a man of remarkable composure. He seemed, in fact, to view approaching death with disdain, as if it hardly were worth his attention, and all who conversed with him were stirred to admiration by his aplomb.

The scene of the execution was the Public Square, and the gallows were erected on the northwest corner of the park, immediately in front of the site of the future courthouse. Scattered all about, indeed, were the timbers and other building materials which would go into the house of justice, and the large crowd that assembled on execution day used the lumber to improvise benches for more comfortable viewing.

The multitude that gave Public Square its very first traffic jam was even larger than had been expected, and the commonly accepted reason for the surprising turnout was the colorful nature of the prisoner. This is not a reference to the established fact that O'Mic was a redskin, such being common knowledge and no rarity, what with redskins darting from tree to tree in large numbers in those days. But O'Mic was colorful in his philosophy and in his speech. He made no secret of his deep-seated contempt for the paleface, and he let it be known that he intended to show white people how an Indian could die. He said he would not even allow his executioners to tie his arms or blindfold him, such being devices to help cowardly whites through their fearful last moments.

When it came to his turn to die, said O'Mic, he would jump off the gallows. Finally—and while he didn't come right out and say as much—his words and the sneer that curled at the corner of his mouth as he talked lent the general impression that he might even do a little *entrechat* as a last fillip to give the big occasion real Indian class.

The word got around the forest fastness in a hurry, sounding from hill to hill and from cabin to cabin, causing the eyes of the frontierspeople to shine with anticipation and drawing them, inexorably, to Cleveland for the big event.

The day, quite properly, began with a religious service, which was held in a grassy clearing in front of Major Carter's house. There were several clergymen present, but the sermon was delivered by Rev. Mr. Darrow of the town of Vienna in Trumbull County.

There also was on hand to embellish the occasion a detachment of the military commanded by a Major Jones, who was admittedly a fine figure of a man in his full uniform, but he could not be described honestly as The Compleat Officer. He ran into his first tough problem as soon as the religious service was ended. The last "amen" was his cue to form a hollow square around the newly painted wagon which bore O'Mic himself, seated high atop his own coffin, but the major either couldn't remember what command to give, or he didn't know.

The prisoner presumably looked down on the ensuing scene of military confusion with a quizzical expression; even, perhaps, a smirk. The palefaces who did not know how to die apparently didn't even know how to conduct themselves when a brave man was about to breathe his last.

The major rode frantically back and forth, "epaulets and scabbard flying," according to one description, but he couldn't summon the magic words. His men, understandably, were completely nettled and confused by the major's wild-eyed behavior and the guttural, unintelligible sounds he was making. Some kind onlooker finally persuaded the major that the simplest solution to the problem was for him to ride to the head of the line and double it around until the front and rear of his forces met. The wagon with O'Mic, meanwhile had gone on a distance, led by the disgusted sheriff, but the major and his men caught up to the wagon and tried the suggested deployment. It worked wonderfully well, drawing a loud cheer from the spectators loping alongside.

Word of the military fiasco sped ahead and the large crowd on the Public Square was in a mellow, appreciative mood when the principals in the hanging arrived on stage. Major Carter, the sheriff, and the prisoner ascended to the platform by a ladder, and it was noted approvingly that the arms of the prisoner were pinioned loosely. There was a rope around his neck and it had a loop in the end. Still another rope was let down through a hole in the top piece of the gallows, and hanging from it was a hook which would be attached to the loop in the rope around O'Mic's neck.

There was a brief conversation among the three men on the high platform and then Carter withdrew, presumably having told the Indian "I told you so," leaving Sheriff Baldwin to attend to the final distasteful formality—the hanging itself.

The sheriff took the traditional cap and pulled it down over O'Mic's face, but when he did, the Indian sprang into action. He seized the cap with his right hand, bending his head low to make this feat possible, and, tugging it up enough so that he could see where he was going, he dove for one of the corner posts of the platform, wrapped his arm around it, and held on for dear life. Which, come to think of it, was precisely the prize at stake.

There was a roar from the crowd, and it was a mixture of approval and disapproval. Some of the spectators who had resented O'Mic's slurs about the courage of palefaces confronted with death jeered loudly, as you might expect. But there were many who cheered the frantic Indian for putting on a more interesting show.

Sheriff Baldwin, nonplused for the moment by the sudden metamorphosis that had changed O'Mic from a docile, cooperative prisoner into a reluctant tiger, tentatively tried to pry the Indian's grip from the corner post but he was unsuccessful. While he was contemplating the situation and seeking a more effective maneuver, Major Carter ascended to the platform and addressed O'Mic, speaking in the Indian dialect. Nobody within earshot understood the conversation that ensued, but apparently the major scolded O'Mic for behaving like an old squaw and appealed to his honor as a brave to be more cooperative in the matter at hand, namely, getting hanged.

O'Mic, it is said, listened attentively, nodding his head gravely from time to time, and when it was his turn to speak, he made a forthright, businesslike proposition. He promised that if Carter would give him half a pint of whiskey, he, O'Mic, would gladly dance at the end of the hangman's rope.

The whiskey was swiftly forthcoming—somebody in the crowd had been providential in guessing there might be need of a stimulant—and it was, furthermore, very good booze; real Old Monongahela, for which, in the words of one historian of that day, "an old settler would almost be willing to be hung, if he could now obtain the like."

O'Mic took the tumbler full of whiskey and downed the half-pint in one savage swallow that brought tears to the eyes of the hitherto dry-eyed spectators. Once again, Carter retired from the platform and Sheriff Baldwin returned to his duties. He drew the cap down over O'Mic's face and was reaching for the rope with the hook on the end when O'Mic gave a repeat performance of his previous escape routine. That is, he suddenly lowered his head, nudged back the hangman's cap, and sprang to the corner post, wrapping his arms around the post in a death embrace.

The crowd roared and Sheriff Baldwin adopted a stance that spoke of his complete exasperation. Even as he shook his head, Major Carter ascended to the platform again and spoke curtly to the Indian. O'Mic nodded in complete agreement with everything that Carter said, but he pointed out that a half-pint of whiskey—even Old Monongahela—is not much, really, when one is about to take his final leave of this mortal coil.

Given another half-pint, said O'Mic, he would see to it the authorities had on their hands a prisoner so compliant and cooperative as to make them marvel.

The offer was accepted, another half-pint was proffered, but this time the sheriff held the tumbler, allowing the prisoner to drink his fill, but holding the rope that pinioned his arms so as to prevent him from lunging for the post again.

Now O'Mic truly had reached the end of his trail. Seconds later, full of Old Monongahela, his body swung out in a long arch toward the lake as far as the rope would permit, swung back again, and after repeating this pendulum motion several times, the limp body twisted in a full circle above the center of the platform and then just hung there, hardly moving.

The silent spectators, who had suddenly lost their holiday mood in the presence of death, sat motionless for a full minute or two, as if awaiting some new dodge by the artful Indian, but the truth finally became clear—O'Mic really was dead. Even as this realization came to the crowd, there was a rumble of thunder, and the first spatter of rain came from the lowering clouds that had been gathering through the execution drama. Now there was a heavy blow from the north-northwest that swayed the virgin forest all around the Public Square and sent the new leaves of summer streaming straight out at the end of heaving branches. Lightning crackled across the sky and left a rumble of thunder that came in off the lake like a breaking wave.

By now the crowd was on its feet and running for shelter in the scattered group of cabins west of the Public Square and alongside the steep trails leading down to the Cuyahoga River. An eyewitness observed that "the storm was heavy and all scampered but O'Mic." But several men, presumably Sheriff Baldwin and Major Carter, lingered long enough to place the body in a rude coffin and to drop the remains in a shallow grave that had been prepared alongside the gallows.

There is a finality, somehow, to this simple act of being returned to the earth that precludes any possibility of further developments, but even so the story of O'Mic had not yet reached the last punctuation mark, the community discovered the next day, when it was ascertained that the grave had been disturbed and that O'Mic's body was missing.

Some of the colonists said, almost hopefully, that O'Mic had not really died, that the storm had prevented the officials from making a real determination of his death and that, under the cover of night and the stormy elements, the wily redskin had recovered and made good his escape into the forest. The officials stoutly denied this unlikely possibility, but they could not present a satisfactory explanation for the fact that O'Mic was missing, nor could they prevent the story of his "resurrection" from spreading like wildfire.

Wiser townspeople suspected that the mystery of O'Mic was one that could be cleared up quickly by any of the several doctors of medicine who were prominent in the crowd attending Cleveland's first public execution. The medical practitioners of that day were desperate for good cadavers. O'Mic was a prime, healthy specimen. It is believed that the sheriff and other authorities chose to look the other way while the doctors abducted the Indian's body.

This story is supported by people involved directly, and indirectly, in the grave-robbing episode. The wife of Cleveland's only doctor, Dr. Long, spoke of the deed with a high degree of candor and a measure of emotion because, as a child living in Painesville, she and John O'Mic had been close friends and had played together "on the banks of the Grand River at my father's old residence."

Mrs. Long was in the crowd on Public Square, watching as O'Mic dueled with the hangman, when she suddenly was assailed with revulsion and, in her own words, thought: "Why should I wish to see my old playmate die?"

"I got out of the crowd as quick as possible and went home," she related. "All the people from the Western Reserve seemed to be there, particularly the doctors. I remember several of them who stayed at our house. Among them was Dr. Allen of Trumbull County, Dr. Coleman of Ashtabula County, Dr. Johnson of Conneaut and Dr. Hawley of Austintown.

"When O'Mic was swung off the rope broke and they were not sure that he was dead, but there was a storm coming on and he was hurried into the grave near the gallows.

"The Public Square was only partly cleared then, and had many stumps and bushes on it. At night the doctors went for the body with the tacit consent of the Sheriff. O'Mic was about 21 years of age, and was very fat and heavy. Dr. Long did not think one man could carry him, but Dr. Allen, who was very stout, thought he could. He was put upon Dr. Allen's back, who soon fell over a stump and O'Mic on top of him!

"The doctors dare not laugh aloud for fear they might be discovered, but some of them were obliged to lie down on the ground and roll around there, before they came to the relief of Dr. Allen."

Mrs. Long's account illuminates an otherwise dark page in Cleveland's history, and makes it clear that there can be a light side even to body-snatching. Furthermore, her words explaining the disappearance of O'Mic's body are supported by other accounts, including testimony from the descendant of Dr. Allen—Dudley P. Allen, author of *Pioneer Medicine on the Western Reserve.*

Speaking of poor O'Mic's remains, Allen said: "The skeleton was placed below a spring, on the bank of the lake, east of Water Street, and remained there for about one year, after which time it was properly articulated. The skeleton was for a long time in the possession of Dr. Long, but was later in Hudson in the office of Dr. Town. From there, it was supposed, it was carried to Penn, near Pittsburgh, to Dr. Murray, a son-in-law of Dr. Town. The writer has made every effort to discover its whereabouts and restore the bones to Cleveland, which should be their proper resting place, but all efforts to this end have proved fruitless."

There can be no real doubt that O'Mic had his final comeuppance in the Public Square that fateful day in 1812, but there still are historians who claim that he made good his escape from the clutches of the white man's law. It doesn't matter much any more, one way or the other, but it proves that he was one interesting Indian. A lot of Clevelanders are very proud today that O'Mic was a local boy, and while they haven't memorialized him with a plaque or a statue or anything like that, the city has established a free-speech rostrum on the approximate Public Square site of O'Mic's hanging. Considering all the talking that O'Mic did before consenting to be hanged, the rostrum isn't entirely inappropriate.

IV

Does Anybody Here Know Kelley?

A STUDENT of the early Cleveland scene once observed that "the population alternated between fevers, chills and hard work"—a summary which certainly must be regarded as being open to challenge once all the fascinating details of life in the little frontier village have been reviewed.

It is true that Cleveland had more than its fair share of fevers, chills and hard work. The Cuyahoga Valley must have developed a new, giant species of mosquito with special penetrating power and sacs dripping with malaria. It was worse than the islands of the South Pacific. Most pioneers who sauntered into the rude settlement came out on the dead run minutes later, flailing their arms and striving desperately for sanctuary on higher ground before they collapsed of malarial fever. Some of them made it and some of them didn't; that's how life was in those early rugged days, and survival of the fittest was the rule that prevailed.

Those who escaped preferred to settle in a thriving little community called Newburgh, which had sprung up about six miles to the southeast of Cleveland. While Cleveland struggled for a foothold in the miasmatic valley, Newburgh flourished on the higher ground, drawing from the older town not only many of its permanent desirables, such as one Samuel Huntington, but even cutting into Cleveland's tourist trade. This state of affairs was prevalent as late as 1816, when a Cleveland visitor named Royal Taylor declared that "Cleveland will never amount to anything because the soil is too poor." Having thus delivered a hard blow to the town's pride, Royal completed his lightning one-two punch by paying sixteen dollars for a barrel of salt and returning to Burke's Tavern in Newburgh to spend the night "because it was the most desirable place for man and beast."

It isn't possible at this late date to know with certainty exactly why Royal was so testy and sharp-tongued, but it is a reasonable conjecture that he was irked by the price of salt. Sixteen dollars does seem high. Perhaps he was right, too, in his assertion that Newburgh was the most desirable place for man and beast. A lot of settlers, certainly, preferred Newburgh to Cleveland, and there are stories to indicate it also was popular among the beasts. One emigrant from Cleveland who already has been mentioned, Samuel Huntington, was a genuine prize, and his defection to Newburgh did a lot to boost that town's stock. Huntington was the namesake of one of the signers of the Declaration of Independence, Samuel Huntington, his uncle. He was regarded by one and all as a lad with a bright future. In time he fulfilled all the high expectations, becoming a member of the Ohio legislature, speaker of the House of Representatives, judge of the state supreme court and, ultimately, governor.

With all these successes, the chances are that Huntington never had a political thrill to compare with the fun he had one night in Newburgh when he was pursued to the threshold of his home "by a pack of howling and ravenous wolves!" If Cleveland had mosquitoes, Newburgh had wolves. At the outset, the pioneers were more inclined to take their chances with the latter; so much so that Newburgh became the big town of the area in the beginning years. Clevelanders occasionally were embarrassed to hear their town pinpointed geographically as the community "six miles from Newburgh." There could have been no criticism as humiliating as this, but there was some excuse for outsiders to regard Newburgh as the metropolis. The population of Newburgh outnumbered that of Cleveland by a wide margin.

If Cleveland did not have the numbers at the outset, it did have quality, including a surprising number of majors for such a tiny place. Lorenzo Carter, who is conceded to be the city's first permanent white settler, carried the title of major. So did Amos Spafford, who had been in Moses Cleaveland's original surveying party.

The first big social affair in Cleveland was held in Major Carter's log cabin on the hillside of the Cuyahoga Valley to celebrate Independence Day, July 4, 1801. Some thirty persons came roaring out of the thickets to join in the fun, which included drinking whiskey sweetened with maple sugar and dancing the scramper-down, double-shuffle, western-swing and the half-moon to the scraping fiddle music of Samuel Jones. *Major* Samuel Jones, if you please!

The two other majors present at that social figured in a perplexing little incident a few years later that perhaps offers the best illustration of just how keenly Clevelanders felt about the footloose type of people who had been giving the town a black eye by running off to places like Newburgh without giving Cleveland a really fair trial.

Major Spafford, it seems, had in his employ a kind of handyman who, from all descriptions, was a fine fellow to have on the payroll. He was quiet, hard-working, well-behaved, and honest. The major, therefore, was a trifle disconsolate one day when he discovered his employee had pulled up stakes and left.

Major Carter happened by and, noticing the glum look on Major Spafford's face, inquired as to the trouble. Spafford told him about the handyman's abrupt resignation and departure.

The story clearly and inexplicably aroused Carter's fury. He roared that the handyman had one hell of a nerve to quit like that and take his leave without going through the niceties of a friendly severing of the ties by serving adequate advance notice.

Major Spafford agreed it had been an abrupt resignation, but, he pointed out reasonably, the handyman hadn't stolen anything, nor did he owe anything, in fact, he was owed about four dollars in wages, and he did have every right to move on if he should so choose. He had so chosen, obviously.

Major Carter's angry reply, as quoted by a pioneer resident, Ashbel W. Walworth, was: "Well, there shall nobody run away from this place, and I'll go after him; I can track him out!"

Whereupon he set out immediately in pursuit of the poor handyman who now had become, without knowing it, a fugitive. Not having any reason to hide or skulk along the trail, he fell an easy prey to Carter, who overtook him about the point where East 55th Street now approaches the lakefront.

The handyman, undoubtedly perplexed and probably frightened, put up only token resistance when the major came roaring up the trail. He did demur when Carter said he'd have to return to Cleveland, pointing out that there was no compelling reason why he should return.

The major was entirely unimpressed by the justice of the handyman's position, but he held his temper in check admirably well. He told the man he didn't care if he returned or not; not really.

"But one of two things you shall do," he said. "Either you must go with me peaceably, or be killed and thrown into this cat swamp, to be eaten by the wolves and turkey buzzards."

The fugitive instantly showed he had been swayed by the major's persuasive pleading and reasonableness.

"Oh," he said, "if you are in earnest, I don't care if I go back."

Upon returning to Major Spafford's place near the river, his employer reproved the man for running away and asked his reason. The handyman explained apologetically that he was "a roving character" and that it was his habit after being in a place for a while "to run away." He was, in short, a roamer.

Both majors brushed aside this weak excuse and chided the man for his lack of stability and manners. They called on him to straighten out before it was too late. And the man, being basically a decent sort, mumbled contritely and went back to his work. He stayed on the job for several months more before his restless feet acted up again and helped overcome his fear even of Major Carter. He handed in his resignation once again, but this time the parting was more amicable. Everybody shook hands a couple of times around; the majors wished him Godspeed, and he pushed off once again. Probably for Newburgh.

Fate has a way of balancing the good with the bad, as some philosophers previously have noted, and it seemed as if every time Cleveland lost a good man to Newburgh, another stout fellow from the East unexpectedly popped out of the woods. Among the more notable of these timely arrivals were Abram Hickox and his five daughters, who joined the Cleveland population about 1808. Abram was a brawny blacksmith, and the territory was sorely in need of his particular talents. He would have been welcomed had he come all by himself, but to win a blacksmith with five daughters! The town reeled with joy and the word spread through the countryside like wildfire.

It is likely that the welcome surprised Abram, and perhaps the cheers went to his head. At any rate, he shortly put up a sign which would make you wonder. It read, "Uncle Abram Works Here." It wasn't the kind of message you could argue with, certainly not when the subject was a blacksmith, but it did have a disquieting ring of immodesty. Abram didn't care. You get the impression he added something more to the little town than merely a talent for shoeing horses and forging implements. All the accounts agree that he was a large, loud, outgoing, cheerful, overwhelming kind of individual and, to top it all, the most enthusiastic patriot in Cleveland. His particular affection was for the Independence Day celebration, and it swiftly became traditional that the Fourth of July fun should begin at dawn—a custom that owed a lot to the brawn of Uncle Abram. He had a positive way of bringing all the townspeople to their feet in patriotic posture at the beginning of that large day by hammering on his anvil as hard as he could. It is barely possible that Uncle Abram had as much to do with the steady migration from Cleveland to Newburgh as the ravenous mosquitoes, but that is sheer guesswork.

Meanwhile, just across the river, a new and more serious threat to Cleveland's supremacy—as it turned out—was being shaped by representatives of the United States Government, the Connecticut Land Company, the Fire Lands Company, and the Indian tribes which held title to the lands west of the Cuyahoga River. The motivating reason for the conference was a familiar one—the necessity of further "extinguishing" the claims of the red people to the remainder of the Ohio empire. In June 1805, a delegation of Indians from the western edge of New York State whose tribes still held claims beyond the Cuyahoga, arrived in Cleveland, which had been appointed as the site for the conference. There they joined a Colonel Charles Jewet, commissioner, representing the United States; General Henry Champion of the Connecticut Land Co.; I. Mills of the Fire Lands Company, and others.

The representatives of the Indian tribes occupying the western part of Ohio balked at traveling to Cleveland for reasons unknown, and after a fidgety wait of several days, the white officials and the New York Indians picked up their belongings and traveled westward to meet the reluctant Ohio Indians on their own ground. They did meet, eventually, but there is disagreement among the historians over the site. Some say it was near Sandusky; others say it was at Fort Industry (Toledo) on the Maumee River.

The reluctance of the Indians to attend the conference is understandable in the light of what happened when the meeting finally took place. A letter from a William Dean, one of the principals at the powwow, to Samuel Huntington in Newburgh tells the story. The note, dated July 7, 1805, said:

"Dear Sir:—On the 4th instant, we closed a treaty with the Indians, for the unextinguished part of the Connecticut Reserve, and on account of the United States; for all the lands south of it, to the west line. Mr. Phelps and myself pay about $7,000 in cash, and about $12,000 in six yearly payments, of $2,000 each. The government pays $13,760, that is the annual interest, to the Wyandots, Delawares, Munsees, and to those Senecas on the land, forever.

"The expense of the treaty will be about $5,000, including rum, tobacco, bread, meat, presents, expenses of the seraglio, the commissioners, agents and contractors. I write in haste, being extremely sorry I have not time to send you a copy of the treaty. You will see General Champion, who will be able to give you further information.

"Having some intention of making a purchase of considerable tracts of land, in different parts of the Reserve, amounting to about 30,000 acres; I beg of you to inform me what I should allow per acre, payments equal to cash; and address me at Easton, Pa. From thence, if I make a contract, I expect, with all speed, to send fifteen or twenty families of prancing Dutchmen."

Another eyewitness to the historic transfer of land from Indian to white ownership was Abraham Tappen of Unionville, Ohio, who made this poignant observation in a letter to Colonel Charles Whittlesey of Cleveland years later:

"x x x The Indians in parting with and making sale of the above lands to the whites, did so with much reluctance, and after the treaty was signed, many of them wept."

The effect of the transaction, however tragic it was from the standpoint of the Indians, was to open up the lands west of the Cuyahoga River to colonization. The territory on that side of the river, immediately across from the struggling settlement in Cleveland, was surveyed in 1809 by Ezekiel Hoover and became known as Brooklyn Township.

The first West Siders, not counting the Indians, were led by a

Groton, Connecticut, man named James Fish, who settled in Brooklyn in May 1812. He must have liked the flat, friendly terrain because in the same year, in response to his reports, two other members of the Fish family, Moses and Ebenezer, arrived. The following year, Ozias Brainard and his family took their place in the new village, while in 1814 six families from Chatham, Middlesex County, Connecticut, settled in Brooklyn and began to hack a home out of the wilderness. In this particular Brooklyn, a lot of trees grew.

All the while, the Cleveland colony was looking across the river and watching its newest rival spring into being with a cold, disapproving eye. Indians on the West Side they could abide, but this was a different kind of threat, this settlement called Brooklyn and its people. Cleveland fretted.

The prevailing Cleveland opinion, for one thing, was that the "avalanche of immigrants" to the new village was made up mainly of paupers, not prancing Dutchmen. Brooklyn being part of the Township of Cleveland (not to be confused with the village), the people of Cleveland feared they might have to support the newcomers through new, heavier taxes. It was decided to send the township constable across the river to—in the words of one historian, James Harrison Kennedy—"drive the invaders out of town."

This move was blocked by Alonzo Carter, the son of the famous Lorenzo. He personally vouched for the new settlers and concluded his statement of support for them with some rather pointed and bitter words in which he assayed the worth of the impoverished Brooklynites as being larger by far than the combined value of all the trustees of Cleveland Township. He endorsement was highly effective in quelling the anti-Brooklyn faction because the name of Carter was the most influential and best-known name in the county. Eventually Carter himself became a West Sider. In 1825, in cutting a new direct channel for the river, eight acres of the Carter farm were separated from the East Side. His cabin was on that acreage, opposite the foot of Superior Lane (now Avenue).

It was on this unfriendly—almost hostile—note that the long and tangled relationship between the towns on the Cuyahoga began. The situation was destined to get worse before it would get better.

A more critical issue than municipal rivalry had arisen at the very time that Brooklyn was coming into being. It was the outbreak of the War of 1812 between the United States and Great Britain. One of the war's early developments, the surrender in August 1812 of the American forces under General Hull to the British in Detroit, led directly to one of Cleveland's most embarrassing episodes. The wild countryside immediately became a breeding ground for even wilder rumors of British invasions. It was just like old times in New England, with wide-eyed couriers riding about atop heaving horses shouting that the Redcoats were coming.

The people of Cleveland took the rumor seriously and there was a mighty scramble for the highlands, with some Clevelanders forgetting their pride entirely and taking cover in Newburgh. It was almost a complete evacuation, except for the soldiers who manned the hastily built Fort Huntington at a strategic site on the high bluff where Water Street and Lake Street met (West 6th Street and Lakeside Avenue). Where the fort once was, next to the Cuyahoga County Courthouse, now is tiny Huntington Park.

It became clear, shortly, that the British were nowhere about and that the invasion report was false, and the residents of Cleveland sheepishly made their way back to their cabins. The soldiers manning Fort Huntington continued their surveillance of Lake Erie and the harbor by night and by day, and once or twice it did seem that the battle might be joined. Two British warships appeared off the mouth of the Cuyahoga River at midday, June 13, 1813. One was the *Queen Charlotte*, a three-master with seventeen guns, and with her was the *Lady Prevost*, a two-master. The *Queen Charlotte*, second largest of all the warships in the British fleet, was one of two ships whose guns later destroyed Captain Perry's flagship, the *Lawrence*, in the Battle of Lake Erie. The two enemy ships turned away from Cleveland harbor when a severe thunderstorm and high winds lashed the area. The following morning, a heavy fog blanketed the lake, and when it had dispelled, the British ships were gone.

There is a story that the guns of Fort Huntington were activated late one night when some ships were observed as they tried to slip into the Cuyahoga River. Some hits allegedly were scored before it was learned that the doughty defenders of Cleveland were pumping cannonballs at American ships.

On the credit side, however, a high spirit prevailed at the fort through these very trying times. Waiting for the enemy forces to show themselves is a very trying game, as every military man will confirm, and it is said that a high-ranking officer of Fort Huntington made it a practice to revive his flagging morale from time to time with visits to an attractive widow who lived near the fort. She was a Mrs. Hungerford, and the soldiers of the post understandably transposed the sound-alike names and called their post "Fort Hungerford" instead of Fort Huntington.

One afternoon they went beyond this sly play on names with a practical joke whose victim was the romantic officer. Several of the soldiers went to the front door of the widow's house, and hammered thereon, loudly demanding admittance, whereupon the back door of the house flew open as the men had hoped it would and the disheveled officer shot out of the widow's house in a frantic bid for escape. But the soldiers, thoughtfully, had placed a large tub of a lard-like substance directly before the back door, and the fleeing lover tripped on it and plunged into the goo, spread-eagle style.

It was, some aver, the high point of the war in Cleveland-town until the day of Perry's great victory over the British in the famous Battle of Lake Erie. This battle took place near the Lake Erie Islands, off the town of Sandusky. The distance from the point where the war-ships met in the decisive conflict is a healthy sixty miles or so west of Cleveland. It hardly seems credible that the sound of the guns could have been heard at such a distance, but a lot of Clevelanders swore that they listened to the noise of the naval battle, and perhaps they did.

One earwitness report came from John Doane, who lived in Cleveland for ninety-seven years (from 1801 to 1898). He died as he neared his one-hundredth birthday.

"The noise of the guns in the great battle at Put-in-Bay, between Capt Perry and Commander Barclay, I plainly heard at my residence, and when the firing ceased I felt assured in my mind that Perry had won," Mr. Doane told a Cleveland author-civic leader, O. J. Hodge.

But the real prize for the keenest ears on the Great Lakes would have to be awarded a man named Velorus Hodge of Buffalo, New York, who testified that "One day in 1813, with several other boys, I was picking blackberries in Buffalo on the hill where High Street is now laid out. Suddenly, in a ravine, where the berries were very thick, we distinctly heard the firing of cannon. It was the day of Perry's victory on Lake Erie and the scene of the fight was two hundred miles away . . ."

No matter who heard what, it was a great victory for our side, and there was a rousing celebration in Cleveland, as there was all over the country as the news spread. The elimination of the British and the Indians as threats to American westward expansion opened a new, exciting era for the Western Reserve; a time of progress and growth.

Little more than two years after the war, Cleveland became an incorporated village—a milestone that perhaps is best honored in the retelling of an eyewitness account of the civic celebration that was staged in the town the night the news was announced.

"On the 23d of December, 1814," an anonymous observer wrote, "the village of Cleveland was incorporated by act of the General Assembly, and was made the occasion for wild and extravagant rejoicing, one enthusiastic citizen adding to its splendors by setting fire to a load of hay which a farmer was bringing to market.

"An old field piece was brought into requisition, and Abraham Hickox

[sic], acting as powder monkey, carried the powder in an open pail, which ignited and blew him as high as the eaves of the houses, but he came down all right and as full of fight and patriotism as a singed cat. In fact, patriotism was on tap and ladled out by the gourd full. At nightfall everyone was comfortably filled up and the most of them too full for utterance."

On the first Monday in June 1815—by which time everybody presumably had sobered up and the tankards of patriotism had run dry—the village held its first election. Twelve voters jammed the polls to elect the following slate: Alfred Kelley, president; Horace Perry, recorder; Alonzo Carter, treasurer; John A. Ackley, marshal; George Wallace and John Riddle, assessors; Samuel Williamson, Dr. David Long, and Nathan Perry, Jr., trustees.

Kelley, the man who led the ticket to become Cleveland's first chief executive, was a significant choice. In picking him, the tiny town elected to start off with a big man. True enough, he was only twenty-five years old at the time, and he had moved to the Western Reserve town from his home in Oneida, New York, less than five years before, but Alfred Kelley had quickly established himself in the town (and the state) as a man who packed a considerable future.

Among other things, Kelley was Cleveland's first practicing attorney—which may or may not be an arguable distinction. He had arrived in Cleveland in 1810 in the company of his uncle, Joshua Stow, a member of the Moses Cleaveland founding party of 1796. It was a timely arrival, for 1810 was a key year. It was, for instance, the year in which Cuyahoga County's Court of Common Pleas was organized and began its sessions. It also was the year in which the county government was set up and its first officers named. They included, as prosecuting attorney, Peter Hitchcock of Geauga, who took office in May. When the newcomer, Kelley, was admitted to the bar on his twenty-first birthday, November 7 of the same year, Hitchcock yielded the county post to him.

Professional men were scarce on the frontier, of course, and when they appeared they were heartily welcomed into the inner circle of community life, as Kelley obviously was. Fortunately for the town, another professional man popped into the Cleveland picture at almost the same time as Kelley. He was David Long, a twenty-three-year-old doctor who traveled from his home in Hebron, New York, to Cleveland in June 1810 to become the city's first resident physician. The two young men hit it off together amiably and in the autumn, when Kelley began to practice law, he and Dr. Long shared office space.

Kelley's chief contribution to Cleveland in the ensuing years was not so much as a lawyer as it was in the field of politics and business. He served as a member of the state legislature, representing Cuyahoga

County, from 1814 to 1822, and in that time he helped to assure Cleveland future prosperity and growth. It was, indeed, Kelley who was instrumental in having the legislature grant a charter of incorporation as a village to Cleveland on December 23, 1814.

He held the top office in the new town less than a year, resigning the post in the following March, 1816, presumably because of the press of business and politics. The town trustees must have liked the Kelley style, however, because they appointed his father, Daniel Kelley, to succeed him as president. He obliged by serving four consecutive terms as head man of the village—becoming postmaster, also, along the way. It was not too difficult for a versatile man to hold both jobs. Cleveland, as defined in the charter of incorporation, extended only from Erie Street (East 9th) west to the Cuyahoga River, and from Huron Street to the lake.

During Alfred Kelley's service in the state legislature the subject of man-made inland waterways, canals, as a solution to the young nation's critical problem of transportation held everybody's attention. The decision to construct the Erie Canal, connecting New York City and Buffalo, gave impetus to the movement in Ohio to build a canal that would connect Lake Erie with the mighty Ohio River. Five natural routes presented themselves as possible choices, one being a 309-mile route from Cleveland to Portsmouth, following the Cuyahoga River south and connecting with the wide Tuscarawas River flowing down to the Ohio.

Two other lake towns, Painesville to the east and the settlement at the mouth of the Black River to the west (Lorain), competed for selection as the northern terminus of the Ohio Canal, as it was called, but Cleveland's best single asset in the argument was Kelley. When, in 1819, the state authorized creation of a commission to study the practicability of the canal and to make recommendations, Kelley was one of the legislators named to the commission. He argued for the canal route that would be anchored on the north by Cleveland, pointing to the vast reservoir of water to the south of the town, the Portage Lakes, as the clincher. Cleveland won—not merely a canal, but assurance of future development and eventual greatness, so important was to be this inland water route in the movement of goods and people.

Governor DeWitt Clinton of New York turned the first shovelful of earth for the Ohio Canal south of Cleveland on July 4, 1825, following a gay reception in the fashionable Mansion House operated by Noble Merwin. It was not until 1832, however, that the full 309-mile-long waterway was finished. It cost $4,244,539.64, making it one of the cheapest investments in the future since Moses Cleaveland took time out to extinguish the Indian claims to the Western Reserve. The canal opened the trade gates of commerce between the south and the Great Lakes, and Cleveland was a key junction. The little town woke up one morning to discover itself a crossroads of commerce, with a traffic jam rapidly developing. Thus quickly did Cleveland feel the impact of the new water route; new wharves were built along the riverfront to accommodate the swarm of sailing ships that converged on the village, but the demand was such that most of the time there were ships anchored in the harbor, awaiting their turn for unloading. Cargo piled up on the docks and spilled onto the wooden sidewalks, blocking the path of the throngs that filled the waterfront—the sailors, longshoremen, merchants, and passengers.

The canal brought romance to Cleveland, as well as business. There was the smell of foreign ports in the barks that put into the riverway, and now strangers walked the familiar streets. The sound of the saw and the hammer persisted sometimes into the night. The inns were filled and housing was short. People slept in the wagons and in the fields, waiting for Cleveland to catch up with the bustling demand of the new era.

As powerful a stimulant as the new canals were to the Cleveland economy, they were no sooner in operation, it seemed, when men began to talk about building railroads to supplant the waterways. Once again, Alfred Kelley was a leading spokesman for the city as the draftsmen of finance blueprinted the future. He became president of the Cleveland, Columbus & Cincinnati Railroad Company, a forerunner of the New York Central System's Big Four Route, and with such Cleveland leaders as Truman P. Handy, Henry B. Payne, Oliver Perry, Frederick Harbach, Amasa Stone, and Stillman Witt, he built the road and put it into operation in 1851. In that year, the wood-fired, brass-trimmed locomotive, built in Ohio City, made its inaugural run from Columbus into the wooden depot at the foot of Superior Street.

Other railroads to serve Cleveland were constructed at that time. The Cleveland, Painesville & Ashtabula Railroad, which became part of the New York Central System, was incorporated in February 1848 as the first leg of a through route between Chicago and Buffalo. Its president was Herman B. Ely, after whom Elyria was named. Construction of this first segment began in 1850 and was finished in 1852. Another new line, the Cleveland & Pittsburgh Railroad (later the Pennsylvania) completed its first section from Cleveland to Hudson on February 22, 1851.

When Kelley died on December 2, 1859, Cleveland was well started on the road leading toward its metropolitan destiny. The settlement of cabins that he had found a half-century before had been chewed up and swallowed, with scarcely a trace to remind those who followed of what had been. The city had come up out of the valley, abandoning it to commerce and industry and the smoke of the machine age beginning. Cleveland was beginning to live on the high bluff and a new city was forming which would be, in large measure, the handiwork of this urban artisan who had brought the world to its doorstep by water and by rail.

Of all the men who contributed to its future, Cleveland was most indebted to Alfred Kelley. Yet, strangely, it has been unwilling to thank him at all. There are no monuments to him, no parks named in his honor, no buildings erected in his name, no recollection of his person or his deeds anywhere in evidence.

But there is the city itself. Alfred Kelley helped to build it.

V

The Battle of the Bridge

THE struggle for municipal supremacy in Cuyahoga County was short-lived, but nonetheless spirited. The addition of Brooklyn to the lists brought about a three-sided competition, but the major threat to Cleveland, man-eating wolves and all, continued to be Newburgh until 1826.

In that key year, the turning point in the Cleveland-Newburgh rivalry arrived when the issue of which town should be selected as the county seat came to a head.

Three county commissioners were to decide the issue, but one of the commissioners died and the two who remained were evenly divided. There was an election and the candidate who favored Cleveland, Dr. David Long, won the office. That resolved the issue in Cleveland's favor, and thereafter there was no question which community was dominant. Now Newburgh found itself slipping into the background, suffering even the final humiliation of being described to travelers as the town "six miles from Cleveland."

But pride does not die easily, and even in the Cleveland of today—in which the old rival is really nothing more than a very large neighborhood with indefinite boundaries—people still speak of "Old Newburgh" in tremulous voices that tell of their loyalty and the unspoken belief that Newburgh someday, somehow, will rise again.

Considering the extent of the rivalry that had obtained between Newburgh and Cleveland, it must be conceded that the losing village took its defeat in a sportsmanlike manner. Only seven years after the critical election that put Cleveland on top, a visitor from England who passed through Cleveland on his way to Newburgh said loudly that for the size of it, Cleveland was the "prettiest town" he had seen in America. The Englishman's name was John Stair, and even though he uttered those inflammatory words while enjoying Newburgh's hospitality, he was allowed to go his way unharmed or unmolested.

Cleveland's main concern at this point had become the town of Brooklyn. It was sprouting new shoots every day, growing at a prodigious rate in the salubrious climate of the times, and it quickly became apparent that Cuyahoga County had another competition on its hands. The immediate prize was incorporation as a city by the state legislature, with all the municipal powers thereto pertaining, and both towns fought hard for the distinction of being first.

This was a race that Cleveland lost, to the surprise of almost everybody involved and to the great chagrin of the older town. Brooklyn was incorporated under the grand new name of City of Ohio on May 3, 1836, and reigned, for five glorious days, as the only officially recognized city in Cuyahoga County. Finally, on May 8, 1836, Cleveland, too, became a city, but by that time some of the thrill was gone.

All this was to happen some ten years after Cleveland and Ohio City, and even Newburgh, had entered upon an era of great expansion and prosperity brought about by the construction of the Ohio Canal.

In addition to the economic effect of the great canal, it exerted a significant sociological influence on the young cities along its route. Cleveland, for instance, until the time of the canal had been populated almost entirely by New Englanders, and it was a city which was as much eastern in its character as any city could be. But the canal drew upon thousands of hard-nosed, hard-working immigrants for its laboring force, and when the job was done, most of these workers stayed on as permanent residents.

The assimilation of the "foreigners"—mainly Irish and German—was slow to come about, and often painful in the digestive process. They represented something strange and unknown in an area whose population had the comfortable homogeneity of a common New England background. The new people with their strange ways, their unknown tongues, their exotic dishes, and their inclination toward Catholicism were suspect in the Puritan-centered community that was a Yankee stronghold in the West.

A new flood of immigrants, mainly Irish, German, and Bohemian, poured into the young city in the middle of the century with the advent of the railroads. These twin developments, new people and magnificent new transportation facilities, gave Cleveland a forward impetus that would, in the following fifty years leading to 1900, establish it as one of the great cities of the nation.

The newcomers of common ethnic origin clustered together in the poorer neighborhoods which became nationality centers bearing colorful, suggestive names, such as "Irishtown," "The Angle," and, in time, "Little Italy." Some of those neighborhoods have retained their nationality character to this day.

With the completion of the canal, Cleveland changed from a sleepy, picturesque cluster of cabins and primitive frame buildings to a bustling, prosperous port. A picture of the city as it appeared to a stranger from the more sedate East is provided in a letter written by the famous educator, Harvey Rice, upon his arrival here in 1824, when the Ohio Canal was under construction.

Rice, a graduate of Williams College who had decided to seek his career in the wilderness country, sailed to Cleveland from Buffalo—a 120-mile trip that took three days—and arrived late at night on September 24, 1824.

"A sand-bar prevented the schooner from entering the river," he wrote. "The jolly boat was let down and two jolly fellows, myself and a young man from Baltimore, were transferred to the boat with our baggage, and rowed by a brawny sailor over the sand-bar into the placid waters of the river, and landed on the end of a row of planks that stood on stilts and bridged the marshy brink of the river, to the foot of Union Lane. Here we were left standing with our trunks on the wharf-end of a plank at midnight, strangers in a strange land.

"We hardly knew what to do, but soon concluded that we must make our way in the world, however dark the prospect. There was no time to be lost, so we commenced our career in Ohio as porters, by shouldering our trunks and groping our way up Union to Superior street, where we espied a light at some distance up the street, to which we directed our footsteps."

The light was in a tavern kept by Michael Spangler and the travelers found lodging there.

"The town," Rice's account continued, "even at that time was proud of itself, and called itself 'the gem of the West.' In fact, the Public Square, so called, was begemmed with stumps, while near its center glowed its crowning jewel, a log court house. The eastern border of the Square was skirted by the native forest, which abounded in rabbits and squirrels and afforded the villagers a 'happy hunting ground.' The entire population did not at that time exceed four hundred souls . . ."

This was the town that was to disappear within a few years under the impact of its sudden development as a strategic center of shipping and commerce, but apparently the change would bring the town an attractive new look. We know that at least one newcomer to the city was impressed by the town. His name was Milo H. Hickox, and he wrote to a friend:

"Cleveland is about two-thirds as large as Rochester, east side of the river, and is the pleasantest sight that you ever saw. The streets are broad and cross each other at right angles. . . . There are between fifteen and twenty grogshops and they all live."

It is not too much to assume that among the very liveliest of all the grogshops was the Shakespeare Saloon, which advertised in the first city directory published in 1837, promising Falstaffian delights to its customers and "an agreeable retreat" in which "every attention" would be paid to their comfort and convenience.

That same city directory of 1837 devoted some of its precious space to a quaintly worded editorial pointing out the need for a city charter, saying:

"Sundry things were done; sundry hills and streets were graded, to the great satisfaction of some and dissatisfaction of others. Some six or eight thousand of inhabitants had come together from the four winds; some wished to do more things and some wished to do things better; and to effect all these objects, and a variety of others, no means seemed so proper as a city charter in due form and style."

That was a very exciting, historic year in Cleveland, that year of 1837. It was not, for that matter, a routine year anywhere, what with the great financial panic that it brought to the entire nation. Cleveland felt that panic in its economic life, but there were other distractions at hand, chief among these being the evidence of a continuing deterioration of relations with Ohio City. The rivalry between the two cities on the opposing banks of the Cuyahoga moved from the ideological and commercial area to the point of actual physical conflict in 1837. It is still remembered by both sides as The Battle of the Bridge.

Cleveland and Ohio City were connected at Detroit Street by a float bridge jointly owned by the two communities. It was a modest, low structure which, however crude and rustic in appearance, served its purpose admirably until the fateful year of 1837, when the City Council of Cleveland abruptly adopted a resolution directing removal of that half of the bridge extending from the east bank to the middle of the river.

This provocative action may be best understood in the light of some backstage finagling by a pair of real estate speculators named John W. Willey and James S. Clark. These two men in 1836 had purchased a large tract of land which clamped around Ohio City like a horseshoe, beginning in the river valley's flatland and swinging around to the south and to the west of Ohio City.

Willey and Clark had high hopes for this enormous tract of real estate which they had given the poetic name of Willeyville, seemingly intending to promote further municipal confusion along the banks of the Cuyahoga. They also had built another bridge over the Cuyahoga River where Columbus Street, far to the south of Detroit Street, came down into the valley. Columbus Street was an important highway linking Cleveland with the farmlands and towns to the south. Its traffic formerly had been accustomed to following Pearl Road to the Detroit Street Bridge, passing through the heart of Ohio City, before swinging over the river to Cleveland.

As the people of Ohio City saw the new Columbus Street Bridge, its sole purpose was to divert the main flow of traffic from southern Ohio away from its streets and into Cleveland. They boiled with indignation that the bridge-builder's art should be so evilly misused, but there wasn't anything they could do about the Columbus Street Bridge.

Cleveland's action in severing its half of the Detroit Street Bridge was something else again. It was a transparent effort by Cleveland to divert all the important through traffic to the bridge south of Ohio City, thereby bringing about a major bypass of the rival community to the west.

A fact which makes this tangled civic situation more understandable—at least, more interesting—is that John W. Willey, one of the two land speculators who brought about this unhappy state of affairs between Cleveland and Ohio City, also was the mayor of Cleveland. He was, in fact, Cleveland's very first mayor under the newly won city charter.

Some students of this situation have gone so far as to suggest, openly, that Mayor Willey was able to exert considerable influence on the Cleveland City Council in its enactment of the bridge legislation so directly calculated to boost the value of lands owned by Speculator Willey. But no matter how it happened, there was a civic crisis now at hand.

There is, unfortunately, no record that tells what happened in the early hours of the morning following the unannounced nocturnal removal of the Cleveland half of the bridge. All we can do is try to piece together the most likely sequence of events based on the laws of probability and fit them in with the unverified legends that live on in neighborhoods on both sides of the river.

It is an unconfirmed legend, but likely enough to believe, that a horse-drawn fish wagon, running late toward the market place in Cleveland, went careening onto the bridge in the predawn darkness through a heavy mist and rumbled noisily toward its watery surprise. The clatter of the hoofs on the loose-fitting boards and the sound of the iron-rimmed wheels could be heard far out into the river, as could the drayman's occasional shouts of encouragement to his high-trotting horses.

Suddenly, earwitnesses testified later, there was a shriek, which they thought came from the throat of the driver, although the fish and the horses weren't entirely ruled out. It was followed by the sound of a large splash, and minutes later moderately big waves were noted splashing in toward shore. The fish wagon had run out of bridge in the middle of the stream.

The driver and the horses swam back to the Ohio City side of the river minutes later, but no part of the fish cargo ever was recovered. They had been freshly caught, and it was the general opinion of the time that most of the fish had seized this golden opportunity to take it on the lam for the lake and liberty.

By dawn's early light, the shore on the west bank was lined with Ohio City residents who had heard the alarming report that the bridge had been tampered with, and it was in this first gray light of the day, through the mists that still lay heavy on the river, that they saw there was only half a bridge left. And, as the drayman had learned, half a bridge was no better than no bridge at all.

A Cleveland journalist, James Harrison Kennedy, relating how the dastardly deed was done at night "while the Ohio citizens lay dreaming of future municipal greatness," went on to describe how "when the morning mists arose from over the valley of the Cuyahoga, they saw their direct communication gone, and realized that to reach the court house and other points of interest in Cleveland, they would be compelled to travel southward and make use of the hated Columbus Street bridge."

Now it was just like the old days when the Indians occupied the west side of the river and the colonists in Cleveland lived tensely, never knowing when the redskins would get out of hand and go on the warpath. Bonfires burned brightly along the west bank of the river, and the people of Ohio City hopped from one foot to the other in their indignation, crying out for aggressive action.

Retaliation was quick. The council of Ohio City declared the hated Columbus Street Bridge a nuisance and ordered the city marshal to "abate" the nuisance "without delay."

The rallying cry of the West Siders summed up their demands: "Two bridges or none!" Streets leading southward to the Columbus Street Bridge were crowded with traffic on both sides of the river as business and normal living came to a halt while everybody in both towns hustled to the river crossing to see what excitement was next in store.

It was Ohio City's move, and the city marshal, flanked by deputies, strode purposefully onto the bridge and planted some heavy charges of powder. He and his men ran back to shore, put their fingers in their ears, and cringed in expectation of the explosion—as did everybody in the crowd. But the worst that happened was several sharp popping noises and several large bursts of smoke. The damage to the bridge was entirely negligible, if not laughable.

Nobody took the risk of joshing the red-faced city marshal, who determinedly called his deputies to his side, conferred with them, and then led them to the Cleveland side of the bridge, where they dug a deep ditch immediately in front of the bridge entrance. Then they returned to the Ohio City side and dug another ditch, equally wide and deep. It was a temporary measure, but the bridge was effectively closed off to those who would use it until more conclusive means could be found to destroy the structure.

A council of war was held in Ohio City and a date was set for an all-out attack on the bridge. In all the excitement, the historians of the time forgot to jot down the chronology of occurrences, but it is widely assumed and generally accepted that D-Day was the day following the failure of the explosives. Word traveled fast and early on the fateful day. It is estimated that nearly a thousand men from Ohio City and other communities of the county—volunteers, so to speak —gathered for the attack. Many of them were armed with clubs, rocks, and rifles, and they even had their own chaplain. Dr. Pickands, pastor of the Presbyterian Church, invoked divine aid in behalf of the stalwart force before it began the march to the bridge site with a lawyer, C. L. Russell, in the lead.

Cleveland was not about to be taken by surprise. Some of its scouts had infiltrated the Ohio City camp and learned of the serious plans for reprisal. When the Ohio City army reached the Columbus Street Bridge, they saw that Cleveland had marshaled a formidable defense. There, across the river, stood a company of militia with muskets in readiness to rake the bridge area. And if this were not enough to quell the Ohio City offensive, Cleveland also had rolled down to the river's edge an ancient cannon which usually was fired as the highlight of the Independence Day celebrations—continuing the tradition of Uncle Abram Hickox.

Before the opposing forces could enter into any hostilities, a peace-maker suddenly appeared on the bridge. He was none other than John W. Willey, mayor of Cleveland and real estate moonlighter, the villain of the piece. A mighty roar shook the Ohio City side of the bridge when Willey stepped forward and held up his hands for atten-tion. Before he could utter more than a few words, a volley of stones drove him to cover, and the fight, you might say, was on.

At either end of the bridge was an apron that could be raised or lowered, and the one at the Ohio City side was let down to provide a shelter for the anti-bridge forces. The men went at their job of destruction with crowbars and axes, ripping up the planks and throwing them into the river with cries of exultation even as the Cleveland militia thundered across the bridge in a charge that would have brought a sparkle to the eyes of Rudyard Kipling. They were greeted with rocks, clubs, and occasional rifle fire.

In all the swirling melee, an Ohio City man named Deacon House carefully picked his way through the Cleveland lines and spiked the old cannon before it had been fired the first time. It is generally acknowledged that his deed was the military highlight of the day and perhaps the very act that saved the entire affair from becoming

a very real tragedy. Had the fieldpiece been fired into the crowd of
Ohio City men, many would have died and the chances for any
future union of the opposing cities would have vanished.

Some men were injured, even as the fight progressed, but nobody
was killed. The battle was brought to a halt by the Cleveland marshal,
who also was sheriff of the county. He stepped between the opposing
armies and demanded a cessation of hostilities. Having achieved as
much, he took possession of the bridge and shortly obtained a court
decree against further interference. Guards were posted at either end
of the bridge to enforce the free movement of traffic.

Eventually the dispute was carried into the civil courts and a peace-
able solution was found—one which provided a multiple choice in
bridge crossings, as the Ohio City people earlier had demanded.

Out of every such dramatic moment in history should issue some
great literature to memorialize the heroism and high deeds that were
achieved. The Battle of the Bridge, it is gratifying to report, found
at least one poet inspired by what had happened. His name was
D. W. Cross, and he wrote an epic poem called "The Battle of the
Bridge," which was published by *Magazine of Western History*.

The poem, in part, sang out as follows:

> On hills, like Rome, two cities might be seen,
> (Meand'ring Cuyahoga flowed between);
> Whose rival spires in rivalry arose,
> The pride of friends, the envy of their foes.
> Each rival ruler of each rival town
> On his would smile, but on the other frown.
> Each sought for greatness, in his rival's fall,
> Regardless that the world was made for all.
> Envy and hatred waxed to frenzied height!
> Naught could appease but fierce and bloody fight.
>
> The culmination came! A peanut stand
> Erected by a "combination" band
> Of desperate men of capital, who swore
> No trade should be diverted from their shore.
> They claimed that Clark and Willey, reckless, sought
> To build a bridge. The right of way was bought
> Already! And they then designed to build
> Columbus street and bridge! This rumor filled
> Their souls with madness, and their eyes with tears!
> To think that peanut stand, the toil of years
> Should for the want of patronage decay
> And trade and barter turn some other way.
> They all agreed this could not be allowed,
> And boisterous bellowing agitate the crowd!

The epic poem goes on in that vein to recite the valorous deeds of that historic event, and upon publication it became the favorite piece of literature in the libraries of Ohio City. It should go without saying that it was especially popular among elocutionists of the area because it offered a wide range to a really talented public speaker adept in the throwing about of arms, kneeling to simulate the firing of muskets, clapping the hand to the head, reeling about, and all the other dramatic gestures that raised oratory to its highest point of development in the nineteenth century.

The memory of the Battle of the Bridge now has faded from memory and literature, and there is hardly a Clevelander on either side of the river who has anything but a vague idea of what happened. Now the Cuyahoga River is alive with bridges of all types and the people cross back and forth, merry as they please, little aware that once it was a real trick to cross the old river.

Seventeen years after the Battle of the Bridge, the existence of Ohio City as a separate municipal entity was ended by annexation. An election to decide the issue was held in both cities on April 3, 1854. Clevelanders voted in favor of annexation by a count of 1892 for, 400 against. The Ohio City vote count was 618 for annexation, 258 against.

Cleveland, by that time, had far outstripped Ohio City in population. The 1850 census gave Cleveland a population of 17,034, while Ohio City had but 3950.

It is plain that there had been a lot of behind-the-scenes dickering between the Clevelanders and the Ohio City people on the actual terms of surrender, and much of this talk must have centered on the old issue of bridge facilities across the Cuyahoga. Immediately after annexation had been approved, Cleveland built the Main Street Bridge, rebuilt the controversial Center Street Bridge, and constructed still another new bridge at the foot of Seneca Street.

The new spans probably were meant to be symbolic of the new union; of the twain becoming one. But the merger didn't work out quite that simply. Ohio City disappeared as a corporate entity, it is true, but in its place appeared the West Side, and the rivalry between the people on the opposing banks of the river has continued to this day.

VI

Raising Dickens—Cleveland Style

PEOPLE retired early in 1842; probably because there was precious little reason to postpone bedtime. Even the grogshops had closed their doors by midnight, and Cleveland was a dark patch on a black plateau as the sturdy steamship with the sturdy name, the *Constitution*, groped for the Cuyahoga River opening and safe mooring in the early hours of April 25th.

Likely there were some curious Clevelanders about as the ship made to. Its arrival had been widely publicized, and the entire town was anxious to see, in person, the celebrated passenger it carried, young Charles Dickens, the English writer.

Dickens was on the final swing of his first American tour when the *Constitution* docked in Cleveland. He had arrived in Boston on January 24, and since had been touring the United States by stagecoach, canal boat, river packet, trains, horseback, and ship. His travels had taken him far into the western country—as far west as St. Louis. He had made his way back east by the Mississippi and the Ohio rivers, debarking at Cincinnati. From the Queen City, he had traveled by coach northward through Ohio to Sandusky, where he had boarded the *Constitution*. It, hopefully, would take him to Buffalo, but not without pausing overnight in Cleveland.

The prospect of stopping in Cleveland did not please Boz.

Boz was angry, no doubt about it, and his attitude toward Cleveland could not be described as anything less than hostile.

During his brief stay in Sandusky, Dickens had picked up a copy of a Cleveland newspaper, the *Plain Dealer*, and his eyes had alighted upon an editorial in the publication which set his loyal British blood boiling. It was, in fact, a reprint from another newspaper, but Dickens either did not notice the credit line, or else he assumed—as he had a right to—that the very act of reprinting the piece was an editorial imprimatur.

The editorial advocated war with England to the death, and said that Britain must be "whipped again." It promised Americans that within two years they would be singing "Yankee Doodle" in Hyde Park and "Hail, Columbia" in the courts of Westminster.

The editorial had appeared originally in an Alexandria, Virginia, newspaper, *Index,* and the editor of the publication, Jesse E. Dow, is assumed to have written the piece which so angered Dickens when he read it in the *Plain Dealer.*

"War With England" was the headline over the editorial, which said: "We must confess we are astonished at the apparent apathy of Congress on the subject of a war with England. . . .

"England must conquer the United States, or she must sink into the grave of nations. Statesmen and diplomats may dream of peace, but the enemy's cannon will ere long arouse them with a thunder note, and then a war of extermination will commence in earnest. . . .

"We pray not for war if we can have an honorable peace, but we cannot have such. The grasping after the wealth of the world by England has destroyed her earlier sympathies and fired the train of her ambition. A hypocrite in the vesture of the church, she preaches the gospel of the world at one moment and lays the world under contribution at the next by force of arms. A harlot in spotless robes of a vestal, she speaks of purity and virtue and then seduces her hearers with her blandishments and honied tones. She has tyrannized over every power of Europe and Asia. Her fleets have scoured the seas, and her flag floats over every wild crag of the ocean. Despised and feared by all, she sits like a surly mastiff in her island kennel thirsting for blood, yet afraid to leave her litter. Her gold conquered Napoleon—her rapacity has caused nearly every war for the last fifty years. She warred with her own colonies because we would not pay her debts, use her stamped hot pressed paper and drink her infernal tea. She hates France because of her manufactures and curses America for having the manliness to tell her to mind her own business. We are ready to war with England. . . .

"Like Sir John Falstaff we can give reasons as plenty as blackberries for a war; and, feeling confident that we must have one, we are desirous of doing the business up handsomely at once, before our ardor cools or our countrymen become callous to insult and invasion.

"Our country teems with strong arms and stout hearts, burning for the fight. The war spirit is up among the people. The old drums of Louisburg, Havana, Bunkerhill, Saratoga, York-Town, New Orleans and an hundred other scenes of American glory are waiting for the signal. Our dark old battleships for the 'beat to quarters.' Then let our reformers, who are now so busy in saving wafers and sealing wax and who sell letter paper in the post office of the House of Representatives at $8 per ream, be up and doing. Congress of American Republicanism, stand to your arms—war is at hand. In less than fifteen days it may be upon us in all its horrors. Pass your militia bill; distribute your arms; authorize your President to grant commissions to privateers; call home your Whalemen; increase your navy; send your commercial agents around the world and bid the American hearts come home. Fight England, if fight you must, with a will to make a business of it, and my word for it, in less than three years the old Grid Iron and the stars will float triumphant over the seas. The people demand war! Our country is insulted and her glory is dimmed by the insolence of England. We should act as a man would act who has been insulted upon the walk. Thank God, the old blood of the Revolution is still trickling in our veins. We whipped England when we were in our infancy; we threshed her again when we arrived at the age of manhood; and with the blessing of God we can in a short time sing 'Jefferson and Liberty' in Hyde Park and 'Hail Columbia' in the scarlet halls of Westminster."

In his *American Notes,* which Dickens published upon his return to England that year, the English author recalled both the editorial and his brief stop in Cleveland, writing:

"After calling at one or two flat places, with low dams stretching out into the lake, whereon were stumpy light-houses, like windmills without sails, the whole looking like a Dutch vignette, we came at midnight to Cleveland, where we lay all night, and until 9 o'clock next morning.

"I entertained quite a curiosity in reference to this place, from having seen at Sandusky a specimen of its literature in the shape of a newspaper which was very strong indeed upon the subject of Lord Ashburton's recent arrival at Washington to adjust the points of dispute between the United States government and Great Britain—informing its readers that as America had 'whipped' England in her infancy, and whipped her again in her youth, so it was clearly necessary that she must whip her once again in her maturity; and pledging its credit to all True Americans, that if Mr. Webster did his duty in the approaching negotiations, and sent the English Lord home again in double-quick time, they should, within two years, sing 'Yankee Doodle in Hyde Park, and Hail Columbia in the scarlet courts of Westminster.' I found it a pretty town, and had the satisfaction of beholding the outside of the journal from which I have just quoted. I did not enjoy the delight of seeing the wit who indited the paragraph in question, but I have no doubt he is a prodigious man in his way, and held in high repute by a select circle."

Although he did not mention him by name, Dickens obviously was referring to the editor of the *Plain Dealer,* J. W. Gray, whose name appeared in the masthead of the newspaper. Gray appears to have taken a bad rap from Dickens, but even though he was not guilty of writing the anti-English editorial, he was just as bombastic and jingoistic in his editorials as was the anonymous author of the piece that offended Dickens. The same month—April—that Dickens arrived, Gray had written:

"The time is at hand when England—*That power whose flag is now unfurled, Whose morning drum beats round the world*—will be humbled; and He who guides the destinies of nations will take vengeance on this 'Disturber of the peace.'"

There was still another welcoming story in the *Plain Dealer* that month. It said: "'Bozophobia' is a new disease which has broken out in the eastern cities. The dandies, dandizettes and fools are running after Boz, alias Charles Dickens. The tickets for a ball recently given him in New York sold for $5 apiece!"

It didn't help one bit, so far as the Dickens' humor was concerned, that the ride across Lake Erie had been distressingly rough. The whitecaps had made the *Constitution* yaw and pitch about, to everybody's discomfort.

"It's all very fine talking about Lake Erie," Dickens wrote a friend, "but it won't do for persons who are liable to seasickness. We were all sick. It's almost as bad in that respect as the Atlantic. The waves are very short, and horribly constant."

In the same letter, written at Niagara Falls on the English side the following day, April 26, Dickens described his brief visit to Cleveland.

"We lay all Sunday night, at a town (and a beautiful town too) called Cleveland; on Lake Erie. The people poured on board, in crowds, by six on Monday morning, to see me; and a party of 'gentlemen' actually planted themselves before our little cabin, and stared in at the door and windows *while I was washing, and Kate lay in bed*. I was so incensed at this and at a certain newspaper published in that town which I had accidentally seen in Sandusky x x x, that when the mayor came on board to present himself to me, according to custom, I refused to see him, and bade Mr. Q tell him why and wherefor. His honor took it very cooly and retired to the top of the wharf, with a big stick and a whittling knife, with which he worked so lustily (staring at the closed door of our cabin all the time) that long before the boat left the big stick was no bigger than a cribbage peg!"

The mayor in question was Dr. Joshua Mills, by all accounts a good physician, a fine mayor, and hail fellow well met—when he was met, that is. In any analysis of the Dickens' visit, Dr. Mills emerges in a highly sympathetic light. Here he was, a simple man trying to perform a simple official function, that of welcoming a great literary celebrity to the city, only to be rudely rebuffed. Possibly he carried a key to the city, tucked away somewhere in his greatcoat, but there is no doubt that his head was swimming with the florid words of a grandiloquent greeting.

What should a mayor do under the circumstances? Most mayors would turn color in embarrassment, harrumph loudly, and stomp off deck and down the rickety gangplank—perhaps even lean out of the hansom waiting to carry them back to City Hall to shake a stick at the cabin of the rude Englishman.

Dr. Mills, clearly, was no ordinary municipal official. He was a doctor and he hardly could be expected to behave in a pattern traditional with politicians. Even so, his behavior was remarkable. Perhaps his medical knowledge had disciplined his temper—assuming his temper had been ired by Dickens' refusal to be welcomed to the city. But the real clue to Dr. Mills, the man, was his simple, direct action in sitting down on the wharf and whittling a big stick down to the size of a cribbage peg.

It was, in a way, a kind of Dickensian situation itself, which had the highest elected official of the port city placidly whittling and covering the wharf with the fine shavings while the great author peeked out—wide-eyed, one would guess—at the scene.

Eventually, Mayor Mills did leave. So did the hundreds of people who had traveled to the dockside in the chill Cuyahoga Valley that April morning. When only a handful of the more determined sightseers still hung on, Dickens emerged from his cabin and even left the *Constitution* for a short "prowl" around the pretty little town in the company of a friend. Along the way, he sighted the building that housed the *Plain Dealer,* the offending journal, but he did nothing more than stare balefully at the structure before turning on his heels and returning to the ship. At nine o'clock that morning, the *Constitution* lifted anchor and steamed out of the river, carrying Charles Dickens away from an occasion of displeasure.

In mitigation of Dickens' behavior toward the mayor and the people of Cleveland, there is the knowledge that, being close to the end of three months of arduous travel, he was fatigued and probably homesick. His trip from Columbus to Sandusky through the Ohio wilderness was mainly on a "corduroy road" made of tree trunks, and the jolting ride left a lasting impression.

"Good Heaven!" Dickens exclaimed in his description, "if you had only felt one of the least of the jolts with which the coach falls from log to log! It is like nothing but going up a steep flight of stairs in an omnibus."

Count the bumps, throw in the hateful editorial, add a bit of *mal de mer,* consider the goofs who insisted on peeking into the Dickens' cabin while he was trying to get dressed, and the author comes back into focus as a human being performing and reacting under considerable duress.

It was November of 1842 before the first copy of *American Notes* was received in Cleveland, and the *Plain Dealer*, which reprinted sections of the book, made this gratuitous observation:

"His [Dickens'] stay in this country was short, his time was mostly spent in barrooms, stage coaches and steamboats; and it is evident from his Notes that he has become acquainted only with such characteristics of our people as float on the surface, and has yet to learn our real characters. However, there is much in this work to amuse and instruct the American readers, although in every page we meet traces of a deep-seated English prejudice."

A few weeks later, the following *Plain Dealer* editorial appeared:

BOZ IN CLEVELAND

Long will be remembered that bright morning in May [sic] when it was announced to the citizens of Cleveland that "the Dickens was among them" . . .

All the dignitaries from the shirtless loafer to his Honor the Mayor met the boat at the foot of Main street, where other famous men had disembarked . . .

When his "Notes of America" were first published, the *would be great men* of this *little* city ordered ten score copies by Hardin & Co.'s express to be brought with lightning speed. The books were opened and all of Cleveland that appeared was the following lines, the glory of which we take all to OUR HUMBLE SELF;

(At this point the *Plain Dealer* editorial reprinted Dickens' commentary on Cleveland quoted earlier in these pages.)

That immortalizes us, that word "prodigious"! How slight the foundation often, on which rests the fabric of human greatness! But for a vagrant copy of The Plain Dealer and the careless penning of a paragraph which proved unpalatable to English taste we might have lived and died in comparative obscurity. But the above "note" has made us the subject of comment by all the Lords, Dukes, Marquises and Ministers of England!

Sluggish the spirit and base the lot of him who is content to plod through a dull life to a fameless grave!

The only thing Cleveland could cheer in the entire episode was Mayor Mills' whittling performance. This was no small thing, really, because Cleveland—like all cities everywhere—has had chief executives without even that minor skill to recommend them. Good whittlers, like good mayors, are awfully hard to find.

VII

Rockefeller in Cleveland

U NLESS you search about carefully, it is almost as if John Davison
Rockefeller, the richest man in the world, never had lived in
Cleveland.

Millions of footprints have almost obliterated the path that John D.
made in his Cleveland lifetime, and the spreading blanket of a modern
metropolis has all but covered completely the old landmarks that once
marked his presence.

The city's memory of its most famous son becomes progressively
fuzzier with each day, and there is already a noticeable vagueness
about the details of his years there, even in the firsthand accounts of
people who knew him. Such memory of him as lives on is tinged with
a mixture of pride and hurt. There is a lingering vicarious sense of
triumph that one of the local boys made it big in the money game, but
isn't it too bad he let success go to his head?

It's a perfectly normal, perfectly American reaction; the indignation
of a hometown scorned. John D., as almost everyone knows, hit it
very large in Cleveland, businesswise, that is, but the time in his career
finally arrived when he became the victim of his own success. Mahomet
at last had to go to the mountain. Rockefeller had created a global
business, the Standard Oil Company, and it was not feasible to have
its headquarters anywhere else but in the financial capital of the world.
In the years from 1877 to 1883, John D., his family, his partners, and
his principal executives moved from Cleveland to New York.

It was an exodus that did not go unnoticed or unresented, even
though the Rockefellers themselves made it clear that Cleveland was
still their real love. Each summer, beginning in 1884, they returned
home to Forest Hill, a lovely seven-hundred-acre patch of greenery in
the high hills of the East Side with its own lake, with dark, clean-
smelling woods, and a vista that took in almost all of the town and the
bright blue waters of Lake Erie to the north. Later, it would have
winding paths for bicycling by moonlight and for the leisurely stroll in
the fresh morning air smelling of dew and the Lake Erie waters. It even

would have its own nine-hole golf course and a network of private roads.

The very perfection of the Forest Hill estate itself was a divisive force in the relationship between John D. Rockefeller and his Cleveland neighbors. With a Shangri-La as his daily environment, John D. had no need nor urge to venture beyond his own acreage. Cleveland therefore saw little of the famous man in his prime years, whether he was in New York or in Forest Hill. If he were in town, though, he could be counted on to emerge with his family on Sunday morning for the trip through the lower East Side to the Euclid Avenue Baptist Church at East 18th Street and Euclid Avenue, the church that he had joined as a fifteen-year-old boy freshly arrived in town and which he gave magnificent moral and financial support throughout his life.

It was in Strongsville, a town on the southern outskirts of Cleveland, that the Rockefeller family first settled in 1853, following a rather abrupt departure from New York State. Among the several explanations for the move, the most intriguing is the story that the head of the family, William Avery Rockefeller, decided to pull up stakes in order to avoid an embarrassing involvement with the law

Ida Tarbell, an acid-penned biographer of the Rockefellers, once wrote of William Avery Rockefeller that he had "all the vices save one." He did not drink. Otherwise, he was depicted as something of a rounder who had little use for religion and lived under a shaky set of ethics.

Father William was, at the same time, the most interesting and the most mysterious of all the Rockefellers. All the fragmented descriptions and anecdotes about him bring forth a personality as far removed from John D. Rockefeller as possible. Where John D., the son, was quiet, religious, conservative, restrained, and proper almost to a painful degree, Father William was outgoing, boisterous, restless, and careless of the conventions that bind.

William Avery Rockefeller made what was seemingly a substantial living as a peddler of patent medicines and miraculous medical cures. He was, essentially, one of the enterprising quacks of his day, even calling himself "Dr. Rockefeller." He sought out his "patients" in the wild western country, spending many months of the year away from home swinging about the frontier with his wagon full of medical goodies and with syrupy assurances of good health for each and every customer. No ailment was beyond his great powers to remedy, judging from one of his handbills, which read:

"Dr. William A. Rockefeller here for one day only. All cases of cancer cured unless they are too far gone and then they can be greatly benefited."

There are dark suggestions in several of the Rockefeller biographies that Rockefeller *père* was not above chasing the girls wherever he could find them, and the evidence hints that this hobby was one of his most enduring weaknesses. In the tradition of playboys everywhere, though, when it came to choosing a wife, William carefully selected a girl of strict upbringing and high moral standards, Eliza Davison, a member in good standing of the Dutch Reformed Church.

In his initial bid for Eliza's hand, William showed a rare technique, if the story of that first encounter is true. It seems that the shrewd elder Rockefeller (who was at that time, of course, the young Rockefeller) could play the role of a deaf mute to perfection. It had been a useful device in cultivating friendly relations—and business, probably—among the Indians, they having a great superstitious regard for anybody so afflicted. When William presented himself at the door of Eliza Davison's house, he pretended this inability to speak or to hear with some piteous gestures, and the sight of the tall, handsome, handicapped boy apparently wrenched the heart of this good woman. It is said that she exclaimed: "If he weren't deaf and dumb, I'd marry him!"

The roguish William held her to her word and they were married.

As demanding as was his job of touring the West in the interest of a healthier America, William still interrupted his field trips often enough to sire a family. His first child was a girl, Lucy. The second was a boy, John Davison Rockefeller, named after Eliza's father, John Davison, a stern Scotsman. The date of the first boy child's birth was July 8, 1839, and the place was Richford. The town later would become famous for the event, and the accent would be shifted to the first syllable of the town name. The family in following years was further augmented by the births of William, Mary Ann, and a set of twins, Franklin and Frances. Of the latter pair, only Franklin survived infancy.

The family moved to Moravia, some forty miles distant, in 1843, and then on to Owego in Tioga County in 1850, finally breaking the home ties with New York State three years later in the move to Strongsville, Ohio. There is nothing to indicate that the selection of Strongsville as the family's home community was anything more than a random choice. William Rockefeller was motivated not so much by a desire to live in Ohio, it seems, as he was by the powerful wish to leave New York State.

John D. was fourteen and his brother William was thirteen when the big move interrupted their education at Owego Academy. There was no high school in Strongsville; indeed, there was but one high school in Cleveland, and that was too far from home—twelve miles or so distant. The elder Rockefeller still was determined to provide his sons with a good education, however, and he could afford to do so. It was decided to have the boys board in downtown Cleveland and enroll in Central High School in the heart of the little lake town to the north.

The enrollment at Central was small, high school being something of an educational luxury in the middle of the nineteenth century, but John and William found themselves among some interesting classmates. One was a sixteen-year-old boy named Marcus A. Hanna. Another was a pretty, shy girl named Laura Celestia Spelman. She would marry John D. Rockefeller one day. He, of course, would become the richest man in the world, while Mark Hanna would become a United States senator, a President-maker and, some say, the most powerful politician in the world.

It was most unlikely that two such future notables should be brought together in the tiny classroom of a small school in a sleepy Ohio village, but there they were, in open defiance of the cosmic odds, together for two years at least. Sometime in that period, John's interest in further educational preparation for the world flagged. He became, in today's parlance, a high school dropout. It was not such a dreadful offense against society then as it is now, and, as a matter of fact, John D. didn't completely drop out of the field of education. He switched from the high school to Folsom's Mercantile College (forerunner of today's Dyke Business School) where, he said later, the foundation for his future business success was laid.

"My business college training, though lasting only a few months, was very valuable to me," he wrote. "But to get a job—that was the question. I tramped the streets of Cleveland for days and weeks, asking merchants and storekeepers if they didn't want a boy. But offers of my services met with little appreciation. No one wanted a boy and very few showed any overwhelming anxiety to talk with me on the subject. At last one man on the Cleveland docks told me I might come back after the noonday meal. I was elated; it seemed that I might get a start.

"I was in a fever of anxiety lest I should lose this one opportunity that I had unearthed. When finally I presented myself to my would-be employer he said he would give me a chance, but not a word passed between us about pay. This was in September, 1855. I joyfully went to work. The name of the firm was Hewitt & Tuttle, wholesale commission house."

The company's office was on Merwin Street in the river bottomland area called the Flats.

"When January of 1856 arrived Mr. Tuttle presented me with $50 for my three months' work—about $4 per week. No doubt it was all I was worth, and it was entirely satisfactory to me. For the next year at $25 a month I kept my position, learning details and clerical work connected with such business. It was a wholesale commission house.

"At the end of my first year's service I became bookkeeper with a salary of $500. The next year I was offered $700, but thought I was worth $800. We had not settled the matter by April and as a favorable opportunity had presented itself for carrying on the same line of business on my own account I resigned."

The "favorable opportunity" was the formation of a partnership in 1859 with a man ten years his senior, Maurice B. Clark. The two pooled their money to finance a commission merchant business dealing principally in the handling of vegetables. Clark, a native of England, had two thousand dollars to invest. Rockefeller had only nine hundred dollars saved, but his father had promised him and his brothers a cash gift of one thousand dollars each when they should reach their twenty-first birthdays. John D. was only nineteen, but his father offered to give him his money in advance, provided he agreed to pay interest on the one thousand dollars until his twenty-first birthday arrived. The promise was given and the firm of Clark & Rockefeller was made possible.

Even as the world looked askance at William Avery Rockefeller in later years, John D. indicated his deep affection and respect for his father, writing: "To my father I owe a great debt in that he himself trained me to practical ways. He was engaged in different enterprises; he used to tell me about these things, explaining their significance; and he taught me the principles and methods of business.

"He used to dicker with me and buy things from me. He taught me how to buy and sell."

William Rockefeller's revealing postscript to this revelation was his statement that "I cheat my boys every time I get a chance. I want to make them sharp. I trade with the boys and skin them and just beat them every time I can."

John D., reminiscing at another time, said his father never carried less than one thousand dollars in his pockets. This at a time when a thousand dollars was a large sum even to have in the bank. John D., who won a reputation himself for carrying a supply of dimes in his own pockets, recalled his father's big money foible with admiration.

Mark Hanna once said his old schoolmate Rockefeller was "mad about money, though sane in everything else."

The Rockefeller family did not stay long in Strongsville, moving on briefly to Parma, another Cleveland suburb, and finally into Cleveland itself, renting a house in late 1854 on the west side of Perry Street (East 22nd Street), near Prospect Avenue. The landlord was Colonel O. J. Hodge.

Hodge leased the house to the William Avery Rockefeller family for one year at a rent of two hundred dollars per annum, payable quarterly.

"Never was rent paid more promptly," Colonel Hodge wrote, "and never did I have, in all respects, a better tenant. On the day the lease expired, the keys were brought to me by Mr. Rockefeller's son, now John D. Rockefeller, the great multi-millionaire. I had become somewhat acquainted with the young man at his father's house, where, to me, he seemed a quiet, unassuming youth. He showed none of that hilarity often seen in boys of his age. Usually he sat quietly in his chair, listening to what was being said. In 1858, three years after . . . I was surprised to see his name coupled with that of Mr. Morris [sic] B. Clark in a business enterprise . . ."

A number of Clevelanders were surprised at the speed with which the teen-ager moved into a position of business independence. By 1863, the firm of Clark & Rockefeller had made enough money that the partners were searching about for a likely business in which to invest their surplus. That their attention should have been drawn to the possibilities of the oil business is hardly surprising. The first oil well had been struck near Titusville, Pennsylvania, in 1859, and it is a matter of record that the production of the Pennsylvania fields had reached two hundred thousand barrels in the following year and continued to leap upward with each passing month.

The nation suddenly was caught in a frenzy over oil, but in few places was it as noticeable as it was in Cleveland, which, during the decade of the 1850s, had left the languorous bliss of a small town for the robust pace of a booming city. The Ohio Canal, although a tremendous boon to the community in the previous twenty-five-year period, now seemed to typify what was being left behind—a slow-moving, quiet, calculating way of life. Now there were no fewer than five railroads clanking through the stirring city, and their tracks scarred meadows and yards, took over the riverbanks and even the lakefront in a kind of arrogant show of industry's pre-eminence.

This was the transition time for the city. The horse-drawn barges still ambled through the canals; the white-sailed schooners still sailed into the harbor; heavily laden wagons and stagecoaches still rumbled and squeaked over the cobblestoned streets, but the picturesque scene was fading. The city was yielding to the vanguard of the Industrial Revolution, and it already was being sullied. Of the mighty flow of petroleum that had been drawn from the Pennsylvania oil fields, thousands of barrels of the viscous wealth had been shipped to Cleveland. Refineries to process the petroleum were springing up all over town, especially in the Cuyahoga Valley area where proximity to the railroads was the strategic advantage.

By late summer of 1863, there were twenty refineries actively at work in Cleveland. The smell of oil was in the air that Rockefeller breathed and it was beginning to discolor the waters of the Cuyahoga River flowing past his office. Little wonder that he and his partner should have considered the advantages of investing in petroleum when they already were swimming in its fumes!

It was John D.'s decision, after a careful study of the situation, that the production end of the oil business was entirely too speculative; too risky to meet his requirements of a sound investment. It was his judgment that he and his partners should skirt this get-rich-quick end of the business and concentrate on the processing and distribution of petroleum and its derivative products, thereby reducing the element of risk in the venture.

Through that wonderfully mysterious element of chance that is almost always a part of every success story, there had arrived in Cleveland at this critical juncture a young Englishman named Samuel Andrews, a candlemaker, no less, by trade. He had developed a new process for refining oil kerosene from crude petroleum, but he needed financial backing to put his idea to work.

The firm of Clark & Rockefeller decided to go into the oil refining business, using the Andrews' process, and the hope of the partners was that this would be a profitable sideline; a diversification which would relieve them of the fears that everywhere follow men who insist on carrying all their eggs in one basket. The offshoot company was called Andrews, Clark & Co.

The venture turned out rather well—better, even, than the vegetable commission house business. It led within seven years (January 10, 1870) to the formation of a joint stock corporation called the Standard Oil Company, which has prospered to this very day. Along the way, it helped to make John D. Rockefeller a billionaire and the most important business tycoon in the world. It established Cleveland as the world center of oil refining—a blessing not without its drawbacks.

William Ganson Rose, a leading Cleveland historian, described it this way:

". . . This was the era of oil. Cleveland had a number of small refineries in operation, and it was estimated that more than one-third of the entire production of the oil region was shipped to local plants.

"The city was flavored and saturated with oil; the river and lake were smeared with it. Oil wagons rumbled through the streets and tanks blocked the railroads.

"Oil fires kept the city firemen eternally vigilant and filled the valley with painful apprehension. Kerosene lamps were instantly popular, replacing feeble, flickering candles and whale-oil lamps.

"Rockefeller and his associates envisioned Cleveland as a great refining center; and, buying up their small rivals, they launched the gigantic Standard Oil empire . . ."

Rockefeller was not the ostentatious type. He and his bride, Laura Spelman, lived well but not extravagantly. He was already on his way to high financial success when they were married on September 8, 1864, being involved in the commission house business and the oil business both at the time. If that doesn't seem much of a start, remember that he was only twenty-five years old and still groping for direction.

In all the years that John D. and his family lived in Cleveland, they occupied only three houses. As honeymooners, they lived briefly with his parents. The first home of the honeymooning couple was on East 19th Street, close to today's Carnegie Avenue. Four short years later, they moved to swank Euclid Avenue and a mansion in Millionaire's Row at the corner of Case Avenue, now East 40th Street. It was a large, ungainly brick house with mansard roof and the usual gingerbread trim, but it met the needs of the young, growing family, and the address was the correct one for a young, rising businessman as the price, estimated at more than forty thousand dollars, would suggest.

Finally, there was Forest Hill, the name given to seventy-nine acres of scenic, wooded land six miles to the east of the city's center. It was high, sloping land topped by a plateau with a magnificent view of the green countryside and the shimmering lake to the north. Rockefeller loved the beauties of nature. He admired the site and he bought the land—not with the thought of extracting personal pleasure from it, but as an investment. Two years after he purchased the acreage, a group of three men became interested in it as the site for a hydropathic sanitarium. Rockefeller joined with them in the project, incorporating as the Euclid Avenue-Forest Hill Association, capitalized at $250,000. The association bought the land from Rockefeller and proceeded to construct a large frame building to house the sanitarium. Before it was finished, however, financial difficulties discouraged the sponsors of the project and it was never carried through. John D. repurchased the land and then entered on what was undeniably one of the strangest episodes of his career. He took a flyer as an innkeeper, turning the building into a private club-hotel.

It was a very large building that the sanitarium association had started out to build, of course, and its adaptability to use as a hotel immediately occurred to John D. His experience in the short-lived venture in that summer of 1877 discouraged him.

"I found that the guests expected Mother to entertain them and act as hostess," he wryly commented later.

The hotel idea was abandoned at the end of that summer and the building, thenceforth, became the Rockefeller summer home. It quickly found high favor with everybody in the family and the big, gloomy mansion on Euclid Avenue in time became nothing more than an occasional stopping place, used mainly on Sundays, when the Rockefellers would ride in from Forest Hill to attend services at the Euclid Avenue Baptist Church. The family would retire to the big house after church and spend a quiet afternoon in the cool, high-roofed parlors, returning in the evening to Forest Hill, the fun spot.

John D. kept adding acreage to his original investment in Forest Hill until it comprised some seven hundred acres of choice land. Even when business compelled him to move the family to New York and to take up legal residence there in 1882, Forest Hill continued to draw the Rockefellers back every summer, and there never was any doubt that this was the real family home. It remained the favorite refuge of John D. until it burned to the ground in 1918.

One of the features of Forest Hill late in the century was a nine-hole golf course which was laid out, not for John D.'s pleasure, but for his wife, Laura, who took up the strange, foreign game three years before he did. It was, of course, Laura's pursuit of par which caught John's interest and led him to take up the game. Her teacher was one of America's pioneer professionals, Joe Mitchell, a native of Scotland who came to Cleveland to be pro at Lake Shore Country Club. Sometimes, during the lessons, John D. would stand apart, listening intently and watching every move. When his wife was playing the course, he often would saunter to the links and study her progress.

One day he called Mitchell aside and gravely asked the question that millions of golfers since have repeated.

"Do you think that I can learn to play that game?" he asked Mitchell.

"Of course," said Mitchell.

"Very well," said the billionaire. "I will send for you at eight in the morning, but you must tell nobody. It must be a secret."

Mitchell agreed and the lessons began. Every morning he would be picked up by the Rockefeller carriage at the Lake Shore Club to be driven to Forest Hill to meet with Rockefeller. Mitchell charged five dollars an hour, portal to portal.

After months of instruction, Rockefeller decided that he was ready to make his competitive debut on the links, hoping thereby to astonish everybody in sight, most of all his wife.

Mrs. Rockefeller and her sister, Lucy, were on the home course early the next morning, ready to tee off, when John D. suddenly showed up. They greeted him and he, with eyes a-twinkle, suggested perhaps it would be helpful to them if he showed them how to hit the ball.

There were the shrieks of womanly laughter and hoots of derision that were to be expected under the circumstances, but Rockefeller insisted this game of golf was simple enough that even he could handle the clubs. His wife and his sister-in-law reacted as he had hoped, challenging him to step up to the tee and take a swing. As he was making ready for his first shot, they repressed their giggles as best they could. They quieted down, though, when John D. flexed the club once or twice and then clouted the ball straight down the fairway.

It was a highly competent performance that stilled all ridicule. There was, in fact, an involuntary cry of admiration from the surprised Mrs. Rockefeller.

"Wonderful! Wonderful!" she exclaimed, clapping her hands.

It may have been one of the happiest moments of the billionaire's life, and Mitchell's description of Rockefeller suggests this was so.

"I'll never forget how the old gentleman looked at me, with those little eyes sparkling, and winked," recalled the professional. "The lessons were to be a secret for all time, and I never gave him away."

Possibly John D. thought his wife's confidence in him needed bolstering every now and then. Laura Rockefeller once, in explaining why she had brought up her children to be modest in their tastes for wordly luxuries, told a friend that, "I have to save my money. John may lose his some day."

There isn't any question but that golf, now such a well-established sport, owes a large debt to John D. Rockefeller. When Rockefeller began to play golf, it was regarded as a strange, senseless British eccentricity; a game to be viewed as a curiosity, but not to be taken seriously. Pictures of Rockefeller at play on the links were a fixed part of American journalism for nearly four decades, and in his pursuit of par he was the American Pied Piper, leading millions of his fellow Americans, rich and poor, into the same feverish chase; one from which there is no escape.

Rockefeller was like any other duffer on the links in the way he went at the game, but there were some subtle differences. For one thing, he had better control of his emotions and his reactive speech than most people.

"When he'd miss a putt," Mitchell revealed, "he'd say: 'Shame! Shame! Shame!' That was his strongest language. But then, no matter who he was playing with, he'd stop and practice that same putt over and over until he dropped it."

Rockefeller was way out in front of the crowd in golf as in business, and he anticipated the modern cart-riding golfing set by his use of the bicycle. He always had a boy and a bike standing nearby as he played. When he made his shot, the boy would wheel the bike to him, and off he'd go across the fairway, a glistening sight in his white straw hat, white shirt, white trousers, and white shoes. He played every day he was home in the summer, except when it rained. The hottest weather would not stay his desire for the game, and no intrusion from the outside world, however calamitous, could interfere with his intense preoccupation in golf.

One day as he was playing along at Forest Hill with Mitchell, a messenger brought word to him that Federal Judge Kenesaw Mountain Landis had fined the Standard Oil Company $29,240,000. John D. listened with interest, nodded his head, and resumed his play with nothing more of a comment than, "Shall we go on, gentlemen?"

Another time his game at Forest Hill was interrupted by one of his staff aides, a Canadian-born youth named Cyrus Eaton; the same Cyrus Eaton who himself became one of the richest men in Cleveland—for that matter, one of the world's richest men.

"I'll never forget that day," recalls Eaton. "Mr. Rockefeller and a group of his assistants and business associates were supposed to leave the following morning for Buffalo to attend the Pan American Exposition there. I was at the main house at Forest Hill when a telegram arrived, announcing that President McKinley had been assassinated.

"In those days, anarchism was in full flower and there was a lot of hate propaganda leveled especially at wealthy men. John D. Rockefeller, being the wealthiest man in the world, was, of course, the prime target and symbol of capitalism. It was an anarchist who shot McKinley and the terrible deed had a double import and significance to Mr. Rockefeller, especially as he was planning to travel to the exposition the next day.

"I rushed up to him on the golf course and breathlessly showed him the telegram. Mr. Rockefeller read it gravely, shook his head and then, without any sign of agitation, he went back to his game."

At one point, John D. developed a bad slice, a dread affliction whose terrible implications can be appreciated only by another golfer. Millions of players have succumbed to the slice, surrendering silently sometimes, or simply whimpering in despair as they slid down to defeat. But John D. did something about his slice. First, he hired a photographer for a Cleveland newspaper to take a series of pictures as he addressed the ball—a sound enough idea, to be followed in later years by coaches in all sports. The idea worked gratifyingly well for John D., but this photographic device failed him in his effort to correct his distressing habit of lifting his head every time he brought his club around. Like golfers everywhere, rich and poor, he wanted to see where the ball was going before it even had left the tee. Again John D. fought back at his own human tendency to err by hiring a young boy to follow him around the course. Each time that the great man started his swing, it was the lad's job to cry out shrilly: "Hold your head down! Hold your head down!" There is no record, unfortunately, to reveal the outcome of this experiment. Most golfers, assailed by such a strident cry in midswing, would be likely to go berserk. In view of John D.'s self-control, however, it may have worked for him.

Golf, as played by John D., was something of a mob scene, what with photographers loping alongside, a boy crying out for him to hold his head down, the caddy, a boy to hold his bike in readiness, and still another boy to hold an umbrella over his head as a shield against the hot sun.

John D. did not regard golf in a completely frivolous light. It was, first of all, physical exercise, which he knew he needed if he were to extend his life-span. It was also a personal challenge and therefore to be greeted warmly by a man who had met and overcome all the other challenges life had thrown at him. It was a sport that called for the kind of emotional control he had and approved of, and it was a test of personal honesty.

"One of the best places to test a minister is on the golf links," he told his Euclid Avenue Baptist Church Sunday School class, after announcing he was to play a game the next day with the pastor.

"Even the best of them often lose their tempers. I am sorry to say that I have met ministers who did not hesitate to cheat a little on the links."

Rockefeller began to teach Sunday School classes at the Baptist church as a teen-ager and continued this Christian duty through the tumultuous, formative years of his business struggle toward world leadership. He had a way of compartmenting his life—so much time for business, so much time for religion, so much time for play—as he divided his money, with religion always one of the main beneficiaries of his philanthropy. He is believed to have contributed about a million dollars in his lifetime to the Euclid Avenue Baptist Church. Over a long period of years, he matched the contributions of all the other members of the church, dollar for dollar.

Rockefeller in 1872 surely was as sorely pressed for time as he was at any period in his career. This was the critical era, as Standard Oil struggled for a permanent footing. But 1872 also was the year when Rockefeller took on additional duties at the Euclid Avenue Baptist Church, accepting the post of superintendent of the Sunday School— a position which he held until 1905.

Throughout his later career as a Sunday School teacher and superintendent, Rockefeller played host at the annual church picnic that was the social highlight of each year. The picnic was held on the spacious grounds of his Euclid Avenue mansion for several years, and then it became an annual fixture at Forest Hill.

It is to be guessed that many of Rockefeller's golf foes found it expedient to let the old man win, and with his keen, analytical mind, he probably knew it. One who did not practice such deception or tact, however you may view it, was a Cleveland physician, Dr. E. B. Rhodes. It is probably no accident that Dr. Rhodes was one of Rockefeller's favorite golfing companions.

"The first time I played golf with him," said Dr. Rhodes, "I was warned that the old man loved to win, but I said I would 'throw' no matches and I never did. In fact, in fifteen years I played with him almost daily I lost only once, and on that occasion Mr. Rockefeller ran into the house and called to his wife: 'Mamma, mamma! I beat Dr. R. today!'

"When we lost a ball, we would call all the caddies and make them look. If they couldn't find it, he would call his partners, and if they, too, failed, he would summon all the gardeners and hired hands and keep them looking until the ball was found."

His refusal to abandon even a possession of such small value as a golf ball was part of Rockefeller's heightened sense of property. He simply regarded the squandering of money or property as wrong.

There are innumerable stories illustrating his careful respect for money and for the principle of full value to be received in exchange for money. One of the favorites of his biographers is his famous barrel bung blast contained in a letter to one of his refinery officials:

"Last month," he wrote, "you reported on hand 1,119 bungs. Ten thousand were sent you at the beginning of this month. You have used 9,527 this month. You report 1,012 on hand. What has happened to the other 580?"

When Rockefeller worked late in his downtown Cleveland office and the weather was bad, he was wont to take a room at the Colonial Hotel on Prospect Avenue—a hostelry, incidentally, which still is in full operation. One such night, when a terrible blizzard was raging, John D. walked into the Colonial and asked for a room.

The room clerk nodded, and as he handed Rockefeller a pen to register, he mentioned that the room would cost two dollars, but would include breakfast. The combined rate, he explained, was a new rule of the house.

"I don't want to eat breakfast here and I won't pay for it," said the great business tycoon, stomping toward the door. There he turned and added: "I pay my coachman anyway." With that parting reminder, he wrenched open the door and disappeared into the driving snow.

Not that John D. did not have his own extravagant little habits; he did. One was his habit of nibbling at little smoked herrings. He always liked to carry a package of the herrings in his pocket in case the appetite for the tidbit should assail him.

He confided one day to his best friend and personal physician, Dr. H. F. Biggar, his suspicion that the member of his household staff in charge of purchases was cheating him.

"The other day," he said, "I saw some herrings in a store window. The price mark was on them. Then I went home and looked up my grocery bills that I had paid. I had been charged eight cents more for a package of these things than they cost at that store, according to the sign that I saw with my own eyes. Now, if they do that with my herrings, they do it with other things. But I have kept quiet about it—only told you. I have given the cook two weeks vacation and now I shall watch how much the second cook charges for these herrings. I know that I have been cheated."

Richest man in the world or not, John D. did not like anybody to play him for a patsy.

Another sport, besides golf, that Rockefeller enjoyed was swimming, and he frequently swam in the large lake on his Forest Hill estate. He was no different from any other swimmer in town, except, possibly, that he was given to wearing his hat while swimming.

One of the favorite games at Forest Hill was bicycling through the twisting woodland roads by moonlight, and many a guest of the Rockefellers who was drawn into the game congratulated himself on getting through the experience alive. It was a "follow-the-leader" game in which each participant was called on to follow the lead cyclist, but no lights were allowed—only such light as the moon and stars gave. Many a guest ended in a clump of forsythia bushes with his bicycle sprockets draped over each ear, but Rocky, Sr., thought it was great fun.

The thirty-five years, especially the many summers that the Rockefellers used Forest Hill, were the wonderful green years for John D., his wife, and their children. Theirs was the utopian summer retreat, and in the lavish outlay of money to make it as perfect as possible, Rockefeller gave the lie to the popular canard about his stinginess. There was nothing stingy about John D., but he did have peculiar notions about getting value for his money.

A Cleveland journalist, John E. Bryan, who is today—of all things!—financial editor of the *Plain Dealer*, recalls a revealing boyhood encounter with Rockefeller. He was standing by while his father, Charles Bryan, chatted with the great John D., when the oil king suddenly broke off the conversation to pat the boy on the head and hand him one of his famous shiny dimes. Young Bryan, showing a financial instinct even at that early age, examined the dime carefully, looked up at the wizened old man, and informed him gravely and candidly that a neighborhood philanthropist always gave him a quarter.

"Ha!" said John D., nodding in understanding. "Now tell me, son, what have you done to earn even a dime?"

As remote a personality as John D. was, even to Clevelanders who knew him, he was a familiar figure compared with his brother William. Two years younger than John, William operated in his brother's shadow and yet he was adjudged by those who knew him as a shrewd, imaginative businessman. Beyond this likeness, he apparently was very much dissimilar to John D., as was the youngest brother, Frank.

Neither of the younger Rockefellers showed the religious, conservative streak that characterized John, and both of them were likened to their father, William Avery, in their physical appearance and in their interest in the material pleasures of life.

William, Jr., left Cleveland in the Standard Oil exodus to New York, severing his ties with Cleveland almost entirely. So far as is known, he returned to the city only a few times after that. He attended Frank's funeral in Cleveland in 1917, and is known to have visited John at Forest Hill at least once, but beyond those occasions, William's separation from Cleveland was total.

The relationship among the three brothers was anything but one of complete harmony. William and John were close friends through the years, but Franklin was more the loner. Some people said he was more like his father, the senior William, than either of the other sons. Frank was a vice president of Standard Oil—so far as the title and the paycheck were concerned, anyway—until 1912, but something had happened around the turn of the century to alienate him from his brother, John. Family biographers are vague on the point. One widely accepted supposition is that there was a quarrel between the men over the questionable behavior of the father, William, Sr. Another strong possibility is that Frank, who had been in partnership with James Corrigan of Cleveland in the Franklin Iron Mining Co. in Wisconsin, was angered by his brother John's treatment of his friend Corrigan.

The mining company had gotten into financial troubles and Corrigan put up twenty-five hundred shares of Standard Oil stock as security for loans from Rockefeller. John D. eventually took over the stock at $168 a share, and when the same shares jumped to five hundred dollars each within two years, Corrigan sued him, claiming the oil king had deceived him about the value of the stock. The legal ruling was unfavorable to Corrigan and the verdict was upheld by the Ohio Supreme Court, but Frank Rockefeller was angered by the transaction.

So bitter was Franklin's feeling toward John that he refused to speak to him in the last fifteen years of his life. He became, in fact, one of John's most outspoken critics. Frank severed his business connections with Standard Oil and his brother in 1899, but was kept on the company payroll for some years thereafter—presumably by decision of John.

He remained a resident of Cleveland, but he also had a twelve-thousand-acre ranch in Belvidere, Kansas, as well as an interest in ranches in Texas and Arizona. He spent five months of each year in Cleveland, but never was known to communicate with John—even though John often was in town at the same time.

"I am Frank Rockefeller, stock farmer—not Frank Rockefeller, brother of John D.," he has been quoted as declaring.

Franklin became gravely ill in February 1917. He was operated on for intestinal trouble in a Cleveland hospital and a fatal paralysis developed. But even as he lay close to death, the bitterness of his feelings

toward John were such that he fretted over the possibility that John
might try to visit him in the hospital. He dictated a statement to reporters which clearly indicated the extent of the breach with his
brother.

"Frank Rockefeller," he stated, "has not sent for his brother John
and will not send for him nor will he advise his brother of his illness."

Franklin had made many statements that must have hurt his brother,
but this one, dictated on his deathbed, must have carried the most
piercing hurt of all; more, even, than Frank's action at an earlier time
in removing the bodies of his two children from the family burial plot so
they would not be near the famous billionaire.

When Frank died, all his grieving older brother could do was shake
his head and say: "Poor Frank. I held him in my arms when he was a
baby."

William Avery Rockefeller, father of the clan, never figured im-
portantly in the civic or social life of Cleveland—probably because excursions out West to sell his patent medicines took him away from the
city so often. His trips became longer and more frequent with the
passing years. From 1860 on, he was rarely seen in the city.

John D. Rockefeller, Jr., once wrote of his grandfather:

"My Grandfather Rockefeller was a most lovable person. My Uncle
Frank, father's youngest brother, had a ranch in Kansas and my grandfather was often there. He would come to visit us at Forest Hill but he
never sent word in advance. He telephoned from the end of the trolley
line and we would send a carriage to meet him. He gave me a .22-calibre
rifle, and the two of us used to shoot marks and targets. Grandfather
was a great storyteller. He played the violin too, holding it down at his
waist instead of tucking it under his chin. All the family loved him. He
was a very entertaining man, coming and going when he felt like it.
He lived a detached kind of life and I didn't know much about it."

When the older Mrs. Rockefeller died in March 1889 at the age of
seventy-six, her husband failed to appear in Cleveland for the funeral.
He was the only member of the immediate family who was missing.

There have been published reports that William lived in New York
City under the assumed name of "Dr. William Levingston" until he died
in 1906 at the age of ninety-six. According to a New York World story
published in 1908, he married a twenty-year-old girl in 1855, and allegedly lived with her in bigamous bliss until his death five decades
later.

Now all the Rockefellers are gone from Cleveland, and Forest Hill has
been swallowed by the city. Part of it is public park land and still re-
tains some of its old natural splendor; part of it is an expensive home
development called "Forest Hills." People always have had the overpowering habit of adding an "s" to the name of the Rockefeller estate.

The wonderful summer retreat was especially loved by Mrs. John D. Rockefeller. She eagerly looked forward to the approach of warm weather because it meant that she soon would be returning home to Cleveland with all its familiar sights, its old friends, and all the pleasures of the family estate. When Mrs. Rockefeller's health began to fail in 1913, preventing her from making her usual pilgrimage to the Cleveland retreat the following year, the end of Forest Hill was in sight. She never saw the Cleveland home again, dying at the Pocantico Hills estate in New York in March 1915.

The family burial plot was in Lake View Cemetery in Cleveland, but Mrs. Rockefeller, ironically, was not able to return home immediately, even in death. The bar to her return was a remarkable show of avarice by a special Ohio state tax commission made up of John D. Fackler and William Agnew. They had ruled that since Rockefeller had been in residence approximately half of the previous year of 1913 at Forest Hill (due to the illness of his wife), he was, ipso facto, a legal resident of East Cleveland and therefore subject to the state personal property tax.

The tax authorities sent Rockefeller notification of their decision and called upon him to provide a list of all his property for the purpose of determining his tax liability. The aged billionaire promptly refused to comply with the request, answering simply that he was a legal resident of New York State and not subject to the Ohio taxation. The Ohio commission held to its position and sent Rockefeller a tax bill based on his estimated personal property holdings of $311,000,000.

Back home in East Cleveland, meanwhile, the tax rate dropped from $1.41 per one hundred dollars of valuation in 1913 to a mere thirty-seven cents per hundred dollars in 1914 in gleeful anticipation, apparently, of the Rockefeller windfall . . . a windfall that never fell. Rockefeller simply refused to surrender to the Ohio tax decision, holding tenaciously to his claim of New York residency.

The death of Mrs. Rockefeller added a macabre note to the controversy, because her husband was unable to take her body to Cleveland for burial. If he had appeared in Cuyahoga County, he would have been confronted by process servers. While his attorneys sought to settle the case, Mrs. Rockefeller's body was placed in a mausoleum owned by John Archbold, Rockefeller's second in power at Standard Oil. After six long months, arrangements were made which permitted the grieving oil king to take his beloved Laura home for the last time; not to Forest Hill, but to Lake View Cemetery, only a short distance away from her favorite home.

Twenty-two years later, on May 23, 1937, John D. Rockefeller died in Ormond Beach, Florida. In less than two months he would have reached his ninety-eighth birthday. His body was returned to Cleveland for the final services and he was interred alongside his wife at the foot of the tall granite shaft that is the tallest monument in the cemetery; to one side of him is his wife and to the other is his mother. Spread out then in a semicircle, fan-like, are the graves of other members of the immediate family—not including either of his brothers, or his father, however.

The erosion of the years has been severe, but it is still possible to find the signs that Rockefeller left along his Cleveland path. There is still the Rockefeller Building, a seventeen-story building that was one of the city's first skyscrapers and continues to be one of the city's most attractive buildings. It sits on Superior Avenue, between Public Square and the Cuyahoga River, overlooking The Flats and Merwin Street and River Street, where John D.'s career was planted and took root. The building was constructed in 1905 and when it was completed, John D. turned it over to his son, John D., Jr., as a gift.

In 1920, the junior Rockefeller sold the classic building to a Cleveland entrepreneur named Josiah Kirby, who later would fall into the clutches of the law for mismanaging the funds of his Cleveland Discount Company. The new owner of the building promptly dropped the name of Rockefeller and renamed it the Kirby Building.

When John D. Rockefeller, the senior member of the family, heard of the transaction and the loss of his name from the tall Cleveland building, he was upset enough to repurchase the building at a reported price of $2,972,000, representing a tidy profit, estimated to be several hundred thousand dollars, for Kirby. His first act was to restore the name, "Rockefeller Building." The building later passed out of the hands of the Rockefeller family again, but there was a provision in the terms of sale that the name of the building must remain Rockefeller. It is somehow appropriate that in this city where the great business dynasty was born, and where the founder of the greatest fortune in American history first made his way and lies buried, that the name of Rockefeller should live on, even in such a small way.

VIII

On the Square

THE Public Square is the most controversial piece of real estate in Cleveland; a civic anachronism with impressive staying powers that has successfully resisted attack, criticism, and almost all efforts at beautification since Seth Pease sketched it in on the first crude maps of the city-to-be. It is believed that it was incorporated into the master plan at Moses Cleaveland's behest.

As it is now constituted, the Square is a ten-acre area which is divided into four quadrants of equal size by Ontario Street, a north-south thoroughfare, and Superior Avenue, which runs east and west. Where these two streets meet, in the middle of the Square, is the geographical heart of the city.

The principal criticism of the Square among progressive Clevelanders is that it is an old-fashioned, hick-townish concept, serving little or no utilitarian purpose and failing even to meet the minimal standards of a civic decoration.

There are the traditionalists, on the other hand, who will fight to the death to save the Square. It is their stout contention that this open area in the center of downtown is one of Cleveland's principal charms, a distinguishing characteristic that links the city with its New England origin and sets it apart from most other large cities of the Midwest.

The Square is no grassy commons, although it was planned as a wide-open meadow where Clevelanders would have a convenient place to graze their cows, ibex goats, horses, and other livestock. The idea is both attractive and sound, but wholly impractical in this day and age. By the time a householder walks his cow downtown and fights his way through the crowded city streets, he has wasted half his day. Now it's entirely possible that wouldn't bother him at all; there are people who enjoy wasting their time, as we all know. But he no sooner gets back to his house than it's time to hop the bus and return downtown to lead the cow home. That means he runs into the rush-hour traffic, and only the man who has tried to walk his cow across the Detroit-Superior High Level Bridge, or the Main Street Bridge, in the five o'clock congestion can appreciate the impracticality of (a) grazing cattle in Public Square, and (b) owning a cow.

As matters stand, each of the four quadrants today is devoted to a different civic purpose. The northwest quadrant, for example, has as its feature piece a statue of Mayor Tom L. Johnson. It is different from most statues of great men in that the sculptor eschewed the usual heroic pose. He is not standing, one leg forward and bent at the knee, with outstretched hand. He is not even seated on a horse. He is sitting in a comfortable armchair and he is staring reflectively out at the Square. It is not what you would call a heroic stare either. Chances are the sculptor probably got thrown out of the sculptor's union for breaking all the rules.

There is an area set aside in Tom Johnson's quadrant as a free speech rostrum in the tradition of London's open-air free-speech area in Hyde Park. Cleveland has provided people who are seized with the ungovernable impulse to speak with a two-step stone rostrum, and it is put to strenuous use. People who are hustling through the Square on their way to work, or rushing for the bus, usually stop long enough to find out what subject the speaker of the hour has selected. They may even tarry long enough to determine if the speaker is making any sense. Very few speakers do. The rostrum seems to draw heavily on the lunatic and fanatical fringe, but there is no harm done and perhaps some good. The Public Square regulars—i.e., the bench brigade—appear to enjoy every word spoken. The pigeons are all for free speech, too, because when a speaker draws a good crowd, it almost always includes some sports who are willing to buy a bag of peanuts from the man with the peanut wagon. When that happens, the pigeons flutter about, wheeling gracefully above in exultation before they descend in a flapping, cooing uproar that almost drowns out the man on the rostrum.

The northeast quadrant is more sedate. Its main feature is a round pool with a weak, hesitant fountain which no doubt used to be a great civic attraction, but which loses considerably in comparison with the many new fountains on the magnificent Mall, which can be seen clearly from this particular section of the Square. But there are shade trees, grass and floral arrangements which please a good many people. It is the part of the Square which is most reminiscent of the leisurely, peaceful atmosphere of the nineteenth century. The nostalgia is heightened considerably by the Old Stone Church (the First Presbyterian Church), which faces the Square from the north as it has since 1834. The mellow chimes in the tower of the church sound across the Square every fifteen minutes, and twice a day, at noon and at 6 P.M., the carillon plays old airs in concerts that often slow the hurrying commuters and sometimes bring passersby to a complete, appreciative halt.

The southwest quadrant, directly in front of the Terminal Tower, which overpowers the entire Square with its height and massive bulk, has the statue of Moses Cleaveland, a band shell, and an information booth of the Cleveland Transit System, a miscellaneous grouping that does nothing to cheer the eyes of onlookers.

But it is the southeast quadrant which draws most of the critical comment. Herein resides the single most controversial element of the entire Public Square—the Soldiers and Sailors Monument. It was born in controversy and there is every likelihood that it will disappear in controversy, but while it stands it will not be ignored. Everybody in Cleveland, resident or visitor, has an opinion on this structure which so dominates the entire central area, and the opinions range from patriotic approval to aesthetic revulsion. The criticism generally is kept to a low undertone because to attack the monument, which has been the artistic centerpiece of the civic area since the turn of the century, is to be classified not merely as a Philistine but as an un-American trouble-maker.

There is one point on which everyone can agree: the monument, conceived as a labor of love by Captain Levi Tucker Scofield, is both massive and unique. Its main feature is a central granite shaft which rises 125 feet in height, topped by a statue of Liberty. Its bulky base is a somber, mausoleum-like structure which has inside it a room with marble panels on which have been inscribed the names of the ten thousand officers and men from Cuyahoga County who served the Union in the Civil War. There also are bronze panels which portray patriotic service. Around this base-building are four splendidly executed life-size battle groups in bronze depicting the infantry, the artillery, the cavalry, and the Navy, all in heroic action.

The monument was proposed in 1879 by a man named William J. Gleason. He, a leader among the Civil War veterans, was instrumental in marshaling support for the memorial and pushing the project through to fulfillment despite a civic furore which became so heated as to project the fear of violence. The dispute centered not on the issue of building a Civil War monument—every hamlet, town, and city in the United States was racing to build memorials at the time—but on the question of where it should be placed. Public Square, the center of the city, was the obvious choice for the largest and grandest monument in town, but there was this minor obstruction—Public Square already had a fine monument. It was the Perry Monument, dedicated to Commodore Oliver Hazard Perry and commemorating his decisive victory in the Battle of Lake Erie in the War of 1812.

The dispute over which monument should win the coveted position on the Square settled down gradually into an argument over which of the wars represented by the respective memorials really was the better war. Some Clevelanders pleaded the case of the War of 1812 quite eloquently, pointing out that there would not have been a War between the States if Commodore Perry hadn't whipped the British on Lake Erie. Furthermore, they added, the proximity of Perry's battle—within earshot of Cleveland—gave it more local interest and significance than any of the Civil War battles.

However eloquent were the supporters of Commodore Perry, they were not able to prevail against the planners of the Civil War memorial, who had tremendous political strength at that time, only a few years after the Civil War. They easily won approval of the Cleveland city administration. The Perry supporters even went to court on the issue, but the Supreme Court of Ohio, in 1892, ruled that the building of the veterans' monument in the southeast quadrant of the Square was legal.

The Perry Memorial was removed from Public Square finally on December 3, 1892. It had held a proud place in the heart of Cleveland since September 10, 1860, the forty-seventh anniversary of the date of the Battle of Lake Erie, when it was unveiled and dedicated in a great civic ceremony.

Harvey Rice, the noted pioneer-educator, had conceived the idea of the Perry Monument, and it was he who made the presentation address at its dedication before a crowd estimated at one hundred thousand persons, including the son of the hero, Oliver Hazard Perry II. Among the newspaper reporters covering the ceremony was a *Plain Dealer* writer named Charles Farrar Browne, who already was winning fame as a humorist under his pen name of Artemus Ward. Browne's account of the dedication was straight and factual, but his sense of humor was irrepressible, finally forcing its way into the story with his observation that "the procession was more than two miles in length, as was the prayer of the clergyman."

At that time, a two-railing fence closed in the entire Public Square, preventing use of Superior and Ontario streets through the area. The fence was a manifestation of another famous Cleveland dispute, one involving the use of Public Square by traffic. One faction held that the Square should be a single, unbroken unit; a park area, not trespassed by streets bearing vehicular traffic. The opposing faction was in favor of allowing the streets to cut the Square into four separate areas rather than inconvenience people by making them travel around the sides of the Square.

Perhaps the best suggestion of the emotional effect of the dispute over the fence around the Square is to be found in some doggerel printed by the *Herald* in 1867 relative to the controversy:

"Let fossils creak their crumbling bones,
Let Dotards shriek in quavering tones;
They cannot stop the tides that flow,
The fence about the Square must go!"

The Perry Monument sat in the geographical center of the fenced-in Square while the argument raged, and while it was not a large monument, it was well executed and was regarded with approval. It was twenty-five feet high, with an Italian marble statue of Commodore Perry eight feet, two inches high standing atop a Rhode Island granite base twelve feet high. An iron picket fence with gas lamps at each corner surrounded the memorial.

On August 21, 1867, the argument over the use of Public Square by the main thoroughfares was settled with the decision that the original plan of the city allowed for such practical use of the land. The rail fence was removed and the Perry Monument was moved from the center of the Square to the southeast quadrant, where, shortly, it came under attack from the promoters of the large Civil War monument. After its removal from Public Square, Perry's peregrinating memorial wandered on to a site in Wade Park, overlooking the lagoon, where it stayed until it was evicted by the construction of the new Museum of Art. It moved again, in 1913, to the bank of the lake in Gordon Park, where it is to this day.

The Soldiers and Sailors Monument was built at a cost of $280,000 and was dedicated on Independence Day 1894, with a great civic celebration that included yacht races in the harbor, a band concert on the Square under the direction of Professor Frank H. Hruby, the firing of cannon, the shriek of whistles and, of course, old-fashioned Fourth of July oratory. The principal speakers at the dedication ceremony were former Governor Joseph B. Foraker of Ohio, who was also to serve in the U. S. Senate, and the future President of the United States, William McKinley, then governor of Ohio.

They must have dedicated the monument well, because it still sits on the Square, a vestigial reminder of another century such as is rarely found in prominent display in larger American cities. While nobody questions its high-minded representation, or the sentiment that inspired it, not even the kindly patina of the weather and the years can conceal its baroque features and bulking disfigurement of the heart of the city. Still, wise politicians hesitate to attack tradition, and this memorial certainly has become a firm part of the Cleveland tradition.

As should be apparent, Cleveland's Public Square, which daily is the scene of some of the most overpowering traffic jam-ups in America, never has been the placid, pastoral retreat that Seth Pease and Moses Cleaveland had in mind when they laid out the town. It has been, instead, a battleground of one kind or another ever since the day that Lorenzo Carter and his fellow townsmen fought to hang the reluctant John O'Mic approximately at the place where all the free speech enthusiasts today denounce the devil, established authority, and our social system.

One of Cleveland's veteran editors, Charles E. Kennedy, liked to tell about the time he was walking across Public Square in the company of a friend when a brilliant light shot out of a building on the southwest corner of the Square. He looked up at the building in surprise, but his friend tugged at his arm and assured him there was no reason to be alarmed.

"It's a young fellow named Brush," he told Kennedy. "He's got a laboratory in that building, and he's experimenting with a newfangled lamp run from a galvanic battery."

It was one of the understatements of the century. Charles Francis Brush, a graduate mining engineer, analytical chemist, and consultant in the iron ore industry, had become caught in the fascinating possibilities of electricity, and out of his experiments emerged the successful arc light and dynamo.

When his invention had reached the point where it warranted a trial outside of his laboratory, Brush fastened the apparatus to the sill of his window facing the Square on the second floor of the little building.

On that particular night, a downtown parade had been scheduled and just as the cavalry rounded the corner, past the Forest City House, Brush threw the switch, causing a purplish bright light to glow in the crude lamp, growing steadily brighter as it burned.

The cavalry horses had never seen an electric light before. Neither had their riders. The horses reared in wide-eyed terror and pranced excitedly about, forgetting military discipline.

Brush, looking out his window in amazement at the light he had caused to flare in the lamp and at the accompanying panic disrupting the parade, was chortling in triumph when he heard a pounding at his laboratory door. It was a huge policeman, a man who was not to be put off his duty by a lot of scientific gobbledygook and legerdemain.

"Put out that damned light!" he roared. The inventor, aware that this was not the moment to explain the significance of the arc light, immediately hastened to comply.

Brush's experiments with electrical arc lighting continued, and finally, in 1879, his work had advanced to the point of experimenting with the new marvel as a means of street illumination. The place for the experiment in the world's first street lighting was Public Square; the date, April 29. The Cleveland Telegraph Supply Company, with which Brush was associated, erected twelve lamps of two thousand horsepower on 150-foot-high poles set about the Square.

Thousands of spectators from cities all over Ohio and Pennsylvania thronged the Square that night, joining almost all the people of Cleveland, to see the promised miracle. Most of the sightseers, forewarned by the newspapers of the blinding glare that might be expected, carried smoked glass to hold before their eyes.

There was an almost fearful hush as the moment for the demonstration approached. Thousands of heads tipped back to look at the opalescent glass globes suspended at the tops of the tall standards when, at 8:05 P.M., Brush signaled for the switch to be turned on. One of the lamps immediately gave off a purplish flickering light, and then all the others followed. The lights grew brighter steadily, losing some of their purple coloring as they did, and the glow from the lamps was sufficient to illuminate the entire Public Square. It was a dim light by modern standards, to be sure, but to the thousands who looked at it that night and who were bathed in its beams, it was a dazzling, blinding glow, and the crowd roared its pleasure and admiration while the Cleveland Grays Band played a number that called for smashing cymbals and the artillery lined along the lakeshore for the event boomed the news of Brush's miracle.

In the six months that followed this demonstration, the Cleveland City Council contracted for Brush arc lights to be installed not only on Public Square, but also adjacent downtown streets, giving the city the distinction of being the first in the world to light its streets with electricity.

It was not the only worldwide first that the Public Square could lay claim to. The world's first electric streetcar was demonstrated on the Square, and began service in Cleveland in 1884. And, earlier, in 1852, the Zion Evangelical Lutheran Church, then on a site facing the Square, set up a candle-lighted Christmas tree in the little church sanctuary during the holiday season. It was probably the first Christmas tree to appear in a church or to be allowed in a church ceremony, according to Historian William Ganson Rose. The innovation allows Cleveland to share with Wooster, Ohio, the credit for beginning the Christmas tree tradition in the United States. A twenty-one-year-old native of Germany, August Ingard, is credited with having installed the first Christmas tree in his home in Wooster in 1847.

The Square, predictably, was the focus point of the city's centennial celebration in 1896—and a flamboyant celebration it was, reflecting the brash, cocky attitude of a community that had grown from a forested wilderness into a metropolis of more than a quarter-million persons in a mere hundred years, making it the tenth-largest city in the United States in the 1890 census. As part of the summer-long observance of the big birthday, a log cabin was built—under the direction of one Bolivar Butts, no less—on the northeast corner of the Square, while in the very center a great arch that closely resembled the Arc de Triomphe in Paris spanned Superior Avenue. The scientific highlight of Founders' Day, July 22, came at 8:15 P.M. when President Grover Cleveland, far away in his summer home in Buzzard's Bay, Massachusetts, pushed a button that somehow, magically, illuminated the great Centennial Arch in Cleveland, dazzling the thousands of celebrators gathered on the Square.

Some people, as we all know, simply cannot leave a good thing alone, so it isn't surprising that numerous attempts have been made over the years to give Public Square a more impressive name, but the people stubbornly have stayed with the original, direct designation. It was proposed that the name be changed to Perry Square, when the admiral's monument was the centerpiece feature, and again it was proposed that the name of "Monumental Square" be adopted, but both efforts failed. In 1861, on April 16, the city fathers yielded to pressure and formally renamed the area Monumental Park, which is the official name to this day, but it never has gained any popular usage, any more than Sixth Avenue in New York has been popularly called "Avenue of the Americas."

Cleveland's City Council hasn't had too much luck in its administration of Public Square affairs over the years—the unsuccessful name change being but a sample—so it does not come as any great surprise to learn that at one time the council officially decided it was an area strictly for the birds. Back in 1859, a rather slow year legislation-wise, the City Council imported twenty pairs of English sparrows directly from their native land in the hope they would be helpful in destroying some insect pests which were attacking the trees in the Forest City. The first results must have been encouraging because the council shortly thereafter purchased an additional fifty pairs of sparrows and thoughtfully built birdhouses on the Square to accommodate the feathered imports in a style to which they certainly were not accustomed.

The councilmen, as everybody knows now, wrought better than they knew. The sparrows flourished and multiplied with dismaying speed, seeming not to care one bit that the city demolished the birdhouses and withdrew the welcome sign. Now they, the starlings, and the pigeons are all over, under, and around the Square, and living with them is one of the city's current problems. The same council body that sponsored their migration to Cleveland occasionally tries to shoo them away, but all efforts along this line have been unsuccessful to date. The most dramatic counterattack by the City Council came in the 1940s, when guns were installed at strategic places around the Square. Every so often, at set intervals, the guns were triggered automatically and the sound of the fusillade boomed and echoed all over the Square.

This was an effective stratagem, in a limited sense. That is to say, the explosion of the guns did startle the birds. Thousands of them would take off at each blast and fly frantically about, their little bird-type brains and nervous systems rattled by the sudden roar. The trouble was that the reaction of the birds was as nothing compared with the reaction of the pedestrians within earshot of the cannonading. Some of them flew higher than the birds. Yielding to the entreaties of the citizens, the council reluctantly withdrew its noisemakers, and the birds took over the Square again. Clevelanders fortunately had chosen a softhearted bunch of legislators to represent them. In another Ohio metropolis, Cincinnati, the city government once offered to pay a bounty for birds brought in by eagle-eyed citizens. When the sound of the gunfire had died away and the smoke had cleared, the Queen City looked like Berlin at the end of World War II.

Clearly, there is something about a big, wide, open space like Public Square that is tempting to politicians. History is studded with stories proving that politicians, like nature, abhor a vacuum. Show them an empty space, like a park or a public square, and they rush to fill it. It is not surprising then that just as a Cleveland city administration in the 1950s would cast covetous eyes on the Erie Street Cemetery for use as a parking lot, or consider using the Mall as the site of a new Hilton hotel, so the city officials of 1895 would consider it absurd to buy land for a new city hall when so much acreage was going to waste in the Public Square. The city at that time was leasing space in a privately owned building, the Case Block on Superior Avenue, just east of the Square.

A new city administration building had been authorized by voters in November 1894, and the only question to be resolved was where to build it. From his temporary quarters in the Case Block, Mayor Mc-Kisson enjoyed a good view of the broad sweep of the Square, and the temptation was too much for his frugal character. With the approval of the City Council, McKisson made his determined effort to grab the land. He sent a swarm of workers onto the Square and they quickly enclosed the two northernmost quadrants with a board fence. That half of the Square would be the site of City Hall.

But the mayor and the council had underestimated the proprietary affection that Clevelanders always have had for their downtown center. A mighty storm of protest from citizens, newspapers, and politicians of opposing parties darkened the skies overhead and drove the city administration to cover. Ground for the new city hall had been broken on June 4, but sufficient opposition manifested itself in the week that followed to cause the McKisson forces to back down. The city filled the hole, removed the fencing, and the politicians retreated to their old rented quarters in the Case Block.

The people had spoken, as they always do in Cleveland when anyone

tries to tamper with their Public Square; even as they did in 1966—
by way of a more recent example—when it was proposed that a
"hospitality building" be erected on the northeast quadrant to house the
Cleveland Convention & Visitors Bureau and to serve as an information
center for visitors wandering aimlessly around the Square. There was
enough public indignation over that project to nip it in the bud quickly,
demonstrating that the fierce sentimentality of the people toward the
old-fashioned open space in the middle of the city still is alive.

A newspaper writer of the 1890s, possibly the same poet who penned
the immortal lines denouncing the fence that had penned the Square in
an earlier year, summed up Cleveland's attitude toward its Public
Square in the following heartfelt lines whose message still obtains:

> Oasis in the city's heart,
> An Islet in the tide;
> While men and decades both depart,
> It stays—a people's pride.

IX

Artemus Ward: His Town

American laughter was lucky laughter
A coonskin tune by a homespun bard;
It tasted of hams from the smokehouse rafter
And locust trees in the courthouse yard,
And Petroleum Nasby and Artemus Ward!
—From "American Laughter" by Kenneth Allan Robinson

ARTEMUS WARD, no ordinary man, lived not quite thirty-three years. Of these, only three were spent in Cleveland. They were the years, though, that showed he was no ordinary man. They set the direction of his brief life and by so doing they added something rich to the lives of all Americans. If Artemus Ward was the "father of American humor," as he has been called, then Cleveland was its birthplace.

The most dramatic illustration of Artemus Ward's power to use words came about at a meeting of President Abraham Lincoln's cabinet in the dark depths of the Civil War. The date was September 22, 1862.

As the cabinet members filed into the meeting room in the White House, the President already was seated. He was grave-faced and preoccupied with a small book. When his aides had seated themselves, he looked up from the book and smiled in greeting.

"Gentlemen," he said, "did you ever read anything from Artemus Ward?" None of the group replied as Lincoln studied their faces.

"Let me read you a chapter that is very funny!" he said as he opened the book to a chapter called, "High-handed Outrage At Utica," and began to read.

The cabinet members listened politely, but some of them showed in their faces that they considered the reading to be inappropriate to the time, the place, and the occasion. Secretary of War Edwin Stanton was open in his look of disapproval.

Salmon P. Chase, Secretary of the Treasury, was another who listened and disapproved. He mentioned the strange episode in his diary.

"The President," he wrote dryly, "seemed to enjoy it very much."

When Lincoln had finished reading, there was momentary silence as the President looked around at his cabinet. Perhaps there were some smiles, but we know there was no laughter from the President's own despairing words.

"Gentlemen," he said, "why don't you laugh? With the fearful strain that is upon me night and day, if I did not laugh I should die, and you need this medicine as much as I do."

The President's tall shiny hat was resting on its top on the table beside him, and even as he spoke, he was removing from the hat an official document which he proceeded to read aloud to his astonished cabinet. It was the immortal Emancipation Proclamation, which would make that date in history one for all men to remember.

Artemus Ward, whose work was the companion piece of the famous proclamation, was in fact one Charles Farrar Browne, a writer and sub-editor of the *Plain Dealer* in Cleveland. Although he and President Lincoln never met, the Chief Executive was one of his most ardent admirers.

Browne, a native of Waterford, in Maine, was a printer in the day, when, to quote Stephen Leacock, the printer "was a sort of troubadour, carrying his composing stick as the troubadour carried his guitar, or Scott's Last Minstrel his harp. Easily enough they changed from printers to composers, from artisans to artists."

That metamorphosis, for Browne, occurred in Ohio, where he switched from the role of printer to that of writer on the Toledo *Commercial*. His career with that newspaper was brief. J. W. Gray, editor of the *Plain Dealer*, was struck by the originality of Browne's writing and hired him in October, 1857, as, of all things, commercial editor of the *P.D.*

The story announcing the hiring of Browne was headed, "An Additional Editor," and it said:

". . . we have felt it due our patrons that a COMMERCIAL EDITOR should be added to our present editorial force, one who will take specially in charge the commercial department and collect and collate market reports from all parts of the world and give in condensed form the most reliable figures to our readers.

"For this purpose we have secured the services of Mr. Charles F. Brown, Esq., lately of the Toledo Commercial, and who comes to us highly recommended as a scrupulously correct and diligent business man, a talented and agreeable writer. Mr. Brown will also have charge of the Local Column in place of Mr. Cleveland, our old and well-tried associate now promoted."

William W. Armstrong, who later would become the editor and owner of the *Plain Dealer*, had employed Browne briefly as a printer for the Seneca *Advertiser* in Sandusky, Ohio, when he was proprietor of that newspaper. Browne's physical appearance intrigued Armstrong.

"I believe," he said, "that he was the gawkiest, greenest-looking young fellow I had ever set eyes on."

Another Clevelander, James F. Ryder, a prominent pioneer photographer, described Browne graphically in his volume of reminiscences, *Voigtlander and I,* published in 1902.

"On going into the Plain Dealer editorial rooms one morning I saw a new man and was introduced to him as Mr. Brown. He was young, cheerful in manner, tall and slender, not quite up to date in style of dress, yet by no means shabby. His hair was flaxen and very straight; his nose, the prominent feature of his face, was Romanesque—quite violently so, with a leaning to the left. His eyes were blue-gray, with a twinkle in them; his mouth seemed so given to a merry laugh, so much in motion, that it was difficult to describe, so we let it pass. It seemed as though bubbling in him was a lot of happiness which he made no effort to conceal or hold back. When we were introduced he was sitting at his table writing; he gave his leg a smart slap, arose and shook hands with me and said he was glad to meet me. I believed him for he looked glad all the time. You couldn't look at him but that he would laugh. He laughed as he sat at his table writing, and when he had written a thing which pleased him he would slap his leg and laugh . . ."

Browne (he added the final "e" after he left the *Plain Dealer*) was twenty-three years old when he arrived in Cleveland in late 1857. His performance as commercial editor and as local reporter must have pleased the management from the outset because very shortly his name appeared on the masthead as associate editor, making him a triple-threat man. As the local reporter, he was expected to write all the local news that was fit to print, and if he couldn't find enough of the genuine article, he was supposed to provide an acceptable substitute.

One of those dry, dull, newsless days that all reporters are familiar with must have challenged him three months later because an item appeared in the *Plain Dealer* saying: "Mr. Artemus Ward, proprietor of the well-known side-show, writes us from Pittsburgh as follows:

Pitsburg, Jan. 27, 18&58

The Plane Deeler:
Sir:
i write to no how about the show bisnes in Cleeveland i have a show consisting in part of a Californy Bare two snakes tame foxes &c also wax works my wax works is hard to beat, all say they is life and nateral curiosities among my wax works is our Saveyer Gen taylor and Docktor Webster in the akt of killing Parkmen. now mr. Editor scratch off a few lines and tel me how is the show bisnis in your good city i shal have hanbils printed at your offis you scratch my back and i will scratch your back, also git up a grate blow in the paper about my show don't forgit the wax works.

yours truly
Artemus Ward
Pitsburg Penny

P.S. pitsburg is a 1 horse town. A.W.

The item delighted readers of the *Plain Dealer*. They chuckled so audibly and so encouragingly that in the months and years that followed, the snail-like progress of Artemus Ward's traveling show toward Cleveland (it never did arrive) and all the many delights it promised continued to be reported in the fine, lugubrious detail of the proprietor's "letters" to Charles Farrar Browne.

Artemus Ward was Browne's creation, of course, but he was so much a part of Browne that the two, in time, became one. And if the world was winning a wonderful new creature of fantasy in Artemus Ward, Browne himself was losing his identity. Almost everybody came to call him Artemus Ward and that, in fact, became his most common name, as uncommon as it was. There is a story that Browne borrowed the name from a half-wit snake charmer who lived near Cleveland.

Among the attractions added to the wonderful road show of A. Ward as it plodded toward Cleveland were "an amoozing Kangaroo and other moral Beests and Snaiks . . . besides several miscellanyous statoots of celebrated Piruts and Murdrers ekalled by few and exceled by none."

There was also the worrisome lion—the one with a vexing problem of hindsight. The lion had had an unfortunate accident, dashing headlong into a pole. The force of the collision had split the poor animal from head to tail. Its owner hastily put the animal back together again, but haste not only makes waste but also strange-looking lions. The owner had put the two halves together wrong-end-to, which may be all right to people who don't take their lions seriously, but it certainly did make for an awkward-looking animal, if a vastly entertaining subject for Browne and his readers.

It is worth mentioning, in any discussion of Browne, that he had come to the right community to try out his wings of wit. Whether the reason is due to geography, the soil, the vagaries of the climate, or perhaps a kind of hysterical reaction to their release from the stultifying Puritan environment, nobody is able to say, but it is a proven fact that Clevelanders do like to laugh. Their record as laughers is long and unsullied. A sense of humor has been an honored attribute in the town since old Moses Cleaveland drew the first big guffaw from his followers by heading up the wrong river, and it has served them in good stead through the years, enabling them to meet all sorts of harrowing situations with the equanimity that is possible only when humor is present to balance pain.

The world knows Charles Farrar Browne only for his stories about Artemus Ward and the amusing lectures that he gave in a later period of his career, but Cleveland was privileged to have Browne inject his sparkling—and, often, devastating—wit into every phase of the community's life in his capacity as a forerunner of the modern-day columnist.

Browne apparently came by his wit naturally because his mother also was known for her fine sense of humor. The two, mother and son, were very close. He always addressed her as "Caroline."

"Be respectful to your mother," she advised him one day. "Remember what the Bible says."

"Well, I expect I ought to," he agreed, "but it is so different from the Plain Dealer, I don't putter with it much . . . a man cannot serve two masters, and I'm a Democrat." The *Plain Dealer* was an outspoken Democratic Party supporter.

Browne frequently showed his serious side, as he did, for example, in his story reporting a lecture on "The Law of Success" by Ralph Waldo Emerson on January 20, 1859, in Melodeon Hall under the sponsorship of the Cleveland Library Association, admission, twenty-five cents.

"He [Emerson] is a man of massive intellect, a great and profound thinker," conceded Reporter Browne, "but . . . his lecture last night was rather a sleepy affair. For our part . . . we had quite as lief see a perpendicular coffin behind a lecture desk as Emerson. The one would amuse as much as the other.

"Mr. Emerson is a great scholar—full of book learning—but, like many other great scholars, he is impractical and visionary. Let mankind adopt his ideas (providing always that mankind can understand what his ideas are) and they would live a strange, weird life—the chaotic dream of a lunatic."

It can be deduced readily from this that Browne was no respecter of great names and in his pieces he often walked close to the edge of irreverence. He was responsible one day for presenting in the *Plain Dealer* three stories whose authorship he ascribed to the "three tigers of the Cleveland press"—the editors of the *Plain Dealer,* the *Herald,* and the *Leader*—boldly using their by-lines over the stories.

Interestingly enough, *Time* magazine, in an article on the success of the *Plain Dealer* in 1965, described the current editor-publisher of the *P.D.,* Tom Vail, as a "tiger," indicating that at least one journalistic tradition in Cleveland lives on.

In each of the stories, Browne had the editor in question taking a position opposite to the one that Browne knew the editor really favored. For instance, the editor of the *Plain Dealer,* J. W. Gray, Browne's boss, was a man who loved to dance, but in the story that the humorist wrote under his employer's name, he had Gray denouncing dancing as an evil which "destroys more people than War, Pestilence and Famine."

After three years on the *Plain Dealer* staff, where his salary had risen to ten or twelve dollars a week, Browne had gathered enough confidence to want to try the larger national scene. By 1860, his name was known all over the country thanks to the habit of American newspapers in those days of reprinting each other's stories and editorials. Artemus

Ward had become one of the favorites of editors in almost all American cities, and they eagerly searched each issue of the *Plain Dealer* for his pieces to reprint.

Vanity Fair magazine took a more direct approach to this popular product in 1859 and made an arrangement with Browne for him to mail his copy directly to them. They, in turn, would pay him at an agreed rate. This arrangement bolstered Browne's confidence and pocketbook, of course, even if it did make Editor Gray of the *Plain Dealer* terribly unhappy when he found out about it.

The writer and the editor quarreled over the issue. Gray wanted Browne to reserve his talents exclusively for the *Plain Dealer*. Browne, in reply, offered to abide by such an agreement provided the newspaper would pay him one hundred dollars a month. Editor Gray's stricken outcry caused sailboats far out on Lake Erie to tack suddenly into the wind and startled wild animals into a dash for cover as far away as Lakewood and Hardscrabble Corners.

The end of the Cleveland chapter in the life story of Artemus Ward came shortly thereafter, when the *Plain Dealer* published the following:

VALE

The undersigned closes his connection with the Plain Dealer with this evening's issue. During the three years that he has contributed to these columns he has endeavored to impart a cheerful spirit to them. He believes it is far better to stay in the Sunshine while we may, inasmuch as the Shadow must of its own accord come only too soon. He cannot here, in fit terms, express his deep gratitude to the many including every member of the Press of Cleveland, who have so often manifested the most kindly feeling toward himself. But he can very sincerely say that their courtesy and kindness will never be forgotten.

The undersigned may be permitted to flatter himself that he has some friends among the readers of newspapers.

Charles F. Brown

Editor Gray acknowledged the defection from his staff with a polite farewell that may or may not have been sarcastic in part, but which certainly hinted that good men to fill the "local" job weren't terribly hard to find.

"Our associate Mr. Brown has had a 'louder call,' as the Reverends would say, and goes to a larger city, where he can enlarge his sphere of usefulness. To do the Locals for a daily paper in a city like this is a drudgery, cramping to such a genius as his, and we cannot blame him for aspiring to a higher position. It is the lot of our Locals to rise in the world. Bouton built himself such a reputation while with us that he went to New York and is now City Editor of the Journal of Commerce.

McLaren, another Local, is now preaching the gospel; and Brown is destined to become either a minister or an author, perhaps both. Our relations are now and always have been of the most agreeable kind, and we part with him with many regrets."

Browne accepted a job on the staff of *Vanity Fair* in New York, and for two years, 1860 through 1862, he—or rather, Artemus Ward—achieved some of his best writing. He was more a national celebrity now than ever before, and the news that Abraham Lincoln was one of his most faithful readers did nothing to detract from his growing reputation.

Shortly after his arrival in New York, Browne had accepted some invitations to speak. He enjoyed the experience so much, and found it so remunerative that before long he was one of the regulars on the lecture circuit, and by 1863 he was lecturing full-time, having left the *Vanity Fair* staff. A collection of his pieces, *Artemus Ward, His Book,* was published and met with "tumultuous success," selling forty thousand copies—a large sale for the day—and enjoyed as much acclaim in England as it did in the United States.

"It was a case," analyzed Stephen Leacock, "of the meeting of extremes. Nothing could be further from the staid classical culture of England than the mind and thought of Artemus Ward; nothing further from the humor of Dickens and his imitators than what Artemus Ward brought from over the sea—irreverent burlesque and burlesque irreverence, Gargantuan exaggeration and the orthography of a printer's delirium. But the English seem to have delighted in the sheer 'cussedness' of the new American humor . . . and they treated him not as a comic entertainer but as a comic genius."

England, indeed, would be witness to the last brilliant flare of that genius. In 1866, while in London on his second English tour, the frail humorist became too weak and too ill to carry on. He died at Southampton the following March, 1867, a victim of tuberculosis. He was not yet thirty-three years old.

On his deathbed in a foreign land, the mind of Artemus Ward wandered back to Cleveland and the beginning of his success. He called for a pad and pencil and wrote:

"Some twelve years ago, I occupied the position (or the position occupied me) of city editor of a journal in Cleveland, Ohio. This journal—The Plain Dealer—was issued afternoons . . ."

He wrote nothing further, for it was at this precise point that Charles Farrar Browne—Artemus Ward, if you please—died. He had returned home, in a sense, with his very last thoughts.

X

Adventures in Journalism

THE world was bemused, if not startled, in 1965, when a newspaper copy editor from Cleveland sailed the Atlantic Ocean, from Falmouth, Massachusetts, to Falmouth, England, in a 13½-foot sailboat. The intrepid amphibious newsman was Robert Manry of the *Plain Dealer*, and his tiny craft was named *Tinkerbelle*.

It was a daring, puzzling feat—a voyage of seventy-eight days' duration over thirty-two hundred miles of ocean in a craft that could be classified somewhere halfway between waterwings and a rowboat. The significance of this admirable derring-do was obvious, certifying as it did that man had not lost entirely his zest for adventure, or the courage to challenge the eternal elements. What puzzled many people was that a newspaperman from inland Cleveland—a copy editor, at that!—should have been such a marine adventurer.

There would not have been such puzzlement had the world known Cleveland newspapermen better, for theirs is a long, outstanding record of adventurous thrusts into the unknown, usually in the face of staggering odds. Sometimes, just to keep the record straight, the newsmen did a little staggering themselves, but that's neither here nor there.

The Manry sea voyage recalls to the mind the earlier, valiant attempt by a group of Cleveland journalists to cross the Cuyahoga River—which offhand does not sound like the kind of feat that should be mentioned in the same book with Manry's heroism until one considers all the facts and the hazards attached thereto.

One has to know, for instance, about Cleveland's High Level Bridge.

The Detroit-Superior High Level Bridge, a major east-west connection over the Cuyahoga Valley, is a two-deck structure which was the largest double-deck, reinforced concrete bridge in the world when it was opened in 1917. It is still an imposing—if overburdened—span with its old-fashioned bulk covering a distance of 3112 feet in length, with twelve concrete arches and one 591-foot steel arch. The top deck is used for regular traffic vehicles, while the lower deck—now sealed off—was reserved for use by streetcars.

To traverse the bridge, the streetcars had to drive down into a subway on either side of the river. There were two subways on the West Side; one having an entrance on West 25th Street, near Franklin Avenue, and the other on Detroit Avenue at West 28th Street. The entrance on the East Side was on Superior Avenue at West 6th Street.

The subways and the bridge together made streetcar riding in Cleveland highly worthwhile. They formed the grand climax to a trip downtown, and they gave the trip west a smashing, exciting beginning. Upon approaching the bridge, the streetcars suddenly left the bright street and dipped down into a dark, steeply graded tunnel at what seemed to be excessive speed, swaying and rocking as they hurtled downward, while the white-knuckled passengers fearfully eyed the concrete walls of the tunnel a finger's length away. There was always the unspoken fear, too, that the streetcar's brakes had failed and that this was a runaway vehicle.

At the bottom of the East Side incline, leading down into the subway, the streetcars had to make a sharp turn, causing the steel wheels to press against the rails with a piercing, screeching sound that added just the right note to the growing apprehension.

Just as the passengers were adjusting to the dim, yellow lights of the streetcar in the dark tunnel, the car would emerge abruptly in the daylight of the open deck, and this was the most thrilling part of the entire ride. Nothing more than a short iron railing guarded the side of the deck, hardly sufficient to keep a streetcar from toppling over. The tracks were laid on a bed of wooden ties, but you could see between the ties to the yellow river below—196 feet below. This perilous ride, or so it seemed, did not last long; just long enough to scare the bejabbers out of the passengers, and then suddenly the streetcar was back in the dark tunnel on the other side, the walls were rushing past again, and you could tell that it was twisting and fighting its way back up to street level once again.

Now the question that had bothered virtually nobody except the curious newsmen was whether an automobile could drive down the ramps, maneuver through the tunnel, cross the open main section of the deck, and still emerge safely at the other side. At first it was merely a kind of intellectual speculation worthy of being discussed in the friendly setting of a downtown pub, as it was one night until one of the newspapermen, a natural leader named Jimmy Lanyon, who was sports editor of the *Plain Dealer* at the time, rose to his feet and announced that he was prepared to meet the challenge head-on by driving his car across the bridge's streetcar deck that very moment.

"Let us be done with the talk," cried Lanyon. "Let us have some action!" Some of his stouthearted colleagues jumped to join him, and in a twinkling the adventurous newsmen were on their way. Their car roared down Superior Avenue, lunged down the ramp like an escaped fury, twisted through the dark tunnel, passing an eastbound streetcar whose motorman jumped up and down on his bell in panic as he stared out with disbelieving eyes, and finally shot out on the open deck where, its tires slashed by the tracks, its innards shaken loose by the jolting drive, it finally wheezed and pitched to a stop.

All streetcar traffic between downtown and the West Side was halted for several hours while transit workers and police effected a rescue of the valiant newsmen and pulled their car out of the way. The incident was reported in terse style by the newspapers the next day. Nowhere in print was there any editorial commendation of the attempted crossing.

Newspapers traditionally have served as havens for men and women who were not completely understood by the outside world; they have provided sanctuary to those who were harassed and pursued by the keepers of the conventions, carefully keeping alive in the editorial rooms the last spark of individuality in a society that grows more regimented by the hour. Sometimes, as in the gallant attempt to drive the streetcar deck, the behavior of newsmen may seem antisocial, or irrational to the outside world. It is not. It is simply a manifestation of the creative spirit at work in material surroundings.

For the first twenty-two years of its existence, Cleveland was without its own newspaper. What little journalistic attention the town received was from a publication called the Ohio *Patriot*, published in New Lisbon, Ohio, southwest of Youngstown, beginning in 1808.

At last, on July 31, 1818, the first Cleveland newspaper, the *Gazette and Commercial Register*, appeared. It was better than nothing, but it followed a fitful schedule of publication, with intervals of up to three weeks between issues. The following year, 1819, the *Herald* was established. From that time on, there was wild confusion on the newspaper front, with new publications springing up left and right even as old ones were going out of business.

In today's Cleveland, with a metropolitan population approaching the two million mark, there are two large dailies, the afternoon *Press* and the morning *Plain Dealer*. There is but one Sunday paper, that published by the *Plain Dealer*.

In January 1842, when the *Plain Dealer* came into being, Cleveland had been a city only a few years and its population, combined with that of Ohio City, was about seventy-five hundred. Serving this handful of people was the new paper, the *Plain Dealer*, the *Herald*, the *Morning Mercury*, the *Eagle-Eyed News Catcher*, the *Commercial Intelligencer*, and the Cleveland *Gatherer* (a weekly); six newspapers in all.

The pity of it all, of course, is that the *Eagle-Eyed News Catcher* was not able to survive. It had a name that deserved to live.

The *Plain Dealer* grew out of the *Independent News-Letter*, started in 1827. It was rechristened the Cleveland *Advertiser* in 1832. When two brothers, Admiral Nelson Gray and Joseph William Gray took over the *Advertiser* at the end of 1841, they gave the paper the unusual name which makes out-of-towners cock their head in puzzlement when they first hear it. Archer H. Shaw, onetime chief editorial writer for the *Plain Dealer* and author of the definitive biography of the newspaper, *The Plain Dealer—One Hundred Years in Cleveland,* recalled that there had been a short-lived New York *Plain Dealer* started in 1836 by William Leggett, who had been one of the editors and a part owner of the New York *Evening Post.* J. W. Gray, who had lived in New York, and who was an avowed admirer of Leggett, presumably was influenced in his choice of the name by the New York publication.

The name traces in origin to an old English expression. A "plain-dealer" was an honest, straightforward type of person, and "plaindealing" was to be desired. Shakespeare frequently used the words within that frame of reference and another playwright, William Wycherley, was the author of a play called *The Plain Dealer* late in the seventeenth century.

"So handy and expressive a title could not long be neglected in other fields," wrote Shaw. "In 1712 a publication named the Plain Dealer was started in London, but only a few issues appeared. Boswell, in his great biography of Samuel Johnson, mentions another Plain Dealer, an English monthly devoted to 'select essays on several curious subjects.' The last number appeared in 1725. It had a successor of the same name and similar character, which appeared in 1763, but soon went the way of the rest."

Winston Churchill, when visiting Cleveland as a young man, spotted the name. "Oh," he said, "there's the Cleveland *Plain Dealer.* I think that by all odds, the *Plain Dealer* has the best newspaper name of any in the world."

In his editorial salutatory, Gray acknowledged the curiosity about the change in name from the *Advertiser* to the *Plain Dealer:*

"We offer no apology for changing the name of this paper," he wrote, "but the Scripture command—'Put not new wine into old bottles, lest they break.'

"This paper is now in the hands of a new editor, with new publishers and proprietors. It is soon to be printed on new type and furnished with new exchanges and correspondents and we hope with new patrons also. This is the 'new wine' that would *burst* the old Advertiser and not leave a trace of its well-earned fame.

"We think the good taste of our readers will sanction the modest selection we have made. Had we called it the *Torpedo* timid ladies never would have touched it. Had we called it the *Truth Teller* no one would believe a word in it! Had we called it the *Thunder Dealer* or *Lightning Spitter* it would have blown Uncle Sam's mail bags sky high. But our democracy and modesty suggest the only name that befits the occasion, the *Plain Dealer*."

Shaw recalled that President Woodrow Wilson used to say he could tell a Clevelander by the way he pronounced *Plain Dealer*. Clevelanders pronounced the name as one word, with the accent on the first syllable. Non-Clevelanders pronounced the two words separately, with the accent on the first syllable of the second word.

In those days when open partisanship was such an important part of journalism, Gray left no doubt where he and the *Plain Dealer* stood. He was a Democrat and the *Plain Dealer* was a Democratic newspaper— and it continued to be such without wavering until 1940 when, after a century in the Democratic lineup, the *Plain Dealer* switched positions and endorsed Wendell Willkie.

There was, in fact, such an intermingling of partisan politics and journalism in the mid-nineteenth century that the two were inseparable. Gray, for example, was chairman of the Ohio delegation to the Democratic national convention in Baltimore in 1852. It is worth mentioning because one of the strangest contradictions in political history pivoted on Gray's action at that convention. Had it not been for this editor of a Cleveland newspaper, one of Gray's fellow Clevelanders undoubtedly would have been elected President of the United States instead of Franklin Pierce of New Hampshire.

Among the strong dark-horse possibilities at the convention was Governor Reuben Wood of Ohio, a resident of Cleveland, and, like Gray, a native of Vermont. When the favorites for the nomination were unable to win the necessary forty-nine ballots, the convention turned its attention to Governor Wood.

All that Governor Wood needed for the nomination was the support of his own state delegation which, by all the rules and traditions of politics, he should have had in his hip pocket. But Editor Gray balked at voting for his own townsfellow because, he explained later, the governor was a "Hunker."

A Hunker, in the political lexicon of that day, was an ultra-conservative Democrat, and Gray didn't like that wing of the party. Some of the political experts of the day interpreted the editor's refusal to vote for Wood as Gray's revenge on the Hunkers for their part in engineering the defeat of New York's Governor Silas Wright in his 1846 bid for re-election. Wright and Gray were lifelong friends, and Editor Gray suspected Governor Wood of having been too friendly with the Hunkers.

When the Ohio delegation led by Gray stunned the party by its incredible refusal to support Governor Wood, the convention immediately passed by the Ohio governor and chose Pierce as its candidate. He was elected President.

Governor Wood accepted an appointment as consul in Valparaiso the following year, 1853, but he held the post only briefly. He retired from politics a year later and withdrew to his estate on Ridge Road in Rockport Township, now Cleveland's far West Side, presumably to ponder what-might-have-been; perchance to dream of the political perfidy of his own townsman.

Editor Gray did not go unrewarded for his part in frustrating the rise of a fellow Clevelander to the nation's highest office. He was named postmaster of Cleveland by a grateful President Pierce in 1853 and he held that political plum until 1858.

One of the most interesting of Cleveland's nineteenth-century editors, and undoubtedly the most powerful, was Edwin Cowles, who came to Cleveland in 1825 from the little Ohio town of Austinburg, in Ashtabula County to the east of Cleveland.

Cowles is remembered for a variety of achievements. Perhaps he should be regarded mainly as the perfect issue of the crossbreeding of politics and journalism. As the editor of the *Leader,* a morning newspaper, he is to be credited with having made that journal the most influential in the city in his time. As a politician, he surely should be remembered as one of the founders of the Republican Party.

The *Leader* grew out of the merger of two newspapers, the *True Democrat,* which was begun in the nearby town of North Olmsted (now a Cleveland suburb) around 1852, and the *Forest City,* which began publication in Cleveland the same year. The owners of the *Forest City* were two brothers from Coshocton, Ohio—Joseph and James Medill. They consolidated their newspaper with the *True Democrat* in 1853 and the result of the merger was the *Forest City Democrat.* George Bradburn and John C. Vaughn had owned the *True Democrat,* and in the merger, Vaughn joined with Joseph Medill and Edwin Cowles in a partnership that lived only a short time—just one year. Cowles became the sole owner of the newspaper in 1854, and one of his first acts was to change its name to the *Leader.* His former partner, Joseph Medill, went to Chicago and started there a newspaper called the Chicago *Tribune,* which is publishing to this very day, according to reports reaching the East.

Cowles, a fiery, outspoken man, was an outstanding catalyst in the civic life of Cleveland during one of the most important formative periods in the city's history. He swung his newspaper as a political club, as did the other editors of the day, but he swung his club faster and fiercer. His running feuds with his competition, especially Gray of the *Plain Dealer,* brought personal-political journalism to its all-time peak in Cleveland. As a matter of fact, Cowles succeeded Gray as postmaster of Cleveland, receiving his appointment from the newly elected President Lincoln.

The *Plain Dealer* did not let that appointment go by without comment. Its editorial said:

"To select so obnoxious an individual personally on the score of being a ruffian Republican is more than even Clevelanders can bear. The appointment of Cowles, personally unfit, simply because connected with a sheet owned and used by the irrepressibles to slaughter the conservatives and put down the liberal sentiments of the party look so much like 'rule or ruin' that the masses are indignant."

The *Plain Dealer* did not always approach the subject of Editor-Postmaster Cowles so subtly. It once said of him, simply:

"The editor of the Leader is the original ass that Balaam mounted."

At another time, the *Plain Dealer* described Cowles as "a catiff wretch . . . one of the most base and infamous of creatures, who, wearing the garb of a human, has nearly all the elements of a demon. . . . A fellow whose fruitful brain can produce a whole catacomb of lies in one single night resembles so much the prince of the regions of Pluto that if he be not his Satanic Majesty in person, he is worst still, being one of his dastardly and treacherous imps . . ."

Other Cleveland editors, caught in this crossfire, still managed to get in occasional potshots at both Gray and Cowles. The Cleveland *Times*, for example, dismissed Editor Gray as a "lying bank pimp—a liar both by instinct and choice."

Even the out-of-town papers, attracted by the noise of all the fun in Cleveland, and perhaps even a trifle envious, tried to get in on the act. James Gordon Bennett of the New York *Herald* declared that "Western editors are all whiskey bottles, their reporters are bottles of whiskey and their papers have all the fumes of that beverage without any of its strength."

The Cincinnati *Enquirer* made an admirable attempt to top everybody when, speaking of W. W. Armstrong, who succeeded Gray as the editor-owner of the *Plain Dealer*, it said:

"When the snarling, ill-conditioned editor of the Cleveland Plain Dealer gets drunk and falls out of the third story window of his boarding house, people in the street who catch a glimpse of his florid face and sanguinary hair cry out: 'Behold, that blazing meteor!' They afterward gather up the quivering, glutinous, odorous mass on the pavement, sweep it up and carry it into the house and put it to bed."

Cowles established himself, editorially, as an enemy of the Democratic Party, an enemy of slavery, and an enemy of the Catholic Church. He was outspoken and vitriolic on each one of those subjects.

"The war between Cowles of the Leader and the Catholic interests in

Cleveland, presided over by that fine old ecclesiastic and citizen, Bishop Richard R. Gilmour, was very lurid and uncompromising," Charles E. Kennedy, later manager-editor of the *Plain Dealer*, recalled in his memoirs, *Fifty Years in Cleveland*.

Kennedy, a Unitarian, wrote:

"Cowles hammered away at the Pope and all his works on the editorial page, but not against individual Catholics, some of whom were on his payroll . . . [he] was front man and head of the Order of the American Union, chief mission of which was the prevention of public office holding by members of the Catholic Church. . . . It died some years before the A.P.A., working along similar lines, came into existence.

"While it thrived, the O.A.U. played quite a big part in politics, especially here in Cleveland, where, in the spring of 1877, the entire Republican local ticket, most of them members of the order, and led by William G. Rose, the candidate for mayor, was elected.

"This ticket was framed up in Cowles' private office in the rear of the Leader's business office . . ."

Ironically, Cowles' daughter became a Catholic while on a trip to Paris, France, as a direct result, it was said, of her father's opposition to her marriage with a titled French suitor.

The really impressive feature of Cowles' success as an editor was that he managed to fight his way to the top in Cleveland journalism despite an inability to hiss. As even little school children are aware, an editor who cannot hiss is like a praying mantis that cannot pray, or a humming bird that cannot hum. Editors depend on their ability to hiss as an aerial acrobat depends upon his trapeze. In some newspapers, the editor's voice never has been heard—only the sound of his hissing as he stalks the halls like a restless steam radiator. It's all part of the game, as they say, and it is likely that if some reporters were not hissed at, they would never produce.

Cowles' deficiency would have been more of a handicap except that he did not *know* he could not hiss during his early career. He didn't find out about it until he was twenty-three years old, when, presumably, it finally dawned on some of his friends—not to mention his reporters— that they never had known a hiss to escape the editor's lips.

A distinguished elocutionist of the day, a Professor Kennedy, was called into the case to determine what was holding Cowles back at a time when competing editors were hissing in such strength that the sound could be heard five miles out in Lake Erie by passing mariners. Henry Howe, a distinguished historian, reported that a thorough examination by Professor Kennedy revealed that Cowles had "so peculiar an impediment of speech that no parallel case was to be found on record."

"It was found," wrote Howe, "that he [Cowles] had never heard the hissing sound of the human voice, and consequently had never made that sound. Many of the consonants sounded alike to him. He never heard the notes of the seventh octave of the piano or organ, never heard the upper notes of a violin, the fife in martial music, never heard a bird sing, and has always supposed that the music of the birds was a poetical fiction."

Once it was known just why the editor never hissed, of course, it was possible to take some remedial action. Which is exactly what Prof. Kennedy did. He spent hours coaching the editor and Howe the Historian is the authority for the word that it produced gratifying results.

"After much time spent in practicing under Prof. Kennedy's tuition," said Howe, "he [Cowles] was enabled to learn arbitrarily how to make the hissing sound, but he never heard the sound himself, although he could hear ordinary low-toned conversation."

All that is left to the imagination is the picture of what pandemonium must have ensued in the Leader city room on the day that Cowles walked in and, without warning, hissed at his staff for the very first time. What a truly historic hiss that must have been!

The nationwide Scripps-Howard chain of newspapers had its beginning in Cleveland in 1878, when Edward W. Scripps founded the *Penny Press*, the forerunner of today's Cleveland *Press*.

Scripps, a picturesque six-footer with a bright red beard and a cast in his right eye that gave him such a baleful look as to frighten friend and foe alike, came to Cleveland from Detroit, where he had been city editor of the Detroit *Evening News*, owned by his half-brother James E. Scripps. With him, to assist in launching the new paper, was his cousin, John Scripps Sweeney, who served as business manager.

The capitalization of the *Penny Press* was ten thousand dollars. Investors in the venture, besides the active proprietors, Scripps and Sweeney, were James and George Scripps, the latter being another half-brother.

The new journal was greeted with ridicule and derision from the established publications because of its smaller, unorthodox size and a generally unkempt appearance. Some called it "the Frankfort Street *Handbill*," after the street where it had its office. But Scripps, nevertheless, had hit on a successful formula that would lead to a newspaper empire. Not only was his publication only half the price of the other papers, he pinpointed the editorial policy in the direction of the so-called working class, as distinguished from his competitors' preoccupation with the moneyed elite. Within a year, the penny dreadful was on a self-supporting basis and within three years it had more circulation than all its rivals combined.

The determination to begin the Cleveland newspaper came to Scripps while he was in Paris, France, traveling with his brother George.

"I determined to be my own boss and run a newspaper of my own, subject to orders from no one," he wrote in his autobiography, *Damned Old Crank*, adding: "I had never been in the city of Cleveland, but that city was only a short distance from Detroit, where I first entered the news business. I knew the size of it and some of its character. I determined I would make my first newspaper venture there."

It was, in a limited sense, a return to ancestral ground because his grandfather on his mother's side, Timothy Osborn, was a wanderer who had settled near Cleveland, on the Chagrin River, where he operated a grist mill and held the office of justice of the peace.

An odd coincidence is that Scripps, the thirteenth child in the family, was born on a farm near Rushville, Illinois, in Cuyahoga County. There he gloried in the title of "laziest boy in Cuyahoga County." When he undertook to publish the *Penny Press* in Cleveland, he must have been the busiest boy in Ohio's Cuyahoga County. And it very well may have been that he also was the busiest drinker in the county, too, because it is his own assertion that until he reached middle age, he consumed daily "enough whiskey to keep three or four men drunk all the time." He estimated his input at a gallon of whiskey a day.

It is understandable that the staid citizens of the community chose to regard this fearsome-looking newcomer with a wary eye. They were apprised very quickly of his casual, if not utterly disrespectful attitude toward the ruling class, and of his disinclination to play the journalistic game of the day according to the established rules.

The best intimation of this came when one of the city's leading citizens, Leonard Case, who also was one of the wealthiest men in town, committed suicide by chloroforming himself in his bed. While the other papers were politely skirting the cause of Case's death and were devoting their columns to the generous terms of the dead man's will, which made a bequest of his considerable fortune for the founding of Case School of Applied Sciences (today's Case Institute of Technology), the *Penny Press* was reciting the unhappy details about the suicide and the causative factors.

This was followed by a sensational episode involving a *Press* reporter named Maurice Perkins, Scripps, and one of Cleveland's most prominent industrialists, Henry Chisholm.

When he came to tot up his life in his autobiography, Scripps chose to tell this story under the dramatic chapter heading: "I Kill Henry Chisholm."

Perkins, while checking the police rounds one night when Scripps was in Detroit, had come across a story involving the arrest of a young man who had been in a street brawl with a woman of questionable repute. The police identified the youth as Stuart H. Chisholm, and Perkins used the name in his story.

The principal owners of the Cleveland Rolling Mills in Newburgh were two brothers, Henry and Stuart Chisholm. Each had a son named Stuart. Henry's son was named Stuart H. Chisholm. Stuart's son was named Stuart Chisholm; no middle initial.

The youth actually involved in the scrape was Stuart (no middle initial) Chisholm, and Henry Stuart was infuriated when the *Penny Press* wrongly involved his son, Stuart H. He sent a messenger to request Perkins to come to his office at the rolling mills to talk over the matter next day. The reporter, a thin, cadaverous type, obligingly presented himself to the industrialist.

Instead of the man-to-man chat he had expected, Perkins was set upon by some of Chisholm's employees who tore off his clothes and painted him from head to feet with black paint, climaxing their brush-work by dumping what was left in the paint can on top of his head. Thereupon, their artistic passion spent, they gave him the heave-ho out of the building. He was picked up by a good Samaritan and taken to his home.

Scripps by this time had returned to Cleveland and had just gotten the news of his newspaper's erroneous identification when he received word of the dreadful experience of Reporter Perkins. He hastily summoned a doctor, fearing that the paint would harden on Perkins and bring about a fatal suffocation. When that danger had been averted and Perkins was quietly hiccuping his way back to recovery, Scripps returned to his office and further excitement.

A mob of men, whom he alleged were drawn from the ranks of the rolling mill employees, had gathered in front of the *Press* office and were threatening trouble. Scripps stood up in his carriage, whipped out a pistol and, florid-faced, turned on them his most baleful look; a wild-eyed expression which startled even him one day when he happened to look at himself in the mirror.

The mob parted, allowing Scripps access to his small plant, and then departed without causing any damage. But shortly a worse threat presented itself—a deputy sheriff with warrants for the arrest of Scripps and Sweeney on the charge of criminal libel.

The two men posted bond and returned again to the *Press*, where they found that all work had been suspended and where another deputy sheriff was waiting to serve a warrant "by attachment" for fifty thousand dollars in damages claimed by Chisholm in a civil suit.

Scripps was told he could not touch the *Press* property until it had been inventoried by court-appointed appraisers and until he had given the court his bond for one hundred thousand dollars—double the amount of the damages sought. The appraisers who showed up turned out to be Edwin Cowles, owner and editor of the *Leader*, and William Gleason, a former *Plain Dealer* employee. Neither felt kindly toward their

maverick colleague and insisted on a thorough, time-consuming inventory—which served, incidentally, to delay the *Press* in its attempt to
publish.

Scripps' major problem, though, was finding somebody who would
stand behind his bond for a hundred thousand dollars. He called a
number of wealthy Clevelanders who had made protestation of their
friendship previously, but all turned him down.

"These men liked my paper and frequently came to me to praise me
for my honesty and fearlessness," he wrote later. "Naturally I turned to
them for help. Naturally enough, they deserted me in my hour of need.
All of them, every last one of them."

It suddenly occurred to Scripps that if he could find an enemy of the
Chisholms, he likely would find a friend of E. W. Scripps. He asked
his attorney, Judge R. R. Paine, for help. Paine was the father of a
youngster on the *Press* staff, Robert F. Paine, who would become editor
of the *Press* and serve in that capacity for thirty years.

Judge Paine took the editor to a shabby house in a not-too-reputable
neighborhood and introduced him to an old, wizened man named
Samuel G. Baldwin, who must have been quite a remarkable character
in his own right. He made a living as a professional bondsman for
thieves and prostitutes and owned approximately a half-million dollars
worth of property in the red-light district. Baldwin, some years before,
had testified in a lawsuit in which Henry Chisholm was one of the
principals. Whatever it was that Baldwin said on the witness stand,
Chisholm did not approve of it, and he allegedly had slapped Baldwin
on the face as he stepped down from the witness chair. Baldwin was
the bona fide Chisholm enemy that Scripps had hoped to find, and he
was more than happy to go bond for the editor, thereby restoring to
Scripps his newspaper and his freedom.

It was the moment Scripps had been waiting for. It was late Saturday
afternoon, and the *Press* missed its usual edition time, but it didn't matter to Scripps; now he was at last on the offensive. By six o'clock
Saturday evening, his newspaper was on the street with the story of
"The Shame of Chisholm," and the team of Scripps and Sweeney saw
to it that enough extra copies were run off the presses to blanket the
city with the story.

That wasn't enough for Scripps. His odd eye was hot with the glare
of a righteous man who had been wronged, and he published the story,
in condensed form, at the top of the editorial column day after day
through the week that followed.

Word came to him that the fury of his attack had had such devastating effect on the great industrialist that his health had been affected,
and that Chisholm, indeed, had taken to his bed. Scripps was visited

by Chisholm's doctor and one of his friends, the president of a Cleveland bank, who begged the editor to relent in his attack.

"I replied bitterly," Scripps said later, "that Chisholm had shown no mercy to the poor weakling Perkins and was entitled to no mercy from Perkins' employer and friend."

The terms of surrender laid down by Scripps was that Chisholm withdraw his civil suit for damages and pay five thousand dollars, which would be given to Perkins, who was still on his sickbed, hiccuping away through all the turmoil.

Chisholm agreed to the terms, through his attorney, and the celebrated case was settled, but not without a tragic anticlimax. Chisholm died only a few weeks later, and his death generally was attributed to the controversy with the *Press*.

"I was shocked by the event," wrote Scripps later. "I believed then, and believe now, that had Chisholm's attack on Perkins killed Perkins, and had Chisholm been successful in suppressing my publicity and hence avoided public contumely, he would have lived many years longer, a leading and respected citizen of the city of Cleveland.

"I may be mistaken, but I never believed that simple remorse killed Mr. Chisholm. But neither have I ever had any doubt that Chisholm's death was caused by me. Had I taken a pistol and shot him to death, I would have felt no more and no less responsibility for that death than I have ever since felt.

"It is true that I did not know I was killing Chisholm when I was killing him. Nonetheless I believe that had I known that I was killing him at the time, I would have pursued the same course. I believe I would have felt no more remorse, no more guilt, under those circumstances than I have since felt, and I have felt none.

"I believed then that I was not only doing what was right, but that I was actually performing a public duty."

As for Perkins, he quit hiccuping the minute that Scripps handed him his five thousand dollars, rose from his sickbed, and went off on a "frolic" that lasted several weeks and cost him half of the money.

Aside from Scripps himself, and Robert F. Paine, no single man personified the Cleveland *Press* more than Louis B. Seltzer, the slight, dapper editor who ruled the paper for thirty-seven years, until his retirement in 1966. He joined the *Press* in 1917 and became editor in 1928. His tenure in that office was the longest in the newspaper's history. He was succeeded by Thomas L. Boardman.

When Seltzer was in his cub years at the *Press*, he wrote under the by-line of "Looey, the Office Boy." Long after he moved past the office boy level he continued to be known as Looey by his friends and even his casual acquaintances. He also was known as "Little Bromo" (Seltzer), usually among his critics, of whom there were more than a few, and "Mr. Cleveland," among those who admired him excessively.

There was a Cleveland legend that Louis Seltzer really ran the city, and there were times when that was no overstatement. He moved the *Press* from its dilapidated old building at East 9th Street and Rockwell Avenue to a glistening new glass-and-white-brick structure two blocks north, at East 9th Street and Lakeside Avenue in 1959. In this new site, the *Press* is just across the street from City Hall, and some political insiders guessed that the *Press* move was to make it easier for Seltzer to run the city by centralizing operations, so to speak.

Until recently, the *Press* had nominal, if not minimal, competition in the afternoon field, but the Forest City Publishing Company, which owned both the afternoon Cleveland *News* and the *Plain Dealer*, inexplicably sold the *News* to the rival *Press* in 1960. By this move, the *Press* was given the afternoon monopoly and picked up some eighty thousand former *News* subscribers. The circulation battle between the *Plain Dealer* and the *Press* had been relatively even until that time, but the death of the *News* shot the *Press* far ahead of the *P.D.*, 390,000 to 310,000. The *Plain Dealer*, put under the direction of a young editor-publisher, Tom Vail, in 1962, has wiped out that imposing lead. Since 1965 the two rivals have been on the fifty-yard line, circulation just about even, glaring at each other again.

As the competition waxes keener between the two newspapers, the city inevitably is reminded of some of the titanic circulation battles that were fought in Cleveland in the past. What makes the comparison even more apt is that both editors, Vail and Boardman, are as fascinated by politics as were the editors of the earlier years when even a homicide was secondary to a political speech—except, of course, when the victim in the homicide happened to be a politician.

Politics and journalism are intertwined in the genealogy of many Cleveland leaders. For example, Louis Seltzer's father, Charles Alden Seltzer, besides being a novelist, was the longtime mayor of North Olmsted. Tom Vail's father, Herman L. Vail, now president of the Forest City Publishing Company, served as a state representative in his younger years. The editor-publisher's grandfather, Harry L. Vail, was himself a newspaperman turned politician. He had been editor of the *Sunday Morning Voice* before he chose to enter politics as a popular county commissioner.

A lot of the fun and glamor went out of newspapers as they matured financially and adopted the cautious, conservative attitude which is almost always the concomitant condition where the money stakes are high. Then editors tend more and more to straddle the editorial fence in the name of objectivity. Not only does such impartiality leave the readers fumbling in the dark as they try to tell the good guys from the bad guys in any specific election campaign, but the modern, unemotional, balanced reporting that is featured in today's newspaper is about as exciting to read as the annual report of an agricultural test station.

A member of the Cleveland journalism scene, briefly, was *Time* magazine, which published out of the Penton Building at West 3d Street and Lakeside Avenue from 1925 to 1927. It was a very young magazine at that time, an experiment in journalism that was still scratching for a foothold. Henry R. Luce and Briton Hadden had launched the enterprise in 1923, but the results after two years of publication were something short of sensational. The circulation at the beginning of 1925 was 34,100.

Cleveland seemed to offer several important advantages over New York, where the magazine was published at the outset: lower costs for printing and office expenses and better distribution. Mailed from New York, as second-class matter, it had experienced embarrassing delays in delivery to subscribers in the populous Midwest, and often did not reach readers in the Far West until a week or more after publication. *Time*, being a newsmagazine, naturally held the timeliness of its product in high regard, and Cleveland, because of its central location, offered the probability of a more effective radius of distribution. More than 60 per cent of the nation's population lived within five hundred miles of Cleveland at that time.

Time made its move to Cleveland in August 1925, and the prime mover was Henry Luce. Hadden was in Europe on vacation at the time, but the magazine did not wait for his return. One day in August a notice appeared on a bulletin board in the *Time* office, notifying all employees that they were dismissed as of August 16. They were informed, further, that all who applied for a job at the magazine's new address, the Penton Building in Cleveland, on August 19 would be rehired.

In his biography, *Briton Hadden*, Noel F. Busch wrote of *Time's* Cleveland adventure:

"While the advantages of centralized distribution amply justified it, the Cleveland move was by no means in all respects an unmitigated triumph. Grave difficulties developed, of which the most dramatic were Hadden's private reactions to his new and strange environment. For Luce, who had spent nearly half of his previous life in China, the differences between one American city and another were relatively small. The salient quality of all of them was that they differed so markedly from the cities he had known in Europe or the Orient, and thus, like most other things about the U.S., tended to excite his approval. Luce was also, by this time, a married man whose comfortable home and diverse social interests enabled him to get along compatibly with the young married set of Cleveland, with whom he had no marked temperamental disaffinity. With Hadden the case was otherwise.

"For the born New Yorker, other metropoli may be interesting, exciting or admirable but there can be only one place in the world that really defines the word city. For an extremist New Yorker, brought up in Brooklyn, this was doubly true. If Cleveland had combined the grandeur of Rome, the charm of Paris and the solidity of London with the exotic glamor of the casbah in Alexandrian Bagdad, Hadden would doubtless have found it a poor substitute for Brooklyn Heights. In point of fact, it seemed to him to lack these charms and to substitute for them what were, in his estimation, defects almost as grave as that of not being Brooklyn in the first place. x x x In Cleveland, he made what was to him a horrifying discovery. This was that Babbitts were not in fact amusing freaks at all but rather, just as Sinclair Lewis had suggested, the backbone of U.S. population . . ."

But if Cleveland did not offer sophisticated pleasures to the urbane Hadden, it did give him a superior opportunity to pursue his big hobby, baseball. He organized a sandlot team, equipped it, and appointed himself manager, captain, and shortstop. The pleasure he found in this sport was not enough, however, to make up for Cleveland's other deficiencies as the headquarter city for *Time*. Most of all, the magazine missed the New York *Times,* the source of so much grist for the *Time* mill. The publishers also missed the wealth of young, intellectual talent then available in New York. And so it came about in spring of 1927, when Luce this time was in Europe on vacation, that Hadden moved *Time* Magazine from Cleveland and returned it to its ancestral home in New York. The two-year sojourn in Cleveland had not been without beneficial effect, entirely. *Time's* circulation had risen to 140,000 by 1927, there was money in the bank, and distribution problems had lessened. Cleveland, baseball, and Babbitry to one side, could take some of the credit for the improvement in the health of the young magazine.

The threat of physical violence hovers over the head of almost every newspaperman at one time or another during his career. The world is full of crackpots and angry people who, for want of a better target perhaps, choose to direct their wretched tempers at the honest men of the press. The history of journalism in Cleveland is replete with incidents of violence attempted on the persons of editors, reporters, and cameramen. There were numerous invitations to the duel at dawn and so many attempts to waylay editors and writers that it is not surprising many of the old-time newsmen, through necessity, were schooled in the use of cane swords and pistols. Edwin Cowles, for example, retired to a back room in his editorial offices for target practice whenever he had any spare time. The thunderous roar of his blunderbuss was as familiar a sound to the staff of the *Leader* as the clanking of the old job press.

It remained for modern times, however, to bring forth the most tragic

realization of violence in the cold-blooded murder of the president and
general manager of the Forest City Publishing Company, John S. Mc-
Carrens, who directed the fortunes of two daily newspapers, the
Plain Dealer and the Cleveland *News.*

McCarrens had joined the *Plain Dealer* executive staff in 1914 as advertising manager, becoming general manager in 1933, the same year
that Paul Bellamy, one of the nation's most respected journalists, was
named editor. It was a formidable team. Bellamy went on to become
the president of the American Society of Newspaper Editors, while
McCarrens in 1939 was named president of the American Newspaper
Publishers Association; two of the highest honors in the American newspaper business.

Then, on the sunny morning of Thursday, July 22, 1943, McCarrens
received a telephone call from a man named Herbert L. Kobrak, asking
for an appointment that day. McCarrens agreed to see his caller in his
office at two-thirty in the afternoon.

Kobrak was well-known to McCarrens, as he was to most publishing
executives in Cleveland. He was a Hungarian native who had come to
the United States in 1908, moving from Chicago to Cleveland in 1917
to become general manager of a Hungarian-language daily, the *Szabadsag.* He frequently identified himself as a Hungarian baron and he was
obsessed, according to one of his acquaintances, "with the dream of
becoming the William Randolph Hearst of the foreign language press."

Kobrak (he also went under the names of Louis Rosenfeld and Louis
Racz) in time became general manager of the Consolidated Press &
Printing Company, publisher of the *Szabadsag* and the German-language
paper, *Waechter und Anzeiger.* In 1939, however, Consolidated went
into bankruptcy and Kobrak was unemployed. From that time on, he
talked almost incessantly to friends and possible financial backers of
starting another newspaper in Cleveland. Among those whom he im-
portuned for assistance in beginning a daily picture newspaper slanted
toward the foreign element in Cleveland was John S. McCarrens.

Kobrak arrived at the *Plain Dealer* Building shortly before two-thirty.
A tense, dark man, he attracted attention on the elevator with his
erratic behavior. He clutched a briefcase to his chest and his chin
trembled. He was admitted to the publisher's inner office a few minutes
after his arrival. The secretary, Miss Jane Hammond, heard voices raised
and then Kobrak closed the door to McCarrens' office. At 3:10 P.M.
four shots were heard in the outer office, the door swung open, and the
publisher staggered out.

"Get an ambulance," he said hoarsely. "I've been shot by a madman!"

C. C. McConkie, comptroller of the newspaper, and two secretaries,
Miss Hammond and Miss Florence Anthony, helped the wounded

executive to the nearby office of Joseph V. Madigan, *Plain Dealer* circulation director and son-in-law of McCarrens.

When they returned to McCarrens' office, they found Kobrak slumped in a chair, near death. He had shot himself in the temple with a .32-caliber revolver, which had fallen to the floor near his outstretched fingers. He died a half-hour after being taken to the hospital.

McCarrens had been shot three times, once in each arm and once in the abdomen. A police ambulance took him to St. Vincent Charity Hospital. On his arrival there, in a moment of consciousness, he told the *Plain Dealer's* advertising manager, Sterling E. Graham: "I'm sorry for that fellow. He's crazy."

The publisher clung to life from that Thursday afternoon until the following Saturday morning. One of the notes left by his assassin indicated that Kobrak had planned to kill McCarrens for several months. Another letter left by the murderer was addressed to "Gentlemen of the Press," and adjured them to consult the records for his history and promised them further big news. It told of his association with well-known newspapers, including the Chicago *Tribune,* and rambled incoherently into speculation over the location of newspapers in heaven and hell, with specific allusions to commentary by Swedenborg and George Bernard Shaw. He concluded by describing himself as a good hunter and fisherman and by revealing that he trained his own bird dogs.

It was the kind of communication that is familiar to newspapermen everywhere. Sick letters from sick people seem to be a fixed part of a newspaperman's life. In the case of Herbert Kobrak and John McCarrens, the sickness led to death.

XI

The Golden Years

THE midway mark of the nineteenth century was the turning point for Cleveland. It was the end of the quaint little New England colony perched primly on the bluff overlooking the beautiful Lake Erie and clinging to Cuyahoga's hillsides. The tiny Connecticut outpost, less than six decades away from the wilderness, suddenly found itself an intersection toward which men and events of destiny were riding hard. They would meet in Cleveland and make it—overnight, it seemed—a metropolis of world importance.

First it had been the building of the Ohio Canal beginning in 1825 that had stirred the little settlement and given it the first pale hint of what the future might bring to this place where the twisting river met the Great Lakes.

But that had been only the promise. The future did not begin to reveal itself until the century began its downhill run, picking up speed as it moved, and carrying the city with it into the twentieth century at breakneck speed. The town that moved into 1850 with a population of 17,034 persons arrived at 1900 with a population of 361,768.

This was boom town, suddenly; the fulfillment of the earlier promise and more; greatness and growth far beyond the conservative predictions of the wise men. Conestoga wagons from the East paraded in steady stream over the mountains and rolled, hub deep, through the muddy streets of the city searching for a place to stop. For many of them this was the end of the great adventure west. Other of the romantic-looking wagons that had arrived earlier were parked in back lots and already had been stripped of their canvas covering, so that their ribs were exposed to the sun and the weather, like bones strewn on the desert.

And still the new people came on—by stagecoach, by canal barge, by horseback, and on foot. Most of all, they came by railroad, the new way to travel and to transport goods. Axes and saws slashed holes through the virgin forests that still abounded over the Ohio country, opening the way for new, profitable railroad routes. Communities everywhere scrambled to entice the rails into their midst, knowing that the trains carried prosperity as well as people; shrugging aside what the railroads were doing to the American paradise.

This was part of the price of progress—tracks that scarred the land and routed beauty; trains that rumbled through the streets, shaking houses and soiling the flowers and the foliage with their soot. Cleveland, like every other town of the time, was happy to pay the price. This port city directly athwart the main routes of travel from east to west, the northern terminal of the great Ohio Canal, was a natural target for the railroads. The silver rails came shooting in from east and west, southeast and southwest. Tracks crossed tracks and crisscrossed the land; they followed the lakeshore and they hugged the bottomland of the river valley as they pushed along in their great trip from nowhere to somewhere, all the while squandering the most precious property that the city possessed in a ruthless assertion of economic and industrial priority.

In recent decades the city has attempted to recover its lost lakefront, becoming locked in a running legal war with the railroads over the complicated issue. Meanwhile, it met its needs by building, in effect, a new shoreline through the stratagem of leapfrogging the tracks and filling in the lake.

The waters of Erie always have commanded the attention of Clevelanders, not just as a gratifying scenic asset but because of the realization that this, one of the largest bodies of fresh water in the world, is the real source of the city's advantage and prosperity.

Perhaps the most important single vessel ever to enter Cleveland waters was the *Baltimore*, which sailed into the harbor in 1852 carrying a cargo that included six barrels of iron ore from the backwoods country of Michigan's Upper Peninsula. It was a token shipment, a forerunner of the future which would establish Cleveland as the largest iron ore receiving port in the nation and the headquarters of shipping on the Great Lakes. Rumors of rich mineral deposits in the Michigan north woods were alive when, in 1847, a Cleveland physician, Dr. J. Lang Cassels, later dean of the Cleveland Medical School, went to the bush country to investigate the reports. He found them to be true. Surveyors running their lines in Marquette County in 1844 had found their compasses behaving erratically, presumably because of the presence of iron ore. Philo Everett, a resident of Jackson, Michigan, went into the remote area near the rim of Lake Superior in 1845 and, with the help of a cooperative Chippewa chief with the unlikely name of Marji Gesick, he pinpointed the rich deposits. He and some friends formed the Jackson Mining Company to exploit the find. Dr. Cassels visited the ore range and then obtained an agreement with the Jackson combine which would allow his Cleveland backers to mine a specific area.

The Cleveland Iron Mining Company, predecessor of today's giant Cleveland-Cliffs Iron Company, was formed in 1850 by a group of prominent Clevelanders that included Samuel Livingston Mather, John Outhwaite, Isaac L. Hewitt, Selah Chamberlain, Henry F. Brayton, and E. W. Clark. With permission of the Michigan legislature, the company began to buy land and to explore for further iron ore deposits in what is now known as the Marquette Iron District. In its evolution, it acquired the interests of the Jackson company.

Mining the valuable ore was not nearly as much of a problem as its transportation to furnaces in Ohio and Pennsylvania. When the first ore was extracted, in the beginning of the 1850s, it had to be hauled by wagons to Marquette, loaded into boats there, shipped to Sault Ste. Marie (The Soo), unloaded, carried by wagons around the rapids of the St. Marys River which connected Lake Superior with Lake Huron, and then reloaded into boats for the final leg of the trip to Cleveland.

Two large projects, Cleveland-inspired, overcame these major difficulties. The Cleveland Iron Mining Company joined with the Jackson Mining Company in the building of a plank road from the mines to Marquette in 1854, and three years later the Cleveland company built the Iron Mountain Railroad to the Lake Superior port. The government, meanwhile, had acted to construct a shipping canal parallel with the turbulent St. Marys River, with locks to compensate for the different water levels at either end. The canal was finished in 1855 and the first shipment was one hundred tons of iron ore aboard the brigantine *Columbia* headed for Cleveland, passing through the Soo on August 17, 1855.

In steadily mounting volume, then, the red mineral wealth of Michigan, Minnesota, and Canada began to pour into Cleveland Harbor, making its way up the Cuyahoga to the steel mills and inland to cities like Warren, Youngstown, and Pittsburgh. Cleveland was where the iron ore of the North met with petroleum and coal from Pennsylvania. The mixture's effect was a form of spontaneous combustion that fired the industrial development of the city. The stacks of the steel mills and the towers of the oil refineries gave the Cuyahoga Valley a new importance.

The cry was for ships and more ships, and Cleveland responded by developing a ship-building industry that made it the most productive center of its kind on the Great Lakes. By the closing years of the century, it was the greatest ship-building center in the nation, ranking next, in world importance, to the mighty yards of the Clyde, in Scotland. Long before that time, though, it had become the world's greatest oil refining center and a leading steel production center.

The homogenous colony of native Clevelanders held tight in the face of the changes brought about by the industrialization of their small city. However they may have regretted the passing of the quiet, quaint town, the freshet of prosperity was more than adequate compensation. The old guard perhaps was most shaken by the invasion of foreigners who

...ıe secure genealogy of the town, but protest was futile
...ın. The newcomers outnumbered all others, and while the
. interests disapproved of the immigrants socially, they needed
...ır brawn and muscle in the gathering battle that was part of the
industrial Revolution. It was a union of convenience, and the old settlers
adjusted themselves to a different kind of life that included the new
people.

Under the conditions of explosive growth that prevailed, life in
Cleveland hardly could be expected to countenance a dull moment.
There was all the gaiety and vitality that are natural characteristics of
a boom town in full growth.

Politics was the chief entertainment of the day, but the theater—
especially the lecture circuit—was coming into its own, and there was
even a touch of literary splendor, as exemplified by the downtown book
mart operated by Moses C. Younglove & Company. It was taken over in
1852 by three brothers named Cobb, which is hardly a notable development in itself except that their full Christian names were Caius Cassius
Cobb, Brutus Junius Cobb, and Junius Brutus Cobb. If this phalanx of
names was not enough to make visitors pause on the threshold of J. B.
Cobb & Company, the three brothers had some classical brothers and
sisters in reserve. They included Lucius Marcius Cobb, Marcius Lucius
Cobb, Lucia Marcia Cobb, Cassius Caius Cobb, Marcia Lucia Cobb,
and, finally and inexplicably, Daniel Cobb.

The lecture platform was in high vogue through the latter half of
the century, and it held a strong lure of money that the most famous
men of the day could not resist. Melodeon Hall, Case Hall, the Academy
of Music, and the Opera House all catered to the public appetite for this
form of *divertissement*. For instance Henry M. Stanley, the man who
braved the African jungles in his successful search for David Livingstone,
told Clevelanders his gripping tale of adventure at least three times
over a period of twenty years, indicating that today's practice of television
program reruns is not entirely new in concept.

Bret Harte painted sketches of frontier towns and recited his most
popular stories of the West, while Buffalo Bill Cody came back to his
onetime hometown in March 1872 to test the public with an acting
performance. He was cast as the star of Ned Buntline's production called
Buffalo Bill, King of the Border Men, but the steely-eyed sharpshooter,
who had stood up to angry redskins and thundering herds of maddened
buffalos, was not equal to the pressures of the stage. He took one look at
his Cleveland audience, his voice faltered, and he broke and bolted for
the wings.

A newspaper critic the next day reported the dramatic debacle and wondered in print: "If it really took Ned Buntline six hours to write Buffalo Bill, I wonder how he managed to fill in the time?"

The old master himself, Mark Twain, enjoyed great success as a lecturer, but Cleveland was not the scene of his greatest platform triumph. On July 15, 1895, he gave a benefit performance in Music Hall for the Newsboys Home, and his lecture was titled, "The Regeneration of the Race."

The audience was demanding enough, but Twain had an added challenge—the stage area behind him had been filled with restless newsboys to serve as backdrop for the humorist. It was a disastrous idea, as Twain noted in a letter he wrote the next day to a Cleveland friend, H. H. Rogers of Standard Oil.

"Last night," wrote Mark Twain, "I suffered defeat. There were a couple of hundred little boys behind me on the stage . . . and there was nobody to watch them or keep them quiet.

". . . Besides, a concert of amateurs had been smuggled into the program, so it was 20 minutes of 9 before I got on the platform. I got started magnificently, but inside of half an hour the scuffling boys had the audience's maddened attention, and I saw it was a gone case. So I skipped a third of my program and quit. The newspapers are kind, but . . . there ain't going to be any more concerts at my lectures!"

Twain possibly had this experience, and others like it, in mind when he wrote in his private papers:

"I remained in the lecture field three seasons—long enough to learn the trade; then domesticated myself in my new married estate after a weary life of wandering, and remained under shelter at home for fourteen or fifteen years. Meantime speculators and moneymakers had taken up the business of hiring lecturers, with the idea of getting rich at it. In about five years they killed that industry dead and when I returned to the platform for a season, in 1884, there had been a happy and holy silence for ten years, and a generation had come to the front who knew nothing about lectures and readings and didn't know how to take them nor what to make of them. They were difficult audiences, those untrained squads, and . . . I had a hard time with them sometimes . . ."

Among the leading citizens of Cleveland most interested in the theater was the famous Mark Hanna, and he indicated his devotion to the stage in tangible ways, including an occasional spin as an actor himself. He starred in the West Side Dickens Club production of *Mr. Pickwick and His Friends* in Case Hall on December 30, 1873, portraying, of course, Mr. Pickwick. Hanna also owned the Euclid Avenue Opera House, which burned down in October of 1892. The theatrical company which was playing the theater at the time included a promising young actress named Marie Dressler. The wealthy Clevelander immediately built a new, larger theater in its place and the opening, September 11, 1893, was one of the social and dramatic highlights of the season. Seats were in such demand they were sold at auction. It was actually more dramatic than Hanna had hoped because the star of the opening production, *Beau Brummel,* was the famous Richard Mansfield, a man of temperament as well as talent. He quit in the middle of the play, stomping off stage in angry frustration and refusing to proceed "in competition with hissing steam radiators."

Mark Hanna's influence on the Cleveland theatrical scene is still strong. The city's only remaining legitimate theater—allowing for an exception of the Roxy Burlesque house—is the beautiful Hanna Theater, named after the famous patron of the arts-politician-businessman.

Surely one of the least remembered Clevelanders of the Civil War period was a man named George Washington Johnson, who joined the staff of the *Plain Dealer* as an associate editor in 1864. Johnson, a young Canadian and a former schoolteacher, came to Cleveland from a position as associate editor of the Buffalo *Courier.* He brought with him his new bride, a pretty girl named Maggie Clark Johnson, also of Canadian birth.

The young couple was deeply in love. Johnson was the demonstrative type. During the Canadian phase of their courtship, in Glanford, Ontario, he had employed his undeniable literary talent to woo her with poetry. One of the ballads inspired by his love for her was published in 1864, the same year he married her.

But the marriage of George Johnson and his beloved Maggie was short-lived. They had been in Cleveland only a few months when she contracted typhoid fever and died after a short illness. She was twenty-three years old. Johnson was plunged into such grief that he resigned from the newspaper staff early in 1866 and returned to Canada, where he resumed teaching as a professor of languages at the University of Toronto. That same year, an English composer named J. A. Butterfield set Johnson's love ballad to music, and it became an instant international standard, "When You and I Were Young, Maggie."

Another well-known song of the nineteenth century had a Cleveland background, having been inspired by a shipwreck off Cleveland Harbor. It was called, "Let the Lower Lights Be Burning," and was written by a leading composer of gospel songs, P. P. Bliss, with music by Ira D. Sankey.

Dwight L. Moody, the Billy Graham of his day, made the song a national favorite by featuring it in his services. He always preceded the rendition of the song with the following dramatic recitation:

"On a dark, stormy night, when the waves rolled like mountains and not a star was to be seen, a boat, rocking and plunging, neared the Cleveland Harbor.

"'Are you sure this is Cleveland,' asked the captain, seeing only one light from the lighthouse.

"'Quite sure, sir,' replied the pilot.

"'Where are the lower lights?'

"'Gone out, sir!'

"'Can you make the harbor?'

"'We must, or perish, sir!'

"And with a strong hand, a brave heart, the old pilot turned the wheel. But, alas, in the darkness he missed the channel, and with a crash upon the rocks the boat was shivered, and many a life was lost in a watery grave. Brethren, the Master will take care of the great lighthouse; let us keep the lower lights burning!"

Of all the entertainments of the time, though, politics by far exerted the strongest attraction. There could have been no busier political arena in the entire Midwest than Cleveland. Fortunately, the fashionable Cleveland hostelries all boasted good, strong balconies at a time when balcony speeches were the vogue. General Sam Houston spoke from the balcony of the Forest City House in behalf of the presidential candidacy of Franklin Pierce, while over on the balcony of the American House, General Winfield Scott was speaking in behalf of his own Whig ticket. When Abraham Lincoln came to town, he was hustled onto the balcony of the Weddell House to make a speech.

President Andrew Johnson, in office only a short time as Lincoln's successor, took to the balcony of the Kennard House upon his arrival in the city on September 3, 1866, as part of his swing around the nation. It was not, incidentally, his most successful public appearance.

Cleveland, whose Edwin Cowles had had so much to do with organization of the Republican Party, was a Republican stronghold. But President Johnson's views on Reconstruction differed from that held by the Cleveland diehards, and he was given a hostile reception.

After speaking briefly about the general policy he intended to follow as President, he lapsed into a more intimate vein, reminiscing about his own career.

"I began political life as an alderman," he recalled, "then became a representative in our state legislature, next a United States senator, and now, by the grace of God, I am your President!"

The applause that the President obviously expected at this point was not forthcoming. As he looked down at the stony audience during the embarrassing pause, a voice, clear and strident, called out from the crowd:

"How unfortunate!"

The President of the United States blinked, made a pointed rejoinder, and withdrew from the balcony.

Illustrative of the relationship between Johnson and the Republican Party in Cleveland, whose nominal leader was Editor Cowles of the *Leader*, is the story of Cowles' refusal to sign a paper of recommendation in behalf of a Cleveland friend, Philo Scovill, who was seeking a government job.

"What?" cried out the editor when approached by his friend, Scovill. "Me sign a paper asking a favor of that old renegade? Not by all the stars that shine and hope everlasting!"

As Scovill's expression fell, Cowles added shrewdly:

"Besides, my signature on your paper seen by Mr. Johnson would kill your political hopes deader than Julius Caesar. But here is what I will do. I'll give Mr. Johnson another flaying and wind it up with abuse of you and the whole Scovill family. You then go to Washington, show the article to Johnson, and it's more than an even chance he will give you anything you want."

Cowles followed through with a denunciation of both the President and Philo Scovill, and it turned out exactly as he had predicted. Scovill was given the federal appointment.

Those were the golden decades for Ohio, politically speaking, as both parties looked to the pivotal Buckeye State for candidates and for leadership. In the national election of 1880, Cleveland came close to having native sons as presidential candidates on both party tickets. James A. Garfield, who was born in Mentor, just to the east of Cleveland in Cuyahoga County, was nominated by the Republicans, and former Congressman (later U. S. Senator) Henry B. Payne of Cleveland made a spirited bid for the Democratic nomination, but lost out to General Winfield S. Hancock.

The nation did not have much time to get acquainted with President Garfield. He was assassinated as he entered the Baltimore & Potomac Railroad station in Washington on July 2, 1881, less than six months after he was inaugurated. He was gunned down by a disgruntled office-seeker named Charles J. Guiteau. The President did not die immediately, but lingered on until the night of September 19. The Fourth of July celebration, two days after the shooting, was a somber affair in Cleveland that year. A mass meeting was held on Public Square and four thousand persons listened quietly to a number of panegyrical speeches even as bulletins on the condition of the wounded Chief Executive were distributed through the crowd by the newspapers.

A reflection of the anger that seized Cleveland with the news of the wanton crime is to be found in the melodramatic language of the Cleveland *Sun and Voice*, which suggested the following as an introductory chapter for the life story of Assassin Guiteau:

"'Twas night and such a night as earth ne'er saw before. Murky clouds veiled the fair face of Heaven, and gave to pitchy darkness a still deeper dye. The moon had fled; the stars ceased to twinkle and closed their eyes, for deeds were doing which they would not behold. For a time the pure streams became stagnant and ceased to flow.

"The hills trembled, the mountains labored; the forests dropped their leaves, and flowers lost their fragrance and withered. All nature became desolate. In glee serpents hissed, harpies screamed and satyrs revelled beneath the Upas. Domestic beasts silently crept near the abode of man. The lion relinquished his half-eaten prey. The tiger forgetful of his fierceness ran howling to his lair, and the hyena quit his repast of dead man's bones.

"Man of all earth's creatures slept, but he slept as if the boding of some half unknown calamity sat brooding o'er his mind. The clock to Time ceased to move. On such a night h—ll yawned and there was spewed upon the earth this monster . . ."

When the news of the President's death reached Cleveland on the night of September 19, all the city's church bells began a tolling that lasted all through the night. Cannons along the lakefront intermittently boomed their tribute to the martyr President until dawn. The following day most of the city's downtown buildings were draped in black and white with the help of the city fire department. Captain George A. Wallace and his men from Hook and Ladder No. 1 also built the catafalque on which the President's coffin would rest in the middle of Public Square.

The funeral train arrived in Cleveland on Saturday, September 24, and the hearse carried the President's body through silent, crowd-lined streets to the measured beat of the military escort. Around the high catafalque on the Square where the slain Garfield would lie in state for two days was an honor guard of the Cleveland Grays.

In like manner only sixteen short years before, a catafalque at the same place had held the martyred remains of President Abraham Lincoln. A canopied pavilion had been erected over the casket which was banked with white flowers. Between early morning and ten that night, more than one hundred thousand persons from all sections of Ohio and surrounding states moved slowly past the casket. It was their last look at the fallen President, and, for most of them, their first look. Some people did not even notice there was a small coffin at the foot of the President's. It held the body of his son, Willie, who had died in 1862, and who would be interred beside his father in Springfield, Illinois.

At least as many mourners—probably more—passed by the body of President Garfield in America's last tribute to him in Public Square, and they included the great names of the nation. Two ex-Presidents, Ulysses S. Grant and Rutherford B. Hayes, came to pay their respects, as did Generals Sherman, Sheridan, and Hancock; all the members of the cabinet and ranking foreign dignitaries.

Reverend Isaac Errett of Cincinnati, a longtime friend of the President, preached the funeral sermon in public services on the Square, and then the body was taken to Lake View Cemetery, close to John D. Rockefeller's Forest Hill estate, in a slow, five-mile procession. The President's body was placed in a private vault until a permanent resting place could be constructed.

It was nine years later, Decoration Day 1890, that the imposing mausoleum-monument to President Garfield was completed in Lake View. Cost of the 180-foot-high stone structure was $225,000, raised by contributions sent in from people all over the world. George Keller of Hartford, Connecticut, was the designer, chosen in a national competition.

The memorial sits on an enviable site, atop one of Cleveland's eastern hills, with a sweeping view of the central city to the west and Lake Erie to the north. It is a formidable monument, with a peaked tower fifty feet in diameter. Fourteen stained-glass windows memorialize the original thirteen states and Ohio, and they ring the memorial chapel of mosaics and marble which features a tall statue of President Garfield, the work of Alexander Doyle, showing the slain President as he looked when he was a member of the House of Representatives.

The dedication of the memorial to President Garfield was a signal for the gathering again in Cleveland of the great names of the day, led by President Benjamin Harrison (another Ohioan). A Cleveland delegation, including Mayor George W. Gardner, Mark Hanna, Liberty E. Holden, publisher of the *Plain Dealer*, and other notables met the presidential train at Alliance, Ohio, where the introductions were handled by the popular congressman from Canton, Major William McKinley, whose possibilities as a presidential candidate already were being explored by the Republican Party.

An estimated ten thousand persons greeted President Harrison and his party in the grand reception that night in the Stillman Hotel, while another thirty thousand jammed Euclid Avenue at the hotel entrance, trying to get in. Dedication ceremonies were held next day—Decoration Day—at Lake View. The procession of celebrities was led, appropriately, by Garfield's old Civil War command, the 42nd Regiment of the Ohio Volunteer Infantry. In the parade that followed the five-mile route were General James Barnett, marshal; General William Tecumseh Sherman, ex-President Rutherford B. Hayes, Chief Justice Melville W. Fuller, and Congressman McKinley.

McKinley was a fine-looking stateman that day, and all the Ohioans who attended the dedication services for the memorial to President-martyr Garfield were proud of the man from Canton. He stood tall and straight and dignified in the sunshine, inspiring trust and respect among those who looked at him. He had that kind of appearance; a kind of nobility in his look and in his posture that prompted William Allen White to say: "He walked among men a bronze statue, for thirty years determinedly looking for his pedestal."

Eleven years from that day in Lake View Cemetery, the services would be for him—another President from Ohio, another martyr of the nation—and he would have found his pedestal at last. But on that day in Cleveland, the sun shone brightly, the future was promising, and he smiled affectionately at his friend, Mark Hanna, when their eyes locked across the platform of dignitaries.

XII

Cassie Was a Lady

NOBODY—not John D. Rockefeller, nor Samuel Andrews, nor Samuel Mather—was able to build a house that attracted the interest of Cleveland as much as the hip-roofed mansion that sat at 8206 Euclid Avenue during the time when the street was awash with wealthy and, oftentimes, eccentric characters.

The public's thoughtful attention here had nothing to do with architectural niceties; it was concerned with a woman named Cassie Chadwick, who briefly made it her home. Perhaps it would be more accurate to call it her base of operations, for Cassie was more a businesswoman than a homemaker.

Cassie and her husband, Dr. Leroy S. Chadwick, lived just beyond Millionaire's Row, but in a fine section still that called for something more than an average income. This condition was well met. Dr. Chadwick had a comfortable practice, and Cassie had means of her own, if that is not too much of an understatement to be allowed.

Curious Clevelanders would meet in little groups along the sidewalk in front of the Chadwick home at certain times of the day and they would stand around, pretending to be in earnest conversation, waiting for a chance to see Cassie make one of her grand exits. Cassie did everything with a flourish, even if it was something as humdrum as walking out of her house and getting into her carriage. It was a terribly fancy carriage, of course, and the horses were fine-looking animals, and Cassie herself carried herself with a regal air.

She was friendly enough. Let there be no doubt of that. She would look up and smile at the people staring her way, and the long plumes in her expensive hat would dip in greeting like an admiral's ensign as she nodded her head toward the onlookers. Everybody agreed that Cassie had a lot of class, but it figured that she would have inherited this much, at least. The science of genetics, which was coming in for a lot of close attention in those days, said as much.

The point was that Cassie Chadwick had let it be known she was the daughter of Andrew Carnegie, the steel king, and in the new aristocracy of the wealthy that was just building up in the United States, this gave

Cassie claim to a place among the nobility. She didn't walk out on her piazza and holler her claim to the world or anything as crude as that. It was a whispered, ladylike assertion; the kind that is made with just the right hint of color in the cheeks behind a fluttering fan.

Everybody was subtly sympathetic and understanding of her delicate assertion to her rightful place in society because it wouldn't really have been any kind of sportsmanship to hold her responsible for the awkward fact that Andrew Carnegie was indisputably the world's leading bachelor. That singular honor necessarily made Cassie an illegitimate daughter, but even a Victorian society was inclined to be tolerant of the peccadillos of the mighty, and such consequences as might spring from same.

Being any kind of relative to the second-richest man in the world was regarded by most enlightened people as an outstanding recommendation for membership in the human race. Thus was society's usual harsh attitude toward illegitimate children softened considerably in Cassie's case by the identity of her alleged sire.

There was a good deal of honest astonishment mixed in with the public reaction, naturally, because Andrew Carnegie's name never had been brushed by any kind of scandal except his scandalous propensity for making money. He was acknowledged to be a moral man of strong religious principles and he had never been identified, certainly, with any kind of intramural footsy.

The story that Carnegie was the father of a middle-aged woman— Mrs. Chadwick was in her forties—was preposterous, but it delighted a good many people, especially those with a strong sense of humor and a lively imagination. And the rumor was readily received by that segment of the people which already was highly suspicious of all millionaires and which already was convinced that men of great wealth, behind their proper public façade, actually were a herd of satyrs.

It is heartening to note that a friendly, charitable view of Cassie's delicate position was held even by the members of the banking fraternity, a group which has suffered too long from the popular public conception of them as flinty, sniffing Scrooges. Their hearts went out to this gentle lady who had been so cruelly wronged by circumstances, and they saw to it that such large sums of money were available to her as she needed to borrow against the triumphant day when she would come into her rightful inheritance. To say this so cooly, so matter-of-factly, does not do the bankers justice, really, when the fact is that most of them fell over one another in their anxiety to advance her hundreds of thousands of dollars. It is true that in almost every instance the loans carried exorbitant rates of interest, but the thing that convinced the bankers that Cassie was a genuine lady of quality was her refusal to quibble over such details.

For her part, this sensitive woman showed in many genteel ways that she was not unaware of the commendable forbearance of society and the unquestioning generosity of the bankers. She was an appreciative soul, and if, in private, she smote her thigh, the popular way to express pleasure in those days, the circumstances justified this unladylike conduct.

Cassie Chadwick, in fact, bore no relationship whatsoever, legitimate or illegitimate, to Andrew Carnegie. She was the gay deceiver of the Gay Nineties, the leading confidence woman of her day, and one of the best in that specialized field of endeavor in American history.

Her real name, given to her at christening, was Elizabeth Bigley. She was born in 1857 in a small Canadian town, Eastwood, Ontario, one of eight children of an erstwhile farmer and railroad section gang boss, Daniel Bigley, and his wife, Mary Ann.

Nothing really notable occurred in Elizabeth Bigley's childhood. She was a heavy reader, it is known, and her favorite kind of literature had to do with successful women. Her parents were heard to complain at times that she was a child with entirely too much imagination. Society, years later, would repeat the complaint.

The first suggestion that Elizabeth was not an ordinary teen-ager came when, at age fifteen, she engaged in a little barnyard dalliance with a hot-eyed young farmer who lived nearby. This in itself is not extraordinary or outside the common chronicle of human weakness, but Elizabeth was said to have held off the swain until he had mortgaged his land to purchase her a diamond ring. Touched by this gesture, she then conferred her favors upon him.

This heady experience must have suggested to the girl the fantastic potential for influencing men that is part of every woman's physiological inheritance and which she explored so thoroughly in later years. Meanwhile, Elizabeth discovered among her other talents a facility for imitative writing which she shortly put to use, writing and mailing a letter to herself over the name of a London, Ontario, attorney. In the letter, she had the fictitious attorney trumpet the glad news that she was heiress to fifteen thousand dollars by the terms of some equally fictitious philanthropist's will.

Elizabeth promptly had cards printed that announced:

MISS BIGLEY
Heiress to $15,000

She put the cards to effective use one weekend shortly thereafter when she left the family farm for a shopping trip to London. In each shop that she entered, she wrote out checks for amounts larger than the price of her purchase. When the clerks hesitated, Elizabeth flashed her quaintly worded calling card as identification, invariably stirring so much good humor in this manner as to dispel whatever doubts remained in the clerk's mind.

The checks bounced, of course, and considering the number she had passed so blithely the bank lobby must have sounded like Wilt Chamberlain dribbling downcourt. She was in her hotel room, packing her bags, when the police arrived the following Monday afternoon. She was taken to the police station where several of the victimized merchants readily identified her as the passer of the bad checks.

Elizabeth was only eighteen years old at the time, and she looked even younger than that tender age. As she stood under the gaze of the glowering police sergeant and the accusing fingers of the merchants, her head dropped upon her chest and her shoulders shook. She was a little, frightened girl suddenly caught doing wrong in a world of towering adults. She was too much for her accusers. They knew she had no money and they had no desire to have her imprisoned. They refused to press charges and she was released with a stern lecture to return home and mend her ways. It was a defeat in a minor skirmish, but it was part of Elizabeth's education and in that sense valuable. Not that it was a complete defeat, either; the merchants let her take with her the clothes she had purchased with the phony checks.

Four years of the quiet, circumspect life on the farm passed and then the twenty-two-year-old Elizabeth made another journey to the city. This time she went to Toronto, where her first move was to go to a bank and deposit a substantial check made out to her as the basis of a checking account. The check she deposited was one of her own authorship, but it showed she had given some thought to the ways of the financial world. She sallied forth then and swept through the shopping district of Toronto on a buying spree of worthwhile dimensions. The next day she was preparing to carry on with a repeat performance when the police stepped in and called a halt. This time Elizabeth Bigley was arrested and tried.

Her first courtroom experience gave the little farm girl an opportunity to show some of the stuff she was made of. She rolled her eyes in their sockets, simpered, smiled, stared vacantly off into space, and generally conducted herself in such a disarranged style that the judge laid aside the charge on grounds of temporary insanity. Then, no doubt mopping his brow in relief, he sent her trundling back to the family homestead. This time, though, her distracted parents would have none of their strange, troublesome offspring. They dispatched her to the home of a newlywed sister who even then was chirping and thrashing about in her love nest on Franklin Avenue in Cleveland.

Elizabeth by now was a changed girl. She somehow had become more thoughtful as the extent of the gullibility of this world of men became increasingly clear to her. She even changed her name from

Elizabeth to Lydia, probably for luck, the way some people throw salt over their left shoulder. Cleveland represented, after all, a new life; at the very least, a new start.

The first thing that Lydia (not Elizabeth) did after taking up lodging with her sister and her new brother-in-law was to mortgage all the furniture in their house, putting it up as security for loans with which to buy clothing and jewelry. Eventually, of course, this particular piece of perfidy was found out as the creditors began to storm the home bastion, threatening to remove the Morris chair, the ironing board, etc., for Lydia's failure to pay on her loans. Her sister was aghast, but being a gentle soul, she was willing to forgive and forget. Not her husband, though; he, obviously something of a hothead, tossed Lydia out into the street.

In the months that followed, Lydia moved from one boarding house to another, mortgaging the furniture belonging to the landladies as she went along just to keep in practice. The money thus gained she put to good selfish use, acquiring one of the finest wardrobes in town and a chest full of fine jewelry, all to make herself attractive to men.

The descriptions handed down indicate that while Lydia Bigley was no stunning beauty, neither was she unattractive. Her main feature of beauty was a pair of large, luminous eyes which she could turn on men in a most appealing expression. A number of suitors applied for her hand along the way, but she was selective. Marriage was a serious affair; a stepping-stone to respectability, a better life, and, hopefully, a higher social position. At last those large luminous eyes alighted on a young, up-and-coming doctor named Wallace Springsteen.

The good doctor didn't have a chance. Not only was he taken by her beauty, but he was gratified to learn that this enchanting creature also was an heiress. Her uncle, she confided, had left her a "large Irish estate." The doctor, probably envisioning himself riding to the hounds in the months ahead, proposed, and without any further romantic falderal, they were wed.

The record will show many marriages have lasted longer than the one that linked Lydia Bigley to Wallace Springsteen—indeed, theirs lasted only seven days, which really isn't much of a record at all. On the other hand, very few marriages have hit the rocks as dramatically as theirs did at the end of that first week.

The smashup came about when Dr. Springsteen arrived home after a hard day at the office only to find that he couldn't even fight his way into the house, there were so many creditors jamming the porch, the hallway, the living room, and even, one presumes, the bedroom. All of them had heard the happy tidings of Lydia's marriage, and they were there to attach everything the good doctor owned, including his stethoscope and forceps.

A divorce was granted to the doctor three months later. Meanwhile, Lydia had hired some lawyers to collect six thousand dollars she said the doctor had promised to pay her for a separation, and while the divorce trial was pending she borrowed large amounts of money from the lawyers. She came out of the legal tangle without a husband, but considerably richer than when it started, which must be something of a course record in itself.

Something impelled Lydia at this time to leave Cleveland, at least temporarily, and the trail that she left between 1883 and 1886 was a faint one. One researcher, a *Plain Dealer* reporter named Lawrence J. Hawkins, who later achieved minor prominence as a painter of water colors, traced Lydia to a farm near Youngstown, where she allegedly lived as the wife of a farmer named J. R. Scott. What happened to destroy that marriage is not known.

"Possibly," mused Hawkins, "she mortgaged his milch cows and was turned out."

Whatever happened, she returned to Cleveland in 1886, this time wearing the name of Lydia Scott, a name she chose to use only a short while. The boarding house on Superior Avenue in which she found lodging was operated by a Mrs. Hoover, who left the city shortly after Lydia arrived. It wasn't long before Lydia had assumed the name of Hoover; and at about that time she gave birth to a son.

The birth of the child was the signal for Mrs. Lydia Hoover to depart Cleveland once again. It is believed she took her little boy to her parents' farm in Canada, and then traveled on, by herself, to Toledo to begin life anew as a clairvoyant, using the name of "Madame Lydia DeVere." She did a brisk business as a fortune-teller, but did not confine herself wholly to peering into the future. Once in a while her crystal ball came alive with the romantic notions of her customers to whom she would confide, in post-passionate moments of candor, her "real" identity. Her own talent for assuming different identities came alive at such intervals, and she became, in turn, the daughter of a British general, the widow of an earl, and still another time, the niece of President Ulysses S. Grant. Her lovers seemed to appreciate her all the more for her distinguished lineage and did their utmost, through money gifts, to make her life more bearable.

Eventually, Madame Lydia met a young, naïve Toledoan named Joseph Lamb, an expressman, who found her irresistible. One of the lures that drew him close to her was her appreciation of the better things in life. The poor Lamb liked nothing better than an occasional session of fun and culture in the parlor of the enchantress. When their passion was spent, they would take turns reading poetry, and that was proof enough for him that he had found an extraordinary woman, as indeed he had.

For her part, Madame Lydia had been studying Lamb and finally hit on a scheme to use him in a fleecing game. What else? She gave him a worthless note for several thousand dollars, signed by a "prominent Clevelander," and persuaded him to cash it for her at a friendly neighborhood bank. He completed this mission so successfully that she drew up another note for him to cash, and still another, and it might have become a regular routine had not the police stepped in. When they totted up the amount that the madame had bilked from the banks, it came to the neighborhood of forty thousand dollars.

Lamb was no help to Lydia at the trial. He bleated freely and expressively, describing not only how he had trustingly served as the instrument of the fortune-teller in trotting back and forth between the countinghouse and the joyhouse, but he also described in a simple, direct statement the details of his love affair with Madame Lydia which left no doubt in the minds of the jurors who was the seducer and who was the seducee.

A happy, faraway look came onto Joe's face as he recalled the happy hours he had whiled away in Madame Lydia's parlor, and his voice strengthened and took on a proud ring as he recalled the poetry readings. In response to questions by counsel, he attributed to Madame Lydia a "strange magnetic power" that made him obey her wishes. The jurors nodded understandingly and acquitted him on grounds of "hypnotic influence," sentencing Madame Lydia, at the same time, to nine years in the Ohio Penitentiary.

The two years that Elizabeth Lydia Bigley Springsteen Scott Hoover DeVere spent in the pen in Columbus constituted something of a turning point period. They gave her the time she needed for quiet recollection of all that had happened in the previous years and an opportunity to judge herself. When the period of introspection had ended, she wrote some letters to the parole board, pleading for a chance to start life anew, and the board acceded to her request. Governor William McKinley signed her parole papers just before Christmas 1893.

So it came about that a proper, quietly attractive widow named Cassie L. Hoover took up residence in Cleveland at that time, and wherever she went, there were nods of approval. She was a nice lady at a time when nice ladies were held in highest esteem by society. Among those who came to admire her the most was a quiet, lonely widower, the respectable Dr. Leroy S. Chadwick, who lived with an ailing mother and an ailing sister. His twenty-one-year-old daughter, Mary, attended an eastern boarding school.

How he and Cassie became acquainted is not known, but the route which their friendship followed to true love was an unusual one. The doctor told Cassie one night about the occasional twinges of rheumatism with which he was afflicted, and she, all compassion, clucked and volunteered to give him a massage treatment. The rubdown must have helped considerably because it wasn't any time at all before the doctor was proposing marriage and being accepted. They were secretly married in Pittsburgh, which seems to be carrying romance rather far, but no matter. Mrs. Cassie Chadwick now had achieved the respectability for which she had hankered so long, and she was about to take her place among the prominent people who had brought Euclid Avenue to a place of such esteem in the nation.

The Chadwick residence was a two-story red brick house with a wooden porch, held up by white pillars, running across its entire width. It had a hip roof topped by a lookout room, or conning tower. It was not the prettiest, or most imposing house on Euclid Avenue, but it was respectable, and that counted heavily in its favor. The interior decoration of the home was attuned to this same somber propriety, or, as one thoughtful looker-on has described it, "chaste dignity." It was, apparently, much too chaste and much too dignified for Cassie's liking, so she arranged a little surprise for her groom.

On Christmas Eve, no less, Cassie took Leroy to a theater party. While they were thus engaged, an army of moving men and decorators rolled up to the sedate mansion and took it over in a fury of activity. By the time the Chadwicks returned, it was no place like home; not the home they had left only a few hours before, anyway, and not like any home that Euclid Avenue ever had seen before, likely.

Every stick of furniture was brand, spanking new. In place of the comfortable old dark pieces with their delicate antimacassar accessories and the frowning portraits of gaunt Chadwickian ancestors, all was gaiety. The prevailing color in the new scheme of things was gold. Lush new Persian rugs now covered the floor, and the dull plush furniture had been replaced by tables and chairs with hand-painted designs, elegantly tooled leather, and artistically carved Circassian walnut cabinets. Dr. Chadwick himself was a pretty hue somewhere between fuchsia and lime green as he groped for his dangling pince-nez and tottered about in aimless shock.

Cassie, now completely taken with the joys of housekeeping, was only beginning. In the weeks and months that followed, she added a lot of little items to make the place seem even more cozy and homelike. She found, for example, a green glass sofa tinted pink and shaped like a seashell, a really rare strike that was, if uncomfortable, a pip of a conversation piece. There was a musical chair that blared out loudly whenever anybody sat on it, and it must have been great fun to watch surprised guests trying to claw their way up the wall after they had vaulted from the trick seat. Beautiful vases were everywhere, on tables, ledges, and even on the floor, while pictures of three-dimensional peacocks and moody maids sniffing flowers covered the wallpaper, one frame touching the next. The centerpiece on a library table in the drawing room was a tall, glass-domed perpetual motion clock, and no matter where one went in the big house, he could not escape the timber-shaking tones of the nine-thousand-dollar pipe organ that Cassie had installed in the small music room.

Now, at last, the sedate old Chadwick mansion was a house to conjure with, as was its mistress. She, as a matter of fact, was ready to undertake her master work of conjuration, and toward that end, she invited a young, but prominent, Cleveland attorney to accompany her to New York City so as to be available should she need his professional advice. She had studied her man carefully, and she knew he was the kind of person incapable of keeping a confidence; in a word, a blabbermouth.

Once in New York, Mrs. Chadwick hailed a hansom and called out an address. The cabbie's route was along Fifth Avenue, and as they were trotting along near 59th Street, Mrs. Chadwick suddenly ordered the driver to halt. She excused herself to the lawyer, promised to return within minutes, and left the carriage to enter a nearby mansion.

The lawyer was startled because the house she had entered was that of the great Andrew Carnegie. The trip to New York had been mystifying enough at the beginning, but this new move heaped mystery upon mystery.

Inside the mansion, Cassie's conversation with the butler did not seem at all mysterious. She had identified herself and explained that she was in New York interviewing applicants for a domestic position in her Cleveland household and that one of the job-seekers had claimed previous experience working for Carnegie. She was simply checking on the girl's references.

The Carnegie butler, while properly deferential to this lady of obvious breeding, was horrified that anybody should have taken such liberties with the Carnegie name. The person, he sniffed, never had been employed in that household and the good lady from Cleveland would be well advised to avoid a scamp of that type.

Cassie thanked the butler and as she departed, she pulled out a large brown envelope from underneath her coat. She came out to the carriage holding the envelope in such a way as to make it conspicuous.

The young Cleveland lawyer was spellbound by this time, and losing the reticence which is the nature of good attorneys everywhere, he admitted his great curiosity over Cassie's visit to the Carnegie house.

Cassie blushed and tried to wag him off, but the lawyer persisted with his entreaties for an explanation and she, giving all the signs of a reluctant girl arriving at one of the great decisions of her life, finally yielded.

"I must tell somebody sometime, I suppose," she sighed, "but you, in turn, must swear eternal secrecy."

"Oh, I do, I do!" babbled the lawyer, beside himself with curiosity.

Cassie searched his face and nodded as if satisfied that she at last had found a worthy confidant. Then she told her story, speaking with downcast eyes, as she revealed that she was the daughter of Andrew Carnegie. Ignoring the gurgling sounds from the throat of the lawyer, she lifted her head bravely and with her large luminous eyes slightly misty, she told how Carnegie really loved her mother, but had not married her because of his deep attachment to his own mother.

"Good God!" exclaimed the lawyer, trying to comprehend the overwhelming news.

"I don't even know who my mother is," Cassie continued, sadder than ever.

"Terrible! Terrible!" barked the lawyer. "Everybody has a right to know their own mother!" On the other hand, he added, the situation could be a lot worse. At least Cassie knew her own father. But did her own father acknowledge her as his own daughter?

"Oh, yes," said Cassie. "Father is very kind. And very generous."

With that, she handed the brown envelope to the lawyer. In it, among other papers, were two notes. One said: "One year after date, I promise to pay to Cassie L. Chadwick $250,000, with interest at five per cent." The note, which carried the large signature of "Andrew Carnegie," was dated January 7, 1904, almost two years in the future. The other note was similar to the first except that it carried the amount of $500,000. It, too, had the multimillionaire's signature.

In addition to those financial goodies, Cassie confided, the envelope contained securities in the value of five million dollars. The hitch was, however, that she could not cash in the securities until several years had passed, orders of Big Daddy.

The lawyer returned to Cleveland several days ahead of Cassie—she wanted to do a bit of shopping—and it was just as she had expected. His performance in those few days still rates as the most spectacular breach of confidence in the city's history. By the time Cassie got back to town, everybody, even the corner newsboys and the shoeblacks, knew of her secret. The lawyer was just a blur as he shot from street to street, spilling the beans wherever he went.

Cassie's followup to this sterling performance was a visit to the staid Wade Park Bank, where she handed over her brown package for safekeeping. She didn't have to tell the treasurer, a respected banker named Iri Reynolds, a thing. The lawyer had done his work well. Every banker in town was hoping Cassie would drop in. Reynolds took her package and without opening it, he gravely wrote her the following receipt:

"I hereby certify that I have in my possession $5,000,000 in securities belonging to Mrs. Cassie L. Chadwick, and that neither myself nor the Wade Park Bank nor any other person has any claim upon the same. Iri Reynolds."

This was the cornerstone on which Cassie Chadwick would build the most fantastic of swindles—a long series of loans pressed on her by bankers in Cleveland, Pittsburgh, Boston, Oberlin, and New York totaling, it is believed, about $2,000,000, give or take a hundred here or a grand there. With Iri Reynolds' receipt in her possession, tapping wealthy men and institutions for loans was so simple as to be embarrassing. She not only used the receipt, she used influential people, and bent them to her purpose.

One such unwitting tool here was John D. Rockefeller's pastor, Rev. Charles Eaton of the Euclid Avenue Baptist Church, whose congregation she had joined upon her marriage to Dr. Chadwick. Cassie confided the secret of her financial dilemma and Carnegie relationship to him, and he, a gracious soul, was thoughtful enough to help her by passing along word to his brother, a Boston lawyer, John Eaton.

Shortly thereafter, Cassie received an invitation to confer with Herbert D. Newton, a Boston investment banker. The conference was eminently satisfactory. He gave Cassie a check for $79,000 and his own note for $50,000. In return, all she had to do was sign a promissory note for $190,000, being careful not to raise her eyebrows over the amount of interest she was being charged.

Back home again, she found her way to the Citizens National Bank of Oberlin, where President Charles T. Beckwith and Cashier A. B. Spear fell all over themselves lending her money, first handing her $102,000 out of their own pockets, and then $700,000 of the bank's funds. A Pittsburgh steel executive gave her $800,000; The Savings & Deposit Bank of Elyria, $10,000; Oberlin College, $75,000, and The First National Bank of Conneaut, $25,000.

So it went, on and on, with nobody, even at this late date, fully informed on the number of loans she engineered or the exact sum of money she mulcted out of banks and individuals. But with $2,000,000 as a round figure estimate, Cassie earned her place in history. What she did with all that money was, from a spectator's viewpoint, more interesting even than the way she got it. Cassie, as a spender, was the female counterpart of Diamond Jim Brady except that she was even flashier. Money, to her, was for the spending.

One day, as Cassie was strolling through a downtown store, her eyes alighted on a handsome grand piano.

"I'll take it," she said to a clerk. Then, laying a restraining arm on the clerk, she added: "How many pianos do you have like this one?"

"Twenty-seven," replied the clerk, after lifting his eyes and doing some lightning mental arithmetic.

"Fine," said Cassie. "I'll take all twenty-seven of them. They'll make nice gifts for some of my friends."

Another time she chartered a train to take a party of her favorite people to New York City for a weekend of fun and theatergoing.

Nobody ever could accuse Cassie of sitting on her money. Nor could anybody attend a dinner party at her house without finding an expensive gift under the napkin. Once she took four young ladies from Cleveland with her on a tour of Europe and paid all their expenses.

Sometimes, of course, her generosity boomeranged on her, as it did when her own cook, upon whom she had lavished much money and fine clothes, including a sable wrap, quit her job in the Chadwick household because it was beneath her station.

She was not the only person to reject Cassie. Cleveland society took a very dim view of her gauche efforts to impress them and generally turned its back on her. But Dr. Chadwick had friends in society and sometimes for his sake, more often out of curiosity's sake, they would attend parties at the Chadwick mansion. They had a great time comparing notes later and regaling the inner circle with firsthand stories of their fantastic hostess.

"Oh, the contrast between Mrs. Chadwick and the other women," exclaimed one gentleman guest after a party, "I'm sure it was apparent to the doctor. He seemed laboring under a constraint all evening.

"If the rooms were almost barbaric in their adornments, Mrs. Chadwick was quite so. Her brown hair, streaked with gray, was piled high and glistened with diamonds. A double necklace of diamonds circled her full throat. There were diamonds on her shoulders and diamonds on the front of her dress. She struck me as being a handsome woman then, though at other times I thought her plain.

"The most remarkable thing about her was her eyes. They were brown, I think, though when I looked in them I was at once filled with such a feeling of strange excitement I cannot swear to the color."

Those large, luminous eyes again!

The house of cards could not stand for long, and it was the Boston banker, Newton, who toppled it. Unable to get any satisfaction from Cassie on the amount owed to him, Newton brought suit in Federal Court in Cleveland on November 22, 1904, for $190,800. The suit also asked that Iri Reynolds of the Wade Park Bank be restrained from disposing of the $7,500,000 it was presumed he held in trust.

All of Cassie's creditors got a nervous spasm when they heard of the suit. Panic is a close relative of high finance, and it was almost a classical Pavlovian reaction when two other bankers jumped into court with their own suits against Cassie, seeking to collect on notes that totaled $67,039.

Now the panic really was on, and it struck immediately at the

Citizens National Bank of Oberlin, which closed its doors while the officers took inventory of the situation. The president of the institution, C. T. Beckwith, a sixty-five-year-old man, took to his bed, ill, after revealing he had given Cassie $240,000 in loans, four times the capital stock of the bank—in addition to $102,000 of his own money.

Cassie's note for $500,000 backing up these loans, explained Beckwith, were indorsed by a man "who can pay it as easily as you or I could pay a nickel," but he refused to divulge to the directors the name of the man. Mr. Beckwith was not only a banker; he was a gentleman. "I can't tell you, I can't," he cried out. "If I lose home, honor, reputation, everything, I must keep locked in my own breast this one secret. I am bound by an oath I cannot break."

Banker Newton also held a $500,000 note. Like Banker Beckwith, he refused to identify the signer. But Banker Newton's attorneys were not hampered by the rules of the banking business. They announced that the signer of the note was Andrew Carnegie.

Now, at last, the big name in the game was in the open for the first time, and reporters called on the steel king for a statement. He replied with a typical Scottish economy of words.

"I know nothing of the woman," said Andrew Carnegie.

Cassie, who had been staying in the old Holland House in New York while she engaged in one of her periodic shopping sprees, suddenly checked out. Rumors that she had committed suicide began to circulate.

Dr. Chadwick and his daughter, cognizant, perhaps, of the impending disaster, embarked for Europe.

Banker Iri Reynolds of the Wade Park Bank was ordered to bring the brown package containing Cassie's $7,500,000 worth of securities into court and to open the package. He complied with the order, and when it became clear that all it contained were worthless securities, he sat down and cried. The judge gently asked him how much of his own money he had loaned Cassie, but Reynolds asked to be excused from answering the question, and it was dropped.

Cassie was arrested, a week later, in the Hotel Breslin in New York. The arresting officer took one look at her large luminous eyes and it immediately became a question as to who was the captor and who was the captive.

"The kindest, gentlest face one would ever want to see," the cop told reporters. "Just such a face as you or I would like to see in our families."

Cassie herself addressed herself more closely to the issue at hand in her statement:

"Public clamor has made me a sacrifice," she said. "Here I am, an innocent woman hounded into jail, while a score of the biggest business men in Cleveland would leave town tomorrow if I told all I know. Yes,

I borrowed money, but what of it? I will even admit I did not borrow in a business-like way. I wish now I had followed old rules a little closer. But you can't accuse a poor business woman of being a criminal, can you?"

A train of tragic events followed. Banker Beckwith, laid low with a heart attack suffered at the time his bank failed, had a relapse which doctors called "paralytic dementia," caused by worry, and finally shot himself to death in February 1905.

The cashier of the bank, A. B. Spear, was indicted for conspiracy with Beckwith and Cassie. He pleaded guilty, served five years of a seven-year sentence, was pardoned, and died in Detroit soon after.

Cassie herself went on trial on March 6, 1905, in the courtroom of Federal Judge R. W. Taylor, who had to fight his way through the crowds surrounding his chambers with the help of deputy marshals. Among the spectators in the courtroom was Andrew Carnegie himself. He stared with frank interest at the woman who had claimed to be his daughter and who had used his name so loosely, but effectively. He did not speak to her, however, nor did she attempt to speak to him.

Somebody asked Carnegie if he were going to prosecute Mrs. Chadwick himself and his reply was: "Why should I? Wouldn't you be proud at the fact that your name is good for loans of $1,250,000, even when somebody else signs it? It is glory enough for me that my name is good, even when I don't sign it. Mrs. Chadwick has shown that my credit is A-1."

The trial lasted six days, and at the end, Mrs. Chadwick's attorney, Jay P. Dawley, made his speech to the jury:

"Here on this beautiful spring morning, when the very elements seem to be arguing with more than mortal eloquence on this woman's behalf, survey the pitiful scene before you.

"A woman stands alone on one side and arrayed against her are all the forces of the great, the powerful, the magnificent United States government, the strongest, the mightiest and the most feared government in the world—and this tremendous crushing power stands as the accuser of this one weak woman . . ."

The United States district attorney, John J. Sullivan, was equally eloquent when it came his turn to address the jury. One reporter wrote that Sullivan "beat on the table with his fist and shouted till the rafters rang." In his plea, he said:

"I shall not do violence to your intelligence. I have studied you, but if I knew human nature as well as she I would know you all. Perhaps the charm of Cassie Chadwick over men has not ceased. Perhaps the seduction of her smile, the music of her voice, the witchery of her eyes—these things of the enchantress—are with her still to influence some of you. I only hope you are beyond the power of this Duchess of Diamonds, this peeress of criminality.

"I say that you have before you a crime which for conspicuousness, magnitude and danger was never exceeded in the annals of the country. You have before you the most dangerous criminal in the world today!"

The jury deliberated for five hours and most of the spectators had wearied and gone home when the moment of the verdict came. Cassie sat stolidly at the trial table, her son seated alongside her, and when the verdict of guilty was announced, he put his arms around his mother's neck and whispered into her ear.

The *Plain Dealer* account of her reaction said:

"A spasm of pain crossed her face, her head gradually fell forward and for a moment she was silent. It was as though the blow had crushed her completely. A few tears welled from her eyes and trickled down her cheeks. She put her handkerchief before her face to stop the sudden flow, but it was useless. Her weeping grew until she was sobbing like a child."

She was sentenced to ten years in the Ohio Penitentiary, but the most telling sign of her complete defeat was that this woman who had borrowed millions of dollars through the years was unable to raise bond pending appeal. She began serving her sentence immediately.

Her career as a prisoner was brief. She was reserved, aloof—some said surly. When the master magician, Harry Houdini, did a benefit performance for the prisoners, she refused to attend; she who had worked so much magic herself. When she talked, as she occasionally did, her speech was full of allusions to a mysterious "trust" fund, which, she said, would be revealed when the time was right.

But time ran out on Cassie Chadwick on October 10, 1907, only 2½ years after she had entered prison. Her death moved one prominent Cleveland banker to wonder aloud:

"What do you suppose she could have done to us if she had had an education?"

XIII

Euclid Avenue

E UCLID AVENUE is Cleveland's main stem and its most famous street. It begins at the southeast corner of Public Square, where the Soldiers and Sailors Monument stands in brooding wonder, and immediately heads southeasterly in a brisk, no-nonsense manner, as if determined to prove that a straight line is the shortest distance between two points.

They didn't name this street Euclid for nothing. It may not have done anything for the straight line theory, but it has had more than its fair share of triangles—including one or two with the most fantastic hypotenuses you'd ever hope to see.

Euclid goes straight until it reaches East 105th Street, a busy uptown intersection called Doan's Corner, where it seems to lose both its resolve and its sense of direction. Some people say it is because when Bob Hope was one of the regular hangers-on at Doan's Corner, he and his cronies used to heckle Euclid Avenue regularly for being so stuffy and so straight until finally the poor old street lost its scientific orientation and was badgered into taking a new tack. From that point on, anyway, Euclid follows a less precise route, but keeps bearing eastward fitfully until it reaches the suburban city of Euclid.

Actually it goes beyond that point. Some people like to say it goes all the way to Buffalo, New York, and because of that contention it was known as the longest street in America. In the earliest pioneer days the route Euclid Avenue follows was called the Buffalo Road.

It will probably surprise a lot of old settlers to hear that the suburb was called Euclid before the famous street got that name. Some of the surveyors who worked in the Moses Cleaveland founding party staged a small mutiny and demanded a more substantial share of the Connecticut Land Company's real estate venture, threatening to walk off the job unless their demands were met. Cleaveland yielded, turning over to them an allotment of land for settlement which they promptly named Euclid, thereby reflecting the honest admiration of the mutinous mathematicians for the great Greek geometrician.

Today's Euclid Avenue is a wide, busy thoroughfare that features the usual traffic uproar, the tall buildings, and the bustling commerce that characterize the main avenues of downtown areas in most American cities. There is hardly anything visible to set Euclid aside as something different or something special in the way of American streets—and yet it is different. And it was special.

If you search, there still are marks to indicate just why it was a street with international fame. They are the few old mansions still standing; some out in the open, still proud and grand; some hidden behind used car lots or the raucous commercial fronts that have been built in front of them, where the greensward once swept down to the sidewalk and the tall trees used to stand.

The famous American traveler, diplomat, and writer of the late nineteenth century, Bayard Taylor, called Euclid Avenue "the most beautiful street in the world," and he was joined in this opinion by people who were in a position to make a comparison. Taylor held that Euclid Avenue's only honest rival for the title of "most beautiful" was the Prospekt Nevksy in St. Petersburg, Russia.

Another strong admirer of Euclid Avenue was a lecturer before the Royal Society of Great Britain, John Fiske, who in 1860 described it in these words:

". . . bordered on each side with a double row of arching trees, and with handsome stone houses of sufficient variety and freedom in architectural design, standing at intervals of from one to two hundred feet along the entire length of the street . . . the vistas reminding one of the nave and aisles of a huge cathedral."

Artemus Ward, who knew Euclid Avenue better than any of those world travelers, wrote of it after he left Cleveland in his usual colorful prose and called it "a justly celebrated thoroughfare."

"Some folks," he wrote, "go so far as to say it puts it all over the well known Unter der Sauerkraut in Berlin and the equally well known Rue de Boolfrog in Paree, France. Entering by way of the Public square and showing a certificate of high moral character, the visitor, after carefully wiping his feet on the 'welcome' mat, is permitted to roam the sacred highway free of charge.

"The houses are on both sides of the street and seem large as well as commodious. They are covered with tin roofs and paint and mortgages, and present a truly distangy appearance.

"All the owners of Euclid Street homes employ hired girls and are patrons of the arts. A musical was held at one of these palatial homes the other day with singing. The soprano and the contralto were beautiful singers. The tenor has as fine a tenor voice as ever brought a bucket of water from a second-story window, and the basso sang so low that his voice at times sounded like the rumble in the tummy of a colicky whale."

The satirical note running through Artemus Ward's commentary un-doubtedly sprang out of his resentment of the snobbery that already was building up on Euclid Avenue in his time in Cleveland. It got a lot worse after he left, even as the street itself became the site of more magnificent mansions. In its heyday, between 1875 and 1900, that stretch of Euclid Avenue extending from Erie Street (East 9th Street) to Willson Avenue (East 55th Street) must have contained the most overpowering concentration of affluence, with all its outward manifestations, in America.

To live in the Millionaire's Row stretch of Euclid Avenue was to be the member of a private club as exclusive as today's Union Club or Tavern Club. The families who lived along the elegant row were formidable members of society and they demanded formidable houses as a mark of their station. All the homes were set back from the sidewalk with a pretty expanse of shady parkland for front lawns and smooth driveways to carry the coaches and carriages to the front steps of the bulking residences. A good many of the homes were in the Victorian tradition, lavished with architectural bric-a-brac, with gables and towers, high-ceilinged rooms, and tall windows to match. There were antebellum-type Greek revival mansions with their im-posing high white pillars, and there were Georgian-style gems, colonial masterpieces, and some great manses that defied classification.

It was an eye-pleasing experience to stroll Euclid Avenue in its heyday. The street was so magnificent as to override the ordinary human weaknesses of envy and covetousness. Even Madame Lafarge would have enjoyed the street. There was so much real splendor to Millionaire's Row that even the poorest of Clevelanders took pride in the street and had a vicarious kind of proprietary interest in maintain-ing it in its full beauty.

Civic concessions toward that end were plentiful, one of the most conspicuous—and controversial—being a rule that the streetcar line could not travel that stretch of Euclid Avenue between East 9th Street and East 40th Street. The streetcars were routed south to Prospect Avenue at Erie Street (East 9th) and had to travel along that thoroughfare until reaching Case Avenue (East 40th), where they swung north to rejoin the Euclid Avenue route. The people of affluence who lived along the stretch of avenue skirted by the streetcars reasoned, and rightly, that the trolley vehicles would be a blight on their picture-postcard scene. Furthermore, streetcars would have interfered with the wonderful sport of winter sleigh races which flourished on Euclid Avenue on a scale of delightful dimensions. Next to New York, Cleveland was the nation's outstanding gathering place for drivers, breeders, and lovers of the best light harness horses in America.

Everybody who lived along the avenue joined in the racing fun, and those who didn't care to race simply jogged along in their sleighs, listening to the singing runners, the clopping of the snow-muffled hoofs, and the song of the bells. It was another era, another world, another universe they lived in, and it would not last long—only until the arrival of the new century, 1900. It must have been enchanting, though, while it lasted.

A recollection of the era by a Clevelander named C. A. Post in a nostalgic volume called *Those Were the Days*, hints at the winter wonderland that prevailed on Euclid Avenue in the twilight of the nineteenth century before the streetcars finally had their way and began to use the Euclid route.

"Every winter afternoon when the snow lay upon the ground (and that was often), and other weather conditions were favorable," wrote Post, "there was a spirited and beautiful sleighing carnival on the avenue, at its height from two to six o'clock. All heavy traffic was, by authority, diverted to parallel streets, and then the many handsome turnouts of one and two-horse sleighs and cutters . . . appeared.

"As I remember very clearly, good carnival form required strict observance of certain rules. One was to drive slowly eastward from Erie Street, then turn at Perry Street [East 22nd], or just beyond there, and drive back to Erie Street at top speed, at least part of the way; perhaps, in the general rush, or . . . by craft or dash, to arrange to have an exciting brush with a friend or foe whom one had singled out as a possible victim to be passed and beaten at the end of the course.

"Above all, we of the common herd, and also the slower drivers of the beautiful turnout with a showy horse or handsome pair of high-steppers without speed, must ever keep an eye open for the real speed kings and give them the right of way.

"Thus, when an Edwards, a Devereaux, a Perkins, an Otis, a Bradley, a Splan, a Dutoon, or any others of the elect, had joined issue with one or more of his class and they were coming like the wind, all of the lesser lights pulled out toward the curb and let the fast ones 'play through' in the center of the roadway, which they did with such speed and dash as to take one's breath away."

The competition in the sleigh racing arranged itself naturally among the wealthy sports according to which side of Euclid Avenue they lived on. It was the north side against the south side, those living on the north side of the avenue calling themselves the Nabobs while their competitors on the south side of the street were known as the Bobs. Prominent among the Bobs were John D. Rockefeller, Charles Harkness, J. M. Hoyt, Fayette Brown, the Chisholms, J. H. Devereaux, and other names familiar to Cleveland society. The most dashing sportsmen of them all apparently, Colonel William ("Billy") Edwards, a prosperous merchant, lived on Prospect Street, just south of Euclid Avenue.

Sometimes the scene took on a dreamy, unworldly beauty; especially when the sleighs raced up and down the avenue at night in a heavy snowfall. The old gas mantle street lamps cast a yellow light that was hardly needed because the night was made so bright by the snow, but they added their own touch of color as the heavy flakes fell on the lawns and the street, adding another white layer to the hard-packed cover that already covered the ground and the cobblestones. The black picket fences that ran along the sidewalks, shielding the big estates from the street, seemed to rise out of the snowbanks as if they were floating high off the ground, and the whitened boughs of the large evergreens sagged with the new weight of the storm.

The sleighs dashed up and down the avenue with singing cutters and jingling bells, the snow whirling in their wake, while the passengers burrowed deep in their seats and pulled the heavy fur robes up above their faces to ward off the stinging wind that drew moisture to their eyes. Just to look at the aristocratic, high-stepping horses and the ornate carriages sliding past was to know beauty. The horses were among the best in the world and sometimes the carriage, like that of Jeptha Wade's, was fancy enough for royalty. His was a two-horse sleigh with a high dashboard topped with red plumes. High above the passengers was the seat of the coachman with his livery of scarlet jacket, shiny top hat, and glistening black leather boots.

The people of substance loved horses, of that there could be no doubt. Racing early became a part of their way of life; a fixture in the Cleveland tradition from such a faraway day that the city has been called "the fountain head of American racing." That claim was made by an associate editor of the *Plain Dealer,* Edwin T. Randall, who wrote: "The history of racing in America is a Cleveland story. But it is a story of trotting horses . . ."

There was a track for the trotters and pacers as early as 1846. It was on Woodland Avenue, between Brownell (East 14th) and Perry (East 22nd). But the most famous track in the nineteenth century, as well as the most fashionable, was the Glenville Track at East 88th Street and St. Clair Avenue. It was built in 1870 by the Cleveland Driving Park Company to be part of the newly organized Northern Ohio Fair, whose grounds were across the street, on the other side of St. Clair. A bridge over the avenue connected the two.

The annual fair proved unsuccessful and was abandoned in 1881, but the track thrived as a fun spot for the town's sporting bloods and racing fans from all elements of the city's population. Some of Cleveland's most famous families kept stables at the track, which was just about as respectable as any place could be. Among the original stockholders of the Cleveland Driving Park Company were, indeed, the three Rockefeller brothers, John, William, and Frank; Howard M. Hanna, Charles A. Brayton, Warren G. Corning, Sylvester T. Everett, and J. V. Painter.

It was at the Glenville Track that the famous Grand Circuit, the major league of harness racing, was born in 1873. It grew out of the Quadrilateral Circuit, composed of Cleveland, Buffalo, Rochester, and Utica, whose meeting was held at Glenville in 1872.

Racing devotees do not find it difficult to recall that the old Cleveland Driving Park track was the scene, on July 27, 1876, of one of the most memorable events in American racing history. It was the free-for-all trot in which Smuggler defeated the great Goldsmith Maid. The trotters, pulling high-wheeled sulkies, ran five sensational heats, with the fifth heat being run almost as fast as the first—2:17¼ and 2:15½.

The race was immortalized in poetry by Oliver Wendell Holmes, who was inspired to write *When Smuggler Beat the Maid*. Both horses enjoyed national prominence, with Goldsmith acknowledged to be the most famous horse of the trotting age. She had been bred by James Roosevelt, father of President Franklin D. Roosevelt, and was foaled in 1857. The amazing thing is that she did not begin her racing career until she was ten years old, but she made up for lost time with a series of epochal performances. At age seventeen, in 1874, she set the world record time of 2:14; at twenty, in 1877, she beat Rarus with a time of 2:14½. Altogether, Goldsmith Maid won ninety-two races and a total of three hundred thousand dollars in her illustrious career. Little wonder that her race against Smuggler drew such attention, especially as Smuggler himself was an unusually interesting trotter. He was known to be a badly balanced horse, given to frequent breaks. He wore sixteen-ounce toe weights in front so his feet would not get out of control!

Again, on July 30, 1885, Glenville Track made an important contribution to racing lore by serving as the setting of a race in which William H. Vanderbilt's famous Maud S. set the world's record for trotting to high wheel sulky—2:08¾. A replica of the mare's head, encircled by a horseshoe, once surmounted the main entrance gate of the track.

It was among the amateur gentlemen drivers, however, that Glenville served its most popular function. The young gentry from Euclid and Prospect avenues in Cleveland had private barns with their names over the door. They had a custom of Saturday matinees at the track, driving across town to St. Clair behind spirited teams hitched to gleaming, costly Brewster road wagons. And after the fun and games, everybody would retire to an establishment known as "The Roadside Club" at the entrance to the park to settle down to some serious drinking and talk about such fascinating subjects as horses and women; presumably in that order.

Officials of the Driving Park Club decided to organize the matinee racing on Saturdays early in 1895. Colonel William ("Billy") Edwards, General D. W. Caldwell, C. A. Brayton, Harry K. Devereaux, O. G. Kent, and W. G. Pollock were the moving forces behind the men's races. The first matinee was held June 1, 1895, with Dan R. Hanna, son of the famous senator, winning the inaugural with Lady Hester. Ordinary high-wheeled road wagons with steel tires were used at first, but club members quickly saw the advantage of buying speed wagons with pneumatic tires, built to order by a famous Cleveland carriage-maker, Frank G. Phillips. Drivers had their own shanties at the track and there they kept their turf trophies on display. Even the losers won at Glenville, though, because it was the custom then that after important cup races, the winners would spring for dinners at the Roadside Club.

"It was expensive to win a cup race," one writer noted, "because at these dinners the cups had to be filled and refilled with champagne and the food was not to be excelled. At the close of every season members had banquets at the club and these were feasts not to be regarded lightly."

The acknowledged champion of the amateur drivers was Harry K. Devereaux, scion of a famous old family and famous himself as the model for the drummer boy in Archibald Willard's "Spirit of '76" painting. The highlight of his racing career was his victory in the Boston Gold Cup Race at Glenville on September 5, 1902. Some twenty-five thousand fans cheered Devereaux to victory in that classic. There were other famous amateur drivers, including Charles A. Otis, whose horse, Dutch Mowrey, was called "the tailless wonder," for the obvious reason that it lacked what horses usually take for granted, a tail. Otis once had an artificial tail made for his racer, but it is said that the horse bridled; just moped about sulkily and absolutely refused to wear the equine mop. The band had to play *Ach du Lieber Augustine* to cheer the horse's spirit after that. Dutch Mowrey was a very sensitive animal.

Another regular among the Glenville amateurs was Frank Rockefeller. This youngest member of Cleveland's most famous family narrowly escaped injury in one race when another driver swerved into his wagon, bending one of the axles. The Rockefeller wagon tilted precariously and careened down the track. Other drivers shouted to him to let loose of the reins holding Nelly Cloud and to jump. Rockefeller hesitated, but finally took their advice, tumbling onto the track, head over shoulders.

The days of fun and glory at the old Glenville track ended in 1908 when the track called it quits. The matinee racing by the amateurs shifted to the elegant new North Randall Track, called The Golden Oval, and continued there until 1916. The sport never was revived after World War I.

If the life led by Cleveland's bluebloods sounds ostentatious, it was meant to be just that. In that heady time of newfound wealth, when the dynasties that would rule Cleveland society and business in the generations to come were still aborning, ostentation was one of the rules of the game. The competition among the elite was not confined merely to racing their cutters down the avenue or their wagons at Glenville; it extended into every phase of living, and was most clearly apparent in the attempts of the city's aristocracy to outdo one another in the size and the rococo trim of the houses that lined the avenue.

Just as one should have guessed, the home of the richest man in the world was not at all the fanciest or most expensive. The Rockefellers lived in a large brick house with wooden porches and narrow arched windows; a spacious house with the high ceilings typical of the day; nice but not showy. It was on a site just west of Case Avenue (East 40th Street), on the south side of Euclid Avenue, and it had a frontage on the avenue of 116 feet. The property was purchased in 1868 from Francis C. Keith for more than forty thousand dollars—a pretty hefty figure for that day.

Eleven years later, in 1879, Rockefeller acquired the Levi Burgert estate immediately to the east of his house, thus extending his property all the way to the corner of Case Avenue and giving him a Euclid frontage of 231 feet. Both of his lots were deep, extending south all the way to Prospect Street. The Burgert house, a large brick residence, was moved at Rockefeller's direction to a vacant lot at the corner of Case and Prospect, where it began a new career of usefulness, serving as a school for young ladies under the direction of a Miss Mittleberger.

Rockefeller's Euclid Avenue home, the birthplace of his children, fell into gradual disuse as the family found life at the Forest Hill "summer" home to be a lot more fun. The house on Euclid was torn down in the 1930s to make way for a parking lot and, appropriately enough, a gasoline station. The large stone stable and coach house were left standing, and old John D. would have been horrified by their use, briefly, as a night club.

The best illustration of just how modestly the Rockefellers lived on this swank street is to be found in the story of one of the other houses on the avenue—this one built, indeed, by a man that John D.'s genius and Standard Oil's generosity to its stockholders had made wealthy. He was Samuel Andrews, one of Rockefeller's early partners.

When Andrews decided to build his new home at the corner of Euclid Avenue and Sterling Street (East 30th Street), it is said he had in mind the hope that he would one day play host to Queen Victoria herself. Nobody today is able to say precisely why he should have harbored this peculiar ambition—though, to be sure, having Queen Victoria as a house guest would be a large feather in the cap of anybody on the avenue—except that Andrews was English by birth and hoped, possibly, to wow the folks back home.

Andrews, at any rate, aspired high and demanded that his new home be fit for royalty. Even Queen Victoria would have flinched though at some of the details that went into the house. It would be hard not to say that Sam went overboard. There are people who claim that his was the most elegant house ever built in Cleveland. Other judges say it was an overwhelming monstrosity. Its cost was said to be around a million dollars, which seems like a fair bundle of the green for a home that came to be known to everybody in Cleveland as "Andrews' Folly."

The controversial mansion was of Victorian architecture (what else?) and contained thirty-three rooms which were cleverly scattered about in a casual pattern that confounded everybody, especially the servants. There were among these rooms five separate and lavishly furnished suites for each of the millionaire's five daughters. Each suite had different color schemes and decorations for each room.

The first floor had six mammoth rooms, with a skylighted court in the center entranceway. A circular staircase with intricately carved railings wound up from two sides of the court, which also featured stained-glass windows especially executed by foreign artisans.

The woodwork in each room was different, and most of it was hand-carved with panels of exquisite workmanship. The wood-carvers and cabinetmakers were brought to Cleveland from abroad by Andrews to ply their genius for his benefit. The floors in each of the large rooms were covered by carpeting made specifically to order for Andrews' house by English weavers. The second floor had the suites for the daughters and the master suite for the parents, while on the third floor was a ballroom and servants' quarters.

It's too bad that Queen Victoria never made it to the Andrews house, even for a quick crumpets-and-tea, because she would have been pleased by the baronial splendor of the house and she probably would have done a royal flip over the butler.

Andrews' butler was English all the way; the real McCoy. He not only acted like a butler, he *looked* like a butler. He wore English knee breeches, ruffled white shirt, velvet jacket, white stockings, and shoes with silver buckles. He was, in brief, all that a butler should be.

Ironically, it was the servant problem that was one of the main factors leading to the undoing of the Andrews' mansion. The big house needed a hundred servants to stay in business, including cooks, chefs, maids, hostlers, carriagemen, housekeepers, and handymen. The architect had craftily designed the house so that the servant quarters were on the third floor while the kitchen, pantries, storerooms, linen rooms, etc. were in the basement. The working day was one long uproar, presumably, with servants running up and down three flights of stairs, lugging pillows, bedclothes, chopped ice, feather dusters, and other such essentials. Andrews found out that even domestics had their physical limitations. The people he hired simply were not up to the demands made on them by his crazy castle, and the consequent turnover in help was dismaying.

If this was not the principal cause of Andrews' quick disenchantment with the grand manor, perhaps it was Queen Victoria's persistent refusal to pop in for a spot of tea. That certainly is a reasonable conjecture, if not as romantic as some of the popular explanations for the family's withdrawal from the house in 1885 after a residency of only two or three years. One story had it that he had built the mansion with the intention of becoming a social lion, but, being one of the *nouveau riche*, society had not given him the immediate and full acceptance which he had anticipated. When his house was finished (so the legend goes), he invited all the leading members of society to a housewarming, but hardly anybody showed up, thereby embarrassing and embittering Mr. Andrews to the point of rejecting both the house and Cleveland itself.

Another interesting, if unconfirmed, story has it that the millionaire had invited society to a grand wedding reception for one of his children, but that the wedding was called off at the last minute. The party went on as scheduled, however, and the guests had a jolly time, filling the large house with sounds of laughter and the clinking of glasses. As the party ended, with the echoes of merriment still traveling through the inner hallways and rooms of the magnificent maze, Andrews locked the doors, had the windows boarded up, and walked away from his towering folly.

The great house stood empty until after the millionaire's death in 1904 in Atlantic City. His son, Horace, head of the Cleveland Electric Railway Company, took occupancy of the house at that time, but only for a short stay. The house simply wasn't much of a home and Horace moved out, taking some of the most exquisite furniture with him. The rest of the expensive furnishings were left to molder and rot in the abandoned old house which gradually became, in the decay of the years, a splendid refuge for bums and sleepy winos. It was finally torn down in 1937 and today the sleek, functional quarters of a television station, WEWS (named in honor of Edward W. Scripps), occupies part of the site.

The grandest survivor, by far, of the heyday of Euclid Avenue is the old Mather mansion which still stands at 2605 Euclid, on the eastern fringe of the downtown section. It has been the headquarters of the Cleveland Automobile Club since 1940, and while its interior has been altered to meet the needs of the club, it is still outwardly unchanged and is a magnificent vestigial specimen of the grandeur that used to be. The home, built by Samuel Mather, was the last of the great homes to be built on Millionaire's Row. It was constructed between 1906 and 1910, after the avenue had passed its peak and streetcars already were rumbling past the mansions that lined the strip. Downtown Cleveland already was pressing eastward into the famous residential section, and the signs of deterioration spelling the end of Euclid Avenue as the paradise of the wealthy were there to be read in 1906. But Mather pressed on with his new three-story brick mansion in spite of those signs. It is estimated that the house cost more than a half-million dollars. It was, when finished, one of the most outstanding residences on a street filled with outstanding residences. Its first floor had a drawing room, library, dining room, kitchen, pantries, billiard room, den, an office for Mrs. Mather, and servants' hall. On the second floor were seven suites of rooms, and on the third floor were eight bedrooms and a large formal ballroom, sixty-five by twenty-seven feet with a sixteen-foot arched ceiling, which would accommodate three hundred persons. There also is a fourth floor, used by the servants and for storage.

The house was built of a reddish-brown brick trimmed in Indiana limestone, and it's worth noting that the bricks were especially handmade, water-struck bricks fired at Gonic, New Hampshire; a duplicate of the type of bricks used by Harvard University in its buildings and gates. Each brick was molded and burned in the method used by early brickmakers. Main entrance to the home, on the west side of the building, led into a large foyer (forty by twenty-four feet) paneled in dark oak, with a beamed ceiling, a marble floor, and a ten-foot-wide stairway, with artistically carved newel posts and railings, rising to the third floor.

The dining room, now the auto club's license bureau, once had as covering for its walls embossed leather, beautifully tooled. It was removed because of the deteriorating effect of the years, but the room still features a ten-foot Elizabethan fireplace and a classic marble figure sculptured by Antonio Rossi of Rome in 1870 that stands as part of a fountain at the eastern end of the room, an area called the "breakfast nook." The statue was purchased by Mrs. Flora Stone Mather's father, industrialist-financier Amasa Stone. Mrs. Mather died before the home was completed.

Hand-carved wood paneling, mostly oak, covers most of the walls in the house, and the floors are of mahogany and rosewood parquet construction. Some of the fine oil paintings that hung in the home during its occupancy by the Mather family still are on the walls. One is Albert Bierstadt's "Emigrants Crossing the Plains," which Amasa Stone bought in 1868 for fifteen thousand dollars; another is "Aurora Borealis and the Statue," by I. Gudin, a French artist, painted in 1865. An Italian-style sunken garden, appointed with imported statuary and complete with arbor and fountain, was directly behind the mansion. A squash court sat to the end of the garden, near Chester Avenue.

No automobile club anywhere in the world is so superbly housed as is the one in Cleveland. Its staff of two hundred employees buzzes about the job of rescuing motorists with stalled batteries and all the other little things that auto clubs do so well, in an atmosphere of Renaissance splendor that is a carryover from an era that was destroyed by the automobile. But the Auto Club has done the city, and all civilized people, a service by proving the old Mather home's usefulness. The American rule for survival is a stern one based mainly on utility value. Let the grand Mather mansion, this illustrious product of artisans and artists and magnificent memorial of the past, waver or falter in its service and the wreckers' claws will be scratching at its sides to-morrow.

But today it still stands, and it embodies the beauty that once filled the sweep of the avenue, winning the hearts of Clevelanders and the acclaim of all who visited the city.

XIV

Mark Hanna vs. Tom Johnson

So MANY strong men sprang out of the Cleveland environment in the city's youthful years it's a pity somebody didn't think of analyzing the soil or testing the air. At the very least, there should have been a Senate investigation.

The situation, as the sunset of the nineteenth century came into view, was that a Clevelander named John D. Rockefeller was cornering most of the money in the world and another Clevelander named Marcus Alonzo Hanna was cornering most of the power in national politics.

But strangely enough, while either Rockefeller or Hanna was capable of shaking the capitals of Europe simply by lifting his little finger, neither one of them had as much influence with his fellow Clevelanders as a portly, curly-haired young man named Tom Loftin Johnson.

Some sticklers for formality among the political science writers of the day insisted on calling him Thomas L. Johnson, which was wrong. He was christened Tom and the name fitted him as no other name could.

Tom L. Johnson today shares the Public Square with Moses Cleaveland. His statue is in the centerpiece of the northwest quadrant of the Square, near the free speech rostrum—no accident of juxtaposition. He was a fierce defender of the public's right to speak out, and something of a free speaker himself.

Hanna and Johnson were born rivals. They competed in business, they competed in politics, and they competed for a place in history.

They were a pair of street railway executives whose political tracks took them to national glory, each by a different route.

They were opposites, but they were also similar. They were strong men, brilliant men, rich men—and they were poles apart in their philosophies of government. If you were a Clevelander, you took your place at the side of one or the other. You were either with Mark or you were with Tom. They left you no middle ground to stand on, nor any kind of a fence to straddle.

Mark Hanna was the Republican; Tom Johnson was the Democrat. Hanna was a prosperous businessman, a millionaire, who plunged into politics in his middle age and helped to shape the Republican Party according to his advanced concept of what a political organization should be.

In that time of industrialization, of new businesses and new fortunes, of growing monopolies and trusts, Hanna fought for laissez-faire government. It was his contention that capitalism would flourish best in an atmosphere free of government-imposed inhibitions, with prosperity benefiting everyone as the end result.

Hanna wanted a businesslike national administration and, by example, he encouraged businessmen to take an active part in politics and to play a forceful role in government. His own role was so active and so forceful that he became the archetype of the political boss, the kingmaker, the boss of bosses. He was the inspiration for the Homer Davenport cartoon of the political boss that since has become a journalistic cliché— the cartoon of the swollen, arrogant, plutocrat-politician with a large dollar sign on his vest, a cigar in his mouth, and a whiskey bottle gripped in his hand.

Johnson, like Hanna, was a businessman and a millionaire. He was, in fact, just the caliber of man that Mark Hanna wanted to see in politics except for some shocking deviations, including the fact that he was something of a political radical. Tom L. was a disciple of Henry George, the champion of the Single Tax, and he entertained strange advanced notions about the need for civic and political reform, social justice, the rights of the public, and even public ownership of utilities.

The clash between the two strong Clevelanders was inevitable. Over a period of twenty-five years they confronted each other in the lists, and every time they rode at each other the ground shook, the trees bent, and small tidal waves formed in Lake Erie.

New Lisbon, Ohio, a small town near Youngstown, was Mark Hanna's birthplace. He was the son of Dr. Leonard C. Hanna and Samantha Converse. His father, the descendant of Virginia Quakers, had been trained as a doctor, but never had practiced because of injuries suffered in mounting a horse. His mother, a schoolteacher, was a native of Vermont and had a sharply honed New England sense of propriety.

Dr. Hanna had entered the family's wholesale grocery business in New Lisbon, and his was said to be the most prosperous household in the town. But the Ohio Canal, connecting the Ohio River and Lake Erie, bypassed New Lisbon and it was almost a death blow to the community. The Hannas finally picked up their belongings and moved to Cleveland in 1852.

Young Mark attended Brownell School and then enrolled in Central High School at the same time that John and William Rockefeller began to attend classes there. The three of them became close friends, and they maintained that friendship through later life.

Mrs. Hanna prevailed on Mark to enroll at Western Reserve College, then in Hudson, Ohio, and he did—briefly. He related the story of how he finished college in four months, instead of the usual four years, when he addressed the college's seventy-fifth commencement exercise.

"I wanted to go to work. My mother said I should go to college. So I went. I was young, innocent, confiding. One day some of the sophomores induced me to help distribute copies of a burlesque program of the exercises of the junior class. I stood on the steps handing them to the audience as they passed in. The President of the college came along. He grasped me by the shoulder and asked, 'Young man, what are you doing?'

"I replied that I was distributing literature in the interests of education and morality.

"I quit college soon after that. The faculty seemed resigned to my absence. One day the [college] president met me on the street. I had on blue overalls and was hard at work. He looked at me with an expression that seemed to say, 'Well, I guess you have found your right place!' And I thought so, too. I liked work better than study. I have been hard at work ever since . . ."

Hanna's first job was working as a roustabout on the Merwin Street docks in the employ of Hanna, Garretson & Company, a wholesale grocery business and commission house owned by his father, his uncle, and a family friend, Hiram Garretson. He was paid twenty-five dollars a month. Close by, on the same Merwin Street, his old schoolmate, John Rockefeller, was working for Hewitt & Tuttle, another commission house. But Hanna quickly shucked the overalls to become a purser on a lake boat, then a solicitor of business for his father's company, a job that took him around the state.

Life was not all work. Mark attended a bazaar one night and met a very attractive girl, Charlotte Augusta Rhodes, with whom he fell in love. That was a romantic thing to do, of course, but there is no doubt that it created a new problem, namely: How to break the news to Papa Rhodes. Daniel P. Rhodes was a remarkable man in his own right. Besides being one of the most successful coal and iron merchants in Cleveland, he also was one of the city's leading Democrats. Young Mark, even then, was unmistakably a Republican, extremely active in the party and extremely outspoken on political subjects.

Rhodes' first sputtering reaction to the news of the romance was that he did not want any "damned" Republican in his family. There were some points in Hanna's favor, though, as Rhodes examined the suitor for his daughter's hand. He was direct, open, and candid—traits that Rhodes treasured—and his mother was from Vermont. Rhodes himself was from Vermont.

Rhodes took pride in his ability to measure men. He was a poker player of sorts and it helped to be able to judge his opponents.

After his scrutiny of young Hanna, Charlotte's father presumably found him acceptable because the couple was married September 27, 1864, in historic old St. John's Episcopal Church, which still stands at 2600 Church Avenue on the lower West Side. Hanna joined his father-in-law's company and his business genius quickly made him a standout. The company prospered, acquired shipping lines and railways for the movement of coal, iron ore, pig iron, and a variety of by-products, and its name eventually was changed from Rhodes & Company to M. A. Hanna & Company. It remains one of Cleveland's most formidable business empires to this day.

Success in business having arrived early, and with relative ease, it isn't surprising that Hanna's eyes were looking about for a sterner challenge and a more interesting way to employ his brilliance. He found it in politics when, in 1880, the Republican candidate for the Presidency was a fellow townsman, James A. Garfield. Hanna's contribution to Garfield's campaign was his organization of the Cleveland Business Men's Marching Club. His original idea for the club was to use it simply as a means of raising money for the campaign, but it beeame more than that. The businessmen who enlisted were willing to give their time and effort in Garfield's behalf, as well as their money. The idea spread to other cities, and Hanna's innovation became an interesting new political instrument.

The most important single result of that presidential campaign, however, was that it ensnared Hanna completely in the fascinating web of politics. He began to enlarge his circle of political acquaintances and to devote more of his time to the role of a student undertaking to master a fascinating new science. Among those whom he sought out was William McKinley, the congressman from Canton. He had reason to remember McKinley from a time several years previous when his company had had a strike. One of the Hanna workers was shot by the state militia and twenty-three of the strikers subsequently were indicted for violence and tried. Their lawyer was William McKinley, and he did a masterful job. Twenty-two of the strikers were acquitted; one was given a short jail sentence.

Hanna remembered the talented lawyer, now a United States Representative, and was even more deeply impressed when McKinley, chairman of the Ohio delegation to the 1888 Republican Convention, demonstrated the one trait that Hanna prized above all others: loyalty. The delegation was committed to Senator John Sherman of Ohio, who, by the fifth ballot, had been unable to pick up enough votes to win, and it was plain that his strength was diminishing. A delegate from Connecticut at that point nominated McKinley, who jumped to his feet and refused the honor, reaffirming the delegation's support of Sherman's lost cause. Now Hanna was convinced that McKinley was presidential timber, and he began, systematically, to promote his personal candidate for the nation's highest office.

He decided that 1892, the next national election year, would not be a successful one for the Republican candidate, and he trained his sights on the election of 1896. He had overlooked a most important hurdle—the congressional election of 1890, in which McKinley was defeated in a major political upset.

Here Hanna showed his battlefield versatility. He immediately revised his plans, knowing that McKinley, to be a serious contender for the G.O.P. presidential nomination, had to be kept in the public eye. The solution was to get him elected governor of Ohio. He directed a masterful campaign, and McKinley won the office in 1891.

Another crisis arose in 1893, when McKinley determined to resign as governor because of a personal crisis. He had endorsed notes for a friend who went bankrupt in the financial panic that swept the country that year, making McKinley personally liable for debts totaling $130,000. Hanna, always the master money-raiser, called on the leading millionaire Republicans to rally around with ready cash and they did. The donors were said to include Andrew Carnegie, Charles Taft, Henry Frick, and Hanna himself.

Their investment was in McKinley's future prospects, and their judgment proved sound in 1896, when the statesman from Canton was elected President of the United States in a national election which was something of an anticlimax, following as it did the tumultuous Republican convention which nominated McKinley. The country was introduced to a new kind of political showmanship and candidate management by Mark Hanna. In boosting McKinley into the White House, Hanna overpowered the political opposition and the voters with an unbelievable barrage of publicity and propaganda.

William Jennings Bryan was the Democratic candidate, and Hanna saw to it that little boys all over the nation soon learned the lines to this singing jingle:

> "McKinley drinks soda water,
> Bryan drinks rum;
> McKinley is a gentleman,
> Bryan is a buml"

In the words of Theodore Roosevelt, Hanna "advertised McKinley as if he were a patent medicine."

Hanna was the first of the high-pressure hucksters, the advance man for twentieth-century Madison Avenue to follow. He was responsible for mailing about three hundred million pieces of McKinley literature to the people of the nation; about thirty million a week, including millions printed in a dozen different languages. He had McKinley's face on drinking mugs, walking sticks, sterling silver spoons, lapel buttons, posters, and badges. He coined the slogan, "The Full Dinner Pail," and, knowing that McKinley couldn't match the silver-and-gold oratory of Bryan, Hanna came up with one of the best gimmicks in the history of national politics—the "front porch" campaign. The porch of McKinley's house in Canton was the homely stage on which he made about twenty appearances a day, each time to a different crowd numbering in the thousands. Railroads cooperated with the G.O.P. in running low-fare excursions to Canton; fares so low, in fact, it was said that it was cheaper for a voter to go to Canton than it was for him to stay home.

With McKinley elected, Hanna attended to his own ambition. He rejected an invitation to become a member of the cabinet (Postmaster General). He regarded the honor of being a senator as second only to the Presidency. McKinley obligingly named Senator John Sherman of Ohio his Secretary of State, while Governor Asa Bushnell of Ohio completed the lightning double play by appointing Hanna to succeed Sherman.

Hanna liked his life as a senator even more than he had anticipated. He was more than a senator; he was, as one observer described him, McKinley's "political prime minister." But the appointment was only for a year's duration. In 1897, he had to win the Senate seat by going before the Ohio State Legislature and winning its approval. At that time, the state legislatures elected the United States senators.

Some experts, indeed, point to the wild Hanna campaign for senator that year as the rowel that pricked a nation's conscience and led directly to the adoption of popular election of U.S. senators shortly thereafter.

Hanna himself was unsure of his own vote-getting ability. He once had said to his attorney, James H. Dempsey: "Jim, I could no more be elected Senator than I could fly."

The Ohio legislature was evenly divided on Hanna's candidacy, and every vote counted. Wavering legislators were wined and dined and wooed by the Hanna side. Once they had proclaimed their fealty, they were guarded against the wiles and lures of the enemy camp; that is to say, they were made virtual prisoners. One solon, slightly soggy from booze, was snatched away from the Hanna embrace by the opposition, who drugged him and stashed him away in one of their own hideouts. The Hanna henchmen struck right back, rekidnaping the bewildered legislator, redrugging him, and re-establishing him as their prisoner.

It was a raw, open political battle for supremacy, and while the nation looked on at the spectacle aghast, Hanna fought with every weapon he owned. On the big day, January 11, 1898, he had his legislative supporters marched under guard through the streets to the majestic, domeless state capitol building, when he was duly elected United States senator.

Hanna's most significant defeat in national politics came after the death of McKinley's Vice President, Garret A. Hobart, who died in November 1899. Hanna was outmaneuvered by two rival political bosses, T. C. Platt of New York and Matt Quay of Pennsylvania, who saw to it that Theodore Roosevelt won the vice presidential nomination in 1900. Hanna disliked Roosevelt, whom he called "that damned cowboy," and he went out of his way to annoy the governor of New York by referring to him as "Teddy." Roosevelt, on the other hand, irritated Hanna by calling him "Old man."

The end of the glory road for Hanna came with the assassination of President McKinley on September 6, 1901 by a man named Leon Czolgosz, who turned a short-barreled .32-caliber Iver-Johnson revolver on the Chief Executive in the Temple of Music at the Pan-American Exposition in Buffalo.

Hanna rushed to McKinley's side as the President's life ebbed away. "William . . . William . . . Don't you know me?" he cried out. Hanna's grief was genuine. Even his critics granted his feeling for McKinley was close to reverence.

Ironically, the anarchist who had murdered the President called Cleveland his home. Czolgosz, the son of a Polish immigrant, was born in Detroit. The family had moved to Orange Township in Cuyahoga County, where Leon and his two brothers grew up on the farm. In 1880, the family moved to Cleveland, where Leon, a brooding type, took to studying anarchistic literature of the day and attending meetings of anarchistic followers. One such meeting was addressed by the leading anarchist spokesman, Emma Goldman, who declared that all governmental rulers should be exterminated.

"This lecture," Leon admitted later, "set me on fire with anarchistic ideas; I could but think I ought to do something heroic."

That "something heroic" he decided on turned out to be the murder of President McKinley.

As if to put the tragedy behind him with hard work, Hanna was the busiest man in Congress during its next session. He proved, further, to be as valuable an adviser to President Roosevelt as he had been to President McKinley. The new Chief Executive's opinion of Hanna shot steadily upward as did his fear of the Ohioan as a possible opponent for the Presidency at the next election. He described Hanna's qualities as "rugged, fearless, straightforwardness of character. No beating around the bush."

When Hanna hesitated to endorse Roosevelt for the nomination in

1903, Roosevelt challenged him to make his position clear, and the break came. Hanna continued his campaign for re-election to the Senate and won by an overwhelming vote. The experts predicted he would make a bid for the Presidency, but there was a perceptible sag in the old kingmaker's attitude. The sparkle seemed to have gone out of politics for him when McKinley was extinguished. He looked drawn and tired. In January 1904, shortly after he was sworn in to his new term of office, Mark Hanna took ill with typhoid and died.

Something else had happened in that dreary last third of 1901 to depress Mark Hanna; nothing so dreadful as the assassination of the President, nor as discouraging as the step-up of Roosevelt, but a political development that was, nonetheless, terribly annoying to him personally. It was the election of Tom L. Johnson as mayor of Cleveland.

Hanna saw Johnson's ascendancy as a menacing portent of things to come. Like most other conservatives of the day, he regarded Johnson as a dangerous radical whose philosophy threatened the security of the established system. He accused Tom L. of being the national leader of the Socialist party. At other times, he called him a "nihilist" and an "anarchist."

The plain fact was that Johnson had been a burr in Hanna's side for some twenty-two years, and his election as mayor of Cleveland was a galling climax of their running feud.

Hanna indisputably was the political mastermind of the nation, but even when people were saying that he was more powerful than the President, and joking about McKinley having to dance at the end of Hanna's string, the Cleveland Republican leader was unable to dominate his own city's political affairs. He was never able to control Tom Johnson. He could not even win an armistice from him.

Hanna found his strongest opponent right at home. Cleveland knew that Johnson was more than a match for Hanna, and so, in time, did the nation.

Johnson's dissatisfaction with the governmental and social order of things puzzled Hanna. From the standpoint of that pragmatist, conditions in the United States hardly could have been better than they were in the last glorious quarter of the nineteenth century when the interests of Big Business were able to bend the government to their will. Among those who had taken advantage of the opportunities opened by monopolistic practice was Tom Johnson himself.

Hanna could understand the discontent of the have-nots, but Johnson was one of the haves. He was as much a capitalist as was Hanna, and he owed the system the same kind of loyalty and service. His defection from the approved path of political and economic orthodoxy made him, in effect, a rogue millionaire.

The first confrontation of the two giants in 1879 had set the competitive tone of their relationship during the twenty-five years that followed. It was a head-on conflict, with a street railway franchise in Cleveland as the prize.

They were unlikely opponents. Johnson was a plump, handsome boy of twenty-four years, gentle in manner and soft of voice. He was a newcomer to the city and a nonentity.

Hanna, on the other hand, was one of the city's leading citizens; a man who counted. It was apparent in his brusque manner, his direct way of speaking, his impatience with underlings.

"Some men must rule; the great mass of men must be ruled," Mark Hanna once said. "Some men must own; the great mass of men must work for those who own."

Johnson wanted to win a place in the tangled transit situation in Cleveland where altogether there were eight different street railway companies in operation. One of these, on the West Side, belonged to Mark Hanna, and his company competed for the same franchise that Johnson sought. Hanna's forces won, even though Johnson's offer was better. The award was predicated on a technicality in the fine type which gave preference to the bidder with an existing service.

Hanna had won the opening round, but Tom Johnson was a quick learner. This was merely the beginning of the fight. It was the kind of challenge he relished; one in which the odds were against him.

The odds had been heavy against Tom L. Johnson from the beginning. He was born in Blue Spring, Kentucky, near Georgetown, on July 18, 1854, the son of Albert W. Johnson, whose career as a cotton grower was ended by the Civil War.

The family began a nomadic existence that continued even after Colonel Johnson returned from the Confederate Army. Except for one year at a school in Evansville, Indiana, the boy had no formal education. In 1869, though, the family finally settled on a farm near Louisville, Kentucky, and Tom, fifteen, got a job in a rolling mill in the city.

That job lasted only a few months. Two relatives of the Johnson family by marriage, Bidermann and Alfred V. du Pont, had purchased the street railroad in Louisville and they gave Tom a job in the office.

The brothers du Pont were grandsons of Pierre Samuel du Pont, founder of the E. I. du Pont de Nemours Powder Company.

Tom Johnson's career with the du Pont railway in Louisville was sensational enough to make Horatio Alger twitch with disbelief. He began as the office boy and handyman at seven dollars a week. At the end of his first year, he was secretary of the company. Two years later, at age seventeen, he was superintendent of the railway. Along the way he also had invented the world's first coin fare box—a glass and metal container that kept conductor and customers alike honest. He profited to the extent of close to thirty thousand dollars from the invention.

At age twenty, he married a distant cousin, Maggie J. Johnson, and two years later he became a full-fledged railway entrepreneur with the purchase of the majority of the stock of the Indianapolis street railway company from William H. English, who later was a candidate for the vice presidency of the United States.

He had approached English with the hope of selling him his fare boxes.

"I don't want to buy a fare box, young man," English said, "but I have a street railroad to sell."

Johnson bought. He financed the transaction with his profits from the invention and a loan from the du Ponts. The Indianapolis railway was a stumbling, deficit operation, and English proved to be troublesome, but the young executive overcame the problems and turned the system into a profitable enterprise.

His appetite whetted by this achievement, he looked around for another battlefield worthy of his talents and decided on Cleveland as his target. The defeat he suffered at the hands of Mark Hanna in his initial bid only made him more determined.

"I was only twenty-five," he wrote later, "and willing to learn."

He purchased the Pearl Street (West 25th Street) Line that ran along that West Side thoroughfare a distance of a few miles to a terminal point at the Market House at Pearl and Lorain streets, just a half-mile short of the Superior Viaduct and the municipally owned tracks on it which would carry a streetcar over the Cuyahoga Valley and into the downtown area.

The trouble was that the precious half-mile of track on Pearl Street between the end of Tom L.'s railway and the Superior Viaduct was owned by the Lorain Street and Woodland Avenue Railway. This was the company in which Hanna was a large stockholder. It was headed by a Captain Elias Simms. They would not give Johnson permission to use their tracks and thus enable him to provide uninterrupted, through service downtown to his customers.

Pending a solution of the problem, Johnson resorted to the use of a horse-drawn bus line to carry his passengers from the end of his line to the center of the city. Meanwhile, knowing that the Hanna-Simms franchise was coming up soon for renewal, he made their blocking of through service on his line a hot political issue. The City Council came under such severe civic scrutiny in the controversy that even though it was normally under Hanna's thumb, it refused to grant a renewal of the Hanna-Simms company's franchise except on condition that Johnson's streetcars be allowed the use of his rival's tracks.

That was Tom Johnson's first victory over Mark Hanna and it had important consequences. It provided him with a firm footing for future expansion in the Cleveland traction field. It gave him civic and political stature as the man who had beat the formidable Mark Hanna. And, as it turned out, it brought about a situation which led directly to still another victory—a quarrel between Captain Simms and Hanna. The partners fell out and Simms was ousted from his railway post.

Johnson, meanwhile, moved quickly toward expansion. He bought a second railway line, the Jennings Avenue Line, and followed with a bid in the City Council for the big prize—a franchise to construct lines on the East Side. If successful in this bid, he would be able to connect the East Side lines with his existing West Side railways and thus provide Cleveland, for the first time, with cross-city, through rail transportation for a single fare.

The concept captured the imagination of Clevelanders, but the odds again were against Johnson. Hanna's influence in the City Council and his calculated willingness "to spread the green" gave him the upper hand. It was a tug-of-war for votes. Johnson and Hanna attended every meeting of the council, directing their opposing maneuvers like a pair of field marshals. A vote was ordered and in the roll call two councilmen who always heretofore had voted in the Hanna interest suddenly shifted to the Johnson side. Their votes were decisive. Johnson won the precious franchise and another sensational victory over the great Mark Hanna.

The happy defection of the councilmen, it turned out, puzzled Johnson as much as it did Hanna—so much so that Tom, reasoning that Hanna's former associate, Simms, might be able to throw some light on the subject, went to the home of his former rival.

Simms came to the door in his shirt-sleeves, squirted some tobacco juice over the bannister, eyed Johnson for a long moment, and finally invited him inside.

Johnson quickly explained the purpose of his visit.

"You're a smart young feller, Johnson," Simms said. "Beat me, didn't ye?"

When Johnson stirred, Simms lifted his hand.

"Yes," he said, "ye beat me. Folks might say I ain't very smart. Everybody knows Hanna's smart, though. Takes more'n a fool to beat Hanna. If you beat Hanna, nobody'll say that any damn fool could beat Simms. Ye beat me; I want ye to beat Hanna."

The explanation of Hanna's defeat was that simple. Simms still retained enough influence with at least two city councilmen to strike back at his old partner and restore some of his shattered pride.

The significance of the Hanna-Johnson conflicts was not the disposition of the prized railway franchises, but the emergence of a strong man who could successfully do battle with the Republican leader—and on his home ground, at that.

In his autobiography, "My Story," Tom L. reveals that the significance of his successful opposition was not lost on Hanna.

". . . I have always thought," wrote Johnson, "that Mr. Hanna anticipated many of the possibilities of the great struggle which was to follow, for it was after my first victory over him in the matter of gaining the right to operate over his lines that he telegraphed me in Indianapolis proposing a partnership and a consolidation of our interests. I wired my refusal.

"When I met him the next time I was in Cleveland, Mr. Hanna asked me why I had declined his proposition, pointing out as advantages to such an arrangement *his* acquaintance and influence with bankers and *his* familiarity with the political end of the game and *my* knowledge of and experience in the street railroad business itself.

"My answer was that we were too much alike; that as associates it would be a question of time, and a short time only, until one of us would 'crowd the other clear off the bench'; that we would make good opponents, not good partners."

He added: "I have never had any occasion to modify that opinion."

Up to that time, Tom Johnson, while admittedly a prodigy to be reckoned with in business affairs, had shown no inclination toward public service. Yet, politics was in the tradition of his family. Among his ancestors he counted some who had been members of Congress and governors, and one who even had been Vice President of the United States—Richard M. Johnson, who served with President Martin Van Buren from 1837 to 1841.

The turning point in Tom Johnson's life came in 1883 when he bought a book called *Social Problems,* by Henry George, to while away the time on a train trip. The book disturbed him deeply, as did another work by the same political economist, *Progress and Poverty.*

George's theory of the single tax—a tax on land values, including the value of all franchises and public utilities operated for private profit—and his fiery denunciation of the way in which the economic system was tilted in favor of the vested interests, whom he grouped under the name of Privilege, came to the twenty-six-year-old capitalist like a messianic call.

He struggled briefly against the call because what George preached was, in effect, a condemnation of the very monopolistic system and the very practices that were making Johnson rich. In the end, unable to repudiate George's arguments even with the help of the best intellects around him, Johnson capitulated. He went to Henry George at his home in Brooklyn in 1885, assured himself of the man's greatness in a series of conversations, and became his lifelong disciple.

It was because of Henry George that Tom Johnson went into politics. His first political speech, a gasping, five-minute struggle, was made in behalf of George's candidacy for mayor of New York. It was symptomatic of the painful readjustment Johnson would have to make in his way of life.

The effect of George's philosophy on him was profound, as his friend, Frederic Howe, noted in his *Confessions of a Reformer:*

"He [Johnson] lived with Henry George whom he loved; had talked every phase of his philosophy through with him. He had its deeper social significance at his finger tips. The single tax had come to him like St. Paul's vision on the road to Damascus, changing a monopolist into the most dangerous enemy that monopoly could have—an enemy not of men but of institutions."

Said Johnson, speaking about Henry George's book:

"If this book is really true, I shall have to give up business. It isn't right for me to make money out of protected industries, out of street railway franchises, out of land speculation. I must get out of business or prove that this book is wrong."

But he did not abandon his business career at that time, nor did he prove George wrong. He continued to shine as one of the most successful capitalists of his generation, but some of the sparkle had gone out of the moneymaking game.

"I continued my business with as much zest as ever," he said, "but my point of view was no longer that of a man whose chief object in life is to get rich."

It was the beginning of greatness for Tom L. Johnson.

Three years after his meeting with Henry George, Johnson projected himself into politics as an active aspirant to office. He won the nomination as candidate for Congress from Cleveland's 21st District on the Democratic ticket. He was defeated handily by the haughty Theodore E. Burton.

He made the same race again two years later against the same opponent, but Representative Burton this time made the tactical error that Richard M. Nixon would make against John F. Kennedy—he engaged Johnson in a series of debates. Johnson gave him a drubbing on the platform. It was a case of old-fashioned political oratory against a naïve kind of candor, and the voters liked the contrasting plain talk. Johnson was elected to Congress and served two terms in which he led the fight for free trade at a time when proponents of high tariff protectionism were riding high in the saddle. He was defeated by his old rival, Burton, in the 1894 election and turned his attention back to business.

Even giving his business part-time attention, Johnson had done rather well. He had invented a grooved streetcar rail and he and his associates, including the du Ponts, had built a factory to manufacture curves, frogs, and switches out of the rail in Johnstown, Pennsylvania; he had bought a railway line in Brooklyn, New York, and in St. Louis. He had rescued the Detroit street railway, which his brother Albert had purchased. Further, he and his associates built the Lorain Steel Company in Lorain, Ohio, which became part of United States Steel Corporation.

Johnson, incidentally, played an important role in the popularization of Coney Island by putting it within reach of the masses through cheap transportation. He merged the Nassau Street railroad with the Atlantic Avenue system and established the first five-cent fare from Brooklyn Bridge to Coney Island. The fare previously had been about twenty-five cents.

One night an old millionaire friend, R. T. Wilson of New York, came to Johnson's hotel room and asked his help through a severe fit of depression that his millions could not relieve, and Johnson suddenly knew that he must escape the net that his many business activities had thrown over his dreams for public service. He began at that time a program of steady withdrawal from business.

On January 8, 1901, Johnson announced at a Jackson Day banquet in Cleveland's Kennard House that he was forsaking business forever and would devote the rest of his life to politics—not as a candidate for office, but as a worker in the ranks "for the principles of democracy."

Less than a month later, on February 1, a delegation of fifty Democrats called on Johnson at home and asked him to be a candidate for mayor of Cleveland. They presented him with a petition with 15,682 signatures. Tom L. found the call irresistible. He was nominated at the Democratic primaries in mid-February.

He was a different kind of politician from the very outset. His use of a circus tent for his meetings—an emergency device at first— became a trademark.

He refused to spend a lot of money on his campaign, even though he was wealthy. He wouldn't even buy a lottery ticket or a ticket to a church gathering.

He wouldn't promise a delegation of City Hall employees that he would continue them in their jobs if elected. When they asked him to pledge the dismissal of all Republicans holding city jobs, he refused.

He declared against granting extensions of street railway franchises to lines charging any fare higher than three cents.

He went on record as a supporter of Henry George's single tax philosophy and promised to try to right an unjust appraisal of real property made the year before.

Big Business took Johnson's nomination calmly, and some members of the Chamber of Commerce thought his election might even be a good thing. One of the most widely quoted reactions was that the election gave Cleveland "a chance to get good government and a hundred-thousand-dollar man for mayor at six thousand dollars a year."

Mark Hanna was not one of the complacent ones. He regarded Tom Johnson as a dangerous man and warned against his election.

The railroad interests also were fearful of Johnson achieving the mayoralty, and they put pressure on the existing city administration of Mayor John Farley and the City Council to reach a settlement on some disputed lakefront land. The land, claimed by the city and the railroads, was worth from ten to twenty million dollars at the time.

"As a citizen," said Johnson, "I had brought suit to prevent the mayor . . . from signing an ordinance passed by a crooked council settling the controversy and conveying the land in question to the railroads without compensation."

Johnson obtained an injunction preventing the city from executing the twenty-million-dollar giveaway ordinance. It was due to expire at eleven o'clock on the morning of April 4. Tom L. was elected mayor on April 1, 1901, defeating his Republican opponent, W. J. Akers, by some six thousand votes. He had three days to win certification of election by the Board of Elections if he was going to block the land gift to the railroads, but it normally took the board from two to three weeks to make its official count.

Johnson prodded the Board of Elections into working night and day to finish the count before the injunction expired. It was a miracle of sorts that they succeeded.

Just thirty-seven minutes before the injunction would die, Johnson took the official oath of office of the city clerk on the third floor of the City Hall, filed his bond, and went directly to the mayor's office.

"Mr. Farley looked up as I came in and mumbled ungraciously; 'Well, Tom, when are you going to take hold?'

"I replied that I hoped he would take his time about moving his belongings, but that I had been mayor for several minutes."

No city ever got such a bargain! A saving of twenty million dollars' worth of precious lakefront land simply by substituting one mayor for another.

The way in which Tom L. Johnson's election as mayor of Cleveland upset the balance of power in the city and shattered the social and political complacency of the entire community is suggested in a recollection by one of Johnson's followers, a former Cleveland city councilman named Frederic C. Howe, who, as a Republican, was one of the new chief executive's opponents in the beginning.

"For the greater part of nine years [Johnson's reign as mayor]," wrote Howe, "Cleveland was an armed camp. There was but one line of division. It was between those who would crucify Mr. Johnson and all of his friends, and those who believed in him. I doubt if any of the border cities like Washington and Covington during the Civil War were more completely rent asunder than was Cleveland during those years. It is doubtful if the wars of the Guelphs and Ghibellines in the Italian cities were more bitter, more remorseless, more cruel than this contention in Cleveland.

"If any kind of cruelty, any kind of coercion, any kind of social, political or financial power was left untried in those years to break the heart of Mr. Johnson, I do not know what or when it was."

Life in Cleveland changed when the stout (260 pounds), curly-haired mayor took office. Cleveland voters had sown the wind and they reaped a whirlwind. Not many of the people in the street had understood him during his campaign as he inveighed against Privilege and hammered words of criticism at monopolistic practices, especially the public utility companies that provided the city's electricity, artificial gas, and street railway service, but they had deep faith in this man who had turned his back on money and privilege to serve them.

The city delighted in the spectacle of the new mayor at work. The people chuckled and applauded when he ordered the parks department to pull up the "Don't Walk on the Grass" signs and invited the citizens to go out of their way to walk on the public greens wherever they found them. They watched admiringly as he ordered new playgrounds, instituted reforms in the city's penal policy, bought farmlands for the rehabilitation of juvenile delinquents, ordered the city to take over garbage collection and disposal (saving the city money in the process), began a new policy of law enforcement, warred on billboards, put whitewings to work cleaning up the city streets, and hammered at county tax policies.

Among those who stood by and watched the new mayor in amazement was Lincoln Steffens, the nation's leading exposer of municipal corruption, who described Johnson's debut in office in these words:

"It was like seeing a captain of industry on the stage. He listened, all attention, till he understood. Then he would smile or laugh, give a decision, and 'Next!' No asking time to 'think it over' or to 'consult his colleagues,' no talk of 'commissions to investigate,' no 'come again next week.' It was no or yes, genial, jolly, but final."

Vice was a prominent part of the Cleveland way of life when Johnson took over; most of it concentrated along the northern edge of the downtown section. The new mayor certainly was no prude, but his sense of civic propriety was offended by what he saw, especially as he recognized that a large degree of police cooperation was an essential element wherever wickedness was able to flourish. He reached deep into the back ranks of the police department and pulled out an arrogant officer named Fred Kohler against whom a number of complaints had been lodged. At first he answered the complaints by sending Kohler to the sticks, but now he decided he had been unfair and that Kohler could be, in fact, a real asset to his administration.

"How would you like to be chief?" he asked the stiff-necked Teuton.

"I haven't asked for it," replied Kohler rudely. He added gratuitously: "I'm a Republican."

"I don't care anything about your politics," said the mayor, "and I know you haven't asked for anything."

Kohler became his police chief. In later years he was to become mayor himself.

There were other appointments like that one, as Johnson crossed over party lines without any hesitation in search of the right men, causing Democratic party regulars to wax wistful. But the bipartisan approach gave him a strong staff of executive assistants, even though his choices seemed to be unlikely—and unwise—to the professional politicians. For example, he named as city solicitor a young man just beginning the practice of law, and he had to withstand loud criticism for his selection. The man was Newton D. Baker, and he turned out to be brilliant in the city's service as law director. Later he also would be an outstanding mayor, a leading world figure as Secretary of War in the cabinet of Woodrow Wilson, and a contender for the Democratic presidential nomination in the 1920s.

Johnson's welfare director was his own minister, Rev. Harris R. Cooley, a great humanitarian with the conviction that society was at least partly responsible for delinquency through its imposition of a life of poverty on so many of the wrongdoers. He believed that society had an obligation to help rehabilitate these people, not as an act of charity but as a matter of justice. The city purchased twenty-five farms with two thousand acres of land during the Johnson administration for the establishment in the country of farm colonies for the care of all city charges—the old, the sick, the young, and the delinquent. This humane experiment in the salvation of unfortunates drew international attention and widespread praise for the progressive new Cleveland city government.

His administration included, as city clerk, a rough-talking former steel puddler from Newburgh named Peter Witt, who first thrust himself into Tom Johnson's awareness by heckling him loudly at a campaign tent rally; a Republican named William Stinchcomb, who put together the city's magnificent Metropolitan Park System and devoted his life to its administration; and Alfred Benesch, a scholarly lawyer who went on to serve as safety director under Mayor Baker and as a member of the city's Board of Education for several decades.

Among the wide-eyed newspapermen covering the Johnson administration was a *Plain Dealer* reporter named W. B. ("Burr") Gongwer. The mayor liked him and persuaded him to forsake his career in journalism to become his secretary. After Johnson's death, Gongwer became the party boss and reigned into the 1930s.

The Johnson administration, in brief, was a breeding ground from which issued most of the city's leaders during the next twenty years, and all of them seemed to be imbued with something of the spirit and drive of the man who was their political mentor. Lincoln Steffens called them "the happiest gang of reformers in America."

Lined up in opposition to those Johnson-led reformers, however, was a strong lineup of those who favored the old Hanna policy of standing pat. They were, in Johnson's eyes, the Princes of Privilege.

Even as mayor, Tom L. did not turn his attention away from his favorite field of battle, the street railway system. All through his four terms of office he fought for the three-cent fare, and it became the rallying cry of all his followers. Eventually it did come about, but not until he had left office, and it lasted only a short while.

He fought monopolism as only an old monopolist would know how to fight it. He fought fire with fire. Instead of engaging in futile denunciations of the monopoly enjoyed by the artificial gas and coal interests, Johnson invited the backers of John D. Rockefeller's East Ohio Gas Company to bid for a franchise in Cleveland. This group had hesitated to try for the prize because its members knew that Mayor Johnson was aware Standard Oil Company, the biggest trust of them all, owned the natural gas wells. They assumed he would oppose their bid, but he disarmed them with his hearty welcome instead. The reason was that he knew the natural gas would be cheaper and that the public would benefit.

The coal and artificial gas interests, meanwhile, had raised a hefty fund to buy the support of the City Council members. This legislative approach, while admittedly crude and dishonest, nevertheless could be impressively effective. One of the council members, a man named Charlie Kohl, had qualms of conscience, though, and confided in Mayor Johnson that a man named Dr. Daykin had offered him five thousand dollars to vote against the natural gas interests.

The mayor interrupted his dinner—a real indication that he thought the information important.

"Charlie," he said, shrewdly, "if you were a really game man, I would suggest a line of action. But I don't think you would carry it out, so there is no use in my advising you."

The councilman pleaded for the chance to prove that he was game and honest. The mayor nodded approvingly and recommended that the councilman return to Dr. Daykin and take as big a bribe as he could coax out of him.

At the City Council meeting that night, the mayor took the floor and made a sweeping accusation of dishonesty against the artificial gas and coal interests. He noted as he talked that Dr. Daykin was among the interested spectators in the council chamber. When he reached the key point in his speech, Councilman Kohl dramatically stepped forward and slapped two thousand dollars in bribe money on the table.

In the pandemonium that ensued, Dr. Daykin hurried toward the nearest exit, but Johnson's booming voice halted him in his tracks.

"You won't get very far, Doctor. Some of my friends are waiting for you outside!"

The East Ohio Gas Company's franchise then was approved and without a dissenting vote—a notable triumph for the mayor. The hapless Dr. Daykin was arrested, tried, and acquitted.

Mayor Johnson also fought fiercely the monopoly enjoyed by the Cleveland Electric Illuminating Company. He tried, unsuccessfully, to get voter approval of bond issues to finance a competitive municipal light plant in 1903. Failing in this, he called for annexation of a small suburb, South Brooklyn, which, fortuitously, already had a small light plant. His campaign to annex the town was fiercely resisted; so much so that the mayor openly charged fifteen Republican members of the City Council with misfeasance and two Democrat councilmen with bribery. Annexation was approved, and the city expanded the municipal plant into a formidable, effective regulator of electric rates charged by the private utility. The latter company, by way of illustration, had charged the city $87.60 annually for each street light in 1900. By the time Tom Johnson left office, the competition of the municipal plant had reduced that cost to $54.96 a year for each light. C.E.I. rates, generally, dropped 20 per cent in three years. The municipal operation has served as an efficient yardstick for some sixty years, saving Clevelanders many millions of dollars over that time, as Tom L. foresaw it would.

He instituted other improvements, among them enforcement of honest weights and measures, the building of grade crossings, construction of public bathhouses, reduction of water bills, adoption of a model building code, inspection of meat and dairy products, creation of a forestry department, a crusade against gambling, the washing of city streets, band concerts in the parks in summer, and skating carnivals in winter.

Cleveland sparkled and danced with the excitement of the Johnson administration. Lincoln Steffens called Tom L. "the best mayor of the best-governed city in the United States." That was the headiest kind of praise, coming from the great muckraker who once had been openly skeptical of Johnson.

In one of his volumes of random reminiscences, *Lincoln Steffens Speaking*, it was written of the Cleveland reformer:

"Tom Johnson, the big businessman who became mayor of Cleveland for an economic purpose, set the precedent for all businessmen and engineers in politics. The ministers and their followers, the good people, called on him to enforce the laws against the saloons, bawdy houses, and petty vice. He refused openly, explicitly, absolutely.

"He said that he had gone into politics to tackle the economic conditions which produced the evils the clergy complained of; he would deal with the causes of riches, poverty, and crime. He would not waste time on the symptoms which engaged the moralists.

" 'I will not be diverted,' he declared to their faces, 'from my larger purposes to your petty purposes. I would rather not be mayor; I would rather stick to the big crooked business you approve than go chasing the miserable men and women you want punished. I shall do the job I was elected to do, leaving your dirty work to you, and, if I have any trouble from you, I will turn aside long enough to show up you and your congregations and your churches and trace your roots to the grafts you are sharing in and living on.'

"They did not know they were in on any graft, so he showed them a little, just enough to frighten them, and they quit. Tom Johnson had no trouble from the churches."

Not everybody in Cleveland agreed with Steffens that Johnson was a great mayor. The man, after all, was a radical; a traitor to his class. He seemed to be intent on upsetting the status quo, and such a man was dangerous.

Men of great influence in the city stirred uneasily as they watched the new mayor. Mark Hanna had no doubts at all about the nature of the threat posed by his old foe. Whenever he could take his eyes off the national scene, he looked worriedly in the direction of Johnson. And when Tom L. made a bid for the governorship of Ohio in 1903, the tired old senator found new strength to fight him around the state.

Johnson was a picturesque campaigner. He took his circus tent everywhere in Ohio, and it was a more efficient auditorium than ever before, giving him the mobility he needed. He roared up and down the dusty Ohio roads and through towns and hamlets in his Winton motorcar, the Red Devil, the long curls that crept out from beneath the back of his black derby blowing in the wind. Ohioans enjoyed the spectacle. And close behind Tom L. came Senator Mark Hanna, the most famous man in the nation outside of Theodore Roosevelt, and he tried to top every argument that Tom L. presented to the voters. He even topped his tent, coming out with one that was bigger than Johnson's.

This was one time that Mark Hanna won over Tom L. Johnson. The voters elected as governor Myron T. Herrick, a fellow Clevelander. It also was the last battle between Johnson and the Boss of Bosses because Senator Hanna died at the beginning of the following year.

Opposition to Mayor Johnson did not die, however. It persisted throughout the four terms he served in office, rising to its highest, shrillest crescendo in 1907 when the alarmed Republican Party waged its most spectacular campaign against his re-election. Representative Theodore E. Burton, the man whom he had engaged in battle over the seat in Congress years before, was selected by the party as the strongest candidate who could be put against the troublesome mayor.

Burton was reluctant to forsake his congressional job, but the party pressured him into accepting the mayoralty nomination. Even President Theodore Roosevelt urged Burton to make the sacrifice, and he agreed.

Cleveland probably had the most interesting mayoralty campaign in its history that summer and autumn of 1907. Burton was known as "the old Roman," and his method of campaigning was directly opposite to the style of Johnson. Burton spoke in long, reverberating, rolling phrases with a classical grandeur to every syllable. He was the statesman and the orator; dignity personified; a visitor from Greek mythology come down to walk among the mortals.

It was at a tent meeting of Republicans in an Irish ward that the congressman made the momentous announcement of his decision to run for mayor.

"*Jacta alea est!*" he cried out, flinging his arm dramatically.

The Irish weren't too sure if that was good, but they applauded dutifully anyway while interpreters rushed around the audience with the translation of the congressman's Latin: "The die is cast!"

Tom Johnson was not the man to let that opportunity slip past. At his next tent meeting, he recalled Burton's Latin quotation and came up with his own interpretation. He said he thought the words meant, "Let 'er go, Gallagher!"

Clevelanders howled with delight.

Congressman Burton doggedly stayed with his formal style of speech, however, opening one evening of campaign oratory with the following preamble:

"I have spoken within the halls of Parliament in London, and in London's Crystal Palace; in Berlin and in the south of France; within the confines of the Arctic Circle, in the valley of the Yukon, Alaska—but kind friends, I am glad to be here with you tonight!"

Peter Witt liked that opening so much that a few nights later he opened a Johnson rally with:

"I have spoken in the corn fields of Ashtabula, in the stone quarries of Berea, and at the town hall in Chardon . . . but kind friends, I am glad to be here with you tonight!"

There was no doubt who won that exchange.

There were a few low punches thrown against Johnson in that campaign, including stories that he was a drunkard, consorted with women of questionable repute, frequented low dives, and encouraged debauches everywhere he went.

The Republicans imported the acid pen of Cartoonist Homer Davenport from New York, and he concentrated all his undeniable talent for violent caricature against Johnson in the pages of the Cleveland *Leader*. Before undertaking the assignment, Davenport, himself a believer in the single tax, came to Johnson and apologized in advance. Johnson told him he understood his position and to go ahead and do his best. "I'll forgive you," he told the cartoonist. Davenport nodded his thanks. "You will," he said, "but my father never will."

Johnson never deviated in his career from a policy of shunning personal abuse.

"There is very great danger," he said, "of having the best of movements sidetracked by the calling of hard names and the personal abuse of individuals. Tactics of that kind will never get anywhere. Throughout the whole of our fight we adhered to our first plan, which was to attack institutions—Privilege, and not men."

Tom L. beat Theordore Burton handily, sending the congressman fleeing back to Washington, and Peter Witt sent President Roosevelt a needling telegram which said: "Cleveland as usual went moral again. The next time you tell Theodore to run, tell him which way."

The campaign had taken a lot out of Tom Johnson, however. His health was beginning to fail, and he had worries. His wife was ill. His daughter had made an unfortunate marriage with a man posing as an Italian "nobleman." His fortune had dwindled steadily away.

His only recreation was an invention he had been working on in his basement during the busy political years—a new system of transporting people in cars suspended from an overhead rail and powered by electromagnetic impulse. His working model was successful and he confidently estimated that his novel railway system would be able to propel people from New York to Chicago in two hours' time—at an average speed of five hundred miles an hour! While the claim still sounds fantastic, engineers of the General Electric Company came to Cleveland from Schenectady at Johnson's invitation to inspect his brainchild, and their judgment was that it was a magnificent concept, basically sound. The G.E. management signed an agreement with Johnson to build a test project, but considerable expense was involved and the idea fell by the wayside of a busy life.

Tom L. had other things to think about.

In 1909, to everybody's astonishment, he was defeated in his bid for a fifth term as mayor. It was an upset that made national headlines, a stunning surprise even to the winner, a former West Side brewer named Herman C. Baehr, who served out his two years and was retired from office. From that day on, though, he signed his name "Former Mayor Herman C. Baehr."

At the end of his term, Tom L. told the new mayor:

"I have served the people for nearly nine years. I have had more of misfortune in those nine years than in any other period of my life. As that is true, it is also true that I have had more of joy.

"In those nine years I have given the biggest and the best part of me. I have served the people of Cleveland the best I knew how."

During Tom Johnson's years as mayor, his personal fortune had dwindled away. An indication of his financial plight was seen in his disposition of the big mansion on Millionaire's Row right after the election. He and his wife moved into an apartment hotel, and he went to New York for medical treatment. In 1910, against the advice of doctors and friends, he made a tour of Europe, where he was hailed everywhere he went—in Great Britain, France, Germany, and Ireland. The climax of his reception was a dinner in his honor in the House of Parliament.

Upon his return to the United States, he was given a public reception and dinner in the Hotel Astor in New York by his admirers on May 31, 1910. He died in Cleveland less than a year later, April 10, 1911.

The Cleveland *Leader*, describing the passage of the simple funeral cortege of six automobiles through the city streets leading to the Union Station, said:

"Two hundred thousand persons saw Tom L. Johnson's last journey through Cleveland. The heart of the city stopped for two hours . . ."

They took Tom Johnson's body to Brooklyn and buried him where he wanted to rest in death—alongside the grave of Henry George in Greenwood Cemetery.

The way Cleveland sorrowed, it was as if a President of the United States had died. There was an instant awareness among the people that a great man had passed their way and paused long enough to brush away the cobwebs of disillusionment that had almost covered the bright, idealistic American dream.

". . . Honesty is not enough," wrote Lincoln Steffens, one of those who sorrowed; "it takes intelligence, some knowledge or theory of economics, courage, strength, will power, humor, leadership—it takes intellectual integrity to solve our political problems. And these Tom Johnson had above all the politicians of my day.

"His courage was the laughing sort; his humor was the kind that saved him tears. He had the instinct and the habit of experimentation, and he had the training of a big successful man of business on the other side of politics. A practical business man, he was a practical politician, too. He knew the game. He could pick and lead a team; men loved to follow him; he made it fun . . .

"He cleared my head of a lot of rubbish, left there from my academic education and reform associations. I asked him one day why he had thought I would not understand him if he told me what he was up to in Cleveland.

" 'Oh, I could see,' he said, 'that you did not know what it was that corrupted politics. First you thought it was bad politicians, who turned out to be pretty good fellows. Then you blamed the bad business men who bribed the good fellows, till you discovered that not all business men bribed and those who did were pretty good business men. The little business men didn't bribe; so you settled upon, you invented, the phrase "big business," and that's as far as you and your kind have got: that it is big business that does all the harm.

" 'Hell! Can't you see that it's privileged business that does it? Whether it's a big steam railroad that wants a franchise or a little gambling-house that wants not to be raided, a temperance society that wants a law passed, a poor little prostitute, or a big merchant occupying an alley for storage—it's those who seek privileges who corrupt, it's those who possess privileges that defend our corrupt politics. Can't you see that?'

"This was more like a flash of light than a speech, and as I took it in and shed it around in my head, he added: 'It is privilege that causes evil in the world, not wickedness, and not men.'

"And I remembered then something I heard him say one day to a group of business men he was fighting, something neither they nor I understood at the time. To a remonstrance of theirs that I do not recall, he blurted out: 'It's fun, running the business of the city of Cleveland; it's the biggest, most complicated, most difficult, and most satisfying business in Cleveland. A street railway is child's play compared with it; a coal mine is a snap; a bank?—bah! There's something that blinds you fellows, and I know what it is. It's what fooled me so long when I was running public service corporations. And I'll tell you something you want to know: How to beat me.

" 'If I could take away from you the things you have, the franchises, the privileges, that make you enemies of your city, you would see what I see and run for my job yourselves, and you'd beat me for mayor and manage the city of Cleveland better than I do.'

"Tom Johnson struck at the sources of the evils, not at the individuals and classes usually blamed, with all his fine intelligence and all the powers of an unusually powerful mayor. . . . He explained his acts with patience, care and eloquence to the whole town; he held the votes of the common people . . ."

There was a mystique to this mayor, as there is around all great men. Those who fell under his spell lived dreamily and fanatically for his cause; they were not so much his supporters as they were his followers. They believed in him and they loved him as few statesmen in the history of the United States have been privileged to receive the faith and affection of the people.

XV

The Valley of God's Pleasure

THERE is a terrible temptation to call Cleveland a jumping town
and then point to Shaker Heights as proof, but the world
might not understand the obscure allusion. Of all Cleveland's suburbs,
Shaker Heights easily is the most famous—and least known.

The modern metropolitan area has more than sixty suburbs, give or
take a town here and there. The precise number depends on the radius
of the arc that one cares to swivel in marking the outer limits of the
metropolitan area.

One urban expert, Noah K. Birnbaum, who swings one of the meanest
compasses in the business, projects his arc so far from downtown Cleveland that it even includes the city of Akron, some thirty miles to the
south. It is known, naturally, as "Noah's Arc," and it infuriates the
proud people of Akron even to hear it mentioned.

The national image projected by Shaker Heights is one of extreme
prosperity and, appropriately enough, utopian living. The irony is that
it started out to be a spiritual Utopia and came to be a materialistic
paradise; a communistic experiment turned into a capitalistic triumph.

This prosperous state of affairs was officially certified by Uncle Sam
in the autumn of 1962, when the United States Bureau of the Census released figures indicating that the Cleveland suburb was the wealthiest
city in the nation in its own population category—cities of 25,000 population or more.

According to the 1960 census statistics, the median family income in
Shaker Heights was $13,933—a nice, round, pleasingly plump median
figure. (Median means the middle income. Half of the families in
Shaker enjoyed an income higher than the figure quoted. The other
half had an income that was lower.)

The average family income in Shaker is more impressive, having
been close to $24,000 a year in 1960. The suburb had 10,402 families
with a combined annual income of $249,000,000.

The median value of homes in Shaker at the time of the survey was
$34,500. The average value was estimated to be around $65,000.

The people who make their home in Shaker Heights are not pleased

to have these sordid details raked up again. It isn't that they are un-
duly secretive or sensitive, but when the news of the community's affluence was published in the nation's newspapers and magazines in
1962, every confidence man in the country grabbed his suitcase and
headed for Cleveland on the dead run. The Shaker Heights police
have gotten rid of most of them, but everybody dreads any publicity
that might bring on another gold rush like '62.

The simple life plainly is far behind for Shaker, but once there was
no simpler life to be found anywhere in the United States.

The Moses Cleaveland party, in plotting the Western Reserve, laid
out four townships on the outskirts of Cleveland and named them, re-
spectively, Euclid, East Cleveland, Warrensville, and Newburgh. In 1822,
when Cleveland itself was nothing more substantial than a clearing in
the wilderness, and packs of gray timber wolves were still snapping at
the heels of the pioneers whenever they ventured outside their cabins,
a group of religious enthusiasts banded under the unwieldy name of
"The United Society of Believers in the Second Appearing of Christ"
chose a fourteen-hundred-acre site in the northwest section of Warrensville Township as the place for their utopian community.

They named their retreat North Union, but they knew it also, more
poetically, as "The Valley of God's Pleasure." It was actually high
ground, several hundred feet above the level of Cleveland, some six
miles to the southeast, but "valley," as used in a symbolic sense by the
sect, meant a place apart from the material world; a spiritual sanctuary.

The Believers themselves were nicknamed Shakers, logically enough,
because they did a lot of shaking in the physical agitations that were
a manifest part of their methods of worship.

A Revolutionary War soldier named Jacob Russell, a native of Windsor,
Connecticut, had been the first to settle the site. He was sixty-seven
years old when he yielded to the lure of the virgin West and purchased
a 475-acre farm in Warrensville from the Connecticut Land Company
in 1811. He and two of his sons, Elijah and Ralph, walked from their
home in Connecticut to the farm near Cleveland in the spring of
1812, planted the fields which they had cleared the previous summer,
and built a cabin. They then walked back to Connecticut, bundled
up their belongings, rounded up the rest of the family (Jacob had
twelve children altogether), and in June walked back to the Ohio
farm.

This should settle any lingering questions as to why the colonies'
ragged armies won the Revolutionary War. Jacob Russell was sixty-eight
years old when he made the two trips to Ohio by foot, rolling up about
eighteen hundred miles on the old shoe leather.

One of the sons, Ralph, became interested in the Shaker movement and late in 1821, after the death of his father, visited a Shaker settlement called Union Village at Lebanon, Ohio.

As he neared home, on his return trip, Ralph had a vision.

"I saw a strong, clear ray of light proceeding from the northwest, in a perfectly straight horizontal line until it reached a spot near my log cabin. Then it arose in a strong erect column and became a beautiful tree."

When Ralph told his wife and his brothers, Elijah, Elisha, Return, and Rodney, of what he had seen at Union Village and of the marvelous vision that had presented itself to his eyes, they agreed with him that he had received a sign from on high to establish a Shaker colony where the family homestead stood.

The Russell farm became the nucleus of the colony, and thirty-two members of the Russell family became converts to Shakerism. Not permanently, however. Ralph Russell himself later renounced his membership in the sect, as did a majority of his and his brothers' twenty-three children.

The Shakers were Christian communists who pooled their belongings and other worldly wealth, drew from a common treasury according to their needs, practiced celibacy and pacificism, dressed plainly, shunned most earthly pleasures like smoking and drinking, prayed hard, and worked hard. Life was the trial and death was the victory. Shakerism was a deviation of Quakerism—"Shaking Quakers" was one of the derisive names applied to their members—and their origin is ascribed to a French religious sect called the Camisards.

Good fortune and prosperity attended the North Union colony in its early decades, and many recruits were attracted to the utopian settlement where no person hungered or thirsted and where the elderly were given tender care. It was, like most Shaker colonies, highly productive. Shakers did not depend alone on agriculture; they also were industrialized, and are credited with some forty inventions, including the flat broom, the common clothespin, and the circular saw.

One field in which the Shakers excelled—and profited—was in the mixture of home medical remedies and tonics. Among their products sold all over the world were skin ointments, porous plasters, lotions, cold creams, liniments and, surprisingly, even a color tint for graying hair. It was called "The Shaker Hair Restorative," and it carried the explanatory legend: "Gray hair may be honorable, but the natural color is preferable."

The Shakers were promoters of the use of sarsaparilla as a blood purifier. Corbett's Shaker Extract of Sarsaparilla, manufactured at the Mount Lebanon colony, was a standard remedy prescribed by doctors all over the United States throughout the last half of the nineteenth century and even into the present century for the treatment of syphilis. Among its ingredients was potassium iodide.

Out of the Shaker experiment came improved breeds of livestock and better seeds, fruit trees, and vines, and some historians say that this sect led the way in the development of the mass production theory in their community workshops.

Nobody would deny that the Shakers were hard-working and their morals were beyond criticism, but the concept of communism, even on such a high level, was repugnant to some of the Shakers' neighbors. The sect's drastic departure from the accepted mores of the day, and some of its strange religious practices caused many outsiders to mock them and others to fear them.

One of the most deplorable episodes involving the Cleveland Shaker colony was the time a gang of persecutors mounted on horseback and carrying lighted torches raided the peaceful community and set fire to many of the buildings. The Shakers philosophically turned the other cheek and bent to the task of rebuilding.

Persons practicing more conventional religions found it hard to reconcile the physical frenzies which were a part of Shaker worship with the restrained reverence of more orthodox sects. It wasn't only the incorporation of dancing into the Shaker worship that astonished and frightened outsiders. There were even more spectacular manifestations of religious enthusiasm which have been catalogued under the names of The Falling, The Jerks, The Dancing, The Barking, and The Singing Exercise.

A student of the Cleveland colony, Caroline B. Piercy, describes the physical agitations in her book, *The Valley of God's Pleasure*, as follows:

"The Falling . . . meant the victims lay apparently lifeless.

"The Jerks . . . Hard to describe. Sometimes affected only a portion of the body of the victim who was under strong emotional stress; again it would affect the whole body when the victim would jerk backward and forward without any control of himself. This movement often took place so rapidly that the onlooker could not distinguish the features of the face. Sometimes the head almost touched the floor in this manifestation. No one could account for these strange happenings and the curious thing was, that many of these were thrown with terrific violence or jerked by some terrible force and although it was awful to behold, no one ever sustained a bodily injury.

"The Dancing . . . usually began with the jerks and affected only the professed religionists as ministers and deeply pious laymen. Such dancing was heavenly to behold. There was nothing in it of levity, nor was it calculated to excite levity in the beholders. The saints of heaven shone through the countenances of these dancers. Thus they moved

(the motion sometimes was very rapid and again it was very slow) in
a set figure until nature seemed exhausted and they would fall prostrate
to the floor. Often during these dances solemn praises would arise, or
glorious exaltations would come from the lips of the performer.

"The Barking . . . the barking exercise was similar to the jerks
especially when only the head was affected. Strange sounds resembling
that of the barking of a dog would be uttered at each jerk. It got its
name from an old Presbyterian preacher who had gone to the woods
for private devotion and was violently seized with the jerks. Standing
near a tall tree, he grasped hold of it to avoid falling as his head jerked
back and forth and he uttered the strange barks. Some wag discovered
him in this position and reported that he had 'found the old preacher
barking up a tree.'

"The Singing Exercise . . . was the most unaccountable of all. The
subject was always in a happy frame of mind and would sing most
melodiously, not from the mouth or through the nose, but entirely from
the chest—the sound issuing forth like from an organ. Such music
silenced everyone and attracted the attention of all. It was actually
heavenly and indescribable. None could ever tire of hearing of it."

The Shaker colony in Cleveland, which had reached a peak population of three hundred believers at one time, steadily declined after
the Civil War until by 1888 there were only twenty-seven remaining
members. The elders of the society decided then to disband North
Union. They moved the twenty-seven persons to other colonies, and in
1889 the site of the Shaker town was sold to a Buffalo, New York, land
development company for $316,000. It was an unhappy end to the
seventy-seven year experiment in communistic living which had contained the seeds of its own failure through its ban on conjugal relations, and its complete dependence on outside recruitment for a continuing renewal of membership.

As recently as 1960, there were twenty-seven Shakers living in the
United States—fourteen at Sabbathday Lake, Maine; eleven at East
Canterbury, New Hampshire, and two at Hancock, Massachusetts. When
the number has dwindled to five, according to an old prediction, the
Shaker movement will revive.

There are few remaining vestiges of the old Cleveland colony among
the elegant tree-shaded boulevards and the sumptuous neighborhoods
of Shaker Heights today. Two stone gateposts still stand at the southwest corner of Lee Road and Shaker Boulevard, and there are two
tiny cemeteries, as well as another burial ground in the yard of a
private residence. But by far the most important existing remainder of
the Shakers is a trio of ponds, the shimmering Shaker Lakes, around
which are grouped some of the choicest properties in this choicest of
suburbs. The lakes were created by the Shakers with the dams which

they built for their grist mills. Some Shakerites with a proper sense of history, members of the Shaker Historical Society, have succeeded in recent years in assembling an impressive collection of clothing, furniture, utensils, and other valuable relics of the ill-fated colony. They are on display in a makeshift museum housed in Moreland School at Van Aken Boulevard and Lee Road.

Sister Mildred Barker, co-trustee of the Shaker Colony at Sabbathday Lake, Maine, visited the museum several years ago and displayed the unfaltering confidence of the religious society when she told the Shaker Historical Society's members that the experiments in Cleveland and elsewhere had not been failures.

"Shakerism is no failure," she said. "It is good, and therefore of God, and no good is ever a failure. The principles and ideals which the Shakers were first to expound have gone out into the world and, like a pebble dropped into the water, we cannot measure the distance of the influence they have borne.

"First in so many things we now take for granted—sex equality, religious tolerance, and so forth—Shakerism is not dying out, nor is it a failure."

XVI

The Vans . . . *Veni, Vidi, Vici*

THE last sad withdrawal of the surviving Shakers from the village they had created in Warrensville Township on Cleveland's eastern flank left behind a ghost town. The fields that once had been tended so carefully and the buildings that had been kept in scrupulous repair told a story of abandonment. Weeds grew in the old furrows, gaunt scrub trees trespassed everywhere, and wooden shingles flapped loose in the wind.

The stage was set for two of the most remarkable men in the history of American business and finance, blood brothers, to make their appearance, play their parts, and give the dramatic story of the Shaker Utopia a happy ending.

How well they succeeded can be deduced from this: In 1930, James W. Gerard, former United States ambassador to Germany, made public a list of the sixty-four men who, in his opinion, "ruled America." These were men whose positions, according to Ambassador Gerard, gave them "a permanent influence in American life," and who were "too busy to hold political office, but determine who shall hold such office." The names of the two brothers, Oris Paxton Van Sweringen and Mantis James Van Sweringen, were on that list.

The Van Sweringens had an act that left almost everybody—especially the bankers—gasping in honest astonishment, adulterated by admiration and envy. Their specialty was building corporate pyramids which were held together by holding companies and interlocking directorates. At each new level they would reach out, pluck fresh money from the benign clouds, and begin building anew.

Everybody applauded, but few understood. Still, one need not understand in order to appreciate artistry. It is enough, sometimes, simply to have the privilege of seeing it.

Of all the men and women to walk the Cleveland scene over the past 170 years, O. P. and M. J. Van Sweringen did more to alter the face of the city than any other private citizens, individually or in combination. They left a deep imprint that shows no signs of eroding. They were the builders of modern Cleveland.

Their only competitors were two public officials—both mayors—Tom L. Johnson, a contemporary of the Vans in their beginning years, and Anthony J. Celebrezze, a more recent influence, who left Cleveland City Hall to become Secretary of Health, Education, and Welfare in the cabinets of Presidents John F. Kennedy and Lyndon B. Johnson.

Tom Johnson's administration conceived and promoted the so-called Group Plan of buildings which eliminated the city's worst tenderloin from Ontario to East 6th Street, between the high lakefront bluff and Superior Avenue to the south, substituting for the ramshackle buildings, saloons, and houses of prostitution a noble group of public buildings that maintained a uniformity of height and architecture. They included the Federal Building, the Cleveland Public Library, the Board of Education, the Federal Reserve Building, the old *Plain Dealer* Building (now a branch of the Public Library), the County Courthouse, the City Hall, and the Public Auditorium.

During Mayor Celebrezze's record-setting five terms in office, 1953 to 1962, the city embarked on its Erieview urban renewal program which, in a sense, takes up where Tom Johnson left off. It begins at East 6th Street and is moving eastward toward East 17th Street in a slow-moving, but continuing, program of demolition and rebuilding.

Strangely enough, it was the Van Sweringens who jumped the traces and frustrated Tom L.'s grand design. In doing so, they shifted the entire pattern and balance of Cleveland's downtown area.

The Van Sweringen brothers were the creators of Shaker Heights. It was their supreme adventure as real estate men who had started out with the modest American ambition to get rich. But their adventure led them down some strange side paths and eventually onward to a glory, wealth, and achievement of which they had never dared to dream.

They ventured into the risky field of real estate speculation at the turn of the century, totally unqualified by background or experience for its perilous paths. They chose as their area of operation the wide-open forested sweep of Cleveland's immediate suburb to the west, Lakewood, and they were promptly clobbered. They had made a down payment on a number of lots on what is now Cook Avenue, but they were not able to sell the properties as easily as they had expected and they soon were hurting for cash. A foreclosure was entered against them, and during the next two years that the judgment prevailed, they were forced to do business under the names of their sisters.

Eventually they were able to settle the Lakewood debt and to resume operations in their own name—but not the same name. They had begun business in Lakewood under the names they had used since birth, O. P. and M. J. Sweringen. Ever after, they identified themselves as the Van Sweringens, reviving the "Van" prefix which had been dropped during the family's Americanization.

Undiscouraged by their Lakewood experience, they shifted operations to the opposite side of the city; to North Park Boulevard in Cleveland Heights, a promising thoroughfare featuring mostly vacant lots, a handsome vista, and a name suggestive of the kind of affluence to come. The Vans subdivided their property into large lots and set their sights for the carriage trade. Their project was an immediate and profitable success, and they turned their eyes to another likely avenue, Fairmount Boulevard, whose chief drawback was its distance from the end of the street railway system.

The Vans persuaded John J. Stanley, president of the Cleveland Railway Company, to extend his car tracks and service to their new subdivision, and that guaranteed their second success, teaching them the value of good public transportation and implementing their wealth so considerably that they were able to act on a dream that had been disturbing their peace of mind for some time.

It had to do with the desolate, moldering ruins of North Union and the overgrown fields of the old Shaker colony.

The Van Sweringens, like the Shakers, were people with vision. They saw beyond the distressing facts of reality to that which was attainable. In 1905, they took options on the first parcels of land in the Valley of God's Pleasure and set about the job of creating the largest and wealthiest real estate subdivision in the United States.

A project of the magnitude they had proposed could hardly be undertaken in privacy; Cleveland's awareness of the Van Sweringens was aroused for the first time.

They were not a prepossessing pair. Neither was an extrovert. Neither was physically impressive. O.P. was the dominant personality and, in build, almost portly. He was the idea man and the spinner of dreams. M.J. was shorter, slimmer, quicker in speech and movement even to the point of appearing restless. He was the practical builder.

Fortune magazine, analyzing the brothers in 1934 when their fortunes were sagging dangerously, said: "The Van Sweringen brothers are conveniently regarded by the business world as one man. And with some reason. For no two men of their prominence have ever so successfully merged their identities. If they had been joined like Siamese twins they could scarcely be any closer . . ."

They were of Dutch ancestry; descendants of Gerret Van Sweringen, the son of a noble family, who left Beemsterdam, Holland, to settle in the New World at what is now New Castle, Delaware, in 1657.

Their father was James Tower Sweringen, who had been wounded in the Battle of Spottsylvania while a Union soldier. After the war he had devoted himself to the pursuit of a fortune that continually eluded him. He came close once in the oil fields of his native Pennsylvania;

close enough to smell the oil that gushed out of the Drake well near Titusville, but not the money.

The meandering course of the Sweringen family took its members eventually to the rolling farmland country of east-central Ohio. There, not far from Wooster, they were given hospitable lodging on the Paxton Downing farm, and it is there that Oris Paxton Sweringen was born on April 24, 1879. His middle name is testimony to the gratitude of his parents toward their friendly hosts.

In a later move, the family settled south of Wooster in a crossroads settlement with the highly picturesque name of Rogue's Hollow. It was the birthplace on July 8, 1881, of Mantis James Sweringen—as his critics delighted to point out in later years.

It was in 1886 that the Sweringen family moved to Cleveland and decided on it as their lifetime home. Besides the parents and O.P. and M.J., there was another boy, Herbert, who was the oldest, and two sisters, Edith and Carrie. The boys attended Bolton and Fairmount Schools, ending their formal education with the eighth grade. Upon graduation, in 1896, they experimented briefly with a bicycle repair shop on East 6th Street before turning to the real estate business and beginning their lifetime career.

The 1366 acres of land that the Shakers had sold to the Buffalo syndicate in 1889 for $316,000 cost the Van Sweringens in excess of $1,000,000 in 1906; not an unreasonable appreciation in the value of the acreage, considering the substantial growth of the central city during the intervening seventeen years. It was, nonetheless, testimony to the supreme confidence and strong nerves of the two young men, still in their twenties, that they were willing to risk such a large sum of money on a purely speculative real estate development idea. Even more remarkable, perhaps, was the willingness of the members of their syndicate to gamble on the business judgment of the two relatively inexperienced brothers. Among the investors were two prominent bankers, J. R. Nutt and Charles Bradley, and two dealers in securities, Warren S. Hayden and Otto Miller.

The lesson that the Vans had learned in Lakewood and in Cleveland Heights was put to use in the planning of the new subdivision. They had lost their shirts in Lakewood trying to sell lots in a middle-income neighborhood, but they had prospered selling streets of expensive homes in Cleveland Heights.

The basic plan for the new development—which they called Shaker Village from the very beginning—called for it to appeal directly to people of means. The idea, simply, was to build a terribly expensive, terribly exclusive, terribly desirable suburb.

The physical concept of Shaker Village did honor to the imagination and good taste of the Van Sweringens and their architects. Instead of the humdrum grid plan of street layout such as Seth Pease and his surveying associates had imposed upon Cleveland in the beginning, the Shaker design envisioned elliptical boulevards, broad, parklike residential avenues; beautiful homes set back deeply and fronted by the green sweep of lawns and trees.

The building code was strict and far-reaching. Commercial establishments were segregated in central areas of shopping, business, and entertainment, and their architecture was uniformly Georgian colonial. The Van Sweringens reserved a veto power over all architectural plans and they had the right to pass on the desirability even of the prospective home buyers (an authority, incidentally, which died with their passing). No two homes could be exactly alike, and it was required that each house had to cost a minimum of $17,500, but builders were not allowed to spend more than $500,000 on a single residence.

To have a fair understanding of this proviso, the minimum cost should be translated into the value of today's market. One expert equates that minimum of $17,500 a half-century ago with $70,000 in 1966 dollars.

The 6½-mile subdivision was incorporated as Shaker Village on October 27, 1911, with the completion of the first-stage landscaping and the paving of the key streets. The tax assessed value of the development was set at $2,525,800. Lots were offered to buyers at $25 a running foot.

Sales were weak at the outset; just a dribble, even though interest in the development among moneyed people was high. The Van Sweringens knew the reason for the hesitation. It was not the restrictive rules that applied, nor was it the high cost of building in Shaker. The flaw in the Shaker plan was the lack of public transportation to link the suburb with downtown Cleveland. The same problem had been overcome by the Vans in Cleveland Heights with the cooperation of the Cleveland Railway Company, but its President Stanley was not at all agreeable to an extension of service to Shaker Village. He had been the loser in the Cleveland Heights transaction with the Vans.

"Such extensions," said the wiser Stanley, "are bleeders instead of feeders." He added that he would not run a Cleveland Railway extension to Shaker Village if the Van Sweringens gave him such a line as a gift.

In casting about for a solution, O. P. Van Sweringen was attracted by the compelling fact that a natural ravine, Kingsbury Run, coursed its way from downtown Cleveland directly over the six-mile route to the Shaker development. He saw it as an ideal bed for a rapid transit line that would whisk Shakerites from their neighborhoods to their downtown offices in an estimated ten minutes. He recognized the development of such a fast commuter system as the key to the success or failure of the costly real estate venture. The two brothers decided to go for broke by building the rapid transit line themselves. They would not have dared to invade the tangled, technical jungle of urban transportation if they had had the pessimistic inside knowledge of the experts. But, knowing virtually nothing about the transit business, they simply went ahead with a plan to do what nobody else had the courage to do. In their case, of course, the moving force was not so much raw courage as it was necessity. They did what had to be done; it was that or surrender their dreams and their investment.

The brothers organized the Cleveland & Youngstown Railroad Company and set about the task of acquiring the needed right-of-way. The purchase of a route through the Kingsbury ravine proceeded smoothly at first. They quickly acquired a route that took their proposed line two-thirds of the distance downtown before they ran into a snag presented by the Nickel Plate Railroad, which owned the final two miles of the right-of-way leading into the downtown area.

The Nickel Plate at that time was owned by the New York Central System, and its executives balked at any agreement with the Van Sweringens to permit the use of its route by their rapid transit line. But, coincidentally, the Interstate Commerce Commission issued a ruling at that time directing the New York Central to divest itself of its Nickel Plate holdings.

The corporate name of the Nickel Plate was the New York, Chicago & St. Louis Railroad Company, but when it was bought by old Commodore Vanderbilt he thought its price was so excessive that he said it might as well have been nickel-plated. The colorful name stuck until recent years, when the line lost its identity in its merger with the Norfolk & Western Railway.

Mayor Newton D. Baker didn't think much of the Nickel Plate at the time the Vans were warily circling about, trying to decide what to do about the line. He tartly described the 539-mile railroad as "a streak of rust; a toy railroad that runs its trains just often enough to make it dangerous."

The price tag on the Nickel Plate was $8,500,000. It was patently an absurd idea for the brothers, already deep in debt, to consider the purchase of a railroad. Everything they owned was in hock, and it seemed as if they had reached the outer edge of their borrowing power. Somehow, though, they were able to arrange the financing with a down payment of $2,000,000 that included $525,000 of their own money. The balance was to be paid in ten promissory notes of $650,000 each, the first payable in five years and the remainder at one-year intervals thereafter.

To raise the down payment, they sold preferred stock in the Nickel Plate Securities Corporation, which they organized for this financing purpose. The fact is worth noting because it represented the beginning of the complicated financial structure which bewildered most of the nation's economic experts following their death.

Of immediate and primary importance to the Van Sweringens and the people of Shaker Village was that the railroad purchase cleared the right-of-way to permit the rapid transit line to proceed all the way downtown.

Construction of the high-speed commuter service began in 1916 and took four years to complete. In its initial phase, the system followed Kingsbury Run to East 30th Street, which it took to Superior Avenue, turning eastward to Public Square. The strategy of running down East 30th Street was that it took the cars through the Negro neighborhoods expected to supply maids for the Shaker families. This route was followed by one in which the Shaker trains surfaced at East 34th Street, turned onto Broadway, north on East 9th Street to Superior, then left to Public Square.

It was a cumbersome, dragging route for what was otherwise a swift-moving service. Once it left its railroad right-of-way and clear ravine route to tangle with the vehicular and pedestrian traffic that cluttered Cleveland's downtown streets, the transit system lost its claim to the word "rapid." Trains that had rocketed from Shaker to East 34th Street decelerated so suddenly at that point as to send the passengers spilling. It was a disappointing climax to the downtown trip.

With the Nickel Plate right-of-way available, the Shaker cars were able to maintain a high-speed route all the way to the heart of the city. This involved a downtown terminal, not only for the rapid transit system, but also for the Nickel Plate Road. The problem took the Van Sweringens into another controversial area. It immersed them in a civic dispute with far-reaching implications for the future development of the city itself and certainly of lasting importance to the Van Sweringens.

Cleveland at that time was in a highly emotional frame of mind about the condition and location of its railroad terminal facilities. One of the city's outstanding eyesores was the soot-covered, antebellum stone monstrosity that was known as the Union Depot. It squatted at the foot of the lakefront bluff, near West 9th Street, in a desolate setting; such an unpretty sight, indeed, that an irate Cleveland outdoor advertising executive, Charles Bryan, had erected a big billboard on the hillside. It proclaimed to all the passengers on the New York Central and Pennsylvania trains that stopped there, or passed through there, this heartfelt plea:

"DON'T JUDGE THIS TOWN BY THIS DEPOT."

There were other railroad stations, some even smaller and meaner in appearance, but they were clustered in the Cuyahoga Valley, just below the southwest corner of Public Square. They were the shabby depots of the Nickel Plate, the Baltimore & Ohio road, the Erie Railroad, and the Wheeling & Lake Erie.

The famous Group Plan devised and adopted during the administration of Mayor Tom L. Johnson had envisioned a grand new railroad terminal at the north end of the new Mall. It was to have drawn together all the railroads into a single, central station which would be, physically, the centerpiece in the whole complex of civic buildings flanking the Mall.

The site of the new railroad depot had been a long-standing civic issue. There were so many ramifications involved in any plan to consolidate the train service under a single roof, including the physical difficulties of bringing the major lines together at any one point and the lobbying of the mercantile interests for a location which would be most favorable to their own enterprises, that an agreement at times seemed almost beyond hope of realization.

Nevertheless, it appeared in 1915 that the administration of Newton D. Baker had wrought the miracle. Representatives of the New York Central, the Pennsylvania, and the Big Four railroads agreed to the lakefront site. The city immediately submitted to the voters the plan for a $16 million Union Station to be built at the north end of the Mall. The way they cast their ballots left no doubt how they felt about the project; they approved it by an overwhelming 6–1 vote. But before this election victory could be translated into a tangible result, World War I intervened, halting all projects but those deemed to be immediately essential to the war effort.

The Union Terminal was shelved until peacetime, when a new, compelling factor was introduced into the railroad terminal issue—the interests of the Van Sweringen brothers. From their standpoint, dictated by the location of the Nickel Plate tracks, the most logical place for a terminal would be at the southwest corner of the Public Square, even though the prevailing trend of downtown business had been steadily eastward, out Euclid Avenue; away from Public Square. Moses Cleaveland's old cow meadow was in danger of returning to that original, primitive use if the trend continued. The Van Sweringens certainly did not want their slickly dressed, briefcase-swinging Shakerites debarking from the rapid transit in the middle of an area that had been passed by progress. They reasoned that a new Union Terminal near the southwest quadrant of the Square would halt the eastward ho! movement, renew the heart of the city, and provide it with a secure anchor.

The Vans campaigned vigorously. Their most vigorous and outspoken foes were the representatives of the Pennsylvania Railroad, whose tracks ran directly past the Mall site, the representatives of the Euclid Avenue merchants who felt a Public Square station would dislocate established

shopping patterns, and some of the loyal, articulate followers of Tom
L. Johnson, original supporter of the lakefront terminal site. The most
vocal of the former Johnson lieutenants was Peter Witt, who would
have succeeded Newton D. Baker as mayor of Cleveland but for an
election system fluke which threw the city hall post to a charming but
inept man named Harry L. Davis.

Again there was a public referendum, but this time the public, en-
chanted by the realization that a depot on the Van Sweringen site
would clean out one of the seediest districts in the downtown area and,
more important, provide a lot of jobs sorely needed, voted in favor of
the Public Square site for the new Union Terminal. The year was 1919.

The Pennsylvania Railroad withdrew its support of a central depot
and announced its decision to continue using the ancient Union Station.
The New York Central, on the other hand, was bewitched by the
ratiocination of the Vans and agreed to use the new terminal, even
though it meant a major resettlement of its downtown trackage and
the construction of a costly new viaduct to carry its trains over the
Cuyahoga Valley and into the new terminal.

Not until the modern-day Erieview Urban Renewal Program came
along has Cleveland known the like of the transformation wrought in
its downtown area by the Van Sweringen brothers. The site purchased,
covering thirty-five acres, was an incredibly corrupt, squalid district;
a rundown rookery that perpetuated poverty and bred a high percentage of the city's crime. It fronted on the Public Square and fell
away to the westward, slumping down the hill toward the river. There
were, on those thirty-five acres, some twenty-two hundred separate
buildings which somehow managed to house a population of more than
fifteen thousand persons.

By 1920, the task of clearing the terminal site was under way,
and the air of the downtown area was filled with the dust of the
falling walls. Unfortunately, some of the city's most historic buildings
were destroyed along with the tumbledown shacks and eyesores. The
old American House on Superior Avenue and the Forest City House on
the Square fell, as did the Central Police Station on Champlain Street,
the Diebolt Brewery and the Gehring Brewery, the Palisade Hotel,
the main building of the Ohio Bell Telephone Company, and Stein's
Cafe. Even the streets, like Champlain, Hill, Columbus, and Diebolt's
Alley (famed for its many restaurants) disappeared. Portions of three
old cemeteries were purchased and the bodies removed to different
burial grounds.

What had started out as the construction of a new Union Terminal
became infinitely more complex as the fertile minds of the Van Sweringens became completely caught up in dreams of a more ambitious
development. They probably were encouraged to lift their sights by the

fact that their other major projects were working out wonderfully well. They had hired John J. Bernet away from the New York Central Railroad to run the Nickel Plate Road and he was doing a superb job. Under his management, the road's gross income increased nearly 130 per cent and the net profit after charges rose from $909,000 to more than $2,000,000. The rapid transit line, which began serving Shaker Village in 1920, was doing for the real estate development exactly what the Vans had hoped it would do—it was drawing buyers at a phenomenal rate.

From 1919 to 1929, Shaker Village added, on the average, 300 new, expensive homes each year. In one year alone, 1925, permits were issued for 556 new homes to cost an estimated $9,128,530. The population of the suburb increased from 1700 to 15,500 in that decade of growth, and the valuation of the property which had been purchased by the Van Sweringens for slightly more than $1,000,000 soared up to $80,000,000.

On the site of the old Forest City House, the Vans constructed the new $8,000,000 Cleveland Hotel (now the Sheraton-Cleveland). On the other side of the terminal a-building, they designed and built another $8,000,000 wing to house a department store—and then bought the old Higbee Company to assure a suitable tenant for the new store. A new street on stilts was built to the south of the department store and terminal, and on it the Vans constructed two new skyscrapers, the Medical Arts Building and the Republic Building.

The keystone structure in this complex, of course, was the terminal building. It originally was planned as a 25-story building, but in the flush of prosperity and the intoxicating thrill of building that only another builder could understand, the Vans changed their design to more impressive dimensions, electing to build a 52-story, 708-foot-high building that was the wonder of the entire Midwest.

The Van Sweringen-built complex that rose on that southwestern corner of downtown Cleveland was the immense kind of project that logically could have been expected of the Rockefeller family and it was, in fact, a kind of Cleveland counterpart of New York's Rockefeller Center which followed it. If the Van Sweringens were out to build a memorial to themselves that could not be ignored, they succeeded as no other men in the city's long history. Their project took eleven years to complete, dating from the time of the election approving the site of the Union Terminal in 1919. Acquiring the 35-acre site and clearing the land took several years. Actual construction began in 1923 and was finished in 1930. Estimated cost: $200,000,000.

Somehow, during this period of feverish expansion and construction, the Van Sweringens became so deeply involved in the railroad business as to become a major force in the industry nationally. Everything they did seemed to draw them inextricably closer and ever faster into a whirlpool of destiny. To make Shaker Village succeed, they built a rapid transit line. To make the rapid transit successful, they bought a railroad and built a Union Terminal. To make the railroad successful, they bought other railroads. Into their ownership, one by one, came such rail holdings as the Chesapeake & Ohio, the Erie, Wheeling & Lake Erie, Pere Marquette, Chicago & Eastern Illinois, and, finally, the Missouri Pacific.

The holding-company structure of the Van Sweringen empire was so elaborate that the precise extent of their holdings still is difficult to ascertain, but it has been estimated that the Vans, at their peak, owned 231 companies with assets of four billion dollars. Among these properties were twenty-four railroads with twenty-seven thousand miles of track and numerous real estate, traction, coal, and other allied companies.

Almost as interesting as their fantastic rise to economic power were the two brothers themselves. They have been described as "men of mystery," and they were, but only in the sense that they were not easily identifiable with familiar American business types. They were modest almost to the point of shyness. They shunned publicity. They avoided society. And they clung tightly to each other.

A Cleveland newspaperman who was hired by the Vans as a public relations man recalled that after he had been on the job for three months—a period of dead calm—he was called into O.P.'s office.

He fully expected a dressing down; perhaps worse. And O.P. began on an ominous note.

"You've been working as our public relations man now for three months," said O.P., weighing his words carefully, "and there has not been a single story about us in the newspapers."

"Well, sir," began the press agent, "you see . . ."

"Splendid work," said O.P. heartily. "Keep it up!"

The Vans lived almost entirely for the pleasure of each other's company and for the fun they got out of their business manipulations—especially their first love, real estate.

They owned a magnificent English Tudor home in Shaker Heights at 17400 South Park Boulevard which they turned over to their two unmarried sisters, Edith and Carrie; they had sumptuous living quarters in the famed Greenbrier Suite on the thirty-sixth floor of the Terminal Tower, where they had their offices, and they had three luxurious private railway cars fitted out for living and for business. Their favorite residence, though, was Daisy Hill in the rolling countryside of Hunting Valley, fifteen miles east of Cleveland, beyond Shaker Heights.

Daisy Hill was a 660-acre consolidation of four farms with a lot of natural beauty, but a sorry record of productivity. It won its name honestly. When the Vans were looking over the property an agricultural expert told them, "It'll never grow anything but daisies!" The Vans wanted the land nevertheless, mainly because it was adjacent to the farm home of their best friends, Ben and Louise Jenks.

If the brothers ever had a hobby outside of their business dealings, it must have been the blooded dairy herd they maintained on the farm until the middle of the 1920s. And if these shy brothers had a favorite person, it probably was the little daughter of the Jenks, Josephine. She called them "Uncle," and they watched over her like doting relatives as she grew up, even to the extent of visiting her when she went away to attend Smith College.

The picture of the sedate, retiring Van Sweringens is almost shattered by the story that Josephine and her classmates used to ride on the running board of the Van Sweringen automobile as they drove through town on those visits. This collegiate informality must have pleased the brothers because they entered into the youthful spirit of things by naming their heifer calves after Josephine and her classmates. And when those calves—Catherine, Helen, Dariel, Janet, Annette, and Beth —were old enough to have calves of their own, each blessed event moved the Vans to send a telegram bearing the happy news to the girl after whom the cow had been named.

The Vans eventually decided to make Daisy Hill their home as well as hobby. They got rid of the dairy herd and instructed Architect Philip Small to go all out in his design of a home for them by making over the barn. It was a massive structure, but what evolved during the seven years that the Vans and their architect worked on their project was even more formidable. The cost of developing their country estate to the level of baronial grandeur eventually achieved has been estimated as high as three million dollars, but the cost apparently was of no great importance. In developing their estate, the Vans were doing something that they liked, and in dragging the project out over a seven-year period they were savoring the delights of the enterprise in the same slow, deliberate way that a gourmet passes a snifter of brandy under his quivering nostrils.

The property included stable buildings, developed at a cost of five hundred thousand dollars, of stone and frame construction with model box stalls for nineteen horses, four living suites, a carpenter shop, a machine shop, and twenty-two garages; a nursery, a greenhouse, and a man-made lake. The barn was converted into a massive and imposing mansion of red brick with a slate roof and a portico with spindle columns. The old silos became decorative towers, lending the building the look of a Norman castle, but the interior was warm and homey with its great beams and early American styling. It was furnished tastefully and expensively. When the furnishings were sold at a four-day

auction sale in 1938 by the Parke-Bernet Galleries, a 220-page catalogue
was needed to list and describe the 1250 items offered.

Typically enough, with all the living space open to them in this vast
residence, the Vans insisted on sharing the same bedroom, in which all
the furniture was duplicated so that each brother had his own bed, his
own dresser, his own chair, and so on.

According to legend, O.P. one morning paused in front of M.J.'s
dresser to check his appearance in his brother's mirror.

"You have your own mirror, you know," M.J. said archly, proving
that even between these "Siamese" brothers there could be moments of
minor friction and petty jealousies. O.P., the outgoing brother of the
two, loved to tell friends of the mirror incident.

"M.J. is so tight," he would say, "he won't even let me get my reflection from his mirror!"

Their home was as elegant and lavish as any house owned by the
elect of Cleveland society, but it never played any role in social capers
of the era because the Vans were removed from society. They had no
interest in society except as a group which furnished the best customers
for Shaker Village—whose name, incidentally, was changed to Shaker
Heights upon its incorporation as a city in 1930. They belonged to the
right clubs, the Union Club, Shaker Heights Country Club, Pepper
Pike Country Club, but they did not participate actively in them.
Neither played golf nor followed any regime of physical exercise, except
for a brief period when M.J. took a mild interest in horseback riding.
If O.P. was the dominant personality, M.J. apparently was the more
venturesome of the two brothers. He took up smoking until O.P. indicated his displeasure, causing him to drop the habit. M.J. once went
for an airplane ride with David Ingalls, a Hunting Valley neighbor
and onetime Assistant Secretary of the Navy, but this adventure
made O.P. so nervous his brother never made a second flight.

When asked by an interviewer once to name his favorite authors,
O.P. is said to have replied: "Rand and McNally."

It probably was an honest attempt to provide an answer rather than
to be witty. The brothers *did* like to look at maps, as all real estate
men do, and wasn't it a map that had showed them the route for their
Shaker rapid transit?

They made a halfhearted concession to culture, however, in one of
the rooms of their mansion called the "Dickens Room." It contained a
valuable library of Charles Dickens' works, including many first or
limited editions. Also featured in the room were the elm and yew desk
chair once used by Dickens, and a square turned-leg oak stool with a
caned top which came from Dickens' furnishings. The desk chair had on
its back a metal tablet with the inscription: "This is the original editorial
chair used by Charles Dickens when he was editor of the London Daily

News, 1846." But so far as their friends knew, neither of the Van Sweringens went beyond this honorary recognition of the English author in their pursuit of literary knowledge. They would sit on Dickens' chair, but it never occurred to them to take time to read his books. O.P. sometimes would read a paperback Western story, and once in a while the brothers would go to the little motion picture house in Chagrin Falls, but business was their recreation.

They tried to interest themselves in the normal *divertissements* of the world about them, but with little success. Their minds insisted on wandering back to the real fun things of life, as illustrated by the time they were persuaded by Horton Hampton, vice president of their Nickel Plate Railroad, to ride to Columbus, Ohio, in a special car and take in a Big Ten football game between Ohio State and the University of Iowa.

Hampton, an alumnus of O.S.U., and M.J. took a keen interest in the hotly fought game, but O.P. looked upon the gridiron goings on with a cool, detached attitude. He seemed to be analyzing the play and determining the strategy while the others were being carried away emotionally.

But O.P. spoiled the illusion he had wrought when, at the most critical point in the game, he leaned in front of his brother to say to the Nickel Plate executive:

"Horton," he said, "do you have any idea how many cubic yards of concrete were used in this stadium?"

"Oh, O.P.!" exclaimed M.J., groaning audibly.

O.P. was the taller and heavier of the two brothers. He was self-assured and, by far, the more articulate. When he spoke, he spoke for his brother as well as himself. That's the way it seemed to be with them from the beginning. When they were youngsters, they themselves would relate; M.J. made the snowballs, but O.P. threw them.

There were other differences. O.P. was dark-complexioned, physically slow, creative. M.J. had a light complexion, high blood pressure, and was the quick, alert type. He had a protective attitude toward O.P., even though he was younger.

They complemented each other as if by design, and there never was a woman who could lure one away from the other, although they were wonderfully inviting targets with all their wealth and influence. When they entered a drawing room at an occasional social function the fluttering of eyelashes flattened the hair on sheep dogs pacing in the rear pasture and made the heavy drapes fill out and billow. The Vans didn't seem to notice. All they needed, apparently, was each other. Throughout their adult lives they even used a common bank account, thereby carrying togetherness to its ultimate.

One morning in 1929 as they were tooling along through the beautiful

Hunting Valley countryside on their way to downtown Cleveland, they began to tot up their worldly wealth and they were astonished to conclude that they were worth one hundred million dollars.

This sober realization of their wealth made the brothers debate seriously the possibility of retiring, but they quickly shook off the notion for several reasons. One was that they were too young—O.P. was only fifty and M.J. was but forty-eight; another was that their lives held very little of interest to them outside of their financial wheeling and dealing.

Life, furthermore, never looked brighter or more promising than it did to these remarkable brothers in the sunlight of that morning in 1929. They were well on their way toward their dream of a railroad system which would rival the existing giants—the Pennsylvania, the New York Central, and the Baltimore & Ohio. They had won control of the Cleveland Railway Company and now owned a monopoly on the metropolitan area's street railways. Their towering Union Terminal project was in its final stages and would be ready for its dedication in 1930. Shaker Heights was booming. Its population had rocketed from 1700 in 1919 to 15,500 in 1929. Their country estates development covering four thousand acres in Hunting Valley was well under way and had shot upward to an estimated value of ten million dollars.

Even the rosiest of retirement schemes paled when laid next to the splendid vista that greeted the eyes of the Van Sweringens everywhere they looked in that grand year of 1929. Indeed, what they had achieved already was drawing the applause of the onlooking world. National publications devoted pages of space to the remarkable Shaker Heights experiment and the forward thrust of Cleveland due to the impetus of the building brothers. An English newspaper tycoon, Lord Rothermere, came to Cleveland to see for himself what the Vans had done, and his lordship was deeply impressed by the splendor of Shaker.

"You have developed the finest residential district in the world," he said, fumbling excitedly for his monocle.

Even while the old, loyal followers of Tom L. Johnson and the spokesmen of the upper Euclid Avenue merchants were condemning the placement of the Union Terminal and its satellite buildings on their Public Square site, other onlookers were sounding the praises of the Van Sweringen project and calling the location they had chosen "inspired."

One national publication, *World's Work* magazine, said in print what a lot of Clevelanders were saying privately; that the changes wrought by the Vans marked "the transition of the city from an overgrown country town to a real metropolis."

It is indisputable that Cleveland had taken on the look of a big city for the first time, thanks to the Vans. It had a skyline now that was the most impressive of any city in the United States, outside of New York and Chicago, and the new silhouette seemed to impart a fresh civic confidence that was almost offensive in its chestiness.

When the time came on June 28, 1929, for the formal dedication dinner and ceremonies to mark the opening of the newest palace of the railroad industry, all the celebrities of the business gathered in Cleveland to celebrate the great occasion. And joining with them were notables from other fields. They came streaming into Cleveland by rail —governors, senators, cabinet members, financiers, and entertainers. It was the most glittering of all gala occasions. The graceful Gothic tower of the Terminal stood high in the sky, clean and proud, a diadem of red lights near its peak, bright floodlights giving it a startling white look from the thirtieth floor to the fifty-second, while at the top, powerful searchlights reached out and probed the horizon. Some enthusiasts, carried away, declared the next day that the tower's lights could be sighted from the Canadian shore, fifty-five miles away on the other side of Lake Erie.

It was, truly, a night to rejoice, and everybody did—everybody, that is, except the Van Sweringens. If they did any rejoicing, it was done quietly and privately because they didn't even show up for the great dedication or dinner. They stayed home that night and enjoyed a sedate dinner in the subdued light of their richly paneled, tapestried dining room at Daisy Hill, just as if it were an ordinary night of the week. The Vans already had had their fun in the planning and the building of the great terminal. The ceremonial rituals attendant to the dedication were a kind of painful public denouement; precisely the sort of thing better ignored by shy men. They, furthermore, had little time to stand around crowing over past accomplishments when there were larger, grander dreams; challenges still to be met—the unification of their railroad properties into a new national system that would challenge the New York Central and the Pennsylvania railroads . . . the extension of the Shaker rapid transit into a citywide, metropolitan rapid transit that would give Greater Cleveland the most modern and the fastest public transportation in the United States.

The stock market crash shivered the nation four months after the dedication of the Union Terminal, and the Great Depression, greater and deeper than any depression the nation ever has known, swept in with a silent roar; like the sound that fills the ears of a drowning man. There were wise men who said later they could see the terrible time coming, and they ticked off the signs and portents that had spelled disaster until it seemed inconceivable that anyone could have failed to know that panic and depression were on their way. But great financiers are not men who waste their time peering cautiously around the corners of time

or worriedly scanning the stars for clues to the future; they ride to glory
and wealth on the wings of courage, losing the timid far behind them.

That's how it was with the Van Sweringens. They were way out
in front and high above the crowd, atop a financial pyramid that was
as much of a marvel, in its own way, as the great pyramids of the
Egyptians. The pity was that the mortar holding the bricks together
had not had time to solidify. The Vans desperately needed time, and
a favorable economic climate, to save their empire.

Their main source of revenue, the mighty group of railroads they
had acquired in a series of overlapping loans and stock issues, fell off
abruptly. Gross revenue skidded from $503 million to $293 million.
Their Shaker Heights real estate sales, which had brought them $5,600,-
000 in 1926, dropped to $65,000 in 1933. In that same year of 1933, two
Cleveland banks which had been closed during the "bank holiday" failed
to reopen. It was reported that the two (the Guardian Bank and the
Union Trust Company) carried on their books loans of almost $14 mil-
lion owed by the Van Sweringen interests and approximately the same
amount owed by interests controlled by Cyrus Eaton.

Shortly after the crash in 1930, the Vans had turned to J. P. Morgan
for financial help, and his house had loaned them $40 million. By
May 1935, it was clear that the Van Sweringen companies were unable
to meet the obligations that matured at that time. The principal and
interest amounted to more than $50 million. The Vans, altogether, were
in the financial hole to the tune of $73 million.

Most of the collateral put up by the Vans as security for their Morgan
loan was purchased by the Mid America Corporation, which was
hastily organized by George Ashley Tomlinson, a colorful Cleveland
lake shipping executive, and George Alexander Ball of Muncie, Indiana, a relative of Mrs. Tomlinson. They purchased for the sum of
$3,121,000 the control of some $3 billion in assets; a group of enterprises employing more than 100,000 persons. And the first thing they did
was to hire the Van Sweringens to operate these, their former properties.

The Morgan "auction" took place at the end of September 1935,
but only one of the Van Sweringens was present—O.P. His brother,
M.J., was in Cleveland, desperately ill and fighting what turned out
to be his last big fight. His high blood pressure condition had worsened
under the events of the time until, in August, he had been forced into
a hospital for treatment. But an attack of influenza had complicated his
condition. He recovered sufficiently to leave the hospital, but not for
long. His condition deteriorated in mid-October and he returned to
Lakeside Hospital, where he died early in the morning of December
13. Those he loved were at his bedside—his brother, O.P., and Ben and
Louise Jenks.

Those who were close to him in those tragic days say that the death of Mantis James Van Sweringen in effect also ended the career of Oris Paxton Van Sweringen. The brothers had been so close that the death of one was the death of both. O.P. went through the everyday motions, but mechanically. He was a man in despair.

Every morning he would go into his brother's old office, adjacent to his, in the Terminal Tower and he would dutifully light the lamp on his brother's desk. Late in the afternoon, as he was leaving for the day, he would switch off M.J.'s lamp. It was a daily ritual.

The lavish home at Daisy Hill became nothing more than a storehouse of painful reminders, leading O.P. to tell a friend one day: "M.J. loved everything about this place. Right now, I wouldn't give you five cents for it."

He walked in mourning for less than a year. In the early hours of November 23, 1936, when O.P. presumably was asleep in a private car of a Nickel Plate train headed for New York, there was a minor accident to the train in the Scranton, Pennsylvania, yards. A switch engine taking a dining car from the train bumped the car in which O.P. was sleeping.

O.P. and two of his companions, William Wenneman, his secretary, and Herbert Fitzpatrick, vice president and counsel of the C. & O., were transferred to another private car furnished by the Lackawanna Railroad. By the time the switch was made and the train got under way again, it was around 8 A.M. The three travelers breakfasted and O.P., saying he was still sleepy, retired to his bedroom for a nap.

The train arrived in Hoboken, New Jersey, at noon. O.P.'s two friends went to awaken him, but they found him dead. It was officially concluded later that the shock of the minor train collision in the Scranton yards had been too much for O.P.'s heart, but some of O.P.'s friends dissented. They said his heart had stopped the previous December, and perhaps they were right. Everybody remembered what O.P. had said after his brother's death:

"I've always been able to see a way, but to this obstacle there is no answer."

The experts—some of them, anyway—are still wrangling over the Van Sweringens; still trying to decide the ethics of their empire and still trying to decide whether to applaud them or hiss them. The pros and cons in the argument by now are reasonably well defined, and much of the bitterness of the people who lost their life savings in the collapse of the Cleveland banks which presumably were weakened by the Van Sweringen loans has died away with the people themselves.

Even before the Vans died, when the Depression was still deepening and the outlook of their empire was as dark and dreary as the dust clouds filling the sky over the Kansas plains, *Fortune* magazine spoke appreciatively of the two brothers.

"They . . . pursued their visions in no plodding fashion," said *Fortune*. "They showed the world how two men starting with a purse of only $500,000 can get control of the largest railroad properties (in terms of mileage) in the U.S. They gave a superbly ingenious demonstration of the use of other people's money and of that corporate conjurer's wand known as the holding company . . .

"Small wonder they are often viewed as historical. . . . The fact is that, while you may condemn the laws, no one has ever been able to impugn the legality of the holding company as practiced by chez Van Sweringen. The brothers still enjoy the status of honest businessmen. . . . The Van Sweringens were as plausible and agreeable and grandiosely scheming as any of them (the big affable superpromoters who are popularly credited with having caused the depression). Yet they are still with us. And the reason is that there was a hard center of achievement in the ambitious fabric of their plans.

"They brought the Nickel Plate up from rust, and the Erie up from dust, and they jammed the Chesapeake & Ohio with rich cargoes of bituminous coal. These are the facts their critics have overlooked . . ."

And on the smaller, local scale, they created a capitalist heaven where a communist Utopia had failed, and they changed the face of a great city, leaving behind them a massive memorial in the concrete bulk of the buildings that form the Cleveland Union Terminal development.

XVII

I, Fred Kohler . . .

O NE of the stars of the Ziegfeld Follies in 1922 was Will Rogers, who was beginning to learn that the larynx can be mightier than the lariat. At any rate, he combined the two talents by roping some notable in the audience and then making his captive the subject of a humorous dissertation that sometimes was devastating.

The loop of his lariat one night sailed out over the audience and fell over the shoulders of the mayor of Cleveland, one Fred Kohler. The crowd applauded and craned for a look, hoping to recognize the celebrity. But this was not a familiar face to New Yorkers. They saw only a stiff-necked man, aging but still handsome, with an orderly profile and blond, wavy hair.

"Here's a fellow from Cleveland who used to be the chief of police out there," said Rogers, shifting his wad of gum. "He was the best chief in the United States, I heard. Then he got into a political squabble and lost his job and a while ago he started to come back, and now they've gone and elected him mayor of Cleveland."

The theater audience applauded.

"I'll say this for him," declared Rogers, "he was better off when he was chief. But you can take off your hats to a fellow who came right back and made 'em like him."

The political pot bubbled and boiled furiously in Cleveland during the early decades of the century, and much of the time Fred Kohler was up to his neck in the hot water; sometimes because of what he had done and sometimes because of what he was. The Prussian character-istics that had enabled him to take a disorganized, disheveled mob of comic cops and expertly whip it into a smartly dressed, highly disciplined, efficient police department were the same characteristics that won Kohler powerful enemies and kept him continually at odds with the leaders of both political parties.

Fred Kohler, in brief, was a hard-nosed, egotistic, arrogant man with all the prototypical traits of Kaiser Wilhelm's favorite field marshals. He sometimes yielded ground to superior force simply as a matter of tactical maneuvering, but he never surrendered and he was always planning the counterattack even as he was retreating.

Not many men would have had the persistence or the ego to stay with the battle as Kohler did, despite a long series of reversals that included his dismissal from the police department following a scandal that engaged the sometimes delighted attention of the entire city, a terrible physical beating by hoodlums, and a series of political defeats that would have discouraged the most insensitive ward heeler.

Kohler lowered his handsome Teutonic head and kept repeating his bull-like rushes into the political arena until finally, to the surprise of everybody but himself, he finally prevailed and won revenge on his numerous enemies on both sides of the party fence. And instead of being conciliatory in defeat; instead of calling on his opponents to close their ranks and bandage their wounds, Kohler slashed away at them even harder, going after the complete rout.

That's the way it was with Fred Kohler. He was a crowd pleaser.

His troubles began after the death of Tom Johnson, who had lifted him from the obscurity of captain to the authority of chief in 1903. Policemen, until then, served whatever political party was in power more than they served the law. They were the bag men of their day; collectors of political graft who were used frequently to harass those who did not contribute to the party coffers and otherwise promote the weal of the incumbent administration. They were conspicuous for their baggy pants, unbuttoned, gravy-stained jackets, and protruding, overhanging bellies. They were slack of jaw and slumped in posture.

They were everything that Fred Kohler was not, as Tom L. Johnson surely must have noted, for the young handsome officer was a stickler for neatness. He gleamed, from the visor of his cap through the buttons on his coat to the tips of his highly polished shoes. Walking or standing, his shoulders were squared and his chin was held high.

Kohler was given a free hand to whip the force into his own image, and he did it with an unemotional, undiplomatic directness of action that won him many lasting enemies on the force—especially among the many Irish policemen whom he seemed to single out as the particular and special target of his dislike. But there is no question that his overall accomplishment in remaking the force into a spit-and-polish military type of organization was outstanding. And timely.

No sooner had he effected this remarkable overhaul of men and machinery than President Theodore Roosevelt arrived in Cleveland to attend the prize social event of the 1903 season—the marriage of Mark Hanna's daughter, Ruth, to Medill McCormick, the scion of the Chicago McCormicks. The way Kohler rose to the great moment made it appear as if he had been pointing to just such an opportunity to show off himself and his men.

The chief, in full uniform, and twenty-four of his men, all mounted, met the President as he stepped off his private car in the Union Station. The policemen saluted smartly and simultaneously—just as Kohler had drilled them to do in more than a month of tedious practice—while the chief doffed his white cap and with a graceful sweep of the arm invited the Chief Executive into the waiting carriage.

The President's itinerary took him all over the city; to the Hanna residence on the far West Side, to St. Paul's Episcopal Church for the marriage ceremony, to the reception at the Union Club, to the hotel, and, finally, to the Union Station. But everywhere Teddy went, he found that Fred Kohler had gotten there just ahead of him. Being something of an actor himself, Roosevelt probably wondered if he weren't being upstaged a bit, especially as frequent changes of costume heightened the effect of the Kohler performance. Along with his other talents, the chief was a quick-change artist. At the Union Station, he was dressed in the full regalia of his police office, but when the presidential party arrived at St. Paul's, Kohler appeared in a masterfully tailored morning coat with wing collar. With his height and bulk, his handsome face and his bright blond hair that looked as if it had been newly marceled, Kohler stood out like a white polar bear at a convention of penguins.

President Roosevelt was impressed by the omnipresent chief, to be sure, and put his thoughts into words as he prepared to entrain back to Washington.

"I believe," he told reporters, "you have the best chief of police in America in Kohler."

The pronouncement undoubtedly pleased Fred Kohler, but it could not have surprised him. He had known all along that he was the best.

One of his most effective devices for the reduction of vice in the city's flourishing tenderloin district was to station a policeman outside gambling joints, saloons, and houses of prostitution. Customers patronizing such places were called on to give their names to the policeman before entering. Some complied, of course, but most people, sensitive to exposure of their private peccadilloes, turned away and sought distraction in more legitimate channels. Kohler took credit unabashedly for the severe curtailment of vice establishments that followed, ignoring the fact that the "Halt! Who goes there?" system had been proposed to him by Mayor Johnson, who, in turn, had borrowed it from his father, the onetime police chief of Louisville, Kentucky.

It was said by some Clevelanders—and accepted by most others—that Kohler had carried the idea past the Johnson concept of discouraging vice by saving the little black books and using them for some quiet political blackmail in later years. He was a tough in-fighter.

Among the people who did not approve wholly, or even partially, of the Kohler police techniques were the tramps and hobos who found themselves in Cleveland. The chief had a way of dealing summarily with any such wanderers who chanced to linger within the city limits. He had what was called his "sunrise court," which was nothing more than an early morning roundup of all vagrants and undesirables available to the police dragnet. They were thrown into paddy wagons, carted to the city limits, and there unceremoniously dumped out with a loud warning not to return. The big flaw in this neat routine was that the people and officials of the suburbs selected to receive Cleveland's human refuse felt that Kohler was imposing on their hospitality. After their protests went unheeded, they began to fight back, especially in Lakewood and in East Cleveland.

Police Chief James Stanberger of East Cleveland would have his men ready and waiting at the Cleveland line each morning. When a new Kohler shipment came their way, they picked up the bums on the first bounce, tossed them into their paddy wagons, and trundled them all the way back to Cleveland's Public Square where, once again, it would be Kohler's turn to pounce on the hapless hobos.

This shuttle service reached a ludicrous peak one day when the same fourteen tramps were transported back and forth between Cleveland and East Cleveland in four separate round trips, at the end of which the bewildered vagrants were staggering around, dizzied by the furious whirl from city to city. All of them presumably got off the merry-go-round eventually and escaped to some saner community, there to reflect on their unusual ordeal. Kohler actually suffered a minor defeat in this episode when the East Cleveland chief obtained a court injunction that forbade tramp-dumping, peremptorily spoiling all the fun.

Kohler's lofty disregard for any laws which might tend to bind him in the pursuit of his duty came in handy to the Johnson administration on at least one occasion. It was at the time of the bitter fight between Mayor Johnson and the Cleveland Electric Illuminating Company over the mayor's plan to create a municipally owned electric plant that would serve to regulate the private company's rate structure. Unable to get voter approval of a bond issue to build a municipal plant, Johnson tried the back-door approach of annexing a suburb called South Brooklyn which owned a small electric plant. The South Brooklyn council voted in favor of the annexation proposal, but Johnson's aide, City Clerk Peter Witt, knew that the action would not be official until the suburb mailed the necessary documents to Columbus. Witt also knew that the utility interest was determined to get the South Brooklyn council to rescind its action. He called on Chief Kohler for help, and what ensued was recalled as follows by Nathaniel R. Howard, then a *Plain Dealer* reporter and later the editor of the Cleveland *News:*

"'Do you ever use a man to go grab something that you ought to have whether you have any right or not?' Witt asked Kohler.

"'Sure,' said Kohler. 'All depends on how fast you move.'

"Witt explained his idea and Kohler called up a policeman.

"'You go with Witt's man to the South Brooklyn Town Hall,' said the chief, 'and do just what you're told. Take your gun along and if anyone wants to get tough draw your revolver and tell 'em to come ahead.'

"With the aid of one of his deputies and the policeman, Witt raided the South Brooklyn Town Hall, confiscated the necessary books and papers, and started in to fill out the annexation forms pronto. The raid was entirely successful, and the village light plant was the city's first blow for municipal ownership. The policeman called the chief at sundown for further instructions.

"'Anybody get tough?' Kohler asked.

"'No,' said the patrolman. 'I heard a lot of talk about their getting their special council meeting tonight in a hurry.'

"'Stay on the job,' said Kohler, 'and keep your gun out. If anyone comes, tell 'em there ain't going to be any council meeting tonight. Let me know if you need help, but I don't see why you should.'

"There was no council meeting."

Tom Johnson's administration annexed South Brooklyn and got its municipal light plant.

Big trouble plainly was building up for Fred Kohler as the list of his enemies grew longer, and the defeat of Tom Johnson seemed to be the signal for the attack. The new mayor, Herman Baehr, had made it clear where he stood on the subject of the controversial chief by using as one of his campaign slogans: "If you don't want more of Kohler, vote for Baehr!"

The new administration had hardly settled in City Hall before Kohler was suspended from office and called before the Civil Service Commission on twenty-five counts of drunkenness, immorality, and conduct unbecoming an officer and gentleman. The trial lasted six weeks, but Kohler, cool and aloof throughout all the sensation-filled sessions, was vindicated. He was exonerated and restored to rank, leaving the city shortly thereafter for a triumphal tour of Europe, where he was feted as an international hero. President Roosevelt's encomium had received worldwide attention.

In 1911, the old organization of Tom Johnson was restored to power in City Hall, with Newton D. Baker as the new mayor. But it wasn't the same, and Kohler brusquely went about making as many enemies in the new administration as he had in the old. The patience of his old political comrades snapped finally in the summer of 1912 when

Kohler horrified the Baker organization at a party picnic with "some unpardonable acts."

A short while later, a traveling salesman filed suit for divorce, and in support of his charges filed an affidavit of several witnesses charging that on a night in June 1912 they and the plaintiff had trapped Cleveland's police chief in the salesman's home on Daisy Avenue S.W. They said they had found Chief Kohler and the salesman's wife under compromising circumstances.

Kohler's enemies danced with joy in the streets, and the entire city giggled at the thought of the dignified police chief being trapped in such an embarrassing situation. On Daisy Avenue, yet. Mayor Baker suspended Kohler on charges of immorality and conduct unbecoming a police officer, and in March 1913 there was another sensational public hearing, held in the City Council chamber, at which the cuckolded husband and a strong supporting cast of witnesses, including many reputable citizens, told how the chief had been caught in *flagrante delicto*.

The chief's defense was weak. He intimated frameup. He said the woman, an old friend, had called him and asked for protection, which he was assiduously trying to provide when the husband and his friends rudely came crashing through the front window.

Fred Kohler was fired as police chief, and almost everybody in the community agreed he was through in public life. Typically, though, he did not cower or ask for sympathy. When the news of his dismissal came, he made his way to his favorite place in the lobby of the Hollenden Hotel and stood there, chin high and his eyes challenging anybody to make a critical remark, until late in the evening.

The Kohler fortunes dropped even lower one night a month later when the deposed chief was set upon by some politically oriented hoodlums as he left the Hollenden shortly before midnight. His path took him into the shadows of Short Vincent Street, behind the hotel, where three assailants fell on him with brass knuckles, blackjacks, fists, and feet. They left him in the street, bleeding and moaning. Somehow he got to his feet with the help of some passersby and he made it home, but he refused to call the police. He was in bed for a week, and it may be that in that week he made up his mind to get revenge on all his old friends and all his old enemies. The only way he could do that was to get back on top somehow; to get power once again.

Kohler became the busiest politician and the most eligible officeseeker in town for the next few years. He ran for City Council in 1913 and lost. He ran for county clerk in 1914 and lost. He ran for clerk of city courts in 1915 and lost. He ran for sheriff in 1916 and lost.

He didn't run for anything in 1917. The chance of a person of his obvious German descent winning an election in that year was not very good. In 1918, though, Kohler returned to the political wars, running for county commissioner. By that time, he had become that political joke, a perennial candidate, and few took his race seriously. That may explain why he won office, at long last. He proceeded immediately to upset the fine balance of two-party politics.

"He turned the office of the county commissioners into a bear pit," wrote Nat Howard. "He was a Republican and the other two men were Democrats. He continually accused them of graft, politics, favoritism on every piece of business that arose; he hurled charges at the clerk of the board, the county engineer, or any county official he could use as a target. He was the sensation of 1919. Wednesday and Saturday mornings when the board met were red-letter days for the newspapers. The Press sent two reporters and a cartoonist to every meeting. One reporter for facts, the other to write color and sidebars. The public impression grew, as Kohler knew it must, that here was one honest man in a courthouse full of shirkers and rascals."

In 1921, inevitably, Fred Kohler ran for mayor, scornfully brushing aside the fact that women were to be allowed to vote in a municipal election that year for the first time. Somebody recalled the scandal that had driven him out of the Police Department and asked him how he thought the women voters of Cleveland would cast their ballots.

"For me," said Kohler.

". . . The women will remember two things about me. That I was a good police chief and kept the town clean, and that when I got into that mess I protected the woman's name right from the start."

Kohler's campaign was a model of simplicity. He walked from door to door in every neighborhood in the city and asked people to vote for him. He mailed bushels of letters seeking voter support. He ran as an independent Republican. He had no use for the organization, and the organization had no use for him.

Just before the election, Kohler brought in a New York public opinion expert to take a poll of voter sentiment—a common enough practice today, but unheard of in 1921. The surveyor posed as a magazine writer and sent out ten thousand cards to registered voters asking their opinion of the proposed city manager plan and asking them to name their choice for mayor. Some 75 per cent of the people polled answered that they favored Fred Kohler.

This finding would have astonished the political experts, who were almost in unanimous agreement that the disgraced ex-chief didn't have a chance. The odds against Kohler's election were running 2-to-1 in the gambling parlors, a fact of which Kohler was keenly aware. Kohler, his friend, Sammy Haas, and an acquaintance of theirs from Toledo, a man named Hayes, quietly covered all bets.

The extent of their operation is revealed in a statement later made by Kohler's nephew, a theatrical advance man also named Fred Kohler.

"Sammy Haas called me over to the Hollenden Hotel in the closing days of the campaign," said the nephew. "He told me he had bet nearly all the money he had in the world on Uncle Fred. He asked me what I thought of the outcome of the election. I told him not to bet another cent, but I did tell him we were going to win. Sammy told me he had bet several hundred thousand dollars on the election; that he had a few thousand dollars left and he wanted to shoot the works, and I told him we were going to win so he shot the works and won.

"When Uncle Fred was elected they collected big money . . ."

Upon the news of Kohler's victory, reporters immediately recalled that when he was booted out of his job as police chief eight years before, he had told the press:

"All right, boys! I'll be leading the Police Department down Euclid Avenue again some day."

Kohler remembered the promise, too. On the day of his inaugural, January 1, 1922, he mounted a horse and led a parade of policemen down Euclid Avenue. He also named one of his old friends on the force, Jacob Graul, as chief, but in reality he was his own chief and the Police Department knew it.

Kohler had based his campaign on a pledge to give the city an economical administration, and he fulfilled that pledge. His first act in office was to fire 850 Republican ward workers employed by City Hall and to replace them with fewer than two hundred persons of his own choosing. The city's finances were in poor condition. The municipal deficit in 1920 had been $926,000; in 1921, $892,000.

Under Kohler's frugal administration, the existing deficit of nearly one million dollars was wiped out the first year and the city had a balance of $558,000. At the end of the second year of his administration, the city had a cash balance of $1,800,000. It was a commendable performance for a beginner in the field of municipal election, even if it was gained at the expense of certain city housekeeping chores, like paving the streets and keeping the parks in trim.

Many of Cleveland's citizens may not even have noticed what a splendid job Kohler was doing to restore the city to solvency; their attention must have been distracted by what he was doing with the paint brush.

Apparently the new mayor was determined that Cleveland never would forget him. He must have known that political fame is fleeting,

and that balanced books have never made the best-seller list. But he
did do something that has kept his memory fresh to this very day.
He painted Cleveland orange and black.

Whenever he was asked where he got the color combination, Kohler
always passed it off as one of his personal inspirations, but the truth
is that he went to some General Electric Company experts at Nela Park
and asked them to recommend to him, confidentially, the most memorable color combination they knew. The experts suggested orange and
black.

No city ever has been splashed with paint the way Cleveland was
under Fred Kohler. His painters sloshed the brilliant orange and black
colors on everything the city owned, including municipal buildings,
voting booths, tool sheds, swings, teeter-totters, park benches, outhouses,
the lifeguard's boat at Edgewater Beach and even, climactically, the
trim on the Christmas tree that the city set up in Public Square during
the holiday season.

Splashed in this early Halloween motif, the people of Cleveland
looked about them in bewilderment and asked the sensible question:
"Why?"

"Well," said Fred Kohler, more mellow and reasonable than usual
on the day a reporter repeated the question, "everybody can see all
the buildings now that belong to the city—to the people. They can
see 'em a long ways off, too. There'll never be any doubt whether
people have got a right to go in the buildings—they'll know they're
at a place they help own and maintain.

"The looks of 'em? You can see 'em, can't you? Well, that's the big
idea. I picked out the colors myself because orange and black are
the most visible colors there are, day and night.

"If a fellow is walking through a park and wants to know in a
hurry where a certain park building is, he can find it now. Nobody's
hiding it from him."

Kohler further assured the permanence of his own fame with a
series of billboards which he had erected around on city-owned property
so as to convey his most important messages to the people directly.
They were sterling messages; simple, uncomplicated and meaningful,
like the message that went up on the billboard at the east end of
the Detroit-Superior High Level Bridge in August 1923, near the end
of his administration.

The message (in orange-and-black combination, naturally) was:

> "I Kept the Wolf From the Door."
> FRED KOHLER, Mayor.

The aging Teuton felt that even the *dummkopf* voters ought to be
able to understand that simple message, and most of them probably

did. But lest anybody get the idea that he had gone soft and was trying to soft-soap the electorate, Kohler put up the following message on another big billboard:

Good or Bad,
Right or Wrong,
I Alone Have Been Your
Mayor.
FRED KOHLER, Mayor

He proved that he alone was mayor time after time by employing the authority of his office in such an arbitrary, dictatorial manner as to enrage half the population of the city. But while that half was fuming, the other half was laughing. He fought with the Irish policemen, with the public utilities, with City Council, with newspaper reporters, with sports fans, and even with the Bohemian crowd that belonged to the raciest organization in town, the Kokoon Arts Club. It was the practice of the club to stage every year a public *bal masqué* in which the merrymakers tried to outdo each other in costumes that fell just short in many instances of complete nudity. Strangely enough, this conservative city with the broad streak of puritanism not only tolerated the Kokoon Club's scandalous affair, but actually seemed to find it amusing. Not Fred Kohler. The onetime star of the Daisy Avenue Follies showed his moralistic side in the spring of 1923 and banned the *bal masqué* on the ground that the previous year's affair had been "too naked"!

Joining the naked ones in the denunciation of the mayor were thousands of sports fans whom he had angered, that same month, by outlawing prize fights in Cleveland. This edict grew out of a fight in Public Hall on April 18, between two 135-pound amateurs named Terry McManus and Morris Kleinman. It was obvious to most of the five thousand fans in attendance (including Mayor Kohler) that the fighters were unevenly matched. McManus was far superior and racked up a big lead on points. Kleinman didn't attract the crowd's affection with the numerous low blows he threw at McManus to slow him down, but it didn't matter. The decision clearly had been won by McManus—except that the judges named Kleinman the winner. Their decision was the signal for one of the best fight crowd riots in Cleveland history. Mayor Kohler stood on his chair and demanded that everybody come to order, but nobody paid any attention to him. That probably angered him more than the raw decision because he announced immediately thereafter that there would be no more fights in Cleveland during his administration.

Morris Kleinman, the crowd displeaser, went on from amateur fighter to professional gambler of national notoriety. He was accused of throwing many low blows at society during his adult career, including rum running on the Great Lakes and shorting Uncle Sam on the income tax returns. He served a three-year term for tax fraud. He was one of the charter members of the notorious "Cleveland gang" that still exerts so much influence in gambling circles in Kentucky and Las Vegas.

These moves by Mayor Kohler make him sound, in retrospect, like a reformer, which he was not. Neither, on the other hand, was he a reckless rake—a rake, perhaps, but reckless, never. A good illustration of his careful approach to illicit pleasure is to be found in his solution of a dilemma which faced him early in his term as mayor. Prohibition had been adopted and it wasn't long before Clevelanders were falling by the wayside as if poleaxed from the effects of the bootleg booze they suddenly found themselves drinking. This perturbed the new mayor deeply and caused him obvious anxiety. It made him wonder about the hooch he himself was buying. One day it came to him, as in a blinding revelation, that as the city's chief executive he had access to the services of one of the city's chemists. He made his arrangements quietly and henceforth it became a part of the chemist's regular duties to analyze Mayor Kohler's bootleg booze to determine if it were safely drinkable. The mayor would drop the stuff off when he got to work in the morning and the chemist, a likely young lad by the name of Julius Kovachy, would return the analyzed spirits to him at quitting time. The system was a big improvement over the royalty's old method of having a taster underfoot all the time to nibble at the king's frappés and pancakes as a precaution against poisoning.

Mayor Kohler one time expressed his views on reformers in a manner which definitely removed him from good standing in any society of do-gooders. His remarks were inspired by a controversy over the acoustical qualities of the vast new Public Hall which was dedicated and opened during the Kohler administration. Just before the opening, a committee of civic experts headed by Professor Dayton C. Miller of Case School of Applied Science had issued a report severely criticizing the acoustics of the great hall.

Kohler rejected the report and its recommendations, and on the opening program, immediately after performances by the police band, the firemen's band, and the German singing societies, Kohler spoke his mind in the following statesmanlike address:

"Ladies and gentlemen of the most wonderful audience ever gathered under one roof in Cuyahoga County, I thank you greatly for your applause. I had hoped that every imbecile that hammered this hall would be here tonight.

"I would like any lady or gentleman who finds anything wrong with the acoustics of this hall to stand up. I have never found it to fail that when a practical man tackles a job, he goes about his business just in the opposite way that a theoretical fool would . . ."

The following night, Kohler warmed up to his subject before another full house in the new hall:

"Because of what they called acoustics, they wanted to fill up all those beautiful panels up there with felt to soften our voices, they said. That would have cost the city about $200,000. We would have been the soft ones to have spent that money.

"There is no place in this community for uplifters and reformers. They go around and find out what a practical man is doing and then take the opposite side. That's the way they get their living. I tell you people I'm always going to be against the imbeciles and bookbugs. Whenever I meet one of them I'm going to walk right away from him and leave him standing in the middle of the street."

One advantage that Kohler had over most Cleveland mayors of the past was that he did not have to worry about re-election. The city already had voted to adopt the city manager plan of government. It was to replace the old mayor-council form of city administration upon the conclusion of Kohler's term of office, taking effect in January 1924. Kohler's flamboyant administration, nevertheless, continued to give the impression that he was running for something, especially in its emphasis on his record of economy.

At the end of his first year in office, the orange-and-black billboards shouted: "The City Now Lives Within Its Income! [signed] FRED KOHLER, Mayor."

When his reign finally was at an end, Kohler put up his last message to the city on a sign that was hung on the revolving orange-and-black Christmas tree on Public Square. It announced that, thanks to Fred Kohler, the city had a surplus of $1,400,000.

The concluding paragraph of his last annual report was a shining example of pure Kohleriana:

"For two years I have kept the wolf from Cleveland's door. Cleveland is again on the map RIGHT. And good or bad, right or wrong, I alone have been your mayor. I gave you the best I had; all of my time, energy, and experience. If my administration has been a failure, it is my fault; if it has been a success, it is also my fault."

The big guessing game in Cleveland was over which direction Kohler would jump after leaving the mayor's chair. He was noncommittal, but at the last minute he went to the Board of Elections and took out two petitions for governor, one for county treasurer, one for coroner, and one for county recorder. Even as the experts were trying to guess which one of these posts he would seek in this political version of Russian roulette, Kohler filed his petition and announced his candidacy for sheriff.

He won the post easily, but promptly aroused a civic controversy over his treatment of prisoners. He was allowed to spend forty-five cents a day on food for each prisoner. It was charged that he spent, on an average, only seven cents per prisoner, and there were unkind critics who claimed that the sheriff pocketed anywhere from fifteen thousand to fifty thousand dollars during his two-year term of office. He was defeated for re-election in 1926.

Kohler ran for governor in 1928, but he was roundly defeated. It was a strange performance, even for Kohler. He not only failed to put on a campaign for the office, but he didn't even bother to stay in the country during the contest. While his opponents were ranging the Ohio countryside, drumming up support, Herr Fred was lolling in the beer gardens of Germany and touring the cities of Europe. It was either a supreme display of confidence, or the most magnificent show of indifference ever exhibited by a candidate for a major political office.

It was his last hurrah. While he gave the impression that he was prepared to run again for mayor of Cleveland as the city showed signs of abandoning the city manager form of government in the beginning of the 1930s, he never did. He suffered a paralytic stroke on board an ocean liner in the harbor of Plymouth, England, in June 1932, and the man who came back to Cleveland to die was not the big, burly, rough-talking Fred Kohler that everybody knew; just a feeble old man who wanted to sit in the sun and reminisce in a quiet voice.

After he died on January 30, 1934, it was discovered that he had left a fortune of nearly half a million dollars in a bank safety deposit box. It was an eyebrow-lifting sum for a poorly paid public servant to accumulate and, inevitably, it inspired all kinds of speculation. But however the fortune had been amassed, the people of Cleveland were not inclined to be indignant. They knew that Fred Kohler had given them a fair run for the money. He alone had been their mayor.

XVIII

The Victory of Laura Corrigan

CLEVELAND's social register is a book that does not open readily to new entries. The names already inscribed in classical script on its vellum pages are kept free of vitiating, deleterious influences from the outside by hasp and lock, and the keepers of the keys are vigilant, anxious guardians. Over the ramparts of Bratenahl, Gates Mills, Hunting Valley, Waite Hill, and Pepper Pike they watch—ready to challenge any wayfarer who approaches too close.

One who made the game approach was a former Wisconsin milkmaid named Laura Mae Whitlock McMartin Corrigan, and her memory is still green, not only in Cleveland society circles but among the Right People of two continents.

Laura deserves a place in history with such enduring notables as One-Eyed Connolly, the gate-crasher, and the man who broke the bank at Monte Carlo. Cleveland society denied her entrance and repulsed her overtures, as did New York society, but Laura was a fighter and a tactician. She succeeded over all to become the reigning international hostess of the 1920s and the 1930s; the Elsa Maxwell and Perle Mesta of continental society; the friend of the rich and the royal.

The way up to that dizzy social pinnacle was not easy.

Somebody once dubbed Laura Corrigan "the Flagpole Kelly of Social Climbers." But she found that somebody had greased the flagpole when she arrived in Cleveland as the bride of young Jimmy Corrigan in 1917. He was one of the city's leading playboys, no mean distinction in a day when playboys were numerous and the competition among them for honors was spirited.

Her arrival in Cleveland was gaudily arranged by her generous groom, who saw to it that she roared into town in a fifteen-thousand-dollar Rolls-Royce, allegedly of lavender hue, driven by the former chauffeur of Jay Gould and accompanied by a liveried footman. The car whisked her and her retinue to the sprawling country home of the Corrigan family, an estate called Nagirroc in Wickliffe, which today is the home of the Pine Ridge Country Club.

It seems only fair to point out that Nagirroc spelled backward is

Corrigan, and vice versa. The Serutan people may as well be good sports and face up to the fact that the Corrigans were spelling things backward long before they were.

There was no noticeable ripple of excitement among the members of Cleveland society upon the arrival of the young honeymooners in their midst; no gay round of parties to welcome Laura to the inside circle. The general reaction could be described as a frosty indifference that concealed real hostility. As Laura and Jimmy quickly learned, the snub was on. There were tentative bids for Jimmy's company at some minor social functions, but his new wife was steadfastly ignored. A lot of Jimmy's old friends felt badly about giving him the pass-by, sometimes known as the old social shuffle, but, dammit, why did he have to go and marry the girl?

They remembered, fondly, the time when the old Jimmy had had that affair with the Pittsburgh girl—wasn't her name Georgiana Young? —and she had sued him for fifty thousand dollars for breach of promise. The case had traveled through two courts and Jimmy had won the verdict in both, but only after some lively testimony, allegations, charges, and countercharges. Jimmy's lawyer had summed it up rather neatly when he had turned to the court, arms outspread, palms turned upward, and announced that his client was guilty of nothing more serious than sowing his wild oats.

Many of his old Cleveland friends liked to think that *that* was the real Jimmy; not the fellow who had gone off and married a girl whose only recommendation, apparently, was her feminine charm.

Laura's background, certainly, was not prepossessing. Some accounts say she was the daughter of a Wisconsin lumberjack; others identify him as a Wisconsin gardener. It wasn't much of a choice, from a social standpoint. But there is no question at all that Laura Mae Whitlock was an ambitious girl, anxious to rise above her station and make her mark in the world. She went from Stevens Point, Wisconsin, to Chicago to work as a waitress, but not for long. She met and married the house doctor at a Chicago hotel, a Dr. Duncan R. McMartin. It was a large step forward, becoming the wife of a doctor of medicine, and most women would have settled for this achievement. Perhaps Laura also would have accepted the life of quiet domesticity if she had not met Captain James Corrigan of Cleveland, a wealthy steel magnate; head of the Corrigan, McKinney Steel Company, which later became an integral unit in the formation of the Republic Steel Corporation. Captain Corrigan was the father of the noted playboy, Jimmy, and he himself was a rousing, outgoing sort. He had once been a partner of Frank Rockefeller in some speculative investments in iron ore property in the Lake Superior district. Along the way he had borrowed money from John D. Rockefeller, Frank's brother. It was John D.'s treatment of

Captain Corrigan in their financial dealings that presumably caused a permanent rift in relations between Frank and John Rockefeller. Captain Corrigan sued John D., claiming deception, but the courts upheld Rockefeller.

Captain Corrigan went on to found the steel company, with the financial assistance of Judge Stevenson Burke and Price McKinney. The company prospered and grew extravagantly, but a terrible tragedy fell upon the Corrigan family before the new century was seven months old. In July 1900 Captain James Corrigan and his brother, Captain John Corrigan, took their families on a Lake Erie vacation trip aboard James' yacht, the *Idler*, which was said to be the finest sailing craft of its kind on the Great Lakes. Just the previous winter he had spent eight thousand dollars on the yacht to keep it shipshape.

Aboard the *Idler* were Mrs. Ida Corrigan, fifty-two, wife of James; Mrs. Jennette Corrigan Rieley, twenty-four, their daughter and wife of Charles F. Rieley of New Brunswick, New Jersey; two other daughters, Miss Ida Corrigan, fifteen, and Miss Jane Corrigan, twenty; Mary Corrigan Rieley, one-year-old infant daughter of the Rieleys; Mrs. Mary Corrigan, wife of Captain John; the captain of the yacht, Charles G. Holmes, and a crew of eight.

The trip hardly had gotten under way when word came that Captains John and James Corrigan were needed back in Cleveland to attend to an urgent business transaction. They got off the yacht at Port Huron, some thirty-five miles west of Cleveland, and returned by train, leaving orders for the yacht to be towed back to home port by a steamship, the *Australia*.

Lake Erie's shallow waters grew choppy as the *Idler* was being towed toward Cleveland on the morning of July 8, and some of the passengers got seasick. Mrs. James Corrigan, it was said later, asked that the captain detach the tow line and sail the ship independently for a smoother ride. Another account states that breaking the tow line was Captain Holmes' own idea. The action, at any rate, was taken.

A hot sun blazed down on the yacht at high noon as she cut through the rough lake, driving the members of the two Corrigan families below deck. Then, suddenly, black clouds moved in and the wind rose. Lake Erie is notorious for its sudden squalls that can whip its waters into a fury in a matter of minutes, and this was one of the worst. There was terror among the passengers huddled below, and there was a frenzy of activity among the sailors as they tried to take down the sails before the big blow hit in its full strength.

There wasn't time. The *Idler*'s foresail, mainsail, and jib were still up when sudden sixty-mile-an-hour winds tore away the foregaff, even as the sailors slashed away with their knives in a futile attempt to cut the halyards. The graceful yacht staggered under the blow and yawed wildly before she surrendered to the force of the gale by rolling over in the water. She capsized only sixteen miles from home port, close to the cliffs that line the water's edge on the western shoreline of Cleveland. Two fishing tugs were at the scene within twenty minutes, but their rescue efforts were not enough to prevent a tragic toll. They could save only the life-jacketed members of the crew and Mrs. John Corrigan. She—the only passenger to survive—was clinging in a state of shock to a cork-filled sofa.

Captain James Corrigan lost his wife, three young daughters, and his infant granddaughter in that Lake Erie tragedy. The only member of his immediate family left to him was his son, James, Jr.

The yacht righted itself the following day, but it was almost plucked apart by souvenir hunters who rowed out to the disabled craft. Captain Corrigan afterward brought formal charges of negligence against Captain Holmes, and the master of the ill-fated boat was arrested and tried. His sailors gave strong testimony in his behalf, however, and he was exonerated.

There are conflicting stories as to the time and place of Captain Corrigan's meeting with Mrs. Laura McMartin of Chicago. One version has it that shortly after the lake tragedy, the captain, with his brother John and his wife, went to White Sulphur Springs to recuperate and that he met Mrs. McMartin at the resort. It was said that they hit it off at once; that Mrs. McMartin not only was attractive, but that she turned a warm, sympathetic personality toward Captain Corrigan in his troubled time. At the end of the Corrigan party's stay, she was invited by the captain to visit Nagirroc soon and she promised she would.

Another story has it that it was Captain Corrigan's former sister-in-law, Mrs. X. Z. Scott, who went to the resort and took a liking to Laura McMartin, and that it was her invitation that brought the Chicago *femme fatale* to Cleveland and the fateful meeting with the lonely captain.

In any event, there is no disputing that Laura did pop up at the old Corrigan homestead in Wickliffe, and there is reliable testimony that she and Captain Corrigan became great and good friends.

During the seven or eight years that this December-and-May friendship flourished, young Jimmy Corrigan was leading the shadowy life of the prodigal son. The breach-of-promise suit against him by the Pittsburgh girl had brought his father's displeasure to the boiling point and Jimmy, a graduate of Case School of Applied Science, left the old family homestead to try to make his way out West. He did some field work in the western mining country for a New York company, managed a telegraph office at Goldfield, Nevada, and eventually made his way to San Francisco where, among other things, he worked as a bartender.

It was there that Price McKinney, a friend of the family, found Jimmy. He had bad news to convey to him. Old and ailing Captain Corrigan had drawn up a will disinheriting his son and, it is said, substituting as his heirs the children of Price McKinney. But McKinney was said to have persuaded young Jimmy to return home and make his peace with his father before it was too late. The junior Corrigan effected the reconciliation and took up life again in Cleveland.

Strangely, even though Captain Corrigan was something of a swinger himself, he had openly disapproved of the way in which his son liked to lark about. He approved of fun as a pastime, but saw no future in it as a full-time career. He continued to be skeptical of Jimmy's ability to adjust to the problems of a man's estate even after the reconciliation. His skepticism was evident in the will he left behind at his death in 1915. He bequeathed his estate to the son, but placed its administration in the hands of two trustees, Price McKinney and James E. Ferris (another friend and business associate), until James, Jr., had reached the age of forty. At that time the future responsibility of the estate would be determined by McKinney, who would have to decide whether the son could be trusted with the fortune.

Laura McMartin came to Cleveland for the funeral and met the son of her old, departed friend. Their acquaintanceship quickly ripened into a much more significant association and short, gasping noises came from behind the fluttering fans in the drawing rooms of Cleveland society. Whatever Jimmy Corrigan's thoughts were about the trustee arrangement set up for him by his late father, they were subordinate to the grand passion he felt for Mrs. McMartin. She by now had divorced her Chicago doctor, and even while Jimmy's friends clucked and society wagged its head in vigorous disapproval, the romance flourished in rather scandalous disregard for the proprieties of the day. Their marriage in 1917, instead of stilling the tongues of outraged members of society, stirred indignation to new heights.

It was quickly apparent that the doors had been closed to Jimmy Corrigan and his bride, his senior by seven years, but Laura did not crumple into a rocker and become a Nagirroc recluse. Life in the Cleveland deep freeze was not for her, and she refused to accept meekly the brush-off from society. After a determined effort to crash through the social stockade, she finally gave up on Cleveland. She had been roundly defeated in the battle, but there still was a war to be won and she was determined to win it. She and her husband moved to New York City to resume the fight on a new and larger battle-ground, one that gave her more room for maneuvering. She plunged back into the fray, feathered plumes flying and diamonds aglitter; presumably hopeful of victory.

Laura would not have been optimistic about the outcome if she had been better acquainted with the interrelated mechanism of American society. In that case she would have known that there are strong links that bind the inner set of Cleveland with the haughty set in other cities like New York, Boston, Philadelphia, Chicago, Detroit, and St. Louis; perhaps even Gallipolis. There are days when the skies between these cities are dark with passenger pigeons winging back and forth carrying coded messages identifying the undesirables. One of the pigeons must have carried a red-hot dossier on Laura Corrigan, judging from the way New York society braced itself and took its position shoulder-to-shoulder with Cleveland society in opposition to her; two cold shoulders united to fend off a single interloper.

Laura spent a small fortune trying to buy her way into the Manhattan register, but without success. It is entirely to her credit that she did not falter or crumple as it became painfully clear that she had been rejected again. She accepted her second major rebuff without a whimper, ordered the family bags packed again, and in 1921 the Corrigans took off for London and still another running jump at the big goal.

Mrs. Corrigan, clearly, was a persistent woman. Once she had set up her residence in the new locale, her persistence and willingness to plunge steeply paid off handsomely. She rented the Grosvenor Street mansion of Mrs. George Keppel, once a favorite hostess of King Edward VII, and with it a household staff that was one of the largest and most skilled in the United Kingdom, outside of the royal establishments. Mrs. Keppel herself gave Laura's campaign to establish herself in society tremendous impetus with her seasoned advice and introductions to the right people. It wasn't long before Laura's clambakes were the talk of London and Paris. Her dinners were the most fulsome repasts that could be brought together on one table, and all her parties radiated class—not to mention class distinction. When Laura served rare roast beef, it had better bleed blue.

There were a number of good, sound reasons why the social climber from Cleveland, Ohio, should have been so cordially received by international society. It would be foolhardy not to count among these the wealth that flowed her way from the counting rooms of the Corrigan, McKinney Steel Company. But Laura's willingness to spend that money to achieve the right effect was equally important. So was her determination to fetch the best people—absolutely the best people—to her festive board and drawing room. Just as money is said to beget money, good company will beget good company.

A possibility that cannot be overlooked is that many of the titled guests who condescended to be entertained by the American hostess were engaging in a bit of social slumming. Sometimes their motive was just plain avarice. Laura was both eccentric and generous. There was always a jeweled gift of some kind next to the napkin at each setting, usually a gold cigarette case for the ladies and gold garters for the men or something equally rare and desirable. At any rate, the lavish scale of her parties did have the effect of setting the *haut monde* back on its clicking heels, and invitations to Laura Corrigan parties soon became part of the accepted scheme of things among the people who counted on the Tight Little Island—including, of course, certain members of the Royal Family.

Even as England was buzzing with amusement—and a little resentment—over the audacity of the lady from Cleveland, some social cutups decided to have a bit of malicious fun. They sent out engraved invitations to a Laura Corrigan party to a select list of people. There was a notation on each of the invitations that the Prince of Wales would be among the honored guests.

When one of those invitations was shown to the prince, he reacted in a way that did him credit. He spotted it immediately as a monstrous kind of joke and upset its calculated effect of embarrassing Mrs. Corrigan by showing up for her party, thereby giving the social stock of the American hostess a tremendous boost. The middle-aged woman from the Wisconsin farmlands who could not make the social grade in Cleveland or in New York was rolling at last and was well on her way to becoming a pacesetter of the smart set in London and in Paris as she shuttled back and forth between the two cities, with occasional side ventures to the Mediterranean, in one of the most impressive demonstrations ever given of the fine art of partying high society.

Once in a while, it is true, Mrs. Corrigan flubbed one, but she was a quick learner and usually overrode her mistakes with a burst of generosity that shortly brought any injured acquaintances back within her orbit in a mood of total forgiveness. It is generally conceded that she pulled her biggest rock when she upstaged two members of Parliament who had been brought to one of Laura's parties by Mrs. Cunningham-Reid, a sister of Lady Louis Mountbatten, by completely ignoring their uninvited presence. Unfortunately for her, the victims of her icy indifference were friends of Prince George, and that royal gentleman was so offended by the incident that he refused to attend a dinner party to which Mrs. Corrigan earlier had invited him.

Laura's *faux pas* did not cause a lasting rift with Prince George; he was among the titled elite who favored her with his company throughout her career, as did King Alfonso XIII of Spain, Princess Marina of Greece, Princess Mary of England, the Duke and Duchess of York, the Duke and Duchess of Kent, and many other members of Europe's reigning families.

As might have been expected, Mrs. Corrigan did not regard Americans as her favorite people, and those of her fellow countrymen who won admission to her list of party regulars always found themselves to be a small minority at any gala. One of those regulars was another expatriate, the Countess von Haugwitz-Reventlow, the former Barbara Hutton.

Even as life moved along smoothly and victoriously in England and on the Continent for the Corrigans, Laura and Jimmy still had the annoyance of unresolved and unsolved problems back home in Cleveland. The life of an international society hostess is one that exerts severe pressures on the old bankroll, and Laura, a practical woman at times, realized that if she were to mount the social summit, as it seemed she would, it could be done only with the help of an unlimited checking account.

With Price McKinney and James Ferris in their roles as trustees of Jimmy Corrigan's inherited estate, Mr. and Mrs. Corrigan were not free to do the things they wanted. McKinney, furthermore, had indicated his disapproval of Jimmy's marriage to Laura by dropping the Corrigan name out of the title of the great steel company in Cleveland, changing it from Corrigan, McKinney Steel Company to the McKinney Steel Company.

Court action was instituted by Jimmy to gain control of his inheritance. He charged in a suit heard in the Lake County courthouse in Painesville, just east of Cleveland, that McKinney was trying to "squeeze" him out of authority in the affairs of the McKinney Steel Company, citing the change in the company name as part of the evidence to support his charge. Corrigan charged further that Ferris was acting for McKinney in his actions and decisions rather than for the best interest of the Corrigan family. He accused McKinney of being so antagonistic in attitude as to make cooperation with him impossible.

The court decided, after weeks of argument, not to grant the five-year continuance of the trusteeship that McKinney and Ferris had been seeking. Jimmy Corrigan was given control, at last, of his father's estate, whose worth was estimated to be at least twenty million dollars; more likely, thirty million dollars.

Jimmy Corrigan now had a 40 per cent stock control, and he was first vice president of the steel company as well as a member of the board of directors, but he did not have control of the corporation. It still rested in the hands of Price McKinney and his associates. Corrigan apparently was resigned to this state of business affairs, but not his wife. Laura never was willing to settle for anything but the role of leader. On the other hand, she knew nothing about business or high finance, and opposing her and her husband were some of the canniest, most experienced men in the steel industry.

Laura, nevertheless, returned to the United States with Jimmy in

1925 and did battle for control of the steel company. It wasn't much of a fight. The family of Captain Corrigan's old associate, Stevenson Burke, held some 13 per cent of the stock in McKinney Steel Company, and Laura persuaded them to part with it for a sum said to be in excess of five million dollars. When she told her husband the price, he was staggered; they simply did not have that much money to invest. The wherewithal was a minor detail, as far as Laura was concerned. She hocked all the family silver, her magnificent collection of jewelry, and then borrowed the rest.

So it came about that one day in May 1925, Jimmy Corrigan strolled into a meeting of the board of directors of the McKinney Steel Company and announced that he was the boss. The former Burke stock holding of 13 per cent, added to Corrigan's original holding of 40 per cent, clearly gave him a tidy total of 53 per cent of the company stock and indisputable control. The company issued a statement that the new president of McKinney Steel Company was James W. Corrigan.

Price McKinney, a very capable steel executive and old friend of Captain Corrigan, went home in defeat and a short while later committed suicide.

As president of the company, Jimmy now was committed to stay on in his old hometown, except for occasional trips to London, where Laura spent most of her time. He changed the company name back to Corrigan, McKinney Steel Company and renewed his acquaintanceship with his old circle of friends in Cleveland. His tenure as a steel executive, however, was short. On January 22, 1928, three years after gaining control of the company, Jimmy left the Hollenden Hotel and walked leisurely to his favorite haunt, the Cleveland Athletic Club on Euclid Avenue, where he planned to have dinner and then bowl with the C.A.C. Indians. He was pulling open the door that led into the C.A.C. lobby when he staggered back as if struck, and dropped to one knee. He pulled himself to his feet again with difficulty and had gotten through the doorway when he fell to the lobby floor. Jimmy Lee, the club's athletic director, and James F. Green, the doorman, carried him into the elevator and up to the Turkish bath on the eleventh floor, where a physician-member, Dr. Herbert L. Davis, pronounced him dead. He was forty-seven years old.

Laura stayed in Cleveland only long enough to attend the funeral and to make financial and business arrangements with her bankers and her late husband's steel associates. She now was in control of the largest independent steel company in the United States, but this gratifying circumstance was not allowed to interfere with her major responsibility; namely, leading international society on to new, loftier heights. Mrs. Corrigan's permanent residence was firmly established in London, with occasional side trips to Paris, and she resumed her social leadership now with even greater gusto—a side product, perhaps, of the security that comes out of the inheritance of more than twenty million dollars.

In the fabulous years that followed, Laura Corrigan established herself as one of those rare persons of whom legends are made. There no longer was any doubt about her pre-eminence as a social hostess, but the accounts of her triumphant performance still had the power to make Cleveland society wince, such as the time the leading prince of India, the incredibly wealthy Gaekwar of Baroda, turned down a previous invitation to attend a party in the home of a leading American family of the "Knickerbocker" set in favor of an invitation from Mrs. Corrigan.

One season, it is said, the Cleveland social reject spent as much as five million dollars on entertaining. Her specialty was the unusual. One party would have an Oriental setting, with real, genuine Orientals imported from the rice paddies for atmosphere, while another would provide a South Seas environment, complete with palm trees, monkeys, outrigger canoes, and whatever else was necessary. She thought nothing of financing the trips of her party guests from all parts of the world, and it was her custom not only to pay the expenses incurred by the guests, but also to provide them with high-priced gifts.

One who knew her well, Winsor French, a popular Cleveland *Press* columnist and himself a member of Cleveland society, wrote of Laura's ascendancy:

"She had a fine time with her money, too. Year after year she rented vast houses at the most expensive resorts, filling them with equally expensive guests. Gold cigaret cases she bought by the gross, to be given away as favors at her dinners.

"Aware that many of her friends had little else beyond their titles, position, and the clothes on their backs, Laura doled out spending money the way one might tip a waiter. She also bought paintings—fine portraits, which in time she came to think of as 'family portraits,' and described them as just that. It is difficult to believe that she could have fooled anyone, but the purchased 'ancestry' gave her a sense of security.

"Whatever else she may have become, however, no one could ever describe Laura Corrigan as a connoisseur of art. One time she gave $25,000 to the Cleveland Museum with instructions it should be used to purchase a fine painting in memory of Jimmy Corrigan. It was, too; a magnificent Cezanne, 'Pigeon Tower at Montbriand.'

"Laura, when she saw it, was so horrified that she tore from the frame the bronze plate describing it as a gift to the memory of her late husband. It was her first and last donation to the museum."

Mrs. Corrigan's career was dimmed and almost extinguished during the brief reign of King Edward VIII, whose dislike she had incurred when he was Prince of Wales at the time she had crossed the Mount-battens. King Edward disliked her and made no pretense of gallantry, repeatedly striking her name off dinner and party lists. No doubt the coolness that prevailed between Mrs. Corrigan and another American woman in London, Mrs. Wallis Simpson, had something to do with the new monarch's attitude and actions.

Laura at one time had embarrassed the Royal Family by giving a mink coat to Princess Marina of Greece at the time the princess announced her engagement to the Duke of Kent. The princess accepted the gift and wore it, thus obligating the Royal Family to invite Mrs. Corrigan to the wedding. It was a dilemma, but wise Laura provided a graceful, face-saving out by booking passage aboard an ocean liner for America at the time the wedding was to be held, just in case an invitation was not forthcoming. The invitation was issued—but it was not delivered to her until she was past the point of no return, in midocean.

When King Edward VIII abdicated the throne, the Corrigan fortunes soared high once again. Laura was a good friend of the new ruling couple, George VI and Queen Elizabeth, and their favor restored her to her leading position as a social hostess. She swept back into the lead again with bigger and better parties.

It was said that Mrs. Corrigan, an intellectually active woman, was especially adept at the art of conversation, this being one of the charms that brought her famous guests back to her table time and time again—that and her generosity, of course. It is recorded, however, that there was one occasion, at least, when her conversation flow was dammed. That came about at the time she was seated at the dinner table between Author George Moore and the Marquess of Donegal. There had been a lull in the party chatter and that was the precise moment that Moore, moodily twisting his goblet of water, suddenly chose to say loudly:

"You know, Mrs. Corrigan, I always think that of all the sexual abnormalities, abstinence is by far the most revolting!"

Laura could only stare at her guest, completely tongue-tied by his *non sequitur*.

Even though her trips back home were infrequent, she still managed to give Clevelanders one of the most interesting sideshows of the entire Depression period when, in April 1938, she transferred her fortune from the Union Trust Company to the vaults of the National City Bank.

This involved the movement of a cool twenty-one million dollars and required the services of three Brinks armored trucks, twenty armed guards to line the block from the Union Trust at Chester Avenue and East 9th Street to the Vincent Avenue entrance of National City, one block west, a large detachment of policemen, scores of plainclothes detectives and, finally, some trustworthy bankers to help carry the load. One bank officer carried a suitcase containing eight million dollars in government securities; another carried a package containing three million dollars in bonds.

Hundreds of Clevelanders lined the route, thrilled by their proximity to the green stuff that was so hard to come by during the Depression. Many of Laura Corrigan's old townspeople took a vicarious pleasure in her success, choosing to believe that her success in the international circles of society represented a kind of victory for the proletariat. They thrilled to society page items, such as this one that appeared in 1938 in the Cleveland *News:*

"Now comes announcement that Mrs. Corrigan (such is her simple way of styling herself) is planning a ball in London which promises to be one of the most lavish of the West End social season. She has taken over the Duke and Duchess of Marlborough's town mansion, known to the postman as No. 11 Kensington Palace Gardens, and will open it on June 23.

"Rumor has it that the king and queen will look in . . ."

A short time before the coronation, Laura visited the United States and was herself the guest of honor at a party held in New York's Waldorf-Astoria. It was a barnyard party which featured a prop cow that yielded champagne when milked, some perfumed pigs, and other interesting livestock imported from Leonard Hanna's farm near Cleveland. One of the highlights of the evening was a hog-calling demonstration. Mrs. Corrigan's memory of Cleveland remained sharply in focus even under the softening influence of high success overseas, as is illustrated by a story that Jerome Zerbe, member of a socially prominent Cleveland family and society editor of *Town & Country* magazine, liked to tell.

Jimmy Corrigan had been a close friend of Zerbe's parents and was a frequent visitor up to the time of his marriage.

"When finally he married his woman friend of many years, the McKinneys and their friends dropped him," wrote Zerbe. "Finding themselves snubbed by those they wanted to know, the Corrigans left Cleveland.

"By 1930, Mrs. James Corrigan was a glittering figure in international society. Her husband's millions had taken her far, and many a king and queen she counted among her friends.

"That year I was seated next to her at a luncheon in Paris. Giving my place card a casual glance, she said: 'Zerbsky! You must be Polish!'

"I replied that I was afraid she hadn't read my card properly. Picking it up, she exclaimed, 'Jerome Zerbe! Why your mother helped drive me from Cleveland!'

"'You must be eternally grateful,' I replied."

It would be incorrect to conclude from Laura's glittering record of success as a hostess that she thereby had won full membership in European society. There is more than a casual collection of evidence to support the belief that in her eagerness to associate with the mighty she had become a kind of court jester. Many of the run-down-at-the-heels members of nobility who accepted her lavish hospitality were among her leading detractors in private and vied with one another in ridiculing her. Laura, on the other hand, provided them with a lot of material to enliven their snickering sessions. She was a woman of strange ways, some of which sprang out of her pathetic eagerness to prove her acquired sophistication. But no matter how deeply she dug into her silk purse, every now and then a sow's ear would fall out to remind everybody that she had been raised on a Wisconsin farm.

One of the minor eccentricities which delighted the blasé socialites was her willingness to enliven a quiet dinner party by standing on her head. And she could be counted on frequently to embroider her conversational contributions with malapropisms of astonishing range and originality. Her former townsman, Zerbe, offers some examples of her virtuosity in this field in his book, *The Art of Social Climbing*, which includes a rather definitive study of Mrs. Corrigan's career.

According to Zerbe, Mrs. Corrigan "always thought that backgammon was a game called Bagatelle," and that upon being introduced to the Aga Khan she volunteered the information that she knew his brother, Otto, quite well. He recalls that Laura attended a John Gielgud performance in *Hamlet*, and was asked by Lady Juliet Duff if she had enjoyed the play. "Oh, yes," Laura is supposed to have replied, "I found it so interesting. You know I am so intimate with the King of Denmark!"

Loelia, Duchess of Westminster, in her book *Grace and Favor*, recalls that among the most memorable of the malapropisms attributed to Mrs. Corrigan was the one in which she allegedly said of a cathedral that "the flying buttocks were magnificent."

All of her slips and misusages were treasured by the malicious ones who gathered around her board and accepted her gifts. Possibly they resented their own weakness that permitted her to buy her way into their company, but at any rate they lost no time in putting the latest Mrs. Corrigan stories into circulation. Among these gossipy yarns there was almost certain to be one related to Laura's hair—or lack thereof.

She had a magnificent collection of wigs in a day when false hairpieces were not the accepted part of a woman's personal effects that they are today. She had wigs of all kinds to meet every occasion and to represent every possible situation, and it was generally believed that she really needed the hairpieces; that she was, in fact, bald. Any number of stories purporting to prove this deficiency circulated freely in the upper levels of continental society, among them a stylishly embellished classic which said that she once attempted a swan dive into a pool at a resort and hit the water with such force that she lost not only her bathing hat but also her hair. But Laura was a spunky one and stayed underwater until she retrieved the headpiece, apparently preferring a watery grave to the embarrassment of emerging with a shiny, hairless noggin.

World War II interrupted Mrs. Corrigan's glittering string of social victories, but it also proved that there was more to the old girl than tinsel and talk. Instead of heading for safe cover at the outbreak of the war, Laura headed straight for her beloved Paris to help out as much as she could. She was handicapped by a shortage of money, of all things, in her efforts to help soldiers and refugees as France reeled under the Nazi onslaught. Her funds in the United States were frozen by the American government, but that didn't stop her. She received a special safe conduct pass from the Nazis and journeyed from Vichy to Paris, where she negotiated the sale of her magnificent collection of jewels to a German syndicate. She used the proceeds to help feed and clothe the French war victims, clumsily at first—one day she ordered sandwiches from the pantries of the Ritz Hotel to supply a Paris bread line—but always in a spirit of wholehearted generosity. Laura Corrigan the Humanitarian almost completely forgot Laura Corrigan the Society Hostess.

"I have sold everything except my pearls (once valued at $350,000), my two wedding rings and my wristwatch," she wrote to a friend. "All I possess here could be put in a suitcase." Her wardrobe at that time consisted of two dresses. Instead of returning then to the comforts of America, Laura left Paris for Vichy, where she continued to help in the war relief work, living in an old pension where she shared a bathroom with six other women.

Winsor French described Laura Corrigan's wartime role thusly:

"After the fall of France during World War II, Mrs. Corrigan discovered that she had hidden reserves of greatness. She forgot the titles and the hangers-on she had supported for years; she forgot herself and her silly ambitions and she went to work. . . . She had her magnificent moment and grabbed it!"

She did not lose her hauteur entirely in France, however. One day as she was riding an elevator in a hotel in Vichy, Hermann Goering got on, smiled, and bowed to her. Mrs. Corrigan looked at him frostily, stared meaningfully at her prized emerald that now glinted on the Nazi leader's fat finger, and refused to acknowledge his greeting.

Society was still struggling to get back on its feet in January of 1948 when Mrs. Corrigan left the ruins of London to visit her sister, Mrs. David Armstrong-Taylor of San Francisco, who was to meet her in New York. Shortly after her arrival, Mrs. Corrigan became ill in her New York hotel. She died on January 22—twenty years to the day after the death of her husband.

Gwen Brewster, writing in the Philadelphia *Inquirer* a few months after the death of Mrs. Corrigan, wrote:

"Laura Mae Corrigan has delivered the snub supreme—posthumously. The books have been balanced by the last will and testament of the one-time Chicago stenographer who married into society, was given the deep-freeze treatment by the swanky sets of Cleveland and New York, then went to England to become London's acknowledged social arbiter. The list of legatees named by Mrs. Corrigan . . . reads like a page from 'Burke's Peerage,' or the 'Almanach de Gotha.' Not a Clevelander or New Yorker is mentioned. Which means, says Society, that Laura Mae Corrigan has snubbed last—and best . . ."

Janet Flanner, writing as "Genet," said in one of her Paris Letters to *The New Yorker* magazine: "Laura Corrigan is one of the most extraordinary American women that the Middle West ever produced and Europe utilized."

They remember her in Cleveland. It isn't likely they'll ever forget the girl who wasn't good enough . . .

XIX

Cleveland's Untouchable

ON THE NIGHT of April 20, 1959, a program series called "Desilu Playhouse" dramatized a "Gang Busters" type of story called "The Untouchables," and America suddenly had a new television hero. He was a government law enforcement agent named Eliot Ness.

It was a good name for a television character; short, euphonious, and rough-hewn in its honesty. Better still, it was a real name and it carried a reputation that could stand alone without the props usually called for from the TV writers. Eliot Ness had been a real man, and if the characterization spun on the tube by actor Robert Stack did not really resemble the original, it is hardly surprising. Copies seldom do, especially in Hollywood.

Out of the two-part dramatization on "Desilu Playhouse" grew a weekly hour-long program series that became the most popular show on the air. The American television audience embraced Eliot Ness, shrugged off the commercials that wreathed over, through, and around his smoking revolver, and relived zestfully the turbulent confrontations of racketeers and lawmen during Prohibition years in Chicago.

The basis of the television series was a book called *The Untouchables,* an autobiographical account in which Ness had the able assistance of a veteran wire service reporter, Oscar Fraley of United Press.

But the book's center core of hard fact was destined to be covered with layer upon layer of fiction and fantasy as the TV scriptwriters labored through the ensuing years to meet the demands of the drawn-out series, and in time the truth was lost in the world of make-believe, and the identity of Eliot Ness came close to being indistinguishable from it.

Chicago was home to Eliot Ness; his birthplace in 1903 and the scene of his most publicized triumphs. But while the story of his conflict with the Capone syndicate was dramatic and flamboyant—including an episode in which he and his men drove a truck through the locked doors of a gangster-operated brewery—this was but the opening chapter in the Ness story. The locale shifted to Cleveland in August 1934, when the celebrated young representative of the "new breed" among law enforcement officers was transferred there as head of the enforcement division of the U. S. Treasury Department's alcohol tax unit.

The arrival of the glamorous young federal agent stirred the attention of some Clevelanders, but it was, in truth, little more than a municipal side glance. The city was too much caught in the toils of the deepening Depression and the many serious problems that plagued the community to get excited over the arrival of a young man to take up a government post that seemed remote and unimportant.

That situation would change dramatically some fifteen months later, in December 1935, when the newly elected reform mayor of Cleveland, Harold Hitz Burton, surprised everybody, including himself, by naming Eliot Ness the city's safety director—the youngest ever to be appointed. It was the signal for everybody in the metropolis to whirl and take a second look.

Most people—those, at least, who were counted among the law-abiding element—liked what they saw. Ness then was but thirty-two years old and the strenuous life he had lived had not yet rubbed the bloom from his cheeks. He was a six-footer, taller than he looked. He was slim and graceful, and he had a boyish face. He parted his hair slightly off-center and brushed it back, often applying a heavy layer of pomade to keep it plastered down in the style of the day. He did not present the formidable, bellicose appearance that Americans expect in their law enforcement officers.

The new safety director not only was an attractive man, physically, but the qualifications he brought to his new job as head of the city's law enforcement and fire-fighting departments could hardly be questioned. They stifled the usual political carping that follows mayoralty cabinet appointments. The naming of Ness was, in fact, a master stroke by the new mayor. He gave the administration a glamor and a glow that it sorely needed.

Mayor Burton himself was a personable gentleman, and one day he would make his mark on the national scene, first as a United States Senator from Ohio, later as a justice of the U. S. Supreme Court. But he was no extrovert showman. He had run for office as an independent Republican, and the voters who had supported his candidacy were encouraged by his action in choosing a safety director who was a professional law enforcement official and removed from the muddy main currents of politics.

Ness was a figure to command attention in every way, and an era which employed loose standards for public officials applauded his background, which included a degree from the University of Chicago, where he had been graduated in 1925. His major fields of study had been commerce, law, and political science.

The newspapers all nodded their editorial approval. The *Plain Dealer* said on December 12, 1935:

". . . If any man knows the inside of the crime situation here, his name is Ness.

"The mere announcement of his selection and acceptance is worth a squadron of police in the effect it will have on the underworld's peace of mind. Racketeers know Ness either by contact or by reputation. They know that he knows. For nine years he has waged relentless war on them for violations of federal law. For him the war goes on, now to be directed from City Hall.

"It is said of Director Ness that he and his agents have smashed a still a day in this district in the federal offensive against illicit liquor. They have brought hundreds under federal charges and seen many put behind prison bars. It was Ness who broke up Al Capone's beer empire, paving the way for Scarface's commitment to Alcatraz . . ."

The editorial writer was right. Cleveland's considerable underworld population stirred nervously when the news about Ness was published. They were not alone. A perceptible undercurrent of fear also passed through the ranks of the Police Department. There had been a marked decline in the standards of the police force that Fred Kohler once had whipped together into one of the nation's finest. All the signs of decay and corruption that had made the old Teuton bristle with rage when he had taken charge years before were everywhere to be seen once again. Policemen had grown careless of their appearance, and it wasn't unusual to see patrolmen walking their beat in unbuttoned uniform coats, unpressed trousers, and dusty shoes. Nor were the men in blue above hoisting an occasional stein of lager while they were on duty. Worse than the infractions in dress and manner was the ineffectual, casual system of law enforcement. It was obvious even to casual students of municipal government that the breakdown in the police power was a serious one and that its inevitable result was lawlessness.

Ness spelled out the situation that prevailed in the Cleveland underworld only a month after he took his oath of office in the Burton cabinet when he addressed the Cleveland Advertising Club. If the members expected to hear some dramatic reminiscences of Ness's encounters with the Capone gang, they were disappointed. Ness talked about Cleveland crime and he laid some startling facts on the line.

The gambling element in Cleveland, he said, was raking in a weekly take of about two hundred thousand dollars. The numbers policy racket alone was yielding some one hundred thousand dollars every week to the operators. Ness reviewed the financial figures in the quiet, disapproving voice of a college professor.

"One of the major problems which the Police Department faces today," he pointed out, "arises from the fact there was a large influx of potential criminals from other cities before Mayor Burton took office. They came here because they knew the rackets were flourishing and because they expected to get jobs. But they found the rackets were all filled up. They had to get some other source of income. A large number of them, then, turned to robberies, safe cracking, extortion . . ."

The policy racket alone had been yielding one hundred thousand dollars a week. Of that amount, Ness said, approximately forty thousand dollars was going to gangsters.

Ness himself had a tolerant attitude toward gambling, but he was a realist, not a reformer, and he knew that the job of cleaning up a city like Cleveland was defeated at the outset if gambling were permitted.

Ness' words were carefully measured by the formidable combine of gamblers who were securely entrenched in the Greater Cleveland area. The leading gambling casino was the Mounds Club in Lake County, some thirty-five miles from the heart of the city, but less than half that distance from the wealthy eastern suburbs like Gates Mills and Shaker Heights. The other leading gambling houses were the Thomas Club and the Harvard Club. All three spots catered to their customers openly and with complete indifference to the illegal nature of their position. Director Ness had every right to wonder about his Police Department.

The inevitable head-on collision between Ness and the gambling forces occurred quickly and dramatically on the night of January 10, 1936, less than a month after Ness first took office.

Ness was attending a meeting of the City Council that night when an aide beckoned him to take a telephone call in his office. The call was an urgent plea for help from County Prosecutor Frank T. Cullitan, an honest and courageous official who enjoyed the respect of the new safety director despite the difference in their party labels. Cullitan was a Democrat; Ness represented a Republican administration.

Cullitan said he was telephoning from a booth in Newburgh Heights near the notorious Harvard Club run by James ("Shimmy") Patton, Arthur Hebebrand, and Dan Gallagher. The prosecutor and a wrecking crew numbering twenty special constables had attempted to enter the club, but despite their warrants they were refused admission by Patton and a bunch of gunmen.

"They're threatening to open fire if we come inside the steel barriers," the county prosecutor told Ness. "We need help!"

Ness was placed in a delicate position by Cullitan's appeal. As safety director of Cleveland, he had no authority outside the city limits, which Newburgh Heights assuredly was. He was new in his post, untried and unproven and very young. A lot of Clevelanders, skeptical of his ability and inclined to dismiss his Chicago achievements as a newspaper publicity buildup, confidently waited for him to expose himself through one or two major blunders.

"I'll be there," Ness assured Cullitan. "I'll come as a private citizen and I'll ask some policemen to go with me as volunteers. Hold everything!"

After sending out a call for volunteers among members of the Cleveland Police Department, Ness called the sheriff of Cuyahoga County, a picturesque, white-maned character named John L. ("Honest John") Sulzmann. Sulzmann, an orator in the wordiest political tradition, was an outstanding advocate of the home-rule policy and had taken a firm hands-off position toward all the communities of the county.

Sulzmann was not in his office. His telephone was answered by Chief Jailer William Murphy.

"Prosecutor Cullitan is at the Harvard Club with several of his staff and their lives are endangered," said Ness. "As a citizen, I am calling on you and the sheriff to send deputies out there to protect the prosecutor."

"We can't send men out there without a call from the mayor of Newburgh," said Murphy.

"Will you go out or won't you?" demanded Ness.

"I'll have to call the sheriff and I'll call you back," Murphy replied.

"To hell with this calling back," growled Ness. "I'll wait on the phone." There was momentary silence and then Murphy's voice said: "No. We won't go out there."

Ness immediately swung into action. By 10:30 P.M. he arrived at the Harvard Club with his volunteers. Eyewitnesses at the scene compared the arrival of Ness and his men with the appearance of the U.S. cavalry at the scene of an Indian ambush. The Ness forces included twenty-nine patrolmen, ten motorcycle cops, and four plainclothesmen. All were armed with sawed-off shotguns, tear gas guns, rifles, pistols, and billyclubs.

The reinforcements must have looked impressive to the gamblers inside. Even Cullitan blanched at the sight of so much firepower and the grim looks on the faces of Ness and his men.

"I don't want any bloodshed," said the prosecutor.

Ness nodded, walked directly to the steel door of the club, and addressed a face at the peephole:

"I'm Eliot Ness. I'm coming in with some warrants."

After several long minutes of silence and inaction, the heavy door swung open to admit Ness, Cullitan, and their men.

This peaceful admission was something of an anticlimax to the tense hours of siege. The only flurry of action inside the club occurred when a Cleveland *Press* photographer, the late Byron Filkins, who was about five feet tall, was pushed from a chair by a gambler who did not want his picture taken. Big Webb Seeley of the rival Cleveland *News*, roaring with indignation at the mishandling of Shorty Filkins, promptly laid a mighty haymaker on the gambler's jaw, stretching him across a crap table.

Ness learned later that one of the nation's most wanted gangsters, Alvin Karpis, had been in the Harvard Club that night, but had slipped out of the law's net during the hours-long standoff that had preceded the safety director's arrival.

That did not dim the glory of the conquest. It was a victory of the first magnitude for law and order; a tremendously effective opener for Ness' career as Cleveland's chief law enforcement officer. It was an incident that deserved a place alongside his dramatic crash-through of the gates of the Capone brewery.

Clevelanders, most of whom had grown cynical and weary during the administration of Mayor Harry L. Davis immediately preceding the Burton election, blinked in surprise and pleasure over the setback administered to the gambling forces. All of a sudden, the contest between law and the lawbreaker, the good guys and the bad guys, had come alive. All of a sudden the issue was in doubt and Eliot Ness was the town hero. His timing was terrific. The city seldom had needed a hero so badly.

In that mid-Depression period, idealism had taken a terrible pounding from the grim facts of day-to-day existence, such as it was. The city's old standards of morality, deeply rooted in the heritage of the New England past and the conservatism of the thousands of central Europeans who had taken up a new life in Cleveland, had collapsed as badly and as dramatically as the stock market, the banks, and the general economy. The heart of the city was a depressing reflection of the times. Panhandlers and prostitutes were out in such numbers they jostled pedestrians right off the sidewalks; some used bookstores openly peddled pornographic literature, and the entertainment level in some of the night clubs that sprang up all over the downtown area following Prohibition's repeal was almost Saturnalian.

It was a time not so gay as it was hysterical and abandoned— except on the hastily filled-in lakefront where for two years, 1936 and 1937, the Great Lakes Exposition gave the city and its visitors—seven million in all—a kind of downtown Coney Island and miniature world's fair jumbled together. Cleveland loved the Great Lakes Exposition because it was the most marvelous diversion offered them through-out the long years of the Depression. Even the jobless could scrape up enough dimes and quarters occasionally to take in the expo and admire its many shows, including one called the Aquacade, that the young Billy Rose had put together with Esther Williams as star.

Next to the exposition, Eliot Ness was the most interesting distraction of the time. He had announced, in a flat, businesslike voice that he was out to get the crooked cops, the numbers operators, the vice rings, and even to reduce the appalling number of traffic fatalities. And Clevelanders who had seen other reform movements go down to defeat chuckled and watched closely to see how Mayor Burton's baby-faced safety director would fare.

They discovered quickly that his approach to crime was about as emotional as an accountant's approach to double-entry bookkeeping; that he was activated more by practical considerations than moral outrage.

"It is debatable whether gambling is morally wrong," he said, "but from the policing standpoint you have an entirely different picture. I am inclined to be liberal in my views of amusements and I do not want to intrude my opinions on others, but as a safety director I must recognize everything which contributes to a lawless situation. By that, I mean major crime.

"Gambling brings into financial power citizens recognized as law violators. They collect large sums of money which must be distributed among many persons, some of them public officials, perhaps.

"We find the lawbreakers growing in power. Gradually, with use of their money, they get inroads into the systems of public protection, perhaps a safety department, perhaps the courts. Other lawbreakers gather under their protection, and you have a situation in which the policeman on the beat, and perhaps his captain, doesn't know what laws to enforce, what persons to arrest, and what persons to avoid. Since his advancement depends on his making no mistakes, he becomes cautious and gradually we find ourselves a city growing more desirable to lawbreakers. That stuff travels.

"A policeman must be able to do police work without having to find out the family background, the connections, of every individual he comes across in his work. His job is complicated enough without that."

Ness harked back to his Chicago days to recall the time he tapped a telephone conversation from the headquarters of Al Capone's brother, Ralph, in a Chicago suburb, and learned that Capone actually was in league with two competing candidates for office. One of the candidates was an out-and-out Capone-sponsored man; the other one was backed by the forces of reform. Capone had both of them in his hip pocket and could not lose.

"In any city where corruption continues," said Ness, knowingly, "it follows that some officials are playing with the underworld. If town officials are committed to a program of 'protection,' police work becomes exceedingly difficult, and the officer on the beat, being discouraged from his duty, decides it is best to see as little crime as possible."

Cleveland's policemen were among Ness' most attentive listeners. He was an unknown quantity, for all his reputation and his heroics in the Harvard Club raid. He didn't fit any known pattern of the day. One thing about him they learned quickly: He wouldn't put up with sloppy, out-of-shape cops.

In the Ness book, a good police officer was defined as one who could qualify as:

(1) A marksman
(2) A boxer
(3) A wrestler
(4) A sprinter
(5) A diplomat
(6) A memory expert
(7) An authority on many subjects

Beyond that seven-point program the policeman presumably was on his own.

The new safety director's first move was not to launch a drive against the city's leading criminals, but to investigate the members of his own Police Department. Two weeks after taking office, he transferred 122 cops to new posts in the biggest shakeup in years. Meanwhile, he was putting together a new band of "untouchables," a group of handpicked policemen to help him in his undercover investigation of the force. No holds were barred, and Ness was able to employ many of the same techniques and devices he had used in his fight against the Capone mob in Chicago—wire taps, investigating bank accounts, hiring stool pigeons, and any other helpful means.

The Cleveland situation was so bad, he learned, that some policemen actually were serving as "enforcers" for the gangsters enjoying monopolistic control of certain rackets, and that some of the police had been known to turn down protection money from independent racketeers, forcing them out of business with frequent raids that drew public applause.

Ten months after he took office, Ness presented a startling hundred-page report on the Cleveland crime situation to County Prosecutor Cullitan. He also presented Cullitan with the testimony of sixty-six witnesses who had indicated their willingness to blab all to the Grand Jury. The report was the work of his new Untouchables and his own investigative perseverance. He had spent one hundred consecutive summer nights following the trail of police crookedness through some of the city's worst dives and some of the metropolitan area's nicest suburbs. He had talked with bums and degenerates and respectable community leaders on the same night about the same suspect.

His investigations had not been without their amusing moments, one of which arrived the night Ness and a reporter walked into a saloon at East 82nd Street and Kosciuszko Avenue. As they walked through the door, a uniformed cop dropped his drink on the bar and dove for the rear of the cafe, racing up a stairway to a short landing. The door at the landing was locked, so the panicky policeman pressed himself flat against the door, hoping he would not be noticed.

Ness, as a matter of fact, had not given any sign that he had seen the policeman. He went directly to the bartender and asked to see the proprietor. The bartender told him the proprietor wouldn't be around until a later hour.

"Who shall I tell him was here?" asked the bartender.

"My name is Ness," said the safety director.

One of the customers at the bar let out a loud, derisive laugh.

"Oh, yeah? I suppose you're the safety director, too!"

"That's right," said Ness.

The customer nudged his drinking partners.

"Listen, buddy," he said to Ness, losing his smile, "go peddle that stuff somewhere else. It just happens the director's a personal friend of mine."

"I see," said Ness. "O.K., buddy, but if you've got any doubts about who I am, just ask that officer who's hiding up there on the landing!"

He turned and walked out of the saloon, the reporter in his wake, leaving behind a bar full of nervous customers and a very thoughtful policeman.

On the basis of the Ness-led investigation, the Grand Jury, under Mrs. Lucia McBride, returned bribery indictments against a deputy police inspector, two veteran captains, two lieutenants, a sergeant, and three patrolmen. All were convicted. The officers received Ohio Penitentiary terms of two to twenty years. The patrolmen received lighter sentences.

Before he stepped down from his job as safety director in May 1942, Ness sent another half-dozen policemen to prison and brought about the resignations of two hundred others. He moved carefully but relentlessly in pressing his campaign against rogue cops, winning the praise of the chief justice of the Ohio Supreme Court, Carl V. Weygandt, for "the outstanding completeness and care with which he assembled evidence against the police officers."

Cleveland had been hopeful, but understandably skeptical, about the apple-cheeked young safety director in the beginning, but his quiet ferocity in showing the racketeers and black sheep policemen who was boss convinced everybody that the law finally had a real champion on its side. Even his worst enemies conceded that Eliot Ness was, in a quiet way, one of the bravest men they ever had known.

"Director Ness," wrote Alvin ("Bud") Silverman of the *Plain Dealer*, a veteran and respected reporter of City Hall affairs, "is as devoid of fear as anyone who ever lived."

Silverman conceded, at the same time, that the imperfections that are characteristic of human clay were easily discernible in Ness. This was no saintly paragon.

"His social habits," Silverman wrote, "which included living in a Lakewood boathouse and entertaining in a most sophisticated manner, had tongues wagging most of the time. Also, he was too handsome and self-centered to be popular with the great bulk of hard-working conservative Clevelanders."

He was, on the other hand, tremendously popular with the working newspapermen in town. Not only did he provide colorful, exciting copy, but he was entirely different from the usual distant, reticent type of public official. He was friendly and trusting, and his trust seldom was violated. Furthermore, he was a young man who liked to have fun, and he found he could have fun in the company of the newsmen his own age. One of his best friends and confidants during his term as safety director was Ralph Kelly, political editor of the *Plain Dealer*.

When it seemed to Ness that the Police Department had rounded into trustworthy shape, he directed his attack toward other targets. One of these was racketeering practices of labor union officials. Ness put four union chiefs into the penitentiary after a short, fierce campaign, and there was a noticeable turn for the better in the behavior of other union firebrands.

Cleveland's traffic safety record at the time Ness took office was one of the worst in the nation. It was open season on pedestrians all the year round, but the Ness crusade against traffic manslaughter and injuries brought gratifying results, with Cleveland winning the National Safety Council's first prize for reduction in deaths and accidents twice during his administration.

The safety director showed some of his insight into mass psychology when he tricked up all the Police Department's vehicles in a garish red-white-and-blue paint combination. There was some ridicule of the bright colors by aesthetes who like their police cars to come on more quietly, but the Ness motivation was more than a whim. He reasoned that the police vehicles would be more noticeable when decked out in the bright paint combination and that the public would be far more aware of their presence on the streets. And that's the way the experiment worked out. It suddenly seemed to Clevelanders that the avenues were jammed with police cars where none had been visible before.

Now the outside world was beginning to tumble to the fact that something unusual in the area of law enforcement was taking place in Cleveland, and Ness, his record as safety director studded with one spectacular success after another, began to receive national publicity similar to the press notices he had gotten in Chicago when he was fighting the Capone mob.

As the excitement of the challenge began to fade away and the tedium of routine began to set in, there were some happenings that tended to take the high glitter off the shiny Ness badge. In the early part of 1939, he was divorced from his first wife, Edna Staley Ness (they had no children), and later that year—in October—he and Miss Evaline MacAndrew, a fashion illustrator for a Cleveland department store, were married in Greenup, Kentucky. She, like Ness, was a native of Chicago, and their friendship had begun in that city years before.

It was in March 1942 that Ness' career received its most serious setback, opening the way to his departure from the cabinet of Mayor Frank J. Lausche. One dark morning, at four forty-five, Ness' car skidded and slammed into an oncoming vehicle on the West Shoreway.

The safety director, his wife, and two friends had been drinking in the Vogue Room of the Hollenden Hotel.

The police report on the accident did not identify Ness as the driver of the car causing the accident, but it did list his license number, EN-1, a very familiar plate to a lot of Clevelanders—and especially to policemen.

The patrolman who had been assigned to the accident said in his report that the safety director had left the scene of the accident and that while Ness had called the hospital where the driver of the other car had been taken, he had refused to identify himself over the telephone.

Sensational headlines blackened the front pages of the afternoon newspapers. The hero had been toppled from his pedestal! Sir Galahad a hit-skip driver? The city was too far gone on Ness to believe the bad tidings, and he, indeed, did have an explanation to offer. It was a candid, reasonable explanation, even if it did present him in the cold light of a fallible human instead of a superman.

"Mrs. Ness had worked until midnight," the director said, "and after calling her, I took her to dinner at the Hollenden. We met two friends and they joined us at our table. I had several drinks during dinner.

"Then we went to the hotel room of one of my friends and chatted with him about his farm and other matters for a couple of hours. I had nothing to drink in the room. When we left the hotel we started for home. It was very slippery and the thing just happened like that . . ."

He snapped his fingers to illustrate the suddenness of the accident.

"My first thought was for my wife because I thought she was the most seriously injured. She had had the wind knocked out of her. After she regained consciousness, I got out of my car and went over to the other driver and told him who I was." The other driver was Robert Sims, twenty-one, of East Cleveland.

Ness then explained that he had returned to his automobile, driven it down the road a short distance, and then changed his mind, returning to the scene of the accident. But Sims was gone, taken to the hospital by another motorist.

"I had told Mr. Sims that we would follow him to the hospital," said Ness, "but Mrs. Ness said she was feeling better and would rather go home. After I got home I immediately called the hospital and talked to someone. I didn't know who he was.

"The person at the other end of the wire [Patrolman Joseph Koneval] asked who was talking and I said the other party [Mr. Sims] knew who I was. I wanted to make sure that the injured man was all right, but I didn't identify myself. I said that I would have my insurance adjusters on the job in the morning. The party very willingly gave me the name and address I wanted. At no time did he say he was a policeman."

Ness' statement about volunteering his assistance to the injured driver and identifying himself was confirmed by Sims under questioning by police and reporters.

"It was," said Ness, "a very unfortunate thing all the way through, but there was no attempt at evasion in any particular."

The accident was a two-day sensation, but it did deep injury to the public image that Ness had enjoyed in Cleveland. The hero worship never went quite so deeply, or so fervently, after that.

The so-called "hit-skip" accident came at an unfortunate time. Various civic elements that had been smarting under Ness' vigorous administration had been trying to undermine his position. Ness had made himself vulnerable to attack by assuming, in 1940, a responsibility as consultant and adviser of the federal Social Protection Program, a campaign to curb social diseases. He became director of the national program before Pearl Harbor and his trips to Washington and away from his safety director's desk became more frequent and prolonged. Ness was a holdover from the two preceding Republican administrations and the new mayor, Lausche, was not enthusiastic about retaining him, but he was fearful of public reaction to the dismissal of a hero. Some labor leaders protested his retention in office, as did some of the spokesmen in the police and fire departments, the labor unions, and Democratic Party headquarters. Each group had a grievance to settle. The county chairman of the Democratic Party, Ray T. Miller, a former mayor, offered dramatically to go to J. Edgar Hoover and get "a real G-man" if Lausche would fire Ness.

At the height of the pressure campaign to oust Ness came the shore-way accident and the subsequent bad press for the safety director. Less than two months later Eliot Ness resigned from the cabinet of Frank J. Lausche to become the full-time administrator of the federal war-time program against social diseases. His career thereafter, private and public, was a checkerboard that challenges analysis. While still in his federal job in 1944, Ness was invited by the heirs of Ralph Rex of Cleveland to represent them in Diebold, Inc., of Canton, Ohio. He was elected to the board and for a while served as chairman until ownership of the company changed hands. He later joined James M. Landis, former dean of the Harvard Law School, and Dan T. Moore, former Ohio securities commissioner and brother-in-law of syndicated columnist Drew Pearson, in a newly formed export trade company, Middle East Company. It, too, was a short-lived association.

It was while he was serving as chairman of Diebold in October 1945 that Ness got back into the public prints with another burst of un-favorable publicity. On October 9 he had initiated a divorce action against his second wife, Mrs. Evaline Ness of New York, on grounds of gross neglect and extreme cruelty. The petition somehow was kept from the reporters covering the courthouse, and the customary notice of the action was not printed in the *Daily Legal News.*

The petition, numbered 555772, could not be found in the files of the county clerk's office, although there was a record that the fees totaling eleven dollars had been paid. Aides said the petition had gone to Common Pleas Judge Frank J. Merrick after last-minute filing, but reporters were unable to catch up to the elusive petition.

When the county clerk, Leonard F. Fuerst, was asked where the petition had disappeared, he said, simply: "As far as we're concerned, it was filed properly and indexed."

"Where is it, then?" asked a reporter.

"Isn't it in the files?" he countered. "Nothing is ever hidden from anybody."

The divorce was granted, at any rate, and less than two months later Ness married for the third time. His new wife was the former Mrs. Hugh Seaver, a sculptress.

It was about this time that Ness issued a significant statement to the press, hinting at his return to the political arena.

"My business affairs are in such excellent shape," he said, "that I can now do as a chairman of the board should—direct policy." His allusion was to his post at the Diebold company. "I am so situated financially that I do not have to worry about a livelihood. I have some ideas about public service—and I want to try them."

The following year, 1947, Eliot Ness was the standard bearer of the Republican Party in the Cleveland mayoralty contest. His opponent was Thomas A. Burke, one of the most popular mayors in Cleveland's history. Burke was seeking his second term in office.

Throughout his career as safety director of the city, Ness had enjoyed high favor among the leading industrialists of the metropolitan area, and now they rallied around with a campaign treasury estimated at $150,000.

Conversely, organized labor regarded Ness as their enemy, and union support went to Mayor Burke.

It wasn't much of a contest. Ness was a political amateur lacking the basic tools. He was a mediocre speaker and he disliked crowds. All he had going for him was a faded reputation as a hero and a lot of courage. Time after time, rally after rally, he described the Burke administration of being "tired, weary, worn and confused," but it looked to perceptive political observers as if he, rather than Tom Burke, were the one who was tired, weary, worn, and confused.

Mayor Burke beat Ness handily, 168,412 votes to 85,990—a 2-to-1 landslide that buried all of the former safety director's political ambitions and made him a dead issue in Cleveland city government.

"We all liked Eliot," says John Patrick Butler, who had been executive secretary to Mayor Burke, "and we all admired him as an honest, thoroughly competent expert in the field of law enforcement. There never was anybody like him in Cleveland. He really captured the imagination of the public in his early years, and he was given a hero worship unlike that given any city official within my recollection.

"But Eliot missed the boat. He should have run for mayor in 1941, against Frank Lausche, who was then a comparative unknown with a name hard to pronounce. He could have beat Lausche then because at that time Ness was the most famous man in the city and the most admired."

Ness's absence from the city and public attention for five years during the war and immediately afterward cost him too much ground. And his two divorces and three marriages had to hurt him in conservative, strongly Catholic Cleveland. Following his defeat in the mayoralty election, Ness dropped out of sight completely for a while.

"Eliot had run out of gas," says one of his old colleagues of the glamor days. "He was still a fairly young man, but he simply ran out of gas. He didn't know which way to turn."

About a year after the election, he appeared in the office of one of the men who had been hired to publicize his campaign for mayor. He looked tired and dispirited. He told his former press agent that he was down on his luck and needed a job.

"I'd regard it as a favor if you could put me on the payroll for about sixty dollars a week," he is reported to have said.

Shortly thereafter he left Cleveland again and this time it was goodbye. Reports drifted into the newspaper gossip columns once in a while of his business activities elsewhere, but they never were specific or easily verifiable. Then, on May 16, 1957, the press associations routinely reported his death, at age fifty-four, in the little town of Coudersport, Pennsylvania. The stories said he had lived there for about a year, and that he had been in business there.

According to records on file at the Potter County Orphans Court in Coudersport, the former crime fighter had died intestate and insolvent. An accounting of his estate showed total assets of $992.50 and total liabilities of $9001.97.

Among his assets was listed two hundred dollars as the value of Ness' royalty contract with the New York publishing house of Julian Messner, Inc., for the book which Ness had written with the help of Oscar Fraley of the United Press. Ness had seen the galley proofs of the book before he suffered his fatal heart attack. The book was *The Untouchables*, and Ness undoubtedly was hopeful that it would sell enough copies to help him out of his financial plight. He could not have dreamed that it would be the vehicle that would make him an international celebrity, through television.

When the news of his death reached Cleveland, somebody remembered a tribute to his accomplishments written at the time that he resigned his safety director's post and left for Washington to tackle his federal assignment. The tribute had been written by Clayton Fritchey, one of his closest friends and an ace reporter for the Cleveland *Press*.

Fritchey wrote that, because of Ness:

"Policemen no longer have to tip their hats when they pass a gangster on the street . . .

"Labor racketeers no longer parade down Euclid Avenue in limousines bearing placards deriding the public and law enforcement in general . . .

"Motorists have been taught and tamed into killing only about half as many people as they used to . . ."

More important than any of his spectacular achievements as a law enforcement officer was this: Eliot Ness was a man who had given the honest people of Cleveland somebody brave and noble to admire. He renewed their faith in the old American tradition that when things look blackest, a hero will ride into town out of nowhere to save the situation.

Which he did.

XX

Short Vincent

SHORT VINCENT does not appear under that name in the Cleveland street guide, which stiffly insists on identifying it as Vincent Avenue N.E. in the unbending manner of street guides everywhere. But the formal tag is not nearly as satisfying or as recognizable as the commonly used name. As Short Vincent, it enjoys mingled fame and notoriety all over the nation among people who make it their business to know interesting streets.

Clevelanders in particular treasure the nickname because an unimaginative city government in 1905 adopted a numbered street system in the interest of efficiency, and in so doing sacrificed a collection of colorful and historically meaningful names. The north-south streets in the downtown area took on such sterile identifications as East 4th Street, East 6th Street, East 9th Street, and East 12th Street, for example, losing the more picturesque designations of Sheriff Street, Bond Street, Erie Street, and Muirson Street. Now the people cling jealously to such interesting names as have been left to them, and Short Vincent, a name of their own coinage, is a leading example.

The fact is that Short Vincent physically is not much of a street as streets come and go. It is, as its name implies, a short, narrow thoroughfare of undistinguished lineage and limited utility value. It travels a mere 485 feet—just over one-eleventh of a mile. Even people who are terribly fond of the street admit its value in the overall pattern of public movement in downtown Cleveland is negligible. It performs only a minor service by providing a kind of passageway for one-way (westbound) traffic between East 6th Street and East 9th Street, but it is not a route that a motorist intent on getting somewhere would seek out, because it really doesn't lead anywhere.

Once, in the formative days of the city, this little mews with the bend in the middle was an alley that served the stables and coach houses of the estates that fronted on Superior Avenue to the north and Euclid Avenue to the south. It came by its Christian name honestly. The land which it crosses was part of the farm of an early Cleveland settler named John Vincent. The soil must have been fertile, judging from the way the street sprouted with life in later years. It became, in the modern era, one of the city's most significant concentrations of facilities for fun and games, not to mention good food.

Much of the credit for this development must go to the influence of the Hollenden Hotel, the largest and gayest hostelry between New York and Chicago, which fronted on Superior Avenue and backed up to the sidewalk of Short Vincent. The old hotel was torn down in 1963 to make way for the handsome new Hollenden House which now sits on the historic site, but silent tears rolled down the cheeks of some Clevelanders when the magnificent old structure was destroyed.

The Hollenden was one of the city's outstanding landmarks; a living memorial of the Victorian period. Even in the rundown condition in which it found itself at the end, it was a magnificent building and it still enjoyed the loyalty, if not affection, of thousands of regular patrons who sentimentally insisted on the Hollenden address whenever they visited Cleveland. It was a fourteen-story red brick towered structure with one thousand rooms and bay windows that bellied out on every floor. Its builder, in 1885, was Liberty E. Holden, the owner of the *Plain Dealer*, whose newspaper building sat diagonally across from the hotel on Superior Avenue at East 6th Street. The former newspaper plant now is a branch building of the Cleveland Public Library. "Hollenden" was the ancestral spelling of the Holden family name. The management of the hotel was inordinately proud of the fact that it was the first hotel in the world which had electric illumination as a built-in convenience. It also boasted one hundred private baths at the time of its opening, which was a pretty sensational feature for the time, as was the fact that it was of fireproof construction.

City Hall was just a short distance west of the Hollenden, on Superior Avenue near Public Square, and the old Courthouse was directly on the Square, and there were several newspapers grouped nearby. These fed the hotel a steady patronage of politicians, lawyers, newspapermen and, in their train, the sporting element of the town. The Hollenden was the community's smart spot and—it follows—it was the center of the downtown social life. Among its more notable features was the elegant Crystal Room, whose mirrored walls and great crystal chandeliers shimmered with brilliance during a formal function; especially one that called for the use of the solid gold service, usually reserved for heads of foreign governments and Presidents of the United States. Five presidents made the Hollenden their stopping-off place: William McKinley, Theodore Roosevelt, William Howard Taft, Woodrow Wilson, and Warren G. Harding. Among those who frequented the Hollenden's dining room regularly was Mark Hanna, the President-maker, and his favorite dish was always on the menu. It was called Hanna Hash.

After living gloriously and proudly through its first sixty years, the hotel, already beginning to give way to the natural laws of physical obsolescence, its financial position weakened by the Depression, fell into the hands of a succession of hit-and-run operators who were completely lacking in respect for the Hollenden's tradition of class and without pride in its history. Their superficial attempts at modernization resulted in a spoiling of the rococo splendor of the hotel. In a vulgar bid to prolong its earning powers, the huge chandeliers were ripped out and replaced by garish fluorescent fixtures; paint was splashed over the shining grain of the mahogany paneling; chrome-and-glass wall fixtures were installed, and in places asphalt tile squares covered the old marble flooring, completing the desecration. The stately old lady of character was turned into a gaudy frump, and when ownership finally was wrested from the hands of out-of-town interests by two Cleveland investors, James Carney and Peter Kleist, they decided it had gone too far downhill to be rescued and would have to be replaced with a new structure.

The demolition of the old Hollenden proved to be one of the most interesting spectacles of the 1963–64 wrecking season in Cleveland. No hotel ever put up a better last-ditch fight. The wrecking company found that slamming its large iron ball against the wall of the hotel only had the effect of turning the heavy ball into a misshapen mass. After pounding the Hollenden a number of times, the ball began to look more like a cube and the wrecker wisely turned to a slower, piecemeal system of destruction. It took him more than a year to level the structure, many months more than had been anticipated, and all the admirers of this holdover from the past applauded the building's last convincing show of quality.

There is, of course, something immature in America's haste to destroy so many of the worthwhile landmarks that connect the present with the past. We admire and revere the ancient cathedrals, inns, houses, and taverns that decorate the cities of the British Isles and Europe; we cheerfully contribute our money to help rescue the temples of Abu Simbel from the flooding Nile Valley, and so many of our millionaires have dismantled old castles in Europe and the United Kingdom and rebuilt them on an American site, stone by stone, that the practice has come to be regarded as hokey. Meanwhile, we are constantly on the lookout for any of our native buildings which may be acquiring the beautifying patina of the years, and when we spot one we order it leveled in the name of progress. It is all part of our impatience with homegrown antiquity, and the American insistence on equating age with obsolescence.

A large share of the life generated within the Hollenden spilled out
the back door onto Short Vincent, helping mightily in the establishment of that street's unique atmosphere and lasting reputation. Taverns
and restaurants crowded along the walks of the quaint cobblestoned
street, and the way was filled with interesting characters. Somehow,
despite the physical changes that have occurred in the neighborhood,
the street has managed to retain its character. It even took on fresh
appeal when an institution that embodied the spirit of the progressive,
liberal forces in Cleveland moved its quarters to a Vincent address.
It—the City Club—is an outgrowth of the rich political climate that
prevailed during the administration of Mayor Tom L. Johnson. It was
formed in 1912 shortly after his death, and its founders included some
of his former lieutenants and disciples, among them Newton D. Baker,
Frederick A. Henry, Professor A. R. Hatton, and John H. Clarke. The
basic tenet of the City Club was open, public discussion of all issues
facing the people. Its credo:

"I hail and harbor and hear men of every belief and party; for
within my portals prejudice grows less and bias dwindles. I have a
forum as wholly uncensored as it is rigidly impartial. 'Freedom of
Speech' is graven about my rostrum; and beside it, 'Fairness of Speech.'
I am accessible to men of all sides—literally and figuratively—for I
am located in the heart of a city. Spiritually and geographically, I am
the city's club—the City Club."

All local and state election campaigns traditionally reach their climax
in the City Club's Short Vincent quarters on the Saturday noon preceding Election Day, when opposing candidates for major office come together in direct confrontation, not only to make their last oratorical
bids for office, but also to undergo an oftentimes grueling cross-ex-
amination by the club's membership. Close races very often have been
decided on the floor of the City Club in the heat of the question-
and-answer period.

In recent decades, Short Vincent has become best known as a re-
treat-in-depth for some of the most interesting characters in the community fold—gamblers, bookies, touts, playboys and playgirls, show
people and sports figures, the broadcasting crowd and the newspaper
crowd, politicians and panhandlers, lovers of jazz music, conventioners,
and a lot of anonymous seekers after excitement.

The establishment that anchors the entire street is the Theatrical
Restaurant, which started out as a hole-in-the-wall some thirty years ago
and developed into a fine place to eat and a preserve for jazz musicians.
The place changes character at the dinner hour when the musicians
come on, and if the diners sometimes have trouble shouting their orders
into the ears of the waiters, nobody really seems to mind that minor
annoyance.

The Theatrical is the creation of a streetwise, amiable little man known to his friends and customers as Mushy Wexler. His nickname springs reasonably out of his right name, Moishe, the Yiddish form of Morris. Some formalists insist on addressing him as "Mr. Wexler," or Morris, but that kind of strained speech makes all the Short Vincenters uncomfortable and even wary. It is a tradition of the street with a nickname that all its people go by a nickname, and the astonishing ingenuity of the people who inhabit the crooked little way has given rise to a sensational collection of sobriquets. Damon Runyon would have loved the street and all its people; he would have admired their colorful speech and savored the quaint names of such celebrities as Shoes Rosen, Honest Yockim, Milwaukee the Book, Fuzzy Lakis, Mustache Mike, Smalley, Russian Mike, Race Horse Richard, Heigh-Ho Silver, Pinky Schulte, and Squeaky Hilow.

Shoes Rosen and Honest Yockim were the Damon-and-Pythias pair of the Short Vincent gambling gentry until the failing health of Shoes impelled him to move to the softer clime of Las Vegas. The breakup of the genial combination was viewed with genuine regret by everybody who knew them. The anecdotes about their many gaming adventures are still told and retold, especially the one about their trip in a flying machine.

Wherever there was an important prize fight, with all its concomitant opportunities for making an honest wager or two, Shoes and Honest almost always were in attendance. It is not surprising, therefore, that they should have decided to attend a big fight which was to be held in Pittsburgh during one of the early years of the 1930s.

Pittsburgh is not far from Cleveland; a mere 125 miles or so, but at that early time there was no Ohio Turnpike to take motorists swiftly to the Pennsylvania border. Neither was there a Pennsylvania Turnpike to take the travelers deeper within the Keystone State. Such roads as there were had to be among the worst roads in the nation. The alternative to driving was flying, which was generally regarded in that early day as a rather risky venture, with unfavorable odds going against the passengers.

It was probably that element of risk that appealed to the pair and led them to take the plane to Pittsburgh. The trip to the Pennsylvania city was a humdrum experience, but the return flight, after the bout, was a Pegasus of a different color. Shortly after the plane took off it ran head-on into a violent thunderstorm that shivered the frail craft and buffeted it about the sky as icy blue slashes of lightning shot all about it, like a Conestoga wagon under attack by burning arrows.

The few passengers aboard the frail craft—perhaps even the crew—were of the same mind: This was the end. As the weather worsened and the little plane bucked and fluttered, sideslipped and shuddered in the grip of the storm, Honest Yockim turned to his old friend and spoke his mind in a voice filled with regret.

"She'll never make it," said Honest.

Shoes, who had been slumped in his seat staring fearfully at the rain splattering the window, sat up with new color suddenly suffusing his cheeks.

"I bet she does," said Shoes.

Honest sneered.

"I got fifty that says she goes down," he said scornfully. "Even money."

The other passengers within earshot whimpered, but Shoes nodded agreement to the terms, and for the rest of the turbulent trip, Honest was pulling for the plane to crash and Shoes was cheering it onward to the safe landing it eventually achieved in Cleveland.

The moral is, naturally, that men who are really dedicated to the fun of gambling will not overlook any opportunity to test the laws of chance. Life is made to order for them because it is made up of opposites. There are two sides to every question, to every game, to every issue; there is life and death, good and evil, black and white, sickness and health, slow and fast, early and late. Any world so constituted had the full approval of Honest Yockim and Shoes Rosen. They simply took sides, made their bets, and waited for the outcome. The subject of the bet didn't matter. The wager was everything.

Some of the life went out of Short Vincent in 1963 when the popular Kornman's Restaurant, owned and operated by the Weinberger family, closed its doors after a vigorous run of approximately half a century. An outstanding seafood restaurant, Fischer-Rohr's, had occupied the site in the early decades of the century, but shifted to new quarters on Chester Avenue, near East 12th Street. Under the direction of the Weinbergers—Mom and Pop and their sons, Julius and Billy—Kornman's became a headquarters for hearty eaters. Even though the restaurant's main entrance was on East 9th Street, it had a side entrance on Short Vincent, next to the communications center of the street, Frank Ciccia's Barber Shop, and everybody regarded the place as part of the Short Vincent establishment. In the afternoons and in the early evening hours, as the night characters came astir, they naturally drifted into Kornman's to exchange the latest news bulletins, such as who was running at Thistledown or the North Randall Track and what were the odds in the crucial night game between the Clevelands and the Chicagos. There was a big, round oak table in the corner, near the front door, that was their exclusive sitting place, and it was close enough to the end of the bar so that they could still hear the classic monologues delivered from time to time by William "Squeaky" Hilow, the most interesting bartender in the city; a gentle Lebanese with a bashed nose, an irrepressible sense of humor, and a burning desire to perform.

Short Vincent was at its liveliest peak in the years immediately following World War II when Bill Veeck arrived in Cleveland to direct the fortunes of the Cleveland Indians and set up, incidentally, a nighttime dugout on the little avenue. The brilliant burrhead took charge wherever he went; he was living in a hurry and there weren't enough hours in the day. He still had two legs when he became a Clevelander, but he was limping badly and he knew it was only a matter of time before the doctors would relieve him of the leg that had been badly smashed by the recoil of an artillery piece when he was serving in the United States Marines. He wanted the leg to take him places while it could—and it did.

People with two good legs couldn't keep up with Veeck, but some of them made a game try, dashing along in his hobbling wake as he shuttled about town almost every night in the week, from Gruber's Restaurant in Shaker Heights to the Theatrical and Kornman's on Short Vincent. Accompanying him most of the time in this spirited routine was a group of loyal and admiring companions, mostly newspaper people, who won the name of the Jolly Set.

One of the uncontested leaders of the Jolly Set, by popular acknowledgment, was Winsor French, the *Press* columnist, a daily commentator on the Cleveland scene who shares his time between cafe society and society-society. He is likely the one who introduced Veeck to Short Vincent, but the baseball celebrity would have found his way there without any help. He, like French, admires unusual personalities on or off the baseball field, and such connoisseurs of characters are drawn to Short Vincent the way a dedicated fisherman is attracted to a sparkling mountain stream filled with gigantic, angry-tailed trout.

It was French, indeed, who was the moving force behind a celebrated scheme to raise funds for charity by blocking traffic off Short Vincent one night in 1953 and using the street for an outdoor bazaar. The date chosen was June 8th and the affair was called "Fun For Funds Fair." Performers from night clubs, theaters, radio and television stations all volunteered their services, as did the town's star athletes and celebrities, including Bob Feller and Hank Greenberg, then general manager of the Indians. Paint was sloshed on the black asphalt street pavement in appropriately gay patterns, wooden booths and platforms were built, public address systems installed, decorative tinsel hung and, as a special touch to publicize the fair, a tall flagpole was installed. This was not intended as a patriotic gesture, but as a roosting place for a Short Vincent bartender named Richard Tuma.

"Cleveland hadn't had a flagpole sitter in a long time," mused French, chairman of the event. "It seemed like a good stunt at the time."

A month before the big street fiesta, Tuma made his way to the top of the pole and settled down to his sitting assignment. All his friends on Short Vincent were bursting with pride to see him up there, and they shared the vicarious thrill of achievement, basking in the afterglow of all the publicity the three Cleveland newspapers gave the city's leading flagpole sitter. They would yell up to him and wave their arms, and Richard Tuma would wave right back. He didn't have the slightest sign of a big head, and that reassuring word passed up and down the avenue.

Finally came the late afternoon of the big day when the "Fun For Funds" bazaar was to be held, and no event ever gave promise of a more complete success. All the newspapers, radio stations, and television stations had gotten behind the project and publicized it mightily. Thousands of Clevelanders made their way downtown, drawn by the big buildup, and there was no question but that it would be a roaring, smashing success.

As it turned out, it was all of that—and more!

The fun-seekers streamed early into the gaily decorated street and carnival sounds filled the air as the gaming wheels spun, concessionaires called attention to their stands, and a girl vocalist, Barbara Page of Station WGAR, sang from a bandstand rigged in a tiny parking lot. The "Fun For Funds" committee, led by Marshall Samuel, former publicist for the Cleveland Indians, was elated at the signs of success, but their joy was tempered by the dead hush of the air and the strange color of the twilight sky, a sickly yellow. Not many of the Short Vincent regulars were alarmed by the sight because it was the first time most of them had seen a daytime sky in years and they naturally assumed that this was the way it always looked. Not so Tuma, high atop the flagpole that he had called home for so many days. He knew, as the committee and many of the fairgoers did, that there was something decidedly strange about the sky. As he peered toward the west, his worst fears were confirmed. The horizon presented a mass of ominous saffron-colored clouds. There could be no doubt that something special in the way of a storm was approaching.

Tuma, appalled by the sight from his vantage place, shinnied down the flagpole and with hundreds of Clevelanders dashed for cover even as somebody pushed the panic button by yelling: "Tornado!"

It was exactly that: A real, honest-to-goodness tornado; a twister from out of the west. It swung lazily into the city from the southwest, touched down near Cleveland Hopkins Airport and, moving steadily in a northeasterly direction, it roared and swayed through the city, dipped down briefly at Short Vincent and East 9th Street, and passed on out into Lake Erie.

After a cautious interval, heads began to peek tentatively out of doorways, barrooms, restaurants, garages, and Frank's Barber Shop. It all had happened so quickly, but the damage wrought by the tornado was unbelievable. The doughty little street was strewn with debris. Windows were smashed, bunting from the carnival stands lay in the puddles, and the stands themselves were nowhere to be found. A beautiful Hammond organ which had been loaned for the street bazaar by the Halle Brothers department store was smashed against a building wall and lay slumped in ruins. A policeman's horse had been picked up, carried through the air, and lay dead in the street. The tall sign that had been firmly attached to the Gillsy Hotel had been wrenched loose and hung precariously over the littered East 9th Street at the corner of Vincent.

In the quiet aftermath, as the silently accumulating crowd of awed Clevelanders looked about at the wreckage, a drunk staggered out of Mickey's Bar, looked up and down in disgust, and posed the most pointed question of the day.

"What's going on here?" he growled as he flapped his arms and moved uncertainly off into the crowd.

For a long time after that spectacular late afternoon catastrophe, Short Vincenters liked to ruminate over what would have happened if Tuma had stuck to his post at the top of the flagpole in the face of the tornado. The general belief was that he would have ridden out the storm safely, and some of the boys were rueful that he had not taken this perilous course because as the only man in history to go through a tornado atop a flagpole he would have given the entire street added national luster.

Several years later, in October of 1958, Tuma gave all his confreres new reason for pride when, in another outburst of public-spirited cooperation, he agreed to participate in a pseudoscientific test to determine if a mere man could outrun a racehorse. Arthur Brisbane, the Hearst editor-columnist, years before had just about proven to everybody's satisfaction that a gorilla could beat a prize fighter, but hardly anybody had even bothered to consider the man vs. racehorse question. Such controversy as there was came about in a casual way.

The Short Vincent bartender, it seems, had been a patron of a rather sorry racetrack called Cranwood at the end of Miles Avenue in Warrensville Heights, and his luck at the two-dollar window had not been good. One night, while standing about the clubhouse with some of the track officials, Tuma moodily volunteered the opinion that all the nags racing at the Cranwood course were bums.

"I could run faster than any horse you've got here!" he asserted, making no attempt to suppress the bitterness in his voice.

Henry Gottfried, president of the track, and John O'Keeffe, general manager, bridled (as good horsemen are wont to do), and their first impulse was to take umbrage. Gottfried, indeed, shouted back at Tuma, "I'd like to see you!"

"Give me a chance!" yelled Tuma.

O'Keeffe, widely known as a race track publicist before moving up the executive ladder, suddenly saw the possibilities for newspaper space in the bartender's challenging statement. He suggested, craftily, that perhaps Tuma was jesting; that he didn't really believe, deep down, that he could outrun a real racehorse.

Tuma replied, heatedly, that he could beat the best horse that was entered in the Cranwood meet. What's more, he said, he'd like the opportunity to prove it.

"You're on!" said Gottfried.

The race, appropriately named the Question Mark Handicap, was arranged to be run between the third and fourth races at the track on October 23, 1958. On the program it was listed as Race No. 3½, one of several inspired touches provided by the track publicist, Ron Lewis.

Instead of having Tuma run against the best horse available, it was decided in the interest of sportsmanship to name as his competition the worst of the Cranwood entries. The significance of this decision can be better appreciated in the light of the knowledge that the horses running at Cranwood possibly were, in the aggregate, the worst racehorses assembled at any one American track that particular year.

The horse chosen for the big race was a three-year-old colt named Hard Luck Joe which, true to its name, had never won a race in its entire career. One reason for this sorry record, possibly, was that Hard Luck Joe's owners had insisted on running him against horses. They finally must have reasoned that he might have a better chance running against a middle-aged bartender.

When the news of the great contest was announced, all the Short Vincent regulars stirred with interest and there was an immediate flurry of betting, with almost all the money going on the horse, except for a few sentimental side bets. The odds were decidedly unfavorable to Tuma, but everybody admired the determined way he went about preparing himself for the big race.

The word was that Tuma was getting up early every morning and running in the park where track spies could not clock his workouts. He even made some test runs on the track between races, much to the delight of the fans. All of these preliminaries were duly noted and reported by the newspapers, of course, and a capacity crowd was at the track when the big day finally arrived. Among the spectators, certainly, was a strong delegation of Tuma's friends from Short Vincent. Even if they were betting on Hard Luck Joe, the bartender, after all, still was their boy!

It had been arranged by O'Keeffe and Lewis that Tuma would have the advantage of a handicap. He was to start his run at the head of the homestretch while the horse was around the track on the backstretch. The way it figured out, Tuma would run only one-eighth of a mile while the horse was running five-sixteenths of a mile. A hard path, furthermore, had been leveled along the outside rail for Tuma's benefit.

Some of the sharp-eyed spectators to the event say that Tuma added to his advantage by jumping the gun. According to their account, the man got such a head start that all he had to do was float over the finish line. At any rate, it was a runaway victory for Tuma. The poor horse, ridden by Buck Thornburg, came thundering down the stretch like Whirlaway riding for the roses, but the bartender beat him by an estimated seventy yards.

The joy was unconfined on Short Vincent that historic night. One of their boys actually had gone out and beaten a racehorse at its own racket, running! Whether or not Tuma had jumped the gun was shrugged off as a mere technicality. From that night on, the bartender was known simply as Race Horse Richard. It was common knowledge, incidentally, that Race Horse Richard, true to the tradition of the avenue, had bet heavily on himself to win, and so had come out of the memorable race with something more tangible and more valuable even than a new nickname.

When he returned to his bartending duties in Mickey's saloon he was as much an attraction of the place as the exotic dancers, which is really saying a lot because the dancers usually doubled as "B" girls and strove mightily to entertain the customers.

Mickey's was one of the most rollicking honky-tonks on the south side of the street—the side of the street reserved for indecorous visitors bent on high jinks. All it took to bring them back in line when they went too far, usually, was a reproving look from Mickey's manager, a man named Fuzzy Lakis.

There is no ready explanation why the street was divided as it was; why the north side should have been endowed with respectability by the Theatrical Lounge and Kornman's while the opposite side of the street bounced with girlie joints, excepting the City Club, of course, and a discreet rear entrance to a Stouffer Restaurant.

"We are separated by the Gaza Strip," Mushy Wexler once noted, borrowing the name of the neutral zone that separates Egypt and Israel. But his allusion carried additional significance. The monotony of the girlie joints across the street—Mickey's Show Bar, The Frolics Cafe, The French Quarter, The 730 Lounge Bar—was broken by an alley which leads to the rear stage entrance of the fusty old Roxy Burlesque Theater. Every time one of the Roxy shows ended, it seemed as if scores of heavily mascaraed glamor girls poured out of the alley in an unstoppable high-heeled herd. There weren't that many, actually; it just seemed that way. It was, in every instance, an eye-popping spectacle for tourists who just happened to be passing by. You could see them looking after the crowd of slim-legged beauties and then peering, tentatively, into the empty alley in sheer wonderment.

Being so close to the City Club, and being partial to politics anyway, as all gamblers are, the Short Vincent regulars were swollen with pride one year when one of their own number, one Hymie Mintz, decided to throw his hat into the political ring. He announced his candidacy for the state legislature, and in due course he was called before the screening committee of the Citizens League of Cleveland, a voters' watchdog association which, among other duties, tries to make appraisals of candidates for public office and to offer recommendations to the bewildered electorate.

The story has it that when Hymie made his appearance before the Citizens League committee, he provided the usual basic biographical information and then answered a series of questions put to him by the committee members. One of the questions was: "What is your position on the Taft-Hartley Bill?"

"I already paid it!" Hymie is said to have replied in a voice quivering with righteous indignation.

Hymie didn't make it up the political ladder, but another man who was well known on the famous little street did. He was Anthony O. Calabrese, an Italian immigrant with a captivating ability to twist the King's English and still make an uncommon lot of sense. He ran for the state legislature, was elected, and surprised most of the political experts by his victory. One or two of the experts, analyzing the results, attributed the Calabrese win to voter confusion. They pointed out, cynically, that there happened to be a very popular mayor of Cleveland named Anthony J. Celebrezze. Their broadly implied insinuation was that some voters who had cast their ballots for Tony Calabrese may have thought they were voting for Tony Celebrezze—the American pronunciation of the two names is very close. The Calabrese forces, unmoved by that argument and refusing to concede any part of the point, countered with the suggestion that the truth was just the reverse; that Tony Celebrezze owed some of his success to the voters' confusing him with Tony Calabrese.

As if the voters of Cleveland were not sufficiently confused by the similarity of these two principals, a number of other Celebrezzes and Calabreses have been active to the city's politics. The former mayor and Kennedy cabinet member, Anthony J. Celebrezze (now a federal judge in Cincinnati), had a brother named Frank D. Celebrezze, who served with high distinction as Cleveland's safety director during the administration of Mayor Frank J. Lausche, and who later was elected to the municipal bench. His son, also named Frank Celebrezze, now is an active politician and was elected a judge of the Cuyahoga County Common Pleas Court in 1965. Meanwhile, Anthony O. Calabrese, Jr., son of the veteran state legislator, came of political age and was promptly elected to the Ohio House of Representatives. In the 1966 election, he unsuccessfully ran for Congress against Representative Frances P. Bolton, a member of the House from Cleveland since the 1930s, when she took the place of her late husband, Representative Chester Bolton.

Time was when as many politicians as horseplayers could be counted on Short Vincent. The lobby of the Hollenden Hotel was a traditional refuge for men of all parties and Manus McCafferty's Artists and Writers Club in that hotel was a time-honored haven for politically oriented citizens. Manus himself, a former amateur flyweight boxing champion and onetime stage union official, held nightly sessions as the Nostradamus of the local party scene.

The glue that held together so many of these interesting and diverse characters in Cleveland's downtown life came unstuck when the old Hollenden closed and submitted to the crowbar and sledge. It was but the first of many hard blows to be directed against the little avenue. One of the worst, outside of the tornado, was the fire that razed the Theatrical Lounge in 1960. That cast a funereal pall over the entire 485 feet of street. Bookmakers, horseplayers, touts, saloon operators, entertainers, and just plain drinking men, all normally optimists by nature, stood back in dismay that verged on despair. The Theatrical was the magnet that drew the conventioners and the money crowd. Fuzzy Lakis, a spokesman for the south side of the avenue, said publicly that Short Vincent was through without the Theatrical; that the little honky-tonks, in effect, could not survive without it. Fortunately for them, Mushy Wexler did rebuild, and his new place, given the more dignified name of the Theatrical Lounge, proved to be even more attractive and popular than the establishment that burned down.

But the blows continued to fall on the little avenue. In 1963, the Weinberger family reluctantly decided to discontinue their famous Kornman's Restaurant. Close on the heels of this dismaying development, the afternoon *Press* went after the tactics of the B-girls in the area's strip joints and it was twilight for Short Vincent as agents of the Ohio Department of Liquor Control pressed charges against one saloon and then another, until the south side of the street was virtually dark at night.

It is really an old story, familiar to every large American city. Nothing is anchored; nothing is stable. The fun centers are continually shifting about, dispossessed by the natural factors of civic expansion, growth, and obsolescence. In Cleveland, it appears that the center of downtown night life is shifting to upper Euclid Avenue; to the outer reaches of that extravagant stretch which once represented the Affluent

Life to so many wealthy Cleveland families of the late nineteenth century.

The present century has been as unkind to Millionaire's Row as it has been to Short Vincent's honky-tonks, thereby proving the impartiality or neutrality of fate, if that is any solace to either side. The great estates and the mighty mansions have come inexorably to an end either disastrous or embarrassing. A number of the large homes became boarding houses, cheap hotels, headquarters buildings for assorted organizations, or merely massive backdrops for used car lots.

Some were summarily abandoned and boarded up. Others were torn down to make way for parking lots. The pattern of demolition was checkered and the effect on the beautiful old avenue was to give it the toothless grin of a withered hag.

Most of the homes mercifully have been removed from the painful present in a recent development which has produced a bright colony of fancy motels, sleek office buildings, attractive restaurants and, of course, a generous sprinkling of watering holes for thirsty travelers along that part of Euclid Avenue.

Once upon a time the gay establishments—the theaters, restaurants, and cafes—were clustered west of Public Square, on the plateau overlooking the downtown flats where the city began. That part of the Flats is still possibly the most picturesque section of Cleveland, but today it looks like the opening scene in a mystery film with its ramshackle old warehouse buildings, the rotting piles of the docks that lay half-collapsed in the oily river, the railroad tracks on all sides, and industrial debris everywhere. The very real mystery is how any proud city could permit such a priceless resource as its very heartland to deteriorate so.

Here and there are signs of interesting life and evidences of a struggle to revive the historic area. There is the old Harbor Inn, a colorful riverside tavern under the towering arches of the Main Street Bridge, and there is Jim's Steak House at Collision Bend, one of the more spectacular hairpin curves of the river, and there is Harry Fagan's Beacon House along the river, at the foot of Lakeside Avenue and West 11th Street—a stronghold of Dixieland music and carefree drinking.

The valley, otherwise, is a scene of urban abandonment and memories. The city travels overhead on the many bridges and viaducts that present such a spectacular scene at night, and very few Clevelanders ever think of looking down at the despoiled river and its littered banks with any measure of compassion.

During the Victorian period the theatrical and tavern district leaped across Public Square to the eastern part of downtown, between the Square and E. 9th Street. The heart of the city vibrated with life then. There were nine or ten theaters providing live entertainment of assorted grades simultaneously, not to mention the halls that provided stages for the thousands of irrepressible lecturers who seemed to abound in those days. Some of the old glory of that time still lives on here and there, as it does in the revived splendor of Weber's Restaurant, now known as The Round Table, a popular hangout of past decades on Superior Avenue across from the old Federal Building.

City Hall once stood on the site of the Federal Building, and in its rented quarters an unknown painter named Archibald M. Willard painted a large oil in 1876 for the centennial celebration of American independence. He called it "The Spirit of '76." One of the numerous "originals" of this painting hangs today in the rotunda of the modern City Hall, and the small park immediately to the east of the center of municipal government is called, in the painter's honor, Willard Park.

Another vestige of the past still living on in downtown is an East 4th Street restaurant called Otto Moser's Cafe. At the turn of the century, when East 4th Street was more appreciatively known as Sheriff Street, this narrow little thoroughfare was the Short Vincent of the day, and Otto Moser's was the most popular cafe among the sporting bloods of the town. It was directly opposite the stage entrance of the Euclid Avenue Opera House, the grandest in town, and all the great, fabled stars of the time patronized Moser's. They are still memorialized by hundreds of dusty, autographed pictures of the old-time stage stars which cover the walls of the old restaurant. Moser's successors, Max and Jack Joseph, former employees of the original proprietor, would not allow anything to be altered or rearranged. The only concession they made to the twentieth century was the installation of a cash register, which they regarded as a painful necessity. Moser himself would not permit one in the place. He just threw the money onto the marble-topped backbar as it came across the counter and let it accumulate or dwindle, as the ups and downs of business dictated.

Next door to Moser's is another survivor of the past gayety, The Rathskeller—not so elaborately theatrical in its atmosphere but still an authentic holdover of the past. Its owner, in the days of its prime, was Henry Grebe, acclaimed as one of the best restaurateurs in the nation.

Among the contemporaries of Otto Moser was a knowledgeable restaurateur of French descent, one Henry Menjou, who ruled over eating places whose names belied his ancestry. One was called The Bismarck and the other, its successor, was called The Berghoff. Each featured menus printed in German, the fashionable language in Cleveland in those days. The Hollenden Hotel ventured to introduce French-language menus at the time, and it was the talk of the town—not the French language but the hotel's audacity. One of Henry Menjou's headwaiters, briefly, was his son, Adolphe, a debonair lad who was completely confident that he was cut out for bigger things in life than feeding hungry Clevelanders. He proved the point to everybody's satisfaction by leaving town to become a motion picture star and creating the universal image of the Man of the World. This was not a small achievement for a kid from East High School, but it may be that Cornell University helped, too.

A young, aspiring music composer named Ernest Roland Ball was among those who stood on the fringe of Cleveland's cafe society in the final years of the old century. Everybody who knew him well called him Rolly, and it was generally conceded that he was a youth with an extraordinary talent for bringing musical notes together in fetching combinations.

Ball was born in Cleveland at 1541 East 30th Street, on the fringe of downtown, in 1878. He attended the Cleveland Conservatory of Music, and, while a student there, worked as a song plugger in a downtown dime store. When he wasn't banging out the new hit tunes of the day on the beatup piano installed on a high platform behind the counter, he occasionally fingered a few melodies that were entirely unknown to the customers. They were his own tunes; random escapees from the rush of music that filled his head. He had begun writing songs at the age of fifteen and it pleased him to note, when he slipped one of his songs into his dime store medleys, that some of the customers beamed and smiled as he played.

After he graduated from the conservatory, Ball went to New York and landed a job in a small music publishing house. He hardly had had time to get settled when one day a slim, personable young man named James J. Walker asked him to set some verses he had written to appropriate music. Ball obliged and the song, "Will You Love Me in December as You Do in May?" became a hit. Young Mr. Walker, as is generally known, went on to become the mayor of New York City.

That was merely the beginning of Ball's spectacular song-writing career, in the course of which he composed some four hundred tunes, including "Mother Machree" (with Chauncey Olcott), "Dear Little Boy of Mine," "In the Garden of My Heart," "A Little Bit of Heaven, Sure They Call It Ireland," "Till the Sands of the Desert Grow Cold," "When Irish Eyes Are Smiling," and "Let the Rest of the World Go By."

"Mother Machree" was inspired by his own mother, Anna (Nannie) Ball, and each Mother's Day the sentimental composer would send the same wire to her: "Today and Every Day I send you my love, my Mother Machree."

Chauncey Olcott and John McCormack sang the songs of Rolly Ball all over the world, making them part of the universal musical heritage, but the Cleveland composer, a brilliant pianist, also was a stage performer and sang his own tunes successfully in vaudeville appearances around the country. In his last stage appearance in Cleveland, at the new, fabulous B. F. Keith Palace Theater, Mrs. Ball sat in one of the front box seats while Rolly serenaded her with "Mother Machree."

"Somewhere out in this great audience is my mother—my own Mother Machree," Ball announced. "Won't you stand up, pretty mother?" But Mrs. Ball was too frightened to stand and the audience applauded in vain.

On May 3, 1927, Ball volunteered to play some of his compositions on a Mississippi flood relief concert program in Santa Ana, California. It isn't likely that he ever played for a more enthusiastically approving audience. Its members gave him a thunderous ovation at the end of each number and he had to take eight curtain calls. As he bowed his thanks the last time, he told the audience, apologetically, that he couldn't come out again. He went to his dressing room, put his head down on the makeup table, and quietly died of a heart attack. He was forty-eight years old. His body was returned to Cleveland and he was buried on a foggy, rainy day in May in Lake View Cemetery, next to the grave of his father. His pallbearers included Irving Berlin and George M. Cohan.

Cleveland had changed a great deal in the quarter-century or so that had elapsed between the time Ernest Roland Ball had left to seek success as a songwriter and the time he had returned for the final requiem. The gay, scintillating theater district around East 4th Street and Euclid, and on Superior Avenue and Prospect Avenue, had been overwhelmed by the mercantile expansion and a building boom that had moved ruthlessly in on the choice sites occupied by old theaters. The motion picture had arrived on the scene and new cinema palaces were the order of the day. Film houses were spotted all over the downtown area, but with the exception of the mammoth Hippodrome Theater on lower Euclid Avenue, the best and the newest of the theaters were in the developing Playhouse Square area, extending roughly from East 12th Street to East 17th Street along Euclid.

Some four miles farther east on Euclid was the increasingly important uptown district where East 105th crossed the avenue; an intersection known historically as Doan's Corner after the original pioneer of the area, Nathaniel Doan. The classiest theater, by far, in this busy district was Keith's 105th. It was in this theater that the show business career of Leslie Townes Hope had its beginning. It was many years later that he took the name of Bob Hope. His mother took him to the vaudeville-movie house to see and hear Frank Fay, then the top monologist-humorist of the day, and the seed was planted. Fay had a way of making show business look easy.

The Hope family came to Cleveland the roundabout way; by way of Eltham, England, where Leslie Townes Hope was born in 1903. He was five years old when Cleveland became home. Life for the transplanted family in the strange and busy American city was a fight for survival, but the Hopes were up to the challenge.

Recalling those beginning days in his autobiography, *Have Tux, Will Travel*, the famous comedian wrote:

"I tried so many different ways of raising a dollar Horatio Alger could have used me for a technical expert. I don't remember whether the paper route was my first job or my tenth. Any job that needed a strong back and a weak mind was where you'd find young Les Hope, pointing the profit motive like a bird dog trying out his nose for distance.

"At one point I sold papers on one of the corners of 102d and Euclid. Three of my brothers had stands on the other corners. I had the Southwest Grocery Store corner, Jack had the Cleveland Trust Company corner, Sid had the Marshall Drugstore corner, Fred the Standard Drugstore corner.

"I had one regular customer whose name I didn't know; all I knew was that he snapped his face open and shut like a wrinkled old coin purse. Not that he talked often. I sold him his paper every night when he went home from downtown in a chauffeur-driven brougham automobile. But we weren't chatty about it. We made our deal with gestures on my part and grunts on his. I'd hand him his paper and he'd hand me two cents. One night he gave me a dime. I told him I was fresh out of pennies, but he didn't say, 'Keep the change. Pay me tomorrow.' It was my rush hour, but I said, 'I'll run and get your change,' and I hotfooted it into the grocery store on my corner.

"It was one of those stores with the cashier in the rear and the change going back and forth in little baskets whipping along on overhead wires. When I came back, my customer said, 'Young man, I'm going to give you some advice. If you want to be a success in business, trust nobody. Never give credit and always keep change on hand. That way you won't miss any customers while you're going for it.'

"I was turning that over in my mind when a streetcar inspector asked me, 'Do you know who that was?'

"I said, 'No.'

"'He is only the richest man in the world,' the inspector said. 'That's John D. Rockefeller, Senior.' He was living in Forest Hill, just outside of Cleveland. There have been times when I wish I had taken his advice."

Hope attended Fairmount Elementary School and Fairmount Junior High School. His high school career was brief and incomplete; he attended East High for a year and a half, thereby posing a continuing problem for school authorities who are still hard pressed to explain to new generations of youngsters impatient with formal education how it could happen that a dropout named Hope could make out so well in spite of his educational handicap.

When he was sixteen years old and one of the leading lights of the Fairmount gang that hung out at the corner of East 105th and Euclid, with special preference for the cozy comfort of the Alhambra Pool Palace, Hope tried out his talents as an amateur boxer, entering a tournament under the ringname of Packy East. One of his good friends, Whitey Jennings, was fighting in the same Ohio State amateur competition under the name of Packy West. The Hope sense of humor already was at work.

Packy East won his first fight, much to his own surprise, drew a bye, and moved into the semifinals against the state amateur champion, one Happy Walsh. Walsh came out of the ring still Happy, but Packy East, the victim of a kayo, came out of the bout as Les Hope once again. It infuriated Hope that his schoolmates had a way of twisting his name around to make it Hope, Les.

It was after that episode that young Hope, a trained hoofer, became an amateur vaudevillian and moved on to stardom in show business. The old gang that used to hang around Doan's Corner with him has thinned out considerably, but those who are left are very proud of his success. They share vicariously in his fame by recalling that they knew him when. Hope is keenly aware of this as he revealed when he wrote in his autobiography:

"People I've never known claim to be my long-lost friends. It's no secret that I used to play pool at the Alhambra Billiard Palace in Cleveland and I meet a lot of people who open with, 'We used to play pool together.'

"I played with many people, but not *that* many."

XXI

Nice Guys Win Sometimes

Race Horse Richard was not the only flagpole sitter to distinguish himself on the Cleveland scene in the years following World War II. Possibly some element in the northern Ohio atmosphere triggered slumbering, latent talents in this highly specialized field; perhaps it was simply that the time was historically right for men to climb flagpoles and pit themselves against nature. At any rate, and whatever the cause, a Cleveland delicatessen operator named Charlie Lupica in 1949 shook loose of the salami and cheddar cheese, bade his pregnant wife a fond adieu, and shinnied to the top of his flagpole for an indeterminate stay.

It was a carefully considered move on Charlie Lupica's part, not an idle, aimless whim, for he was a fan of the Cleveland Indians, and Cleveland sports fans are traditionally a no-nonsense band. Lupica was depressed by the uncertain fortunes of the Indians in the early stage of the 1949 pennant race. The team was, in fact, floundering about in the vicinity of seventh (then next-to-last) place when he made his fateful decision. Once aloft, he announced to the world that he intended to remain there in splendid isolation until his beloved Indians had fought back to their rightful place of honor at the top of the American League.

Through that long, hot summer of 1949, Charlie Lupica held to his promise while the Indians, champions of the baseball world only the previous season, stumbled and staggered through a most unsuccessful time. It should have inspired them that Charlie Lupica was up there, like a brooding eagle, waiting on their fortunes through storm and calm, and even through the birth of his fourth child. Finally, after 117 days, the management of the Indians in the person of Bill Veeck mercifully prevailed on Lupica to end his outstanding demonstration of faith and loyalty. The flagpole to which he still clung was uprooted and transported through city streets, precariously dodging live electric wires and the like, all the way to Cleveland Stadium. There, in center field, Lupica descended to the cheers of thousands of fans and to be greeted by his wife, who smothered him with kisses, and by Bill Veeck, who smothered him with gifts. Near the flagpole was some freshly turned earth where only a few days before, the pennant that the Indians had won the previous year had been interred in a suitably grave ceremony, while Veeck and a stadium full of mourning fans stood by with bared heads.

That's a suggestion of the way it was in Cleveland when Veeck ran the baseball team called the Indians. It was a typical Bill Veeck stunt; the sort of thing Cleveland had come to expect and to enjoy under this master promoter who had reawakened the interest of the people in major league baseball. Even more, he had made the immediate postwar era in Cleveland the liveliest, most flamboyant, most memorable period of sports success ever experienced, perhaps, in any American city.

Veeck always denied that he had any part in Lupica's flagpole adventure other than to applaud it and help bring it to a suitably ceremonious end. It is likely that he spoke the truth because he was a remarkably candid man. The fact is that Veeck had set into motion a kind of sports madness in Cleveland that engendered its own eccentricities. And that burial ceremony in center field was more appropriate than anybody could have known because the wonderful Veeckian outburst, as colorful and as ephemeral as the fireworks displays he liked to stage in the stadium after a ball game, already was dying. Shortly after the end of the 1949 season, the ownership of the Indians passed into new hands and the era was officially closed.

The magic number in Cleveland sports history probably always will be 1948. That was the year the madness reached optimum level and the heady wine of victory set the populace reeling in the streets. That was the year the baseball Indians won their first American League pennant in twenty-eight years in what probably was the most thrilling race in the history of the American League. At the end of the 154-game schedule, the Indians were tied with the Boston Red Sox. The pennant was decided by a playoff game with the Red Sox in which the Indians capped their storybook year with a decisive victory.

The World Series between the Indians and the Boston Braves was something of an anticlimax, but again the Cleveland team triumphed. Even as the players and management of the Indians were exuberantly pouring beer and champagne over each other's heads in the wake of victory, the attention of many Clevelanders already had switched to the professional gridiron, where the hometown representatives, the Browns of the All-America Conference, had been quietly rolling to one victory after another under the leadership of Coach Paul Brown.

The Browns never did get around to losing a game in 1948. It was, as has been suggested, that kind of a year in Cleveland. The Browns played fourteen games and won all of them, a feat which has not been matched since in professional football. Then they beat the Buffalo Bills by a score of 49–7 for their third championship in the AAC in as many years.

Even Cleveland's entry in the American Hockey League, the Barons, had skated to a loop title in the winter of 1947–48 and then went on to win the Calder Cup playoff by way of an encore. This was the first suggestion that 1948 would be a very special time in the history of sports in Cleveland. The poker-faced bookies realized it more quickly than anyone else, and they made it highly unprofitable for anyone to bet on a Cleveland team on the grounds that it no longer constituted a gamble to do so. Sportswriters who had lost their objectivity early in 1948 unabashedly referred to their beloved hometown as "The City of Champions," and this became the rallying cry of the whole community. Some city councilmen even toyed with the idea of passing an ordinance which would make losing in any sport illegal, but cooler heads persuaded the city fathers that the idea was impractical, perhaps un-American, and decidedly unsportsmanlike.

To view this giddy time in its true perspective, it is necessary to know that victory hitherto had never been anything more than a casual, sometime visitor to Cleveland, in spite of the fact that the history of sports in the city abounds with great names and heroic deeds.

Cleveland got into the baseball act early. Its original professional team, the Forest Citys, opened play on June 2, 1869, against the Cincinnati Red Stockings. The local nine dressed in white pantaloons and bright blue stockings, while the redoubtable Cincinnati squad, the nation's leading exponents of rounders, also set the pace in style by wearing racy knickerbocker-type pants for the first time. The game was played on Case Commons, an unfenced park on Putnam Avenue (East 38th Street), between Scovill and Central avenues. It was a contest that should have been a tipoff to the rather bleak years ahead; the Cincinnatis beat the Clevelands by a score of 25–6. The same two teams played again later that summer and another hard-fought battle ensued. This time the visiting Red Stockings beat back the Forest Citys 43–20.

Historian William Ganson Rose has traced the formal beginning of baseball in Cleveland to 1865, when the first amateur team was organized. It, too, was called the Forest City Club and it, too, had something less than an auspicious debut when it lost to a team from Oberlin, 67–28.

Cleveland's second year in professional baseball, the 1870 season, was highlighted by a sparkling exhibition between the home nine and the Atlantic Club of Brooklyn, New York, in which the hometowners dazzled the visitors with their expert play, and especially their batting punch. The score at the end of the fifth inning had the Cleveland team out in front, 132–1. The Forest City players admittedly outdid themselves in that one, thanks to a big first inning (fifty-two runs) and another spirited rally in the third inning (fifty-four runs).

The nation's first professional baseball league, the National Association of Baseball Players, was formed late in 1870 and Cleveland was represented in the 1871 season, as were Rockford, Illinois, Fort Wayne, Indiana, Troy, New York, Washington, D.C., Philadelphia, New York, Boston, and Chicago. It was the beginning of a series of haphazard league affiliations, an in-and-out association that prevailed during the following three decades—the formative years of American baseball.

After dropping out of play in mid-1872 because of financial problems, the city won a new National League franchise in 1879 and held it until the end of the 1884 season, moving to the American Association in 1887. Again, in 1888, Cleveland returned to the National League with a team called the Spiders, a nickname stemming naturally out of the spindly physiques of the players. But in 1890, the city hit the jackpot by fielding two teams in two professional leagues—the National League Spiders and an aggregation of players who wore the Cleveland colors in the new Brotherhood League, a short-lived loop, also known as the Players League, that went out of business the following year. One of the leading figures in this unusual experiment in sports, with players and management sharing profits, was Al Johnson, brother of Cleveland's Tom L. Johnson, future mayor.

The most noteworthy baseball happening in that 1890 season in Cleveland was the purchase by the Spiders, for $250, of Denton True Young, who was pitching for a team in Canton, Ohio. Young, a native of Ohio's Tuscarawas County, was untutored in the pitching skills, but he was roaring fast—so fast the sportswriters quickly hung the nickname of "Cylone" Young on him. That was inevitably shortened to "Cy," and under that tag he went on to become one of baseball's real immortals. His career in the majors lasted until 1912, most of those years with Cleveland, and when they totted up the totals at the end of the trail, they found that Cy Young had won 511 victories against 315 defeats.

From 1891 through 1896, Cleveland had one of the classiest teams in the National League. The Temple Cup playoff of that time was the forerunner of the modern World Series, and the Spiders made the finals in 1891 against an Eastern powerhouse called—straight stuff—the Boston Beaneaters. The Beaneaters were too much for the Spiders, and little wonder. But the team rallied and fought its way back into the Temple Cup playoff again in 1895. This time their opponent was the Pittsburgh team, whose manager, a likely young comer named Connie Mack, acknowledged the Spiders' victory in that series by saying: "I am happy that gentlemen have won the Temple Cup." It was Cleveland's first professional championship, but the glory was brief. The team lost the cup to the old Baltimore Orioles the following season. Presumably, though, they continued to conduct themselves like gentlemen.

As far as Cleveland baseball fans were concerned, that 1898 season marked the end of the Gay Nineties. The owner of the Spiders, Frank DeHaas Robison, late that year became the owner of two teams in the National League when he landed a franchise also in St. Louis. That winter of 1898–99 he sent most of his Cleveland stars to stock his new club; men like Cy Young and the team's great catcher, Chief Zimmer. The Spiders, plundered of their talented players, were dubbed "the Misfits" by Cleveland fans. Franklin Lewis, describing the season that followed in his history of Cleveland baseball, *The Cleveland Indians*, wrote:

"The fans, scorching because Robison had removed from League Park all the old favorites, stayed away from the grounds in such large numbers that, after 27 games there, the team became a road troupe exclusively. It probably was the worst professional team of all time. Its record of 134 defeats and only 20 victories stands out like a festered lip on baseball's strong face."

The city was completely disenchanted with its National League misfits when Ban Johnson, president of the Western League, visited Cleveland in 1900 with his plan for another major league—the American League. It was a most propitious time for him to advance his idea. A baseball enthusiast, Davis Hawley, president of the Cuyahoga Savings and Loan Association and onetime secretary of the Spiders, introduced Johnson to a pair of young sportsmen-businessmen, Charles W. Somers and John F. Kilfoyl. They readily agreed to organize and support a Cleveland team in the new league.

The team they put on the field followed local tradition by wearing blue uniforms and was named, in fact, the Cleveland Blues—but not for long. Too many fans took to calling the players "Bluebirds," a cognomen which displeased the baseballers mightily, leading the management to rename the team the Bronchos in 1902. Again, in 1903, the team adopted still another name, the Napoleons, or "Naps." The name was chosen by the vote of fans in a newspaper contest. Their choice was, of course, signal recognition of one of baseball's legitimate superstars, Napoleon Lajoie, who had been acquired by Cleveland in 1902.

Lajoie, a fancy-dan second baseman and a powerful hitter, was one of many players who jumped from the National League to the new circuit. He and Pitcher Bill Bernhard had deserted the Philadelphia Phillies to join Connie Mack's Philadelphia Athletics. In his first year as an American Leaguer, Lajoie won the batting championship with a .422 average. Facing legal pressure from the Phillies, Mack sold the two stars to his dear friend in Cleveland, Charlie Somers, who earlier had acquired another Phillies star, Elmer Flick.

Charlie Somers was the dear friend of almost every other team owner in the American League. It might truly be said that, at the time, he *was* the American League, for without his generous, unstinting support, the league would have died. It is estimated that he drew on his own financial resources to the extent of a million dollars during the first three years of the American League venture. He loaned money to Charles Comiskey to finish construction of Comiskey Park in Chicago, thereby enabling the White Sox franchise to gain a foothold. He loaned money to the owners of the St. Louis club, the Boston owners, and—with Ben Shibe, a sporting goods manufacturer—he supplied financial assistance to Connie Mack in Philadelphia.

Somers' lavish outlay of money for his own Naps brought together a team that was the most feared in the league by 1903. In addition to Lajoie, Bernhard, and Flick, the Naps also had purchased the previous year a tall, graceful pitcher named Adrian C. ("Addie") Joss, who quickly established himself as one of the best hurlers in baseball. With all these stars, the Naps were favored to win the pennant year after year, but they consistently disappointed the experts and their followers, although they came as close to victory in 1908 as any team could when they lost the pennant by only four percentage points. The finish that year was so dramatic that it still stirs the memories of baseball fans. The Naps, Chicago White Sox, and Detroit Tigers arrived at the closing days of the season virtually in a dead heat. Chicago and Cleveland opened a two-game series in League Park that likely would decide the race. Addie Joss pitched for the Naps, Big Ed Walsh for the White Sox. It was a classic pitchers' battle; a head-on meeting between two masters of the mound whose performances that day brought the pitching art to its highest level of achievement.

Big Ed Walsh, who had pitched and won both games of a doubleheader just three days previous, allowed Cleveland four hits and struck out fifteen in that "crucial" game. But Addie Joss was better. He threw a perfect game—up to that time only the fourth in the history of professional baseball—and the Naps won, 1–0. The city celebrated that night, to be sure, but the roses were strewn prematurely on the streets. The Naps had won a spectacular battle but, as it turned out, they would lose the war. They dropped the second game to the Sox and then lost to the St. Louis Browns, finishing behind the pennant-winning Tigers in the final standings by those four percentage points, a margin so slim as to be hardly measurable except with a slide rule.

The letdown was almost too much for the fans, and apparently the defeat took some of the heart out of the players as well. At any rate, in the following 1909 season the Naps dropped to sixth place, slumping in spite of the fact that owner Somers had brought back to the Cleveland fold not-so-young Cy Young, who performed the incredible feat that season of winning nineteen games for a second-division team at the age of forty-two. This, plainly, was a troubled team. The classy Lajoie, who had been manager since 1905, discovered that one of the facts of baseball life in Cleveland, as in most cities, is that the fans have very little patience with a manager who does not deliver victory. He submitted his resignation as manager late in the season, staying on in the lineup as a player while one of his former coaches, Jim McGuire, took over the managerial reins.

Purely as a historical sidelight to indicate how far baseball has traveled in its trip to the place where the Don Drysdales and the Sandy Koufaxes can negotiate for contracts totaling a million dollars, Lajoie in 1909 was paid ten thousand dollars and was acknowledged to be the highest-paid player of his day. In return for that princely salary, he managed the Cleveland team, played the greatest second base perhaps of anybody in the history of the game, and batted .324. When the word got around that he was paid ten thousand dollars, everybody wondered what the world was coming to when a baseball player could make that kind of money.

Lajoie stayed with Cleveland as a player for five years after quitting the managerial post, but even though he was back in the playing ranks, the team name continued to be the Naps—and he continued to be the big man on the field. In 1910, for instance, he batted .384. It wasn't until 1915, following his departure, that the Cleveland club took on the name of the Indians.

That was a year of significant change in the fortunes of Cleveland baseball. Charlie Somers reluctantly sold the Indians to Sunny Jim Dunn of Chicago because his baseball philanthropies had mired him in serious financial difficulties. Ironically, the success that had eluded Somers during the fifteen years of his ownership came rather quickly to his successor. One of Dunn's first moves—purchase of the holdout star center fielder of the Boston Red Sox, Tris Speaker—proved to be the key to the team's successful future.

The prematurely gray Speaker made Dunn look like a genius in his very first year in Indian uniform, 1916, when he batted .386 and beat out Ty Cobb for the batting title. The manager of the team that year was Lee Fohl, a longtime Clevelander. He was popular and competent, but when he yielded the managerial reins to Speaker halfway through the 1919 season, such was the popularity of the Gray Eagle, as Speaker had been nicknamed by the sportswriters, that the fans approved the change. Perhaps they sensed that Speaker was the man Cleveland had been awaiting to lead them into the Promised Land of baseball. He did not disappoint them. In his first full year as manager, Speaker led the 1920 Indians to the city's first American League pennant and then on to the ultimate heights, a World Series victory over the Brooklyn Dodgers.

There never had been a more interesting, satisfying baseball year than 1920. It was a time filled with interesting characters, high drama on and off the field, unbelievable heroics and, finally, full triumph. But there also was tragedy. It occurred on the hot afternoon of August 16 in the Polo Grounds in New York. There, in a game with the Yankees, the popular Cleveland shortstop star, twenty-nine-year-old Ray Chapman, was hit in the temple by a ball thrown by pitcher Carl Mays of New York. Chapman was the leadoff batter in that inning and the ball that struck him was the first pitch. He fell immediately to the ground, unconscious. Umpire Tom Connolly took one look, turned to the stands, and called for a physician. Players from both teams gathered around the fallen player, among them Yankee catcher Herold "Muddy" Ruel, a coach and front-office executive with the Indians in later years.

Chapman recovered consciousness after a few minutes, following the ministration of two doctors who came onto the field, and he tried to talk, but no words became audible because the blow had caused a paralysis of the vocal nerves. His teammates helped him to his feet, finally, and with the assistance of two of them he began to walk toward the clubhouse. When he was partway across the infield, his legs collapsed under him again and he had to be carried the remainder of the way, to the waiting ambulance.

At the hospital it was discovered Chapman had suffered a multiple skull fracture. As his pulse grew steadily weaker, surgeons decided on an emergency operation. Chapman's condition seemed to improve immediately after the operation, but shortly before dawn he had a relapse and died.

The news shocked the nation. Never before in the fifty-year history of the sport had any player died as the result of an accident on the professional baseball diamond. More shocked than anybody, of course, were Chapman's teammates. They heard the news with disbelief, and more than one of them joined Tris Speaker in weeping openly. The fallen player had been one of Speaker's best friends and he had been something of a counselor to the younger players. Only twenty-nine, he nevertheless had been considering retirement when the season opened, but had stayed on in the belief he could help the Indians to their first pennant. The previous October, Chapman had married Kathleen Marie Daly of East Cleveland, daughter of Mr. and Mrs. Martin B. Daly. Her father was president of the East Ohio Gas Company.

With word of Chapman's death, some players on the Detroit and Boston teams began to draw up petitions asking for the banishment of

Carl Mays from organized baseball. Word of this movement drew angry comment from Speaker.

"I do not hold Mays responsible in any way," he told reporters. "I have been active in discouraging my players from holding Mays responsible, and in respect to Chapman's memory, as well as for the good of baseball, I hope all talk of this kind will stop.

"I can realize that Mays feels this thing as deeply as any man could, and I do not want to add anything to his burden. I do not know what prompted the action of the Boston and Detroit players. For my part, I think it is deplorable."

Speaker's surmise about Mays' reaction was accurate. The New York pitcher had paced the floor of his locked hotel room all night, refusing even to talk with his teammates. When he heard that Chapman was dead, he was unconsolable.

The Cleveland manager was among those who accompanied Mays to the office of New York's assistant district attorney, John F. Joyce. The pitcher gave the following testimony on the previous day's happening: "It was a straight fast ball and not a curved one. When Chapman came to bat, I got the signal for a straight fast ball, which I delivered. It was a little too close and I saw Chapman duck his head in an effort to get out of the path of the ball. He was too late, however, and a second later he fell to the ground. It was the most regrettable incident of my career, and I would give anything if I could undo what has happened."

All the festivity went out of the 1920 baseball season with the death of Ray Chapman, and the American League stood still. The game between the Indians and the Yankees, scheduled to be played on the afternoon of the shortstop's death, was canceled. The Cleveland team went home to attend the funeral service which was held in St. John's Cathedral. Some two thousand persons crowded the cathedral for the solemn high requiem mass, celebrated by Reverend William A. Scullen, chancellor of the Cleveland Catholic Diocese. More than three thousand other Clevelanders stood outside the church, blocking East 9th Street and Superior Avenue during the service.

The last sad rites ended, the Indians entrained for Boston and a return to the pennant race. Three teams were in competition—Cleveland, New York, and Chicago. The loss of Chapman had to hurt the Indians' chances. Chapman had been the team's star shortstop for eight years, the best in the league at that position. He also had been a .300 hitter and a dervish on the base paths—his record of fifty-two bases stolen in a single season is still a team mark. A reserve infielder named Harry Lunte replaced Chapman in the lineup, but when he hurt his leg in a Labor Day doubleheader, the desperate Indians called up a promising rookie on the roster of the New Orleans farm club, Joe Sewell. And in an effort to bolster the pitching staff, the Tribe officials also called up a left-handed submarine pitcher, Walter ("Duster") Mails, from Portland in the Pacific Coast League. With these two moves, as it turned out, the Indians turned the tide of fortune. Sewell proved to be a brilliant shortstop and Mails won seven games, without defeat, in the tension-packed final weeks of the tumultuous season.

All through that eventful 1920 American League race there had been an unsettling, ominous undercurrent of rumor about dishonest doings at the World Series crossroads of 1919. There was, *sotto voce*, persistent talk about a "fix" the previous year—a dishonest deal that had enabled the Cincinnati Reds to beat the Chicago White Sox. The ugly rumors finally came to the surface and were given official recognition in late September, just as the Indians and White Sox were about to begin an important three-game series in Cleveland. When the two teams came together on the field of League Park on the afternoon of Thursday, September 23, they were separated by 1½ games, with Cleveland in first place. But suddenly the outcome of the game and the series, however influential in deciding the pennant winner, was secondary. Cleveland and Chicago were playing in fine, clear weather, but a heavy, dark cloud hung low over the field. It was put there by a statement issued by the president of the American League, Ban Johnson.

"I have evidence," Johnson said grimly, "and much of it is now before the Grand Jury, that certain notorious gamblers are threatening to expose the 1919 World Series as a fixed event unless the Chicago White Sox players drop out of the current race intentionally to let the Indians win. These gamblers have made heavy bets on the Cleveland team."

Johnson's words were linked with other startling allegations that Cleveland had become the center of a far-flung baseball betting racket. President John A. Heydler of the National League, who visited Cleveland for a personal investigation of gambling, charged that one hundred thousand dollars or more was wagered daily in the city on baseball.

The biggest scandal in sports history finally broke out in all its sordid detail on September 28, as a Chicago grand jury returned indictments against eight White Sox players who had appeared in the 1919 World Series. Baseball was plunged into the darkest days it ever has known. The White Sox team that hitherto had commanded so much admiraton now found itself contemptuously renamed the "Black Sox." Of the eight players named in the indictments, seven had been active members of the Chicago squad. They were summarily fired by owner Comiskey.

The Indians, the Yankees, and the weakened White Sox played out the few remaining games, but now there was no longer a question of Cleveland's eventual victory. In the final standings, the Indians topped second-place Chicago by two games, New York by three.

It probably was the best outcome that baseball could have asked. The game desperately needed some players cast in the heroic, clean-cut mold to renew the romantic image of the national pastime. Cleveland, in large measure, answered that need. Much was made of the fact that Ray Chapman, a prototype of the clean-cut, high-minded athlete, had given his life playing the game to the hilt. Pitcher Jim ("Sarge") Bagby had won thirty-one games for the Indians that year. George Uhle, a native of the city, had gone into a Cleveland uniform directly from the sandlots and won a place on the pitching staff immediately. Pitcher Ray Caldwell, who had to fight the bottle as well as the opposing teams, came back to win twenty games for the Indians by way of rewarding Tris Speaker for his faith in him. And, on the hitting side, the Cleveland club had ten batters sporting a season average of .300 or better!

The 1920 World Series turned out to be baseball's best reply to the cynics; the best possible antidote to the poisonous scandal. The Indians and the Brooklyn Dodgers slugged it out, toe to toe, in a seven-game series that still stands out as a classic. Cleveland won the first game; Brooklyn took the second and third, and the Indians won the fourth. In the fifth game, played on Sunday in Cleveland's newly renamed Dunn Field (League Park), Burleigh Grimes started for the Dodgers and found himself in trouble in the first inning. Charlie Jamieson singled. Bill ("Wamby") Wambsganss singled. Tris Speaker bunted and was safe at first when Grimes slipped and was unable to field the ball.

The Cleveland right fielder, Elmer Smith, was the batter in this bases-loaded situation. Grimes worked the count on him to one ball and two strikes before he threw the pitch that would help Smith make history. The Cleveland batter connected with the ball solidly and sent it high over the right field screen, far into Lexington Avenue beyond. It was a blow heard around the baseball world—a grand-slam homer in a World Series game! It had never happened before.

But the same game produced still another sensational feat to thrill fans everywhere, even the sad-eyed Brooklynites. It happened in the fifth inning. Cleveland's pitcher, Sarge Bagby, had put himself in the record books in the fourth when, with two runners on base (Steve O'Neill and Doc Johnston), he hit a slightly Oriental home run inside the temporary bleachers that encroached on right-center field. Possibly Bagby was still enraptured with the thrill of the achievement when he took the mound in the fifth inning. At any rate, the first two batters, Pete Kilduff and Otto Miller, hit singles. The Brooklyn pitcher, Clarence Mitchell, was the next batter. He got hold of the third pitch and drove a hot liner toward right-center field. Second baseman Wambsganss leaped into the air and caught the ball, stepped on second base to double Kilduff and then, spotting the surprised Miller standing in frozen disbelief on the base path between first and second, Wamby ran to him and touched him with the ball.

It took a few seconds before the Dunn Field crowd, and even the players, realized what had happened. It finally came to them that they had just witnessed the first and only unassisted triple play in World Series history, and the old park became Bedlam. People spilled into the streets as the word spread around town—there was no radio—and the city rocked in a delirium of joy.

The remaining games of the 1920 series, all well played, were anti-climactical, as one would expect. Pitcher Stanley Coveleski joined the company of heroes with three victories and Cleveland went on to win the world championship and in so doing helped to restore some of the sheen to a sport that had been so recently tarnished. Another twenty-eight years would pass before the Indians would taste the heady draught of a pennant victory. They were not uneventful or uninteresting years, though, nor were they without hero-athletes. The roster included such outstanding players as Jack Graney, Mel Harder, Wes Ferrell, the Sewell brothers, Joe and Luke; Steve O'Neill, Lew Fonseca, George Burns, Joe Shaute, Willis Hudlin, Earl Averill, Dick Porter, Johnny Burnett, Odell ("Bad News") Hale, Joe Vosmik, Hal Trosky, and Johnny Allen.

On the managerial side, Tris Speaker gave way to Jack McCallister after the 1926 season, followed by Roger Peckinpaugh in 1928. Then came Walter Johnson, 1933; Steve O'Neill, 1935; Oscar Vitt, 1938; Peckinpaugh again in 1941; and Lou Boudreau in 1942. The favorite description of Cleveland by that time among baseball men was "the grave-yard of managers." If this were not actually true, it hardly could be said, nonetheless, that the bubbling waters of the Cuyahoga effected any noticeable prolongation in the lives of the managers who dared to hold the reins of the Indians during the 1920s and the 1930s.

Change was the order of the period, and it reached even into the non-athletic department housed in the front office. Sunny Jim Dunn died in 1922 and his widow turned active direction of the club over to E. S. Barnard, who became president of the American League five years later, in 1927. That same year, a syndicate of wealthy Clevelanders, including John Sherwin, Sr., George Martin, Percy Morgan, Joseph C. Hostetler, Newton D. Baker, and two sets of brothers—Alva and Charles Bradley and O. P. and M. J. Van Sweringen—purchased the Indians for approximately one million dollars. Alva Bradley, a real estate-shipping tycoon, assumed the club presidency.

The most notable development in Cleveland baseball of the 1930s—perhaps even the Depression-struck city—was the completion in 1932 of the largest and most impressive stadium in the United States. Cleveland Stadium was built at a cost of $2,640,000 on lakefront fill land north of downtown, directly below the high bluff on which City Hall and Cuyahoga County Courthouse sit in massive dignity. Beyond its worth as a home for baseball and football, the stadium was a civic asset of incalculable value. Built in a time of economic disaster, it was a symbol of a city's faith in its future. Its location in the very heart of the city and its extravagantly large dimensions were bold innovations that won national attention. The horseshoe-shaped stadium, a two-deck structure, had 78,129 permanent seats—about three times the capacity of old League Park. The playing field was the largest in the major leagues; so large, indeed, that Babe Ruth, upon viewing the great pasturage, was moved to comment: "The only way a man can play this outfield is on a horse."

The first athletic event—if such it can be called—to be held in the still unfinished stadium was not a baseball game but a championship heavyweight fight between Max Schmeling, the German titleholder, and W. L. ("Young") Stribling, Jr., the American contender. It was held on July 3, 1931. The crowd of 36,936 persons was almost lost in the great arena, but presumably they comforted themselves with the knowledge that even if the fight were a ho-hum affair they were participating in a historic occasion. Which, to be sure, they were.

It wasn't until more than a year later, July 31, 1932, that the Indians played the first baseball game in the stadium. There were 80,184 fans on hand, as well as most of the celebrities of the game. The Philadelphia Athletics were the opponents. Lefty Grove pitched for the A's and Mel Harder for the Indians. With such great pitchers, and the wide open spaces of the vast stadium wasteland, it isn't surprising that a pitchers' battle ensued. Philadelphia won, 1–0.

Next to the construction of the stadium, the most noteworthy baseball happening of the Depression was the arrival in Cleveland in 1936 of a seventeen-year-old farm boy with rolling gait and peach fuzz on his face. Robert William Andrew Feller of Van Meter, Iowa, had been discovered the previous year by an Indian scout, Cy Slapnicka, a fellow Iowan. Before being shipped off to a minor league club, Fargo-Moorehead, the high school boy was called in for a once-over inspection. His first performance in Cleveland was on a sandlot diamond in Woodland Hills Park, where he pitched for the Rosenblums, a team sponsored by a downtown clothing store and competing in the city's amateur class A division. He won a 3–2 victory in twelve innings. The next day, recalls Feller in his autobiography, *Strikeout Story*, Slapnicka opened the door to his future.

"You looked very good," said the scout. "Now, I've got a big surprise for you. How would you like to pitch against the St. Louis Cardinals?"

The Indians had an exhibition game scheduled with the famous Gas House Gang on July 6 in League Park. The St. Louis lineup included Frankie Frisch, Dizzy and Paul Dean, Joe Medwick, Pepper Martin, Leo Durocher, Terry Moore, and Rip Collins—an array of talent calculated to disarrange the composure of an experienced major leaguer, much less a seventeen-year-old who never had pitched a ball in a professional game.

"Don't worry," said Slapnicka.

Veteran George Uhle pitched the first three innings against the Cards. Feller was to pitch the middle three innings, with Manager Steve O'Neill catching.

O'Neill's instructions to him were simple. Feller simply was to throw fast balls. He followed his orders without question. The first batter, Catcher Bruce Ogrodowski, struck out. So did the second batter, Leo Durocher.

"I was fast that day," Feller wrote. "Probably as fast as I ever was or ever will be. I didn't try curves. I just kept pumping the fast ball up there and the Cardinals kept swinging . . ."

In three innings, the schoolboy struck out eight of the famous St. Louis Cardinals. The sports world blinked and took note. After the game, a photographer asked Dizzy Dean if he would pose for a picture with young Feller. The man who was at that moment the greatest pitcher in baseball replied: "If it's all right with him, it's all right with me. After what he did today, he's the guy to say."

The performance ended Feller's minor league career before it began. On August 23, 1936, Manager O'Neill announced that Feller would start for the Indians against the St. Louis Browns. The boy responded by making baseball history that hot Sunday afternoon in League Park, striking out fifteen of the Browns as he won, 4-1. His total in that game was within one of Rube Waddell's American League strikeout record, set in 1908. It was the highest strikeout total in the American League since Bob Shawkey struck out fifteen men in 1919.

Master Feller had been a curiosity before, but now he was a celebrity. The best was yet to come, however, in that sensational first season of his. On Sunday, September 13, Feller struck out seventeen in a game with the Philadelphia Athletics, setting a new American League strikeout record and tying the major league high set in 1933 by Dizzy Dean. Feller had to wait until 1938, his second full season in the majors, to set a new mark of eighteen strikeouts in a game with the Detroit Tigers. All things considered, though, it was agreed in 1936 that he had established himself as a pretty promising lad.

Feller fulfilled that promise in the years that followed. His was a long, record-studded career, of such distinction as to make his election to baseball's Hall of Fame the surest ballot bet since Alf Landon ran against Franklin D. Roosevelt. It spanned twenty-one years, including four years in the Navy in World War II—four years subtracted from his career when he was at his physical peak. Rapid Robert, as he was identified by the sportswriters, still managed to pitch three no-hit games (a feat matched only by Sandy Koufax of the Dodgers and Cleveland's Cy Young), twelve one-hitters (the previous record was seven, held by Cleveland's Addie Joss), and to set a new season's record for strikeouts, 348, in 1946. The previous record, 343, was held by Rube Waddell. Feller kept company with the great from the very beginning, and he more than held his own in the select circle of baseball's pitching superstars.

The postwar era in Cleveland baseball will be remembered always in the city's sports annals as the time when Bill Veeck limped onto the scene and took over control of the Indians. His reign in Cleveland was short—a mere 3½ years—but neither the Indians nor the old sport were quite the same thereafter. Neither, for that matter, was the city.

Veeck, young and husky, came into Cleveland with a leg that throbbed from a service-incurred injury, and some burning ideas on how a major league baseball club should be operated. Before he sold his interest in the Indians in 1949, he had lost the leg, but had won a pennant (1948), a World Series (1948), and, most of all, he had won the affection of the fans.

The blond burrhead with the corrugated forehead limped and thumped his way up and down the city's avenues in open-throated splendor, laughing at the rain, the snow, and all the other club owners as he preached his unorthodox tenet that baseball was a game and should be fun. It is no overstatement to say that he shook the national baseball establishment as it had not been shaken since the Cincinnati Reds daringly experimented with knickerbockers in place of pantaloons. For the great American pastime was—and still is—in the hands of an element more conservative than is to be found in the halls of high finance or in the groves of the Academy. Under their sober direction and cautious counsel, a simple game has been turned into a complicated contest, clothed in conservative gray flannel and encumbered with strategy and statistics until it is nigh on to death at the hands of the sobersides.

Contrarily, under the ministration of Veeck, baseball in Cleveland stirred and fought the bonds of civilized restraint that had made the game about as exciting as a Sunday outing of the Watch and Ward Society. He put comedians on the playing field (sometimes intentionally), gave away nylons and automobiles to the fans, introduced fireworks exhibitions after the ball games thereby, incidentally, distracting attention away from the score, and shuffled ball players in and out of town in such bewildering numbers that at times even the scorecards were obsolete because the linotypes were lagging hours behind his trading maneuvers.

The Indians went right on losing ball games in 1946 under Veeck, but he had caught the attention of the fans. There was interest, if not hope. But everybody recognized that Veeck's brand of baseball was

fun and games, in that order. Clevelanders and fellow Ohioans responded to this advanced philosophy in stirring numbers. When Veeck
took over, close to midseason, the team had drawn 289,000 persons. In
the ensuing laughter and confusion, another 763,289 fans fought their
way into the ball park, raising the season total to 1,052,289. And hardly
a man or woman in the vast outpouring thought to be critical of the
ball club for its failure to rise above sixth place, probably for fear
of being called party poopers. Such was the spirit of the time. League
Park and the lakefront stadium, used on weekends and for special
games, were *the* places to be seen in those giddy days, and the object
was a good time.

Veeck, the iconoclast of the front office, knew wisely that 1946 was
but prelude and that in 1947 he would have to provide a different
kind of a season; one that included a better showing on the field. The
clowns in motley would have to yield to the shining knights in armor;
amusement would have to yield to admiration; laughter would have to
make way for cheers. In the words of the old aphorism, faith without
works crashes, and Veeck knew he had to justify the faith the fans
had shown in him with a more effective baseball machine if he was to
hold their attention. He put it this way, spelling out his philosophy for
the shocked eyes of the wing-collar camp in his autobiography, *Veeck
—as in Wreck:*

"We did not draw crowds simply by putting on a show. Cleveland
had been without a pennant winner for 26 years, the longest of any
American League city, and we communicated our determination to produce one. I agree completely with the conservative opposition that you
cannot continue to draw people with a losing team by giving them
bread and circuses. All I have ever said—and, I think, proved—is that
you can draw more people with a losing team plus bread and circuses
than with a losing team and a long, still silence."

The Indians, considerably improved by trades and purchases, finished
fourth in 1947 and drew 1,521,978 persons. The following year, 1948,
the team won the American League pennant in the thrilling finish that
called for the first playoff game in league history and then won the
World Series. Attendance in that fateful year was 2,620,627, a new major
league attendance record. In that same season, the Indians set a new
high mark for single game attendance with a crowd of 82,781 on June 20.

Of all Veeck's precedential moves during his brief tenure as owner of
the Indians, perhaps the most significant to the future course of the
game was his smashing of the color barrier that had prevented Negro
players from winning a place on an American League team. Branch
Rickey had pioneered in the National League by hiring Jackie Robinson, but it took Veeck to blaze the way in the junior circuit by signing
a promising infielder named Larry Doby, who eventually developed
into a hard-hitting, fleet center fielder for the Indians. Doby joined the

team in early July 1947. The following July, 1948, Veeck hired the
legendary Satchel Paige over the protests of the stuffed shirts—some of
whom were upset not so much by the fact that Paige was a Negro, but
that he was somewhere in his forties—a very old man, as baseball years
are counted. They accused Veeck of another hippodrome stunt and of
making a mockery of the game. Old Man Satch provided Veeck's de-
fenses by winning six important games for the team in the final stretch of
the pennant drive.

The stunts, the entertainment and, most of all, the aura of victory
that Veeck created in Cleveland were significant contributions to the
city's well-being. It was not a happy city that he found in 1946. The
downtown area was run down at the heels and the mood of the people
was troubled. It was a kind of melancholia that had been a long time
growing; too much depression and too much war; too much subsistence
living and subsistence dying. The wheels of the urban economy were
still turning, but slowly and squeakingly. The people were querulous
and impatient with one another and with the city in which they
lived.

Cleveland, in short, needed the encouragement that comes from being a winner. The Indians and their colorful front-office boss gave the
city something to cheer about and the opportunity to bask once again
in a favorable national light. What it came down to was a matter of
civic pride and self-respect, and most people were grateful to Veeck for
this, even recognizing that he had his own selfish motives, as all enterprising people do. But he was not ordinary. He was singular in his appearance, disarming in his approach, genuine in his determination to
succeed. He never wore a hat or an overcoat or a tie, no matter what
the weather or the occasion. Dining room captains winced at his informality and some of them protested, but it did them no good. They
should have known that an individual who will not wear another man's
collar will be just as quick in his refusal of another man's tie. The
informal accouterments favored by Veeck represented his way of ex-
pressing his own protest against the kind of formalism and convention
that tend to hem in and bind us all. The stuffy-style dictators, the
pompous and petty dining room managers, the selfish, myopic traditionalists in major league baseball—all were natural foes to Veeck and
while he fought them, thousands of little people cheered. People love
a free spirit. They take heart from the brave and the venturesome.
And there never was any question—even among the many who disapproved of him—that Bill Veeck was both—in good measure.

Veeck sold the Indians in 1949 at the end of the baseball season to
a syndicate headed by a Cleveland insurance executive, Ellis Ryan.
Hank Greenberg, who had been an aide to Veeck as well as a stockholder,

stayed on with the new regime and became general manager. In this post, he dared to do at the end of the 1950 season what Veeck had wanted to do in 1947, and luckily had not—he fired Lou Boudreau, the people's choice as manager of the Indians. His successor was Al Lopez, who had been waiting in the wings. The *señor* from Tampa, Florida, was a natural leader and the Indians flourished under his expert guidance, placing second five times and winning the pennant once. That triumph came in 1954, a memorable year in which the Indians set an American League record for the most victories in a season, winning 111 games. The only thing that baffled baseball experts was how the team could lose even forty-three games with a pitching staff that included Bob Feller, Early Wynn, Mike Garcia, Bob Lemon, and the best relief pair in the game, Don Mossi and Ray Narleski.

The pennant-winning 1954 season unfortunately was blighted by the distressing series of happenings at World Series time; namely, four consecutive defeats at the hands of the New York Giants, who did not figure to do much more than show up in full uniform. It was a humiliation that shook the Cleveland organization all the way down to its farm system roots. Out of that system, the next year, emerged two rookies named Rocky Colavito and Herb Score. The latter, whom the sports writers refrained from dubbing "Hasty Herbert" with considerable restraint, was a fireball-throwing lefthander who made the varsity immediately. He won twenty games in 1956 and led the American League in strikeouts. Seldom has baseball seen a more brilliant prospect. Some very wise observers predicted Score would be better than Bob Feller, better than Walter Johnson, perhaps better than any pitcher who had come before him.

Herb Score, in short, could not miss—but he did, through no fault of his own. The 1957 season hardly had gotten under way when, in a game in Cleveland, a New York Yankee infielder, Gil McDougald, caught hold of a Score fast ball and drove it right back at the young pitcher. It happened too quickly for Score even to raise his glove to protect himself. The ball hit him in the right eye with a cracking sound that could be heard all over the stadium. Score fell to the ground, blood running out of his nose and mouth, clutching that part of his face around the eye.

The wonder of the accident, to those who saw it, was that Herb Score was not killed on the pitcher's mound that night, or that he did not lose his eye. He recovered and the sight returned to his injured eye, but the career leading him to certain immortality as a baseball superstar was ended by that shot off McDougald's bat. Score returned to pitch, but he had lost the precious something that had made him great. After two lackluster years in an Indian uniform and a few poor years with the White Sox, he retired to become a television broadcaster.

The decade that followed the pennant-winning season of 1954 was full of changes and frustrations for the Indians. Manager Lopez moved on to take over the White Sox helm in 1957, and the parade of his successors began that season with Kerby Farrell. Bobby Bragan took over for part of the 1958 season, yielding to an old Indian hero, Joe Gordon, who lasted as manager until August of 1960. At that time, the general manager of the Cleveland club, Frank Lane, pulled off the first managerial trade in baseball history—Manager Joe Gordon of the Indians for Manager Jimmy Dykes of the Detroit Tigers. Mel McGaha took over from Dykes in 1962, followed in 1963 by George ("Birdie") Tebbetts, and in late 1966 by Joe Adcock.

If there was confusion on the playing field—and there was—the same kind of restlessness prevailed in the front office. Myron H. ("Mike") Wilson succeeded Ellis Ryan as president of the club in 1953. Financier William R. Daley, once an usher at League Park, became principal stockholder and board chairman in 1956. Gabe Paul took over as general manager of the club in April 1961, and as principal stockholder and president in 1962, and began anew the quest for the magical combination of men and circumstances that can turn a staid city into a frenzy through their victories on the baseball playing field. Vernon Stouffer, nationally known restaurateur, purchased control of the Indians in late 1966, but Paul remained as general manager.

What a city seeks, in tying its emotional hopes to the ups-and-downs of a collection of grown athletes in modified knickerbockers, is precisely the hallucinative type of joy that gripped Cleveland in 1948, when all the world looked good in spite of the contradictory facts to be found in reality.

What Cleveland has been seeking since 1948 is just what Bill Veeck described in his autobiography when he told of being offered a "tremendous sum of money" at the peak of his Cleveland success if he would run for the United States Senate against the distinguished incumbent, Robert A. Taft.

Veeck, a Taft admirer, refused the political invitation, but expressed his conviction that if he had chosen to run against the famous senator, he would have been elected.

"You still don't think I'd have a chance against Taft?" he wrote. "Well then, you weren't in Cleveland during those three-and-a-half years when the Indians pushed the world news from the front pages. You weren't in Cleveland in those years when the Indians brought the people of the city so close together that it was as if everybody was living in everybody else's parlor. You weren't in Cleveland in those days of cheer and triumph when every day was Mardi Gras and every fan a king."

XXII

The Greatest Show in Football

THERE was another important sports development to gladden the hearts of Clevelanders as the city struggled to find itself after World War II—the emergence of the Cleveland Browns, the most successful football team of its time; a team that would come close to achieving in professional football the kind of consistent superiority that the New York Yankees had established in baseball.

Cleveland, only fifty miles from the birthplace of professional football in Canton, was one of the founding cities in the predecessor league of the National Professional Football League (NFL) in 1920. In that year, in Canton, the American Professional Football Association was formed, with Jim Thorpe, the famous Indian athlete, as president. Stan Cofall, a former Notre Dame grid star who in later years became a prominent Cleveland businessman, was vice president of the new league. The member teams included the Canton Bulldogs, the Cleveland Indians, Dayton Triangles, Akron Professionals, Massillon Tigers, Decatur (Illinois) Staleys, Chicago Cardinals, and teams representing Rochester, New York, Rock Island, Illinois, Hammond, Indiana, and Muncie, Indiana.

All through the lean years of the 1920s and the 1930s, when the professional game was having so much difficulty establishing itself in the American scheme of things athletic, Cleveland was represented intermittently by play-for-pay teams, including the Indians, the Bulldogs, the Panthers, and the Rams. The 1924 club won the NFL championship (the league name was changed in 1921), and this aroused an enthusiastic response among football fanatics, but the followers of the professional game were few in number.

This failure of the Cleveland sporting public to embrace the pro game was enough to make a promoter cry out in anguish—and perhaps it did—because it was apparent that the city loved football. There was high enthusiasm for the game as it was played by the big universities, even though Cleveland itself was without representation among the collegiate grid powers. Once, in the early 1930s, Western Reserve University ventured into big-time football under the tutelage of Coach

Sam Willamen, and the Red Cats did fairly well until somebody got carried away with their minor successes and booked a game with Ohio State University. The powerful Buckeyes, then the leading exponents of "razzle-dazzle" football as taught by Coach Francis Schmidt, won by a score of 81–0, leaving thousands of Clevelanders in a pensive mood.

After that debacle, Reserve settled for friendlier enemies close to home, like the John Carroll University Blue Streaks, the Case Tech Rough Riders, and the Baldwin-Wallace Yellow Jackets. These "Big Four" contests drew respectable crowds, but the city's principal interest in football was attuned to the major colleges and universities, especially Ohio State and Notre Dame. There still are large rooting sections for those two institutions in Cleveland.

The modern era of professional football in Cleveland began in 1937, when the Cleveland Rams were organized, giving the city its first NFL team since 1931. The principal stockholder in the Rams was a businessman-attorney named Homer Marshman. The year of 1937 was not a good time, really, to begin a new enterprise. It was a year of recession within a depression, which would not be dissimilar to Winston Churchill's riddle wrapped in a mystery inside an enigma in terms of emphasis. The Rams struggled on the field and off, meeting with indifferent success in either place until 1945.

It was in 1945 that the Rams, led by glamorous Bob Waterfield at quarterback, won nine out of their ten games to win the NFL's Western Division title. The championship game with the Washington Redskins was played in the lakefront stadium on a bitterly cold December day. Considering the weather conditions that prevailed that day, the turnout of 32,178 fans was quite sensational. The Cleveland Stadium is not the most comfortable place to be when the north winds are piercing in off the lake and the temperature is hovering around the zero mark. Fortunately, it was an exciting ball game with a gratifying conclusion. The hometown Rams eked out a 15–14 victory and Cleveland had a championship.

That achievement could have been the beginning of a new, profitable era for the Rams in Cleveland. There was, for the first time, a mass awareness of professional football. The colorful NFL champs had endeared themselves to the city by their heroics in the 1945 season—and it didn't hurt one bit that Bob Waterfield's wife was the gorgeous movie star, Jane Russell, and that she had moved to Cleveland to be near her husband. All of a sudden pro football was a much more interesting game to a lot of discerning Clevelanders.

But even as the cheers of the fans were still resounding, the Rams were saying a final goodbye to the city. Daniel F. Reeves, who had become principal owner of the team, announced he had received permission from the league to shift his franchise and players to Los Angeles.

Cleveland stood as a city scorned and more than one indignant fan cried perfidy, but the move took place.

As humiliating as this development clearly was, the departure of the Rams proved to be for the best. It cleared the Cleveland playing field for the debut of a new football club that had been assembling quietly on the sidelines for some two years. Reeves and Waterfield were gone, but in their places Arthur B. McBride and Paul Brown were suiting up and completing their last-minute plans to surprise not only the city but the entire sports world with a fantastic demonstration of instant success, football-style.

Of the two principals in the ownership and management of the new team, strangely, Brown, the non-Clevelander, was much better known in Cleveland than the longtime resident, McBride. The latter was known only by name—"Mickey" McBride—and little more. Yet, Mickey McBride rates as one of the most interesting and most influential of the city's men of finance in the middle years of the twentieth century. He had come to Cleveland in 1913 at age twenty-three, a tough, smart, streetwise boy wonder of the newspaper business of Chicago, lured from his job as acting circulation manager of Hearst's Chicago *American* to become circulation manager of the Cleveland *News* and the *Leader* at a reported salary of ten thousand dollars. It was a time of circulation wars in Cleveland newspaperdom and McBride knew how to fight. His salary was quickly upped to fifteen thousand dollars. One of his assistants at the *News* was an old friend, James Ragen, who some years later was murdered by Chicago gangsters in a fight over control of the race wire, Continental Press, then owned by Ragen and McBride.

McBride stayed with the *News* until 1932, when he resigned in a dispute over policy, shortly thereafter investing most of his ready cash in the Yellow Cab Company of Cleveland, becoming a partner of Daniel Sherby. Most of McBride's money was tied up in real estate, the purchase of which had been his prime hobby through the years. It was said he spent his happiest weekends touring the city with Mrs. McBride, looking over likely real estate purchases.

"The town was growing," he explained later. "Everything you bought was increasing in value. You didn't have to be smart."

Once, it is said, he owned every parcel of land on the north side of Lorain Avenue, a main thoroughfare, from West 117th Street to West 130th Street. He owned acreage in all parts of the city and outside of the city, especially in Miami and Coral Gables, Florida. He had a distinct flair for acquiring unimportant real estate that insisted on becoming terribly valuable. Something of that instinct for scenting success must have guided him in his other business adventures. In time, his cornucopia was filled with a successful taxicab monopoly in Cleveland and several nearby cities, a profitable race wire service, a printing company, a radio station, and miscellaneous other goodies. Thanks to the happy confluence of profits that kept pouring into his coffers, he was in a position by 1944 to listen without blanching to a highly unlikely suggestion by Arch Ward, sports editor of the Chicago *Tribune*, that he, Mickey McBride, finance a Cleveland professional football team in a new league, the All-America Conference.

The Cleveland financier only a few years before that time probably could have claimed the distinction of being the city's leading non-football fan. It is said he never saw a football game until 1940—the same year, significantly, in which his son, Arthur B., Jr., became a student at Notre Dame University. It is a fact that football is highly regarded at Notre Dame. It is also a fact that the father of any N.D. student who fails to take an interest in the football fortunes of the Fighting Irish stands in peril of being drummed out of the club. No doubt this fact, added to the urgings of young Arthur, spurred McBride into becoming a rooter. But he was not the kind of a man to do things halfway. He did become a fan, but rooting was not enough; the passive role of spectator was not satisfying. McBride became interested in gaining some kind of a proprietary role in the game, and it was toward that end, in 1942, that he made an unsuccessful bid to buy the Cleveland Rams.

Ward's plans for a new team in a new league had McBride's interest. Mickey was still a scrapper, and the turndown by Reeves of the Rams rankled. If he had his own football team, he could give the Rams a run for their money.

"O.K.," McBride told Ward, "but if I'm going to field a team in Cleveland, it will have to be the best team in the country."

There was plenty of time for him to plan his conquest. The All-America Conference could not become a reality and begin its fight with the NFL team until another fight—World War II—was settled satisfactorily. McBride, however, saw no reason to wait until the war was over to put together an organization and do some long-range planning. To do this, he needed a top executive.

"Who's the best football coach in the country?" he asked a veteran *Plain Dealer* sportswriter, John Dietrich.

"Paul Brown," unhesitatingly replied Dietrich.

Thousands of football experts in the country probably would have argued with Dietrich's choice, but few of them would have been Ohioans. Coach Paul Brown of Ohio State University, then on military leave and serving as coach of the Great Lakes Naval Training Station team, was only thirty-six years old, but he already had proved himself to be an authentic gridiron genius to Ohioans; first at Massillon (Ohio) High School and then at Ohio State. In his second year at OSU, admittedly one of the toughest, most demanding coaching jobs in collegiate football, Brown in 1942 had steered the Buckeyes to the Big Ten title and a national championship.

The Ohio State coaching post was one toward which Brown long had aspired during his years as a high school coach, and already he was the campus idol. He was reluctant to give up his budding college career to become general manager and coach of a club that did not exist, in a league that never had played a game. Mickey McBride could not compete with the romance or glamor of collegiate football, but Mickey's financial oratory was overpowering. Among other inducements, he wanted Brown to go on his payroll immediately and draw a princely salary of one thousand dollars a month all the time he remained in service, no matter how long the duration.

There was a popular joke that enjoyed currency at that time. It seems Australian girls had proven to be very popular with American servicemen, and somebody asked a G.I. what it was that Australian girls had that American girls did not.

"Nothing," answered the G.I., reasonably. "But they've got it *here.*"

It was that way with McBride and Brown. What the Cleveland mogul had to offer the servicebound Brown was present and tangible reward, plus the promise of twenty-five thousand dollars a year when the team came into being. The young coach capitulated and agreed to put together a professional football team in Cleveland. It wasn't long before McBride learned that Brown, in his own way, was just as resolute and determined a man as he himself. Speaking at a civic luncheon in Cleveland, Brown turned to McBride and said, unsmilingly:

"We will build a winner and make it go here if it takes every cent you've got!"

Paul Brown was much more than just another good football coach. He was an organizational genius and an outstanding judge of football flesh. The first player he signed was a fellow serviceman named Otto Graham, former Northwestern University star. He also hired, as backfield and defensive coach, one of his own aides at Great Lakes, a Paris, Kentucky, high school mentor named Blanton Collier. And as the months passed and the war neared its end, Brown gradually added new names to the growing roster—Mac Speedie, Jim Daniell, Edgar ("Special Delivery") Jones, Lou Rymkus, Dante Lavelli, Lou Saban, Eddie Ulinski, Lin Houston, John Yonakor, Cliff Lewis, and Lou Groza, as well as some established NFL players on the Cleveland Rams squad who were reluctant to move to Los Angeles. They included Center Mike Scarry, Tackle Chet Adams, and three backfield men, Tom Colella, Galen Smith, and Don Greenwood.

Brown's most significant player announcement, though, was that he had signed Marion Motley to play fullback and that he had invited to the team's training camp a husky All-American named Bill Willis, who had played briefly for him at Ohio State. Motley and Willis were Negroes, and up to that time professional football was punctiliously observing the color line. The action of the Cleveland club's management in signing Motley and Willis was something more than a violation of the agreement that had kept the racial doors closed in professional football; it was a repudiation of the discriminatory policy—a significant social milestone, as important as the breakthrough made possible in baseball by Branch Rickey and Bill Veeck.

Brown could not have cracked the color line, it's worth pointing out, without Mickey McBride's complete support. Even as some of the other club owners in the league a-borning were gasping in horror at Cleveland's plan to open its ranks to Negro players, McBride quickly silenced any objections that may have been forming.

"I employ Negroes in all my other business ventures," he said, "and if any competent Negroes want to compete for a job on my football team, I will not deny them that chance. If the All-America Conference doesn't like what I am doing, it can have the Cleveland franchise back again."

The All-America Conference (AAC) patently needed Mickey McBride more than Mickey McBride needed football. The other owners accepted the new racial ground rules laid down by Cleveland, and the league that never had played a game discovered that it already had passed a football milestone. And it wasn't long before Motley and Willis were making Coach Brown look so good that the old-line prejudices soon were forgotten as the other teams hustled furiously about, searching for good Negro talent. So also, shortly, did the teams in the rival NFL.

Cleveland's team took on the name of the "Browns" after the name of their coach, and thus borrowed a page from the history of the Indians, who, early in their history, had been named the "Naps" after their manager-star, Napoleon Lajoie.

The new football team's first game was played in late summer of 1946. It was an exhibition contest in which the Brooklyn Dodgers were their opponents before a sensational crowd of 35,964 fans in Akron's Rubber Bowl. It was a winning debut: Browns 35, Dodgers 20. It was the first victory of many. It quickly became apparent that the All-America Conference didn't have a chance of surviving its infancy with the Browns as members of the league. Cleveland dominated the play so completely during the years the AAC was in existence, 1946 through 1949, that the statistics are almost unbelievable. In those four seasons, the Browns won fifty-two games and lost only four. They played three tie games.

That year of 1948, that glowing time for professional sports in Cleveland, was the high point for the Browns as it was for the Indians and the Barons. Paul Brown's 1948 team played fourteen games and won fourteen games—the last professional football team to go through a full sea-

son undefeated and untied. The Cleveland club won the AAC championship in each of the league's four years and when, weakened unto death
by the domination of the Browns, the league folded at the end of the
1949 season, the Cleveland club was eagerly absorbed by the NFL.

There had been a lot of conjecture during the years the Browns were
breezing along to one victory after another in the AAC over what would
happen if ever they were pitted against a strong NFL team. Some
devastating wit was employed by some of the officials in the older
league to describe the carnage that would ensue when such a clash
occurred. Now the stage was set for the football Armageddon at last;
now was the time for the showdown battle that would decide the old
argument and establish at last just how good the Cleveland Browns and
Coach Paul Brown really were.

To make the test even more conclusive, the first opponents the
Browns would face in their NFL debut in 1950 were the Philadelphia
Eagles. The Eagles were the NFL champs of the previous season as
the Browns were the AAC champs. It was like starting the season with
a World Series battle, and the attention of the whole football world
was fixed on Philadelphia's Municipal Stadium when the teams clashed.
Some eighty-five thousand fans, most of them Eagles rooters, crowded
the great bowl that day and looked on in stunned disbelief as the
Browns efficiently went about the job of proving that all their past
achievements in football had been valid ones. The final score was
Cleveland 35, Philadelphia 10.

One of the Philadelphia stars, Pete Pihos, was quoted after the game
as saying: "I guess we finally met up with a team from the big league!"

It was a highly significant victory and a highly encouraging one to
fans seeking an augury. But a whole season of play against the best football players in the nation lay ahead and, as it turned out, it was such a
rugged season that at the end the Browns had to meet the New York
Giants in a playoff game to decide the American (Eastern) Conference
title. The Browns won with a Lou ("The Toe") Groza field goal and a
safety in the closing seconds of play, 8–3.

The championship game of the 1950 season pitted the Browns against,
of all teams, the Los Angeles Rams. The game was played in Cleveland Stadium and, at last, the prodigal Rams would come home again;
this time as the enemy. If an amateur dramatist had tried to rig up a
hokey situation like that, he'd have been hooted out of the theater.
But there it was—the old Rams, still led by Bob Waterfield, still cheered
on by Jane Russell, going against the new Browns, led by Otto
Graham.

It wasn't an easy victory. The Browns had to go down to the last few
seconds of the game to win, and again it was Lou Groza who gave the
team its 30–28 margin of victory by booting a field goal from the eleven-

yard line at the very end, making the Cleveland team the undisputed champion of the football world at last. It was a most satisfying achievement and Cleveland hugged the Browns warmly to its civic bosom.

Years later, when the American Football League made its appearance and the old arguments sprang up over the relative and comparative strength of the teams in the new loop and those in the senior league, most spokesmen of the NFL clubs were understandably restrained in their comments. They remembered the Browns, no doubt, and they remembered especially that season of 1950 when Paul Brown and his men taught all the taunters and jibers a lasting lesson in humility.

Proof that the Browns' opening season triumph in the NFL was no accident was provided in abundance in the years that followed. At the end of sixteen seasons of NFL play, 1950 through 1965, the Browns had won the Eastern Conference title nine times and had worn the crown of world champions four times. In that period, the team racked up the best won-and-lost record in professional football, winning 142 times against only 54 losses and six ties—a percentage of such class, one would guess, to insure all kinds of domestic tranquillity, but it was not so.

The Browns dominated the NFL's Eastern Conference in their first six years of membership as they had dominated the AAC. The genius of Paul Brown was freely, openly acknowledged by the football world, and his name gradually rose to the rarefied level on which you will find such names as Knute Rockne and Pop Warner. His star players— Otto Graham, Marion Motley, Lou Groza, and Jimmy Brown—were properly enshrined among the superstars of the game. But the Browns had their troubles. There was an undercurrent of protest among the players against Coach Brown's aloofness; the coolly impersonal attitude he turned toward them most of the time. It was said, indeed, that he held this same aloof attitude in his dealings with Mickey McBride and shunted the owner out of direct and general participation in the team's affairs, on and off the field, to such an extent that McBride gradually lost interest in the Browns. Whatever the reason, Mickey McBride in 1953 unloaded the club for six hundred thousand dollars to a syndicate headed by a Cleveland industrialist, Dave R. Jones.

Brown continued as coach and general manager with full authority under the new owners. His genius, meanwhile, had not gone unnoticed among the other coaches. As the Browns victoriously rolled along to one conference title after another, and three world championships in their first six years of NFL play, the imitative process set in. Competing teams borrowed Brown's techniques; such characteristics as the Cleveland club's high degree of organization and discipline, classroom schedules and homework demanded of the players and elaborate film review of team play, as well as intensive scouting procedures—all became standard league practice. The effect was that the margin of superiority that had enabled the Browns to dominate most of the league gradually shrank, and victories came harder.

Cleveland fans, accustomed to victory, were shocked in 1956 when their team lost the conference title to the New York Giants and dropped to a disgraceful, for them, won-and-lost record of five victories, seven defeats. It was the only time in the history of the team that the Browns had failed to play at least .500 football, and it was a sign of the trouble ahead. The team snapped back in 1957 to win the conference title, but the championship game with the Detroit Lions was a humiliating rout, with the Lions doing all the routing, 59–14.

For the next six years, the Browns played respectable football, placing second in their conference four times, but everybody expected something more than respectability from the orange-shirted invincibles. The fabulous past came back to reproach the team, and for the first time there was a questioning note when the conversation swung around to Paul Brown. They asked if the not-so-old master were too inflexible to meet the changing pattern of league play. They wondered if his personality were a hobbling influence on team morale and performance. The rest of the NFL apparently had caught up with the Browns by borrowing from Paul Brown's book. Now many of his followers wondered if the great coach could reach out and open another new chapter that would again establish his mastery.

Early in 1961, after three consecutive second-place finishes, the Browns were purchased from the Cleveland syndicate by a group headed by a young (thirty-six) New York advertising executive, Arthur B. Modell. The price paid was $3,925,000, a considerable increase over the $600,000 that Mickey McBride had received only eight years earlier. Modell hastened to assure reporters of his respect and admiration for Paul Brown. The famous coach and general manager would remain in those posts, he said, and would continue as the boss of the team. For his part, Brown spoke in noncommittal terms of the change in ownership, emphasizing only that he was still in charge. By way of stressing the point, late in that autumn of 1961, after the club's third-place finish, Brown traded the star halfback, Bobby Mitchell, to the Washington Redskins for draft rights to the Syracuse University backfield star, Ernie Davis. Modell was not consulted on the deal.

The tragic story of Ernie Davis had an important effect on the Paul Brown legend. The big halfback (six feet two inches), an All-American and winner of the Heisman Trophy given each year to collegiate football's outstanding player, perhaps would have restored the Cleveland coach to a position of pre-eminence in the professional sport had things gone as expected. On the basis of his record at Syracuse, Davis gave promise of being an even better football player than another Syracuse grad, Jimmy Brown, the greatest pro footballer of his day—some say of any day.

In midsummer of 1962, Davis, while in the training camp of the College All-Stars, getting ready for the annual All-Star Game in Chicago against the NFL champs, developed a swelling in his neck. It was thought, at first, he had the mumps. Then an examination disclosed that the brilliant rookie had monocytic leukemia and the medical guess was that he had only about a year to live!

The estimate of the doctors proved to be optimistic. Ernie Davis, the Browns star who never played a game with the team, died in University Hospital in Cleveland early in the morning of May 18, 1963, and his uniform number, 45, was retired by the Browns. A city which had not known the player nevertheless sorrowed in the death of the man. There had not been such deep, heartfelt emotion over a fallen athlete since the death of Ray Chapman of the Indians.

The Davis tragedy came at a time when the Browns and all their followers already were in a state of shock over the dismissal of Paul Brown as coach and general manager of the Cleveland club that bore his name. Legends simply are not fired and Paul Brown, clearly, was a legendary figure in the world of football. He was in the record books to stay, and his achievements as coach of Massillon High School, Ohio State University, and the Cleveland Browns were beyond compare. But Paul Brown's team had not won even a conference title since 1957. His last world championship had been won in 1955. So it was inevitable that in 1963 there should be raised the cynical question that has plagued men of achievement since the beginning of time: "What have you done lately?"

So long as his teams continued to dominate, Paul Brown did not need the approval or affection of others. Their respect for his genius was enough. But the Browns had not been winners for five years in a row. Unquestioning respect had given way to doubt, and some of the players were grumbling openly. Some of the experts began to say that the rival coaches were playing the Brown system better than its originator. Yet the great coach stood coldly and uncompromisingly in his lonely position of complete authority until finally, on January 7, 1963, Art Modell astonished everybody by announcing that Brown was through as coach and general manager of the team. He was invited to stay on as a vice president until the remaining six years of his ten-year contract expired, making him, surely, the best-paid vice president in all professional football history at $82,500 a year.

Blanton Collier, Brown's coaching protégé from Great Lakes Naval Training Station and a member of the Browns coaching staff for many years, took over as the new boss. Paul Brown was gone, but the Browns continued.

Whether the change in coaches came at just the climactic point in the rebuilding process that had been under way, or whether the warmly human touch of the fatherly Collier was the missing element in the Browns' equation, none could say. It was a fact, though, that the faltering team seemed to take strength from the change. Cleveland that season again became a power in the Eastern Conference and achieved a good 10–4 record, fighting the New York Giants right down to the last whistle for the title.

In 1964, Collier's charges went all the way. They won the Eastern title handily and then, to the surprise of all the experts, they annihilated the highly favored Baltimore Colts in the championship game, 27–0.

It was a thrilling comeback for the team—the vindication that Modell needed desperately to answer those who criticized him for firing the greatest coach in football. And if he needed further support for his action, the Browns won the Eastern title again in 1965, which was achievement enough, even if they did drop the title game to Green Bay's Packers. Furthermore, the great lakefront stadium was filled almost to capacity at nearly all of the seven home games each season, an average of about eighty thousand persons a game.

The slogan of the Browns from the team's beginning has been: "The Greatest Show in Football!"

It comes as close to being the truth as any slogan could.

XXIII

The Man in the Tower

IT IS a highly appropriate circumstance that the office from which Cyrus Stephen Eaton directs his vast financial empire should be high in the Terminal Tower, in a suite of oak-paneled rooms on the thirty-sixth floor which once were occupied by the Van Sweringen brothers and, later, by another business genius, Robert R. Young.

The point has been made that visiting dignitaries from the Soviet Union are unusually fond of the great tower. But a Cleveland subject commanding even more of their admiration is Mr. Eaton himself, the man in the tower.

This is, of course, a contradictory situation. Communists are not supposed to think kindly of capitalists, much less admire them. Capitalists, in turn, are supposed to abhor the followers of Lenin; they are supposed to regard all proponents of Marxist-inspired ideologies as the enemy.

These are the long-accepted ground rules, but the modern-day Reds and Capitalist Eaton simply have not been playing the game according to the rules. They have been bussing and embracing in public and smothering each other with flattering words for a number of years, much to the confusion of the onlookers.

When Anastas Mikoyan stopped off in Cleveland to visit Eaton in January 1959, he presented the best wishes of Nikita Khrushchev, and added gratuitously: "When Mr. Khrushchev talked about you, his whole face was beaming!"

Eaton has made the leaders of the Soviet Union beam more than once by his friendly overtures and his sympathetic words. On the other hand, he has also made many of his own countrymen wince with his numerous critical pronouncements on American international and domestic policy.

The frequent alignment of this capitalist, so wealthy he has been called "The Cleveland Croesus," with the governments of the Communist world has been a matter of genuine puzzlement to spectators at the international game of power politics. During the troublesome decade that began in 1955, America has tried to analyze and rationalize this paradoxical state of affairs without real success.

If it is any comfort to the political experts, Eaton also has made a practice of baffling those who have undertaken to decipher his words and actions throughout his business career. He is as much of a riddle to students of finance as he is to students of international affairs. He is a man whose words and actions do not yield easily to elucidative analysis. The Cleveland multimillionaire has remained what a *Fortune* magazine writer, Robert Sheehan, called him in 1961—"No less an enigma than the Soviet Union itself . . ."

Whatever Cyrus Stephen Eaton is, in the final judgment of the world, his spectacular life has been inextricably intertwined with the development of modern Cleveland, the city he has called his home since one June day in 1901 when he stepped off the train at the lakefront station. He was a seventeen-year-old boy with twenty dollars in his pockets and the ruddy glow of the windswept Nova Scotia farm country on his cheeks.

He had traveled to Cleveland to spend the summer with his uncle, a Baptist minister, Reverend Charles Aubrey Eaton, and, hopefully, to earn some money to cover expenses at McMaster University in Toronto, where he had enrolled for the fall term. The Rev. Mr. Eaton lived in the old Euclid Hotel, not far from the Euclid Avenue Baptist Church, of which he was the minister.

As young Cyrus registered at the hotel, he made known his intention to seek work in Cleveland, and asked the desk clerk to keep him in mind should he hear of any openings. The clerk said he understood the hotel management was looking about for somebody to handle desk duties at night. Cyrus applied for the job immediately and was hired, but his career in the hotel business was short-lived.

The most prominent family in the congregation of the Euclid Avenue Baptist Church was, without challenge, that of John D. Rockefeller, who served as a trustee of the church and as the Sunday School teacher. He was the principal benefactor of the church, of course, but besides contributing financial support, the world's richest man also took a direct, personal interest in every phase of the institution's well-being. John D. especially took pride in knowing the ministers of the Euclid Avenue Baptist Church perhaps better than they knew themselves. He studied them in church, on the golf course, on rides in his carriage, and in his home.

The Rev. Mr. Eaton enjoyed Rockefeller's high favor. He was a young man, more like a brother to young Cyrus than an uncle, but he had demonstrated qualities of intellect and character that had impressed the old oil king. Upon hearing that the minister's young nephew was visiting him, John D. insisted that Rev. Eaton bring the boy with him to Forest Hill for Sunday dinner that weekend.

Mr. and Mrs. Rockefeller both were taken by the handsome young Canadian lad with the bright smile and unusually formal manners. In the course of the get-acquainted conversation, Cyrus recounted—probably with a touch of pride—how he had landed a place on the hotel staff.

Mrs. Rockefeller was disturbed, if not horrified, by the news. A hotel to this genteel, highly religious woman was a distasteful place; a breeding ground for evil, outlandish capers; the refuge of nymphs and satyrs. She obviously felt strongly about the minister's nephew being exposed to such a place, and she turned to her husband and called upon him to save the boy through a counteroffer.

"Isn't there something that Cyrus can do around here?" she asked.

Rockefeller, an amenable spouse, nodded. He indicated that he could find room for young Eaton on his Forest Hill staff.

"Thank you," said Cyrus, gravely. "I shall try to obtain a release from my agreement with the hotel manager."

That minor technicality was easily handled, although the hotel manager understandably was incredulous when the newly hired youth told him that the famous John D. Rockefeller sought his services. Once convinced, the hotel man offered to exchange jobs with Eaton.

Life on the Rockefeller range at Forest Hill was both pleasant and interesting. Eaton served in a combination of capacities. He was an office boy, the watchman over the telegraph room into which flowed messages from all the financial capitals of the world, a messenger, and a social companion. In this privileged position, he sat in the throne room of international finance, and it is not too farfetched to say that it was here that he learned the primer on making money and wielding power.

After two full summers on the Forest Hill staff, Eaton was transferred to a job with Rockefeller's new East Ohio Gas Company, which John D. had organized to bring natural gas into Cleveland and the surrounding area. The company was hard at its basic job of laying gas mains all over the city, and Cyrus, following his indoctrination in the science of ditch-digging, shortly was placed in charge of a crew of workmen. By summer's end, he was directing four hundred workmen in the laying of gas mains under Woodland Avenue and other sections of downtown. When he is in a reminiscent mood today, Eaton takes visitors to one of his thirty-sixth-floor windows and points down at the Public Square.

"I helped to lay the gas mains under the Square," he says, and the note in his voice unmistakably is that of pride.

Tearing up a town to put down the gas pipes is a messy job. The gas company's efforts, while indubitably in the best interests of the city, were not appreciated entirely by the people of Cleveland. Theirs was a pretty city, remember, and they were justifiably proud of its parklike appearance and the elegance of avenues like Euclid and Prospect. They were not unaware of the importance of the natural gas service to the community, but their quite human reaction to the network of ditches that suddenly scarred the lawns and boulevards was anger and outrage. Somebody in the gas company had noticed Cyrus Eaton's talent for quiet, diplomatic speech, and he was given a new responsibility—soothing the irate householders and business people whose grounds had to be torn up to receive the gas supply pipes.

The natural urbanity and sophistication of Cyrus Eaton that enabled him to step smoothly into the pace of big city life and to take his place among the people of high finance is especially surprising in light of his native environment. Eaton was born in Pugwash, Nova Scotia, on December 27, 1883, the son of Joseph Howe Eaton and Mary McPherson Eaton. His father operated the village store and did some farming. His mother was a descendant of New Englanders whose loyalty to the Crown had prompted their migration to the bleak Canadian maritime province in 1782. It was her hope that Cyrus, the fifth of nine children, would follow in the vocational footsteps of his cleric-uncle in Cleveland.

Throughout Cyrus' apprenticeship period under John D. Rockefeller, he continued to attend McMaster University and to pursue the study of philosophy, a natural approach to theology, and it appeared that his mother's wish for him would come true. But a struggle was shaping in the youth's mind. The world of finance and industry in which Rockefeller was the central figure had captured Eaton's fancy. So had the quiet preaching of the old multimillionaire, who repeatedly impressed on his young protégé that there was a spiritual value in the creation of wealth so as to provide more jobs and a better livelihood for humanity.

In a reminiscent mood, not long after his eighty-first birthday, Eaton recalled that Rockefeller—he referred to him as "Mr. Rockefeller," in the respectful voice of one speaking of his elder—wanted him to join Standard Oil headquarters staff in New York City.

"I'm sure," Eaton said, "that if I had gone, I eventually would have become president of Standard Oil. But I didn't want to go to New York City. I wanted to stay in Cleveland, and I did."

Probably the only time of indecision in Cyrus Eaton's life came at the time he graduated from McMaster University with an A.B. degree in June 1905. Theology and big business both beckoned to him. He took a job as a cowboy on a ranch in Saskatchewan to give himself time to make a decision. Late in the autumn, he returned to Cleveland to visit Uncle Charles, intending to spend the Christmas holidays with him. But his uncle told him of a church post that was available—a position as lay minister of the newly organized Lakewood Baptist Church—and Cyrus accepted the job.

Eaton's career in the suburban Cleveland church was brief, and if it was marked by any flashes of ecclesiastical enthusiasm, they went unrecorded. Not long after he had cast his lot with the church, he was approached by some Rockefeller associates who wanted him to undertake a special business mission in their behalf.

The small syndicate wanted him to go to Canada and there, acting as their agent, obtain gas and electrical utility franchises in the young, growing cities of the northern nation. Eaton accepted the assignment and returned to his native land. Within a short time, he won the right to build an electrical power plant which would serve the city of Brandon, Manitoba. When he returned to Cleveland with the good news, he found the syndicate had grown wary of further speculation and had withdrawn from the Canadian investment because of the financial panic which had taken hold of the nation in that year, 1907.

His own enthusiasm for the project undiminished, Eaton managed to borrow enough money in Canada to finance the construction of an electrical power plant in Brandon. Once the plant was in operation, in 1909, he sold it for a significant profit. With this as his stake, he turned his efforts toward the acquisition of utility franchises elsewhere in Canada and the cities of the Middle West of the United States. One franchise led to another, and in a surprisingly short time Eaton's Continental Gas & Electric Company, a Kansas corporation, was a significant factor in the utilities field.

Success came to Cyrus Eaton with such a rush and flurry that he didn't have time to sit down and assess his real wealth. He says it came as something of a surprise to him when, in 1914, he learned he was a millionaire. The realization burst upon him one day when he was offered two million dollars for his utility properties—an offer he refused, incidentally, in favor of a further expansion of his holdings.

Eaton likes to recall that his father journeyed to Cleveland from the old family home in Pugwash about this time. Cyrus met him at the station and as the two rode along toward home, the son posed a question.

"Father," asked Cyrus, "what would you do if you had a million dollars?"

"I'd satisfy all my worldly wants, I think," said the elder Eaton. "Why do you ask?"

"Because I have between two and four million dollars and I don't know what to do with them," said Cyrus.

Eaton's solution to his dilemma was to plow his money back into the utility business, reinvesting and expanding his corporate empire until eventually the companies he controlled were the suppliers of gas and electrical power to some eight hundred communities in the United States and Canada. The holding company he formed, United Power & Light Company, became one of three giants in the national field, a competitor with the combine headed by Samuel Insull of Chicago and Sidney Mitchell's Electric Bond & Share.

The battle for supremacy between Eaton and Insull reached the decisive stage between 1926 and 1930. The victory apparently went to Insull in January 1930, when Eaton sold him his stock interest in Chicago's Commonwealth Edison Company and the People's Light and Coke Company for an estimated fifty-six million dollars.

Some financiers later were sharply critical of Eaton for making this particular deal, alleging that he knew it would prove to be too much of a burden on Insull's strained finances. Eaton, who professed a friendly feeling toward Insull, argued that he had supposed his rival knew what he was doing at the time. At any rate, Insull's financial base was so weakened by his expensive purchase of Eaton holdings that he was unable to meet the demands and crises of the Depression. His utilities empire collapsed and Insull, a broken man, fled to Greece to avoid prosecution.

The complicated financial life of Cyrus Eaton was only partly taken up with the problem of utilities during the 1920s. He had begun to make his influence felt in the steel industry, starting in 1924. The following year he walked into the executive offices of the Trumbull Steel Company in Warren, Ohio, and stated that he was interested in purchasing control of the floundering corporation.

When the Trumbull executives allowed skepticism to creep into their voices over Eaton's ability to swing such a large investment, the Clevelander made a very gaudy suggestion.

"Why don't you call the Cleveland Trust Company and ask if Cyrus Eaton's personal check for twenty million dollars will be honored at that bank?"

One of the startled steel officials took him up on the challenge and called the Cleveland bank to pose the question. There was no hesitation at the other end of the line. The president of Cleveland Trust quickly replied that it would be a pleasure and a privilege to cash one of Cyrus Eaton's checks for that amount.

As it turned out, only eighteen million dollars was needed to purchase control of Trumbull Steel, and Eaton gladly paid the price. It gave him his keystone piece for a design which, if successfully completed, would give him a steel combine to rival or surpass the largest existing corporation in the nation, namely, United States Steel.

Eaton now was operating along the classic lines laid down by his mentor, John D. Rockefeller, some sixty years earlier. The oil tycoon successfully and systematically had gone about the job of eliminating competition in the refining business through merger and purchase, swallowing one rival after another until Standard Oil had reached gargantuan size and dominated the oil industry. Now the pupil was challenging steel. In a determined series of transactions, he bought control of United Alloy Steel Company, Central Steel, and Republic Iron & Steel, and merged them into a new production unit called Republic Steel Corporation. It represented, finally, an amalgam of eight different steel companies. This creation of Cyrus Eaton suddenly stood forth as the third-largest producer in the steel industry—a tremendous achievement, but still short of the Cleveland financier's goal. He wanted Republic to become the giant of the industry.

The simplest and most direct route toward that treasured end was the merger avenue, and now Eaton aimed his sights at the plumpest prize of all, Youngstown Sheet & Tube, a company in which he was a stockholder of importance. It was believed that his strategy would be to merge Sheet & Tube with Inland Steel of Chicago, followed by a quick marriage with Republic.

Whatever his plan, it was jarred by the dramatic entry on the scene of another suitor interested in wooing and winning Youngstown Sheet & Tube—Bethlehem Steel Corporation. The bidding for control immediately became spirited, and it was obvious that money was a secondary factor. Eugene Grace, president of Bethlehem, underlined this point when, in raising the financial ante, he said:

"What are a few million dollars more or less in a deal of this magnitude?"

It appeared at last that Bethlehem had won the prize. Stockholders of Youngstown Sheet & Tube were called to a meeting to vote their approval of the merger. At this critical moment, Cyrus Eaton appeared on the scene holding 35 per cent of the Youngstown company's stock— enough to block the merger. He had purchased some fifty-one thousand shares of the stock, about 4 per cent of the total, on March 22, the closing date for transfer of ownership on the company's books.

The question of Eaton's right to vote the stock immediately became a legal issue, and the struggle for control of Youngstown found its way into the courts where, after a series of bitterly fought battles, Bethlehem finally called off the proposed merger. Of this classic clash and the Eaton strategy, one Cleveland financier was quoted as saying:

"For boldness, for careful calculation of mathematics and the law of the problem, put it down as one of the unforgettable incidents of American finance."

It was, however, a costly victory for Eaton. The acrimony of the legal give-and-take had lost him some old friends and supporters high in the aristocracy of Cleveland finance. The battle also had been a distracting influence at a time when the worst economic storm in

American history was developing. Had Eaton been free to prepare for the Depression, it is possible he might have battened down the hatches, pulled in his sails and, perhaps, ridden out the storm with a minimum of damage and loss.

In the process of putting together Republic Steel, Eaton had used a most effective welding instrument called Continental Shares, an investment trust which he organized in 1926. Riding high on the crest of one achievement after another, Continental stock soared to three hundred dollars a share by 1929, and the predictors of its future were unconfined in their optimism. A year later, at the time of the court's decision in the Bethlehem fight, Continental Shares was quoted at eight dollars a share, and in 1932, when a stockholder, half in jest, offered a hundred shares of Continental for a pack of cigarettes, he found no takers. This investment trust, which owned at its peak, capital and surplus of 150 million dollars in 1929, was able to distribute only sixteen million dollars among its eighteen thousand shareholders when it was liquidated in 1933. Many thousands of those unfortunate investors were Clevelanders, and it goes without saying that Eaton's stature in his home city was diminished considerably by the financial fiasco brought about by the Depression or, as Eaton himself described it, "the economic tornado of the 1930s."

A short time before the crash, Eaton dropped in on Charles A. Otis, a founding partner in the Eaton-controlled investment banking firm, Otis & Company. According to Otis, their conversation ran as follows:

EATON: "Do you know how much we are worth today?"

OTIS: "No."

EATON: "Two hundred and seven million dollars."

OTIS: "Don't you think we ought to sell some of that?"

EATON: "No. We will hold on, and some day it will be four hundred and fourteen million dollars!"

It didn't happen that way. Eaton, ever the gambler, went for double or nothing and ended with nothing; at the very best, he was left with only a trifle more than nothing as his fantastic finances were figured.

It was said that Eaton personally was worth one hundred million dollars in 1929. When the dust had settled after the 1930 debacle, the accepted estimate was that the Cleveland financier was left with a mere one hundred thousand dollars—a nice, impressive figure in many respects, but hardly comparable in majesty, might, or purchasing power with one hundred million dollars.

The full extent of Eaton's setback in that year of depression is not known, but among his losses were control of Republic Steel, heavy investments in utilities, working control of the Goodyear Tire & Rubber

Company of Akron, largest rubber company in the world, and sizable stock holdings in two competitor companies, Firestone and Goodrich. At the time the Depression struck, Eaton was well on his way toward a merger of those three companies, a move which would have created a colossal organization able to dominate the rubber industry just as, through merger, he had planned to make Republic Steel dominant in the steel industry.

Complicating Eaton's financial situation at the time was the quick and forceful way in which eastern bankers called his loans, forcing him to liquidate many of his investments at the sacrifice level to meet his cash obligations. He never forgot. It was apparent in his bitter resentment of the New York banking houses in the years that followed. *Newsweek* magazine, in a biographical study of the Clevelander in October 1945, mused: "Historians may well find that the depression would have ruined Eaton anyway. . . . There was a suspicion, however, that the [New York] bankers were harsher to him than they might have been out of dislike for his trouncing of Eugene Grace and Charles M. Schwab in their efforts to merge Youngstown Sheet & Tube with Bethlehem Steel. Eaton has always maintained that his attempts to build a Midwest industrial empire were based on the idealistic desire to make that region independent of New York financial control. He says he resented the way 'New York' squeezed the Seiberlings out of Goodyear Rubber and tried to take over Henry Ford."

Recalling this low point in the career of the Cleveland financier, *Business Week* magazine (March 12, 1955) made the following observation that is so often overlooked, but which is vitally important in separating Eaton from run-of-the-mine millionaires: "The loss of his fortune did not bother him nearly so much as the loss of personal prestige. Before the 1930s he had been in constant demand by railroads and industrial companies in need of directors and advisers. Now he found himself being ousted even from companies he had helped create."

If the Depression spoiled Eaton's carefully constructed grand design for success, it did not break him. He still controlled Otis & Company, and the investment banking house became his comeback vehicle. By 1942, approximately ten years after the collapse of his financial empire, Eaton was back in the front ranks of successful international investment speculators. His plunge that year on a remote piece of Canadian real estate in western Ontario may have been the most important risk of a career studded with gambles.

World War II was making an extreme demand on the dwindling high-grade iron ore reserve of the fabulous Mesabi Range in Minnesota in 1942, and the United States and its allies understandably were concerned by the signs indicating that a rich new source would be needed to sustain the steel industry of North America in the foreseeable future.

Tests of iron ore known to exist in abundance in the area of Steep Rock Lake in Ontario had proven the deposit to be of a very high grade, but there was pessimism over the ore's accessibility. Steep Rock Lake was in an unspoiled wilderness. It was a shimmering blue centerpiece in a hunter's paradise, far from civilization and without easy access, except by the planes of the bush pilots. Survival there was a touch-and-go matter in wintertime when the temperature had been known to drop to fifty degrees below zero. The most serious problem, however, was that the main deposit of iron ore was underneath the lake itself.

This was the challenge and the opportunity that caught the imagination and enthusiasm of Cyrus Eaton. The reward awaiting the person or syndicate that could devise a practicable, economical method for extracting this ore was so great as to be almost beyond estimation; precisely the kind of superstake that would find a bidder in the Cleveland financier.

Eaton supported a plan which called for Steep Rock Lake to be drained. The boldness of the concept staggered the engineers. Most of them said it couldn't be done. Eaton insisted it was the *only* feasible method to get at the ore. It required the boring of a three-thousand-foot tunnel under the lake to its very center point, curving upward there to the lakebed. At this point, a final blast of dynamite would create a hole into which the waters would descend, to be drained away as a bathtub is emptied.

But Steep Rock Lake was no bathtub. It was a large body of water, fifteen miles long and four miles wide. The engineers said the rocks and boulders on the bed of the lake would quickly plug any hole created by a man-made blast. Eaton took the position contrary to that held by the technical experts. The hole would remain open, he predicted, and the water would flow out the underground tunnel. He proceeded to sell the theory to the United States Government, and the government of the Dominion of Canada. The United States extended him a five-million-dollar loan. Canada allocated twenty million dollars for the project, and Otis & Company chipped in $2,250,000 realized from the sale of debentures. The gamble was on.

When the boring crew had completed the three-thousand-foot tunnel under the lake and had approached within twenty feet of the lakebed, dynamite fuses were planted and the workers hurried back to safety on shore. At the given signal, the plunger was pushed and the dynamite was exploded.

It was one of the most dramatic moments in industrial history, and it certainly was one of the most critically important moments in the life of Cyrus Eaton. The water in the middle of the lake suddenly rose in a great bubble, there was a roaring sound, and rocks and boulders shot high into the air. All at once the onlookers knew that the plan had succeeded. There was a quickening whirlpool in the center of the lake, and it was obvious that the water from the lake was rushing downward through the underground tunnel. The gamble was won and the riches of Steep Rock basin were ready to be exploited by man. It stands out now as one of the principal sources of high-grade iron ore for North America—a treasury containing an estimated two billion tons of ore.

Further extending his holdings in this basic field, Eaton went on to gain control of iron ore deposits in the Ungava Peninsula of northern Quebec Province, regarded as the future supply source of Europe's iron and steel industry. There, in the subarctic tundras, Eaton's Ungava Iron Ores Company, formed in 1958 in association with Alfred Krupp and four other West German steel tycoons, holds title to reserves estimated at ten billion tons.

"Undoubtedly," said Fortune magazine in 1961, "Cyrus Eaton controls more iron ore than any other man in the world."

The London Daily Mail, in tacit recognition of this distinction, referred to him dramatically as "The iron master of North America."

The Clevelander's pace seemed to step up after World War II contrary to the expectations of his foes, most of whom entertained the logical supposition that advancing age would slow the Eaton gait. He organized the Portsmouth Steel Corporation in 1946 and made it a successful operation. He bought the floundering National Refining Company for ten million dollars and reportedly peddled its component parts for twenty-five million dollars. He borrowed twenty-six million dollars from the United Mine Workers of America and used the money to buy control of the West Kentucky Coal Company and the Nashville Coal Company. In 1954, he paid $3,630,569.75 for 108,854 shares of C. & O. stock and succeeded Robert R. Young, one of the successors to the fabulous Van Sweringen brothers, as chairman of the board of the highly profitable coal-carrying C. & O. In the 1960s, Eaton was able to merge the C. & O. with the Baltimore & Ohio Railroad.

It wasn't any real surprise that the United Mine Workers union should have been willing to lend capitalist Cyrus Eaton millions of dollars from its treasury. He long enjoyed a rare distinction among men of finance and industry—the reputation of being a friend of organized labor. Among his close friends for many years had been John L. Lewis, the shaggy-browed leader of the miners, one of the few men in Eaton's circle of acquaintances who could hold his own with the erudite Clevelander in arguments over classical literature. In his moments of philosophical relaxation, Eaton likes to quote Spinoza's line: "No regrets, no fears!"

Eaton also persuaded the United Mine Workers to invest money in two utilities in which he has major holdings, the Cleveland Electric Illuminating Company and the Kansas City Power & Light Company, as well as the C. & O. Railroad, in which the union invested $9,421,518 in 1951. According to a 1960 report by John Owens, UMW secretary-treasurer, the C. & O. stock doubled in value after its purchase by the union. Furthermore, the two large coal companies, Kentucky Coal and Nashville Coal, whose control Eaton purchased with money borrowed from the union, had been organized by the UMW with Eaton's approval. Up to the time of the report, the companies had paid fourteen million dollars into the union's welfare fund and the employees had paid the UMW eighty-one million dollars in dues. Thus, the Eaton-UMW arrangement resulted in a happy, profitable alliance for both parties.

A British reporter, searching afield for the right words to describe Cyrus Eaton, finally concluded that he was "the tycoon who looks like a cardinal." It was an apt similitude, in a class with others which have likened him to a college dean or a university professor.

Eaton is, in appearance and formal manner, more the churchman or educator than the financial speculator; still handsome, even in his eighties. He is a slim, erect six-footer with snow-white hair, and he has the appearance of an ascetic. His eyes are a pale, faded blue, and the eyelids are heavy. His manner of dress is predictable—a dark blue double-breasted suit, a white shirt with French cuffs, and a dark, conservative tie. At the beginning of each working day, there is always a fresh-cut rose in a bud vase on his desk.

Whatever fanciful writers see in him, Eaton himself supplies the most accurate identification tag to hang on himself.

"I guess you could call me the last of the tycoons," he says, aligning himself firmly with the old giants of finance—the Rockefellers, the Jay Goulds, the Commodore Vanderbilts, and the J. P. Morgans. He is a tycoon, and no doubts cloud his claim to the distinction. But he is an unusual tycoon—indubitably the only one who ever qualified also as an authority on the literature of seventeenth-century France. When he travels, he usually carries with him some exotic literary bonbon from a play of Jean Racine, say, or the translation of one of Pierre Corneille's plays.

Among other signs of Eaton's scholarly bent are his membership in the American Philosophical Association and his zestful participation in collegiate affairs as a trustee of the University of Chicago, Case Institute of Technology in Cleveland, and Denison University in Granville, Ohio. Throughout his long life, he has shown a marked preference for the company of educators, authors, and other front-runners in the world of culture. At the same time, he has established a record of friendly association with members of the working press—another departure from the norm which stirs a storm of sniffs from his peers in the Union Club. The storm would reach its height late each summer in the years when the financier made it his custom to open the fields of his Acadia Farms home in Northfield for a picnic to which he invited the members of the Cleveland professional chapter of the Sigma Delta Chi journalism society, and their families.

The most substantial expression of Eaton's friendliness toward newspaper people came in the wake of World War II when he extended a loan of $7,600,000 to the 850 employees of the Cincinnati *Enquirer* to enable them to buy the newspaper. His motive in this transaction has been challenged by critics who allege that he was moved to advance the money more by a spirit of malice than generosity. Among the prospective buyers of the Cincinnati property was a rival publication, the *Times-Star*, owned by the Taft family, and it must have pleased Eaton to block the purchase. There was no love lost between Eaton and the leading member of the Taft clan, the late United States Senator Robert A. Taft.

The clash between Eaton and Taft happened in the late years of the Depression and centered on a twelve-million-dollar bond issue which had been proposed to finance the Cincinnati Union Terminal. Taft was chairman of the terminal's finance committee. When Eaton approached him to apprise him of Otis & Company's interest in participating in the issue, Taft dismissed him, according to Eaton, in rather uncomplimentary language.

"Preposterous!" Eaton quoted Taft. "We've already made a deal with people we trust—and I resent your coming in here!"

This very custom of negotiated agreements between underwriting companies and their clients which prevailed at the time, and which was illustrated in the Cincinnati Union Terminal issue, was a sore point with Eaton. He had held the system to be one of the powerful— and profitable—devices which enabled Wall Street firms to hold dominion over finance and industry in other parts of the nation. Clients inevitably, it seemed, chose a New York investment house to handle their issues even when they had more attractive offers from firms in the hinterland.

Eaton wanted to break this monopolistic state of affairs with a competitive system in which investment firms would have to submit sealed bids in seeking to underwrite bond issues of private clients. Such a system would open the way for an expansion of business for midwestern financiers, of course, but it also presented a valuable advantage to the clients. In 1938, for example, Eaton's friend, Robert R. Young, head of the Chesapeake & Ohio Railroad, had allowed competitive bidding on the railroad's thirty-million-dollar bond issue. The best offer was a joint bid by Otis & Company and Halsey, Stuart & Company of Chicago, which saved the railroad an estimated two million dollars. Eaton's profit from the deal was not considerable, but it probably was secondary to the satisfaction he derived from edging out Wall Street's Morgan, Stanley and Kuhn, Loeb combine.

Refusing to admit defeat in Cincinnati, Eaton, more determined than ever because of Taft's curt dismissal, outflanked his fellow Ohioan by seeking help from the administration of President Franklin D. Roosevelt, with whom he was on friendly terms, still another reason for his fellow capitalists to dislike him. He went to Jesse Jones, head of the Reconstruction Finance Corporation, which had extended millions of dollars in financial aid to many of the nation's ailing railroads, and prevailed on Jones to rule in favor of the principle of competitive bidding for railroad bonds. RFC aid was made contingent on the use of the bidding practice.

Eight railroads controlled the Cincinnati Union Terminal. Some already were indebted to the government agency and the others certainly were aware of the wisdom of staying in the agency's good graces. The terminal bonds were put on a competitive bidding basis. Eaton's Otis and Company was among the bidders, of course, but, ironically, he lost the issue to another investment house. At the same time, he scored the larger victory in helping to establish the principle of competitive bidding as an accepted, established practice. Later it was made mandatory by the Interstate Commerce Commission. Furthermore, he had beaten Taft.

They say in financial circles that Cyrus Eaton is a tough foe and a bad enemy; that he never forgets a slight and that he never forgives. Generalizations such as those are best questioned or avoided, but there is ample evidence of Eaton's quite human disposition to even the score with those who have crossed him or otherwise disturbed his personal designs through the years. It is possible, for instance, that Senator Taft lost a lot more than merely a choice of terminal underwriters in his joust with Cyrus Eaton. It may be that his brusque rejection of the unorthodox Clevelander also lost him the Presidency of the United States—or, at least, the nomination for that office by the Republican Party. Eaton worked against him behind the party scenes whenever he approached that most precious of political prizes. It is conceivable that but for Eaton's opposition, Taft would have turned the tide and ridden it to success.

It was part of Cyrus Eaton's wisdom and success that early in his career he recognized the importance of the political factor in the adroit and effective use of the capitalistic system. He studied politics and politicians so as to learn the system fully, even on the city level. Toward that end, he often took time to observe the Cleveland City Council in session. While he never ran for any office himself, he did busy himself in the city's political life in a behind-the-scenes role.

Among his limited community involvements was service as one of the founder-directors of the famous Cleveland City Club, an open speech forum. He also served as a ten-year trustee of the Cleveland Metropolitan Park Board. In this latter capacity he was among the men responsible for the establishment of the Metropolitan Park system, which must rank as one of the most magnificent natural recreational areas within any American city; it is a forest of some seventeen thousand acres, an unspoiled garland of greenery that loops the entire urban area.

Eaton helped to found the Cleveland Museum of Natural History, and his old town house on Euclid Avenue at East 89th Street, a large brick mansion in a fading neighborhood became the home of the Cleveland Health Museum. He was among the strong supporters of the YMCA Evening School, where he studied accounting in his younger days, as it evolved into Fenn College and then into Cleveland State University.

Cleveland is the city which gave birth to the Community Fund, and Eaton once was asked about his seeming lack of willingness to participate as one of the leaders in the annual fund drive. His answer provided an insight into his civic sense of values.

"I haven't the time to be active in the Community Chest," he told his interviewer, "but I feel that I've done my share by helping create tens of thousands of jobs. Regular employment is what makes it possible for people to live a happy life and contribute to the Community Chest."

Eaton's basic contribution to the city, as he suggested, does spring from his creativity as a financier. Through his efforts, Cleveland has the Republic Steel Corporation, third-largest steel producer in the nation; Sherwin-Williams, great paint manufacturer; Fisher Body's huge Cleveland works which he made possible by financing the Fisher brothers of Norwalk, Ohio, with a ten-million-dollar base; National Acme, Eaton Manufacturing Company, and Cleveland Cliffs Iron Company. He also kept Cleveland the headquarters of the C. & O. Railroad after its marriage with the Baltimore & Ohio road.

The influence of Eaton has been a vital factor in the historic growth of all Cleveland's utilities. His contribution to the East Ohio Gas Company has been described, but he also figured significantly in the rise of the Cleveland Electric Illuminating Company, in which he owns a major stock holding, and the creation of the modern Ohio Bell Telephone Company by merging his Ohio State Telephone Company with the struggling Bell company. In the same way, Eaton is credited with helping boost the Cleveland Trust Company into its position of banking dominance in Cleveland by wielding his influence as a director of the Lake Shore Bank to bring about the merger that put Cleveland Trust in the lead.

Eaton is a country gentleman in the old, almost anachronistic sense of the title. He lives on an 870-acre estate called Acadia Farms in Northfield, a little town in Summit County halfway between Cleveland and Akron, some twenty miles from his office in the Terminal Tower. The 150-year-old white frame farmhouse was built by the original owner of the land, a Connecticut pioneer named John Wilson. Eaton purchased the farm in 1912 when he was still in his twenties and presumably still working on his first million dollars.

Acadia, a natural, unspoiled beauty spot with rolling hills, groves of trees, and placid ponds, was to be the family's weekend retreat and a summer vacation place. It served as such until 1930, when the collapse of the Eaton empire brought about a general retrenching that included the sale of the elegant town house. Henceforth, Acadia Farms became the year-round estate. It is not a rich man's showplace, however, but a working, producing farm on which Eaton raises prize-winning pure-bred Scotch Shorthorn cattle, as he does also on his three-thousand-acre Deep Cove Farms in Upper Blandford in his native Nova Scotia.

Eaton married Margaret House, member of a prominent Cleveland family, on December 29, 1907. Their marriage lasted almost twenty-seven years, ending in divorce on August 16, 1934. They had seven children, five daughters and two sons. It was not until after her death in Cleveland clinic in March 1956 that the financier remarried. His second wife was Anne Kinder Jones, an attractive thirty-five-year-old Cleveland socialite who had been crippled by an attack of poliomyelitis in 1946.

Anne Kinder was graduated from Vassar (one of her classmates was the future Mrs. Cyrus Eaton, Jr.) and taught, briefly, at Cleveland College of Western Reserve University. Like Eaton, she has a deep interest in philosophy and poetry. She is, by Eaton's testimony, the "politician" in the family.

Eaton always had a close but passive interest in international events, as one would expect of a financier whose dealings crossed national boundaries as frequently as the lines of latitude and longitude. He did not become an active figure in the Cold War, however, until 1955. Ironically enough, the United States Government played the matchmaker's role in bringing the Soviet Union and the multimillionaire together in the beginning of what turned out to be a beautiful, if sometimes embarrassing, friendship.

A Soviet agricultural delegation was touring the United States in 1955 and the State Department asked Eaton if he would entertain the group at Acadia Farms, show them his Scottish Shorthorn cattle and, incidentally, let them get a close-up look at a genuine capitalist. Eaton was pleased to accept. The visit was a diplomatic success and the exchanges between the Soviet technicians and the capitalist were cordial.

Eaton's real immersement in international politics came in 1957 at the third of his own Pugwash conferences; gatherings of intellectuals and world leaders in diverse fields which he had instituted in 1955 and which originally were intended to be held annually at his Pugwash, Nova Scotia, estate. That third conference was held in Lac Beauport, Quebec, because the time of the meeting—March—usually is marked by inhospitable weather in Nova Scotia.

It was the first time nuclear scientists from all the great powers on both sides in the Cold War had come together in any kind of discussion of mankind's most fearsome scientific discovery. Eaton listened closely to the portentous utterances and the melancholy predictions of future disaster if the nations of the world continued to drift in the international political currents leading toward a global holocaust. The conference, in the words of *Fortune* magazine, "set Eaton afire."

A second meeting of the nuclear scientists of the world was held in the autumn of 1957 in Vienna under the joint sponsorship of the Clevelander and the Austrian Government. It was while he was en route to this fourth Pugwash Conference, far from the homely hills of Nova Scotia, that Eaton's itinerary took him into Russia for a ten-day visit and his first meeting with Premier Nikita Khrushchev. The Soviet leader gave signal recognition of Eaton's unique position in world politics by making a special flight from Yalta to meet with him in the Kremlin. The world's No. 1 Communist and one of the world's leading capitalists presented a study in contrasts when they were introduced. Khrushchev was the peasant revolutionist, short and stocky, blunt-fingered and blunt-talking; Eaton was the cultured aristocrat, tall and slim, with tapered fingers and graceful speech. But these two opposites hit it off together famously in their first meeting. The Soviet leader gave the financier an audience that lasted ninety minutes, and it was reported that they had touched on many different subjects of international significance.

They had other meetings in the years that followed and their strange friendship continued, even in the face of adversity. The most trying test, one presumes, came in 1959 when the planned Paris summit conference between Khrushchev and President Eisenhower was toppled by the shooting down of an American U-2 "spy plane" by the Russians twelve hundred miles inside their territory and the capture of the civilian pilot, Francis Gary Powers, on Soviet soil. Khrushchev's reaction was a violent public tantrum that was climaxed in Paris by his refusal to meet with the American President who already had arrived in the French capital and was awaiting the top-level conference.

But if Khrushchev would not meet with the President of the United States, he was delighted to meet with Cyrus Eaton—and did so, at Orly Field in Paris, where he greeted the financier upon his arrival from Cleveland.

It was an inopportune moment for Eaton to display his friendship with the Communist world, and to demonstrate, in particular, his warm camaraderie with Nikita Khrushchev. All America was blushing over the embarrassing U-2 *faux pas* and all America was smarting under the Khrushchev tongue-lashing and the humiliating sight of President Eisenhower's rejection by the Red leader. The news pictures of Eaton and Khrushchev shaking hands and smiling in their warm reunion at Orly Field served only to stir the public mind and emotions against the Clevelander.

After a tour of such Soviet satellite nations as Poland, Czechoslovakia, Hungary, and East Germany, Eaton landed in London, was met by the press, and promptly captured the headlines once again with a series of inflammatory remarks. Among these was his statement that the United States was "more of a police state" than any of the countries behind the Iron Curtain.

Writing on the same subject in the Moscow magazine the *Progressive*, Eaton, according to Scripps-Howard columnist Henry J. Taylor, said: "The only country where people look over their shoulders to see who is listening is the United States. It is we in America who created the picture of a police state. . . . The president of one [American] company told me he has been fingerprinted so often he can't get his hand dry."

"The only people in the United States who believe that communism is a menace," Eaton told reporters, "are the boys on the payroll of the F.B.I."

Whatever Eaton's reasons for his pro-Soviet outbursts, and they are still open to analysis, he was guilty of a tactless disregard for the opinions and feelings of his own fellow Americans on a number of occasions, of which the Paris meeting was but one. Indeed, only a little more than a month after that historic blowup, and while the public memory still retained a clear recollection of the airport meeting, Eaton accepted the Lenin Peace Prize in a ceremony held in Pugwash on July 1, 1960, Dominion Day. The Soviet wire service, Tass, in reporting the ceremony, described Eaton as "a public figure whose activity is an example of public service to the lofty idea of the peaceful coexistence between peoples."

The year of 1960, all things considered, was a red-letter year in Soviet-Cyrus Eaton relations. In September, Nikita Khrushchev journeyed to New York to attend a session of the United Nations and set that world body on its ear with his undiplomatic utterances, coarse threats and, finally, his shoe-pounding tantrum—a high mark in parliamentary crudity even for the tough little Ukrainian.

The Cleveland capitalist earlier had invited Khrushchev to visit Acadia Farms during his visit to the United States, saying: "It would be a good thing for them to see a typically American city like Cleveland. I believe in America. I have faith in democracy and the capitalist system. I would like to show them off to these influential men who disagree with us . . ."

The State Department was not of the same mind, restricting the Soviet leader to Manhattan during his visit to the United Nations. But Eaton was determined to play host to Khrushchev. If Mahomet could not come to the Mountain, then the Mountain perforce must go to Mahomet—and did. On September 26, the capitalist played host to the Communist leader in a ballroom on the nineteenth floor of the Hotel Biltmore while official Washington presumably fumed. Some 150 guests attended and heard Eaton speak in behalf of an expansion in Soviet-American trade while Khrushchev's remarks, in the main, were concerned with the advisability of international disarmament.

The positive side to Eaton's extended series of indiscretions over the years in the arena of international politics is that by playing the role of the devil's advocate, it is quite possible he helped America to keep its democratic balance and perhaps acted as a moderating influence on Nikita Khrushchev and other Soviet leaders. No spokesman for the capitalist way of life ever penetrated so far into the heartland of communism or won the ears of the Soviet chieftains the way Cyrus Eaton did.

In this favored position, able to command the respectful attention of the men in the Kremlin, Eaton may have done more for the cause of international understanding and peace than any of the hot-eyed critics who denounced him for consorting with the enemy.

The Pugwash nuclear conferences were decisive in convincing Eaton that science had rendered another world war so catastrophic as to be unthinkable, and his was one of the influential voices that helped to convey this belief to Khrushchev, a force leading the Soviet premier to the alternative policy of coexistence.

Eaton continually preached the merits of American agricultural methods, with their high rate of productivity, and Khrushchev listened. It is believed that Mr. K.'s insistence that the farmers of the Soviet Union borrow the methods and machinery of the West, coupled with his praise of Western efficiency, caused some of his critics in the Communist Party to accuse him of being too much of an admirer of the United States. Some experts have said that this was one of the important factors leading to the downfall of Khrushchev.

A highly placed State Department official told a writer for *Parade* magazine in 1963 that Eaton's influence with the Kremlin had been helpful in bringing about a thaw in the Cold War. It was also said that his intercession had saved captured U-2 pilot Francis Gary Powers from a Soviet firing squad and later resulted in the melodramatic swap of Powers for the Russian master spy Rudolf Abel on a bridge in Berlin.

It can be pointed out that no matter how severely Eaton criticized his own country's leadership in the Cold War—sometimes unfairly—and no matter how much praise he was willing to pay the Soviet rulers—oftentimes unwarranted—he was consistent in defense of his basic beliefs in democracy and capitalism.

"I live happily and I hope productively by the doctrine that intelligent and enlightened private ownership and operation provide the ideal system of economics for my country, and that the greatest possible separation of politics from economics is desirable."

Describing his philosophy to a British television interviewer in 1960, Eaton said: "I'm a dyed-in-the-wool capitalist, both in theory and in practice, but I'm also old enough to realize that no one has yet found the final answers to all the problems of life. While I would not be a practicing Communist, or socialist, I do respect adherents to these systems for having their own convictions and ideas. I am sure they can go along with their own system of communism and we in America with ours of capitalism and we can get together if we want to."

Again, in 1961, upon his return from Bulgaria where he shared the reviewing stand with Russian cosmonaut Yuri Gagarin at a parade celebrating the Bulgarian national holiday, Eaton spelled out his ratiocination of the troubled world scene and his role in it:

"I'm as dedicated a capitalist in theory and practice as there is in the world. My chief interest is to save capitalism in America from nuclear war, which would turn to dust all the industry I'm associated with and annihilate my family and friends.

"I feel that in America too many people take the narrow view that all connected with socialist countries is wicked and that everything we stand for is of the highest noble order. That attitude is not shared by our allies or neutral nations. Because I say these things doesn't imply I favor communism. But I'm sure as anything that no power we possess can shift the socialist countries from communism. We ought to take the realistic view, get along with them instead of trying to destroy them."

In the midst of the clamorous disapproval of Eaton's position as an apologist for the Communist nations and their leaders, there occasionally has been sounded a contrary expression in praise of his efforts. Such a pro-Eaton position was taken in the *Catholic Herald* of London, England, on January 15, 1965 in a column written by a member of Parliament, Norman St. John-Stevas, under the heading: "Lunch With Mr. K's U. S. Friend."

The column said:

"Last week I had lunch in Cleveland, Ohio, with Mr. Cyrus Eaton, the American industrialist who became a close friend of Mr. Khrushchev, and with whom Mr. Khrushchev stayed during his visit to America.

"Mr. Eaton is a millionaire but certainly not a typically American one, and his understanding of what is going on in the Communist world is, alas, all too rare amongst American businessmen. In the mid-West especially, the rigid anti-Communism of both business and public opinion has altered very little since it was adopted in Stalinist days.

"The American attitude (although not the State Department's) to world Communism is still dangerously oversimplified. Cyrus Eaton is regarded by many as an eccentric but he is in fact a prophetic pioneer of the dialogue between East and West.

"Mr. Eaton is a remarkably vigorous 81, and perhaps before he retires he can do something to bring about a change in the attitude to China of the leader of the Western alliance. If so mankind is likely to be permanently in his debt."

The man who is perhaps the world's busiest octogenarian is visibly irked whenever anybody makes a point of underscoring his age or speaking too heavily of him in the past tense. It is Eaton's firm conviction that his most outstanding achievements are yet to come, and nobody who knows him is betting that he is wrong.

On his eighty-second birthday in December of 1965, Eaton mounted a horse and took his usual canter over his Northfield acres. When he returned to the stables, he took time to pet the horses of his troika team, a gift from Nikita Khrushchev, and then retired to the library of his country home for a newspaper interview.

"Time does some things to us that we don't like," he conceded to Joe Collier of the Cleveland *Press*, "but it makes a lot of things clearer if one keeps his eyes open and does some reading. Every room in this 175-year-old house is a library . . . and they contribute to the pleasure of living.

"Twenty years ago I had a rule to read nothing that was not a hundred years old and proved trustworthy. But I have given up that luxury.

"The way to destroy capitalism is to get into wars all over the world, create crushing tax burdens, create ill will by compelling the less fortunate nations to adopt our way of life. You can't, by force, permanently control men's minds and devotions.

"The way to discourage communism is to make capitalism an outstanding success—to put U.S. bankers and investors into enterprises in every part of the world, taking risks and making available our genius.

"For war, we must substitute forbearance and patience. Let time do something for us."

Whatever else time may do, there is no doubt that it will yield a place to Cyrus Eaton as one of the most remarkable men in Cleveland's history and one of the most unusual men of our time; the last of the old-fashioned tycoons certainly—and perhaps the first of a new breed of socially and politically concerned businessmen.

XXIV

In Search of an Image

A COMMUNITY image is a sensitive thing, not to be tinkered with casually or to be taken lightly, as I learned several years ago while riding a railroad across the Great West.

The train I was riding was the Santa Fe Railroad's *El Capitan,* which has its very own image. It is kind of a fun train; an all-coach streamliner in which passengers perforce snuggle cozily together in their reclining seats at night and sometimes become great and good friends as they roll toward their destination.

My seat partner in this adventure was an interesting little man of advanced years who had no disposition toward sleep and an extraordinary willingness to talk about the most intimate events of a long, uneventful life. He was a sort of man-child; his skin was smooth and pink and his pale blue eyes shone with naïveté and apprehension. He spoke in a half-apologetic manner as if expecting to be rebuffed, as likely he had been many times, and only when he lifted a gnarled, heavily veined hand to brush aside a lock of his neat white hair did his age assert itself.

Charlie was his name, and he was returning to St. Louis after having visited his sister in a satellite town of Los Angeles. It had been many years since he had seen his sister, and he was delighted that he had been able to make the trip. Now he was returning to his home, a farm near St. Louis, and to the loving wife—his second—who awaited him there. He called her the Widder Woman because that's what she had been when he married her. He chuckled as he told how the Widder Woman had swept him off his feet. She really had thought that she had ensnared him with her wiles, but all the while he was playing a game and letting her win. The Widder Woman was an outstanding captor by his honestly practical standards. She had a nice chicken farm and a fair bank account.

"She had what I calls a nest egg," he said, half-raising in the recliner seat to allow a laugh to bubble out of his stomach. "Get it? A chicken farm and a nest egg?"

Then he sank back, reflectively, and said the only trouble with his marital setup was the Widder Woman's son by her first marriage. The lad apparently was a real trial, having been involved in a long series of extralegal scrapes.

"He even runs around with a gunslinger from Kansas City," said Charlie. "That's the worst part. Once, him and the gunslinger came running home to the farm, and no sooner had they arrived, all nervous, when we could see the sheriff's car coming down the road raising such a cloud of dust you could hardly see the whirling red light. The kid and the gunslinger dove under one of the chicken coops, and the police looked all around, but they never looked under the chicken coops. The Widder Woman said she had not seen the boy in weeks and the cops went away.

"That was funny, in a way, but the gunslinger hung around for a couple of days afterward and I was nervous every minute. You can't trust anybody from Kansas City."

I was half-asleep when he said that, but I had to have an explanation.

"That's a broad statement," I said. "There must be a lot of nice people in Kansas City."

"Maybe," he allowed, reasonably. He really was a decent old man. "Maybe. But you can't tell me about their gunslingers."

"Years ago, I suppose," I said, "but not now."

"I wouldn't bet on it," he said. "Nobody will ever get me into Kansas City again. Never. I was there once and the town was full of gunslingers. They were everywhere, walking up and down, their fingers just itching to shoot you. All you had to do was look sideways at them. Not that I had any trouble with them, or anything. They seemed to like me, probably because I was so small, but I wasn't happy until I got out of that town, believe me!"

About that time there was a stirring up front and in the dim light you could see the conductor making his way down the aisle, stopping every now and then to lean down and shake some passenger. He finally reached us and he put a penlight to a card in his hand and looked down at us.

"Kansas City?" he said, and I heard Charlie choke a little.

"Chicago," said Charlie.

"Chicago," I said.

"Kansas City," repeated the conductor. "You get off at Kansas City." And he flicked his light at Charlie, who, by now, was sitting upright.

"Your ticket is to St. Louis," said the conductor, "but you have to transfer at Kansas City."

"Nosiree!" bleated Charlie. "I go through to Chicago and transfer there."

"Sorry, old-timer," said the conductor. "You've got ten minutes before we arrive. Better get your things ready." He passed on, and there was an awkward silence.

"It's too bad," I told Charlie, "but this is 1958. Kansas City is a big, modern city. Perfectly safe."

"Well, there's one good thing," he sighed. "You don't have to get off. It's bad enough as it is, but I've been around a long time. I guess I can take care of myself in Kansas City. The gunslingers there used to like me, years ago."

He reached up and pulled down an old brown valise and shook hands very formally with me before he got off. My window was at the wrong side of the train, so I didn't even get to see him after that, but I stayed awake for a while after *El Capitan* resumed its journey and I remember thinking to myself that old Charlie was one of the bravest men a person could be privileged to meet. The way he got off that train in Kansas City and walked right into the teeth of all those gunslingers was absolutely magnificent.

Not that I accepted the image of Kansas City that Charlie projected. Everybody I ask tells me it is a fine community and a great place to live, even if the baseball team is pretty bad. The very fact, though, that I went out of my way to inquire about Kansas City shows what strong medicine an image is, good or bad.

Cleveland has an image, like every other city, and in its own way it is just as grotesquely inaccurate as old Charlie's conception of Kansas City.

The very worst problem that a person is likely to encounter in trying to correct Cleveland's image, though, is straightening out some of the Clevelanders. An awful lot of them have been led astray into a never-never land by an enterprising public utility, the Cleveland Electric Illuminating Company, which unwittingly has induced giddy and outsized delusions among some of its own customers with an advertising campaign designed to entice new industry to the Greater Cleveland area.

The slogan of the campaign confronts the people of the nation in full-page advertisements in national magazines and on billboards, such as the one that air travelers see as they wheel out of the terminal area of the Cleveland Hopkins International Airport and onto the Berea Freeway leading downtown. At this junction a large billboard welcomes them to "Cleveland—The Best Location in the Nation."

It is common knowledge among psychologists, of course, that this happens to be the worst possible way to welcome visitors. It should be obvious, even to the local chamber of commerce, that people who do not call Cleveland home and who most likely have formed an unhealthy attachment for some other town will be affronted by this slogan. Some of them even may choose to read braggadocio into it, and there have been recorded instances of visitors actually bridling. It is said that a tourist from Sioux City, Iowa, felt so strongly about the billboard that he demanded to be let out of the airport limousine and returned to the field to take the next plane back to Iowa.

That sort of reaction is extreme, of course, and should not be considered typical. But it is a fact that the slogan does tend to put visitors in a thoughtful mood. Some even will slump back in the airport limousine with their eyes hooded and their lips curled back ever so slightly in an expression that says, "Show me!" It is an attitude that challengingly calls on the entire metropolis of Cleveland to produce one single feature that the visitors will like.

This is not a good mood for visitors to be in. It places a city at a terrible disadvantage. Visitors rightfully should be shiny-eyed, joyful of countenance, and keenly anticipatory of all the delights that may or may not be in store for them.

Just to make things a trifle more awkward for Cleveland, the motor drive from the airport to downtown is a tedious, trying route that is calculated to depress the spirits of any free man. The already-cynical tourist discovers that the Berea Freeway is merely a short burst of superhighway. It is succeeded, after a mile or so, by a succession of grim business streets slashing their way in a diagonal across the West Side and doggedly fighting their way downtown.

Like so many other American cities, Cleveland has waited too long on the automobile. There is a vast and comprehensive pattern of limited access highways currently under construction. The new roads will, when completed, change the traffic situation drastically—some traditionalists say for the worse, as in Los Angeles. Nobody denies the almost frantic need for the new superroad system, however, and the expressways already are looping around and through the city, following an army of bulldozers that is still determinedly pushing the past out of the way.

Commuters between downtown and Cleveland Hopkins Airport soon will be able to overlook the highway situation entirely, if they choose. The municipally owned Cleveland Transit System is building the last link in a rapid transit line connecting the airport with the Public Square downtown. High-speed trains will be whisking air travelers and other airport visitors to the heart of the city in approximately twenty minutes at any time of the day or night, no matter how bad the traffic or the weather, by 1968. Plans call also for baggage and freight cars on the rapid transit trains.

Meanwhile, it is not only the visitor to the city who is disturbed by the unfortunate slogan of "Best Location in the Nation." It bothers a lot of loyal, patriotic Clevelanders as well because it can be taken as an absolute axiom that there is no harsher critic of Cleveland anywhere than a native son. The objectivity of the people who make their home in this city and their ability to recognize their own shortcomings is really remarkable. It may be said that the people of Cleveland are opposites to the people of Texas; instead of boasting about the city's attributes, they dwell eloquently on its deficiencies to the extent, often, where outsiders feel compelled to take up the Cleveland cause in a curious reversal of normal American procedure.

A typical commentary was made by Arthur A. Watson, general manager of the National Broadcasting Company's radio and television stations in Cleveland (WKYC) shortly after he had taken up residence in the city in 1965.

"I'm puzzled," he said. "When I found I was being transferred from Philadelphia to Cleveland, I made it a point to talk with as many Clevelanders as I could. I wanted to know about the city and they told me—they told me everything that was wrong with it. But here I am and I have found it a delightful place; a really beautiful city. Sure, it's a pleasant surprise after what I was led to believe, but I'm puzzled when people run down their own city."

As a matter of fact, the "Best Location in the Nation" slogan began as a much more modest contention. Robert H. Bridges, a spokesman for the Cleveland Electric Illuminating Company, recalls the circumstances.

"We first began to promote Cleveland-northeast Ohio in national publications in 1944," he said. "The slogan wasn't developed until the second ad. The slogan read as follows: 'Cleveland-Northeast Ohio . . . The Best Location in the Nation for many industries.' There was a subhead which read: 'No other area in the U.S. offers this unique combination of advantages.' And we listed the advantages.

"The New York *Times* refused the ad on the grounds that no area could support such a claim. We provided them with our research and requested them to check it out.

"This they did, and so the first of many, many 'Best Location' ads appeared in the New York *Times* and later in most of the major national business publications.

"In those wonderfully uncomplicated days following the war, the Cleveland newspapers, recognizing a good thing when they saw it, latched on and began to give the slogan a real fine *free* ride. However hard the reporters tried to be accurate, alas, they found that the headline writers simply would not use the slogan in its entirety. Since the function of our area promotion was and is purely and simply to attract new business and industry to this area and to enlist salesmen in the effort, we felt it would be ungrateful of us to be critical of this shortened version.

"In time we adjusted ourselves to the diminutive. Indeed, we even felt a little author's pride now and then. Besides, we had by then

amassed considerable evidence that BLIN was a resounding success in
getting the attention of prospects. You know, people would say, 'What
impertinence!' and then go on and read the ads and ask for more information, or send a salesman and that sort of thing . . ."

The point is still valid, though, that slogans, like nicknames, must
be used with discretion. There are so many variables in any municipal
equation that today's paean may be tomorrow's pain. Cleveland found
that to be true some years ago, when it was flushed with unbelievable
success and found itself one of the world's fastest-growing cities. By
1920 it had become the fifth-largest city in the United States and,
inevitably, the title "Fifth City" was picked up for wide use as a
synonym for Cleveland. Newspaper writers sprinkled it throughout their
stories; politicians liked its explosive sound and incorporated it in their
bombast, and the Chamber of Commerce orators fell in love with the
designation completely.

None of those uses really was risky, but the indiscreet people were
the manufacturers and merchants who, in the flush of the hour, adopted
"Fifth City" as part of their company names. As if a population rating
had any kind of permanence in a nation with a lot of young cities
still growing and developing! In 1940, Cleveland was elbowed out of
the fifth city position and fell back to sixth position. In the 1950 census,
it became the seventh city; in 1960, the eighth city. Almost everybody
was able to adjust to the new population ratings quickly, bruised egos
to one side, except companies which had allowed local pride to creep
into their official names. Consequently, it is possible to find in the
Eighth City today such vestigial evidence of past census glory as the
Fifth City Furniture Company and the Sixth City Wire Works, the
Sixth City Body Company, and the Sixth City Salvage Company. But
the businessmen of Cleveland are learning, at last, the transitory nature
of civic glory, it seems. Nowhere in the Eighth City is there yet to be
found a company called the Seventh City anything, or an Eighth City
anything. The merchants at least are more cautious than they used to
be.

All of Cleveland, in fact, has learned an important lesson in recent
years, and it has to do with the national confusion of civic values in
which size and numbers have been equated with greatness. Cleveland
rode hard in the population derby and held the inside of the track for a
long while, from 1850 to 1920, when it sprinted hard and spurted far
ahead of a lot of cities which were older, wiser, and a little bit tired
of the pace. The largest city in Ohio exulted and pranced each time
it gained the lead over a competitor city, and it seemed as if this
young giant were unbeatable.

The Depression that began in 1930 hit Cleveland a solar plexus
blow that brought the city to its knees and sharply reduced its popula-

tion growth. No less astute an observer than Cyrus Eaton believes that Cleveland was hurt more by the Depression than any other major city in the United States, and it is his opinion that Cleveland in the mid-1960s is still in the convalescent stage, still recovering from that terrible business slump. There are other experts who share this belief. It is plausible enough to people who remember the exuberant, dynamic Cleveland of pre-Depression days and who can compare it with the somber, convalescent city that walked with a dragging gait and a querulous expression until recent years. The Cleveland that the world knew from 1930 to 1955 was a hurt town and it showed in many ways. There was a disposition toward petty bickering among the civic leaders over petty issues, while the large issue of Cleveland's future went untended and the sprawling downtown area turned gray and shabby.

The revival actually began in the administration of Mayor Thomas A. Burke in the late 1940s, but it was slow to enlist the active support of Cleveland's influential families. Mayor Burke led the way in the development of the first major municipal projects since the Roaring Twenties, when the fabulous Van Sweringen brothers were remaking the face of the city. He sponsored construction of a downtown airport on fill land to the east of the East 9th Street pier, and he activated the dormant plan, actually conceived and begun by the Van Sweringens, for a system of rapid transit lines. The monuments to his four-term administration, from 1944 to 1952, are the Burke Lakefront Airport, which now accommodates more than three hundred takeoffs and landings every day, and the Cleveland Transit System's nineteen-mile rapid system, extending from the Windermere Station, near Euclid and Superior avenues on the East Side, to a temporary western terminal at West 140th Street and Lorain Avenue. When the extension is completed in 1968, making the Cleveland Hopkins International Airport the terminal on the West Side, CTS officials will press for activation of long-standing plans to push the rapid system into every part of the metropolis.

Burke's successor as the city's chief executive was Anthony J. Celebrezze, the first representative of Cleveland's large Italian colony to reach the high office, and while he was irreverently known up and down the street as "The Mustache," he also was acclaimed as an outstanding performer. His major accomplishment as mayor was arousing the town's drowsy fat cats, most of whom were brought to their feet simply by his election. Their nervous consensus was that there was something slightly un-American in having a mayor with such a foreign name. It was almost too much, following so closely on the heels of the wartime administration of Frank J. Lausche, a gentleman of Slovenian descent. The Union Clubbers were really only getting the hang of the Lausche pronunciation (it rhymes with how-she) when he up and got himself elected governor of Ohio.

As it turned out, they needn't have worried about the pronunciation of the Celebrezze name because almost everybody settled for "Tony," and the mayor readily answered to this informal address—which illustrates what a really smart politician he was. He showed this talent in many different ways in his record-breaking five consecutive terms in office, but it is apparent that Celebrezze's major contribution to the city was in the conception of a plan for a drastic face-lifting of downtown Cleveland. Out of his urging arose the plan for Erieview, which called for the demolition of some seventy-six acres of shabby, down-at-the-heels downtown.

That urban renewal program, still under way, has given Cleveland a new physical image. It has sent new skyscrapers like the Erieview Plaza Tower (forty stories) and the Federal Building (thirty-two stories) shooting high into the air, adding new elements to the Cleveland skyline for the first time since the Terminal Tower was finished in 1930. It has added new beauty with its parks and plazas and malls, its reflecting fountains and its splashing pools, and its lofty concept has given Clevelanders themselves a sense of pride and success that some thought they had lost forever.

But there is something else to this image business which, in Cleveland's case, cannot be overlooked. It is, simply, the city's insistence on looking like everybody's hometown.

The most surprising illustration of this phenomenon is, of course, the experience of the visitors from the Union of Soviet Socialist Republics. In Cleveland they see, readily, Moscow, Minsk, Leningrad, and Odessa. Czechs, conversely, see something of Prague; the Hungarians blink back their tears at the resemblance to Budapest, and so on. In like manner, American visitors to the city cannot help but see on all sides reminders of Terre Haute, Boston, Hartford, Chicago, Ashtabula, New York, Los Angeles, and Pine Bluff. It leaves some of them unnerved and a trifle thoughtful to find a slice of home so far away from home.

Safe enough to say, however, that not all visitors are happily surprised. Suppose a man has traveled two thousand miles from Los Angeles to Cleveland, and wakes up in the morning eager to take in the sights and study the costumes and mores of the natives. He leaps out of his trundle bed, springs to his window and looks out, just in time to see a girl walking past with an oversized beam and wearing an undersized pair of orange capris, and he falls back in utter confusion. This is just like home, you see, and he has a devil of a time reassuring himself that he is somewhere other than Los Angeles.

Nobody likes to be disappointed in his quest for exotic surroundings, and, conversely, nobody likes to be homesick. Either one of those two things can happen to a casual visitor who tries to swallow Cleveland in a swift, down-the-hatch way, with a quick look here and a quick look there and his eyes watering all the time. It doesn't do the city's image one bit of good, you may be sure, for those quickie-type visitors to leave town with their eyes still watering. That reaction leaves the way open for wide misinterpretation by onlookers.

It is a matter of common knowledge that the people who least understand and least appreciate Cleveland are those who live close by—i.e., other Ohioans. Diplomatic relations between Cleveland and other communities in the state have been shaky and tentative, at best, for the past hundred years. There is commerce back and forth, and there are polite interchanges of small talk, but there is very little communication in the real sense and nobody, certainly, ever would dare to describe the relationship that exists as a hearty camaraderie. In the minds of most Ohioans, Cleveland is a strange outland concentration, the land beyond the pale. It is to them the Colossus of the North, where strange tongues and even stranger customs prevail, and where the simple Buckeye type had best be wary.

Understand that Ohio, unlike Cleveland, is mainly midwestern in its character. Where it is not a midwestern state, it is laced with a strong flavor of the South—so much so that a kind of southern accent flourishes among the people who live in Columbus, Springfield, Middletown, Dayton, Cincinnati, and other cities of the central and southwestern part of the state.

The preponderance of native-born Americans in the population of most of Ohio has given the rest of the state a homogeneity that is strikingly absent in Cleveland. The differences that separate the largest city in the state from the main territory are represented in the sound of foreign tongues, the strange accents, and the hard-to-spell, hard-to-pronounce names; in a subtly different appearance of the people, in attitude, in outlook, in customs, in clothing, and even in homes.

To the rest of Ohio, Cleveland is the city of foreigners—and in that category they bracket New Englanders with the Lebanese, Slovenians, Hungarians, and other exotic representations with charming and ingenuous impartiality. Whatever is unknown and speaks a strange tongue is, ipso facto, a foreigner.

The population of the Cleveland metropolitan area at the beginning of 1966 was 2,057,400, making it the eleventh metropolitan market in the nation. One of every three Clevelanders either was born abroad or was a first-generation American. It has been said that outside of New York and Chicago, Cleveland is the most cosmopolitan of American cities. In the sense of the worldwide origin of its population, this is true, but Cleveland is not a worldly city within the usual meaning of cosmopolitan. Its personality has not had time to jell. This is the most heterogenous of cities; one which has been force-fed with population from abroad like a Strasbourg goose, and it simply has not had time to digest the diverse groups which it has received during the past century.

A perceptive observer of the Cleveland scene, Emerson Batdorff of the *Plain Dealer*, once wrote: "Cleveland's melting pot does not, it seems, convert its stock to a thin and ordinary gruel. While the second and third generation is naturally much more American in its ways than the old folk, even the third generation of Clevelanders of mid-European descent retain an affinity for the polka. Those of Italian descent still have religious parades. The Scots and the Irish still make the air wild with their music and the pipe major can be seen on occasion treading his stately measure down Euclid Avenue as the sun glints brightly on the dirk in his sock. Greeks still dance fiercely, the men alone as is their custom, to shrill music in night clubs that feature belly dancers. In Greek coffee houses patronized only by men, old folks meditate upon their destiny as they survey the new world over a hot cup . . ."

The international influence is everywhere apparent—from the turnip-shaped church spires that overlook the Cuyahoga Valley on the southwest side to the brick tower of the mammoth West Side Market, where rosy-cheeked women wearing babushkas and old men with caps shop at the open stands for fruits, vegetables, freshly killed chickens, exotic cheeses, garlic-scented sausages, and all the other ingredients for their native-style meals. They cling to their old custom of shopping in the open market place even as they cling to their old churches where they can worship in a tongue which allows them to be articulate. Europe is never far away when you are in Cleveland, and the traces of the origin of its people are on all sides—in the chain of cultural gardens in Rockefeller Park honoring the diverse nationalities which have settled in the city, in the strange-sounding roll call of names in the news stories of the metropolitan newspapers, and, plainly, in the faces of the people themselves.

There are more Hungarians in Cleveland, it is said, than there are in any city in the world outside of Hungary itself. An educated estimate places the number in Cleveland at eighty-five thousand, many of whom came to Cleveland as refugees after the aborted Hungarian Revolution of 1956. The Hungarian colonies are to be found in the Buckeye Road-Woodland Avenue area on the East Side and along lower Lorain Avenue neighborhoods on the West Side. Like so many of the nationality groups, however, they are beginning to venture outside of their old, established territories to take up residence in the suburbs—especially on the West Side.

The Germans, whose number is estimated around one hundred thousand, have left their original nesting neighborhoods to disperse into the suburbs, mainly Lakewood, Rocky River, Fairview Park, Brooklyn, and Parma. The Poles (160,000 strong) have fanned out from the Flats and the lower West Side toward the southern neighborhoods of the city and the suburbs of Garfield Heights and Parma, with some side streams trickling into the western suburbs. The Slovenians, Croats, and Serbs (as they prefer individually to be identified, rather than as Yugoslavs) have been shifting from their old St. Clair Avenue neighborhoods into newer neighborhoods in the northeast side and in the suburb of Euclid. Theirs is a sizable element, numbering more than forty thousand.

Czechoslovakia's delegation, part of a steady migration reaching back to 1860, is counted today around seventy thousand. The main strength of their group is strung out along Broadway S.E. and into Garfield Heights, Seven Hills, Brecksville, and Parma. The Italians, currently estimated around sixty-five thousand, have a Little Italy on Mayfield Road, off Euclid Avenue, on the East Side and another Little Italy near West 65th Street and Detroit Avenue on the West Side. They, too, are beginning to disperse into many of the suburbs in strength, as already have the Irish, once clustered (with the Welsh) in old Newburgh and in such picturesquely named settlements of the near West Side as the Angle, Irishtown, the Cheyenne, the Grove, Achill Patch, and Windy Gap. The sizable Jewish representation in Cleveland, numbering close to one hundred thousand, once clustered around East 105th Street, but in recent decades they have favored Cleveland Heights and Shaker Heights.

Lithuanians, some thirty thousand strong in the mid-sixties, had a fairly tight-knit community in the northeastern area of Cleveland and suburban Euclid, as well as in the neighborhood of East 55th Street and Wade Park. The Slovaks were to be found on the West Side, in Lakewood and to the south, on Broadway. An estimated thirty-five thousand Romanians, whose first colony was in the vicinity of Detroit Avenue and West 54th Street, have begun to spread into the southwestern suburbs of Brecksville and Parma.

The first significant inflow of immigrant stock into the little settlement of New Englanders came in the 1820s when the Ohio Canal, providing a through waterway from Cleveland to the Ohio River, was under construction. Thousands of laborers employed on the great project—most of them Irish—were impressed by the pretty little town on the Lake Erie bluffs and settled in and around the young community.

Approximately twenty-five years later, the construction of railroads into Cleveland resulted in another large influx of laborers—Irish, Welsh, German, Czechoslovakian—and now it seemed the immigration pump was primed. The following half-century was marked by the arrival of many thousands of Europeans seeking a better life in the Ohio boom town.

There is still a thin, steady stream to keep alive the nationality stock in Cleveland; nothing to compare with that which reached flood stage in the second half of the nineteenth century and the opening decades of the current century, but still sizable enough to keep Cleveland's naturalization rate at a level of twenty-four hundred new citizens a year. Occasionally some extraordinary event causes the stream to swell, as it did at the end of World War II and again after the Hungarian Revolution of 1956. The trend, nevertheless, is one of continuing diminution in the number of new residents from foreign countries, and it is already apparent that the process of assimilation is blurring the once clear-cut outlines of the fifty or more nationalities which set up colonies here in years past.

Assimilation should not be made synonymous with elimination in the evolution of a cosmopolitan city, for much of the foreign flavor introduced by thousands of immigrants fortunately is of a lasting nature. These people from the faraway lands change a city, even as the city changes them. Once the two elements are joined, nothing is ever again the same—neither the people nor the city. It is part of the mystery and wonder of America that there still is no such animal as The Typical American, nor is there, truly, a Typical American City. The metamorphosis continues, as Cleveland makes evident, changing shape, form, and size with fickle disregard for the calculations and predictions of the experts. In all the swirling evolution, though, some institutions and characteristics of the nationality groups persist. The foreign-language press in Cleveland still has a substantial readership for its numerous publications, and the nationality-oriented newspapers which are printed in English claim a significant number of readers among descendants of the pioneer immigrants. There are still such newspapers as the *America Romanian News; Amerikanski Slovenec* (Slovenian); *Dirva* (Lithuanian newspaper); *Hungarian Daily Szabadsag; Hungarian Weekly Magyar Vitag; Kuryer,* a Polish bimonthly publication; *La Voz Hispana,* the Spanish paper; *Novy Svet,* the Czechoslovak daily; *Zwiazkowiec,* a Polish bimonthly; *Slovenian Daily News;* and *Waechter Und Anzeiger,* a German weekly, formerly a daily.

Somebody with time on his hands has counted no fewer than 576 fraternal and social welfare lodges based on nationality in Cleveland, and their membership total was figured at 304,600 persons—about half of the foreign stock in the metropolitan area. Further bolstering the entertainment and recreational scene are some 191 nationality-oriented groups devoted to drama, music, and singing. The Slovenians were far out in front in this department with twenty such groups, followed by the Germans with thirteen, including a brass band.

Of more universal interest are the restaurants featuring exotic cuisines aimed at the nationality trade and adventurous Cleveland gourmets, but this field, truthfully, is not what one optimistically may have expected. There are some fine restaurants with foreign specialties, especially Hungarian, Italian, and German menus, but not nearly the number nor variety that the cosmopolitan character of the city would seem to justify. The conclusion of some disappointed eaters who have surveyed the scene and analyzed it is that too many of the immigrant families who found their way to Cleveland were of frugal, thrifty, plain stock to allow for such a capricious, extravagant custom as "eating out." So long as the aging mother or grandmother from the old country is still around to cook up some tasty kluskis or chicken paprikash, the family will continue to eat at home. The restaurant situation gradually is improving, though, and with the widespread nationality base that exists in the city, Cleveland one day could emerge as a power in the eating department.

Of steadily increasing significance in the Cleveland social scene is the city's large Negro representation, estimated in early 1967 to include some 318,000 persons in the metropolitan area. Almost all live in Cleveland itself and almost all live on the near East Side, although there are a few Negro neighborhoods on the lower West Side—in the vicinity of West 25th Street and in the Linndale section, between West 117th Street and West 130th Street, off Bellaire Road. The Linndale colony, an enclave in the otherwise white section of the city, is of long standing, tracing its beginnings to the nineteenth century when the Linndale Yard and the Linndale Station of the New York Central Railroad came into being. The Negro movement into the suburbs is most noticeable in the Ludlow section of Cleveland and Shaker Heights, in Cleveland Heights and East Cleveland, in Twinsburg and in Oakwood Village.

Cleveland enjoyed for many years the reputation of being one of the most advanced cities in the United States in its race relations, and as recently as the 1940s and 1950s, it was hailed as the leader in the field. But the Hough Area riots which broke out in the East Side neighborhood in the late summer of 1966 made it clear that the same racial problems which were besetting other American communities existed in Cleveland, especially in the areas of housing and employment. Between 1960 and 1967, the Negro population in Cleveland increased by nearly seventy thousand, heightening the severity of those long-standing problems, perhaps the most challenging issues to confront the city administration thus far in the latter half of the twentieth century. But the Negro voice in Cleveland long has been articulate and the Negro representation in civic life long has been prominent. Some of the voices, like that of Poet Langston Hughes, have gone far beyond the city's borders.

As of early 1967, ten of Cleveland's thirty-three City Council members were Negroes, directly reflecting the race's total of one-third of the city population. One of the councilmen, Charles V. Carr, serves as leader of the Democratic majority in Council and has been a member of the body since January 1946. Another veteran in the municipal legislature, Leo A. Jackson, has held a seat representing Ward 24 since the beginning of 1958. Their colleagues in the 1967 Council included John W. Kellogg, Warren Gilliam, George W. White, John C. Armstrong, James H. Bell, Craft C. Carter, Jr., and George L. Forbes. M. Morris Jackson served in the Council until early January 1967, when he took a seat in the Ohio Senate. But the real veteran among Negroes in City Hall was Harvey Atkins, Assistant City Clerk and Clerk of Council, whose tenure began in 1930.

The administration of Mayor Ralph S. Locher saw the nomination of Ralph Findley to the post of Health and Welfare Director, making this longtime civic leader the first Negro to hold a cabinet position in city government. When he was named director of the Economic Opportunities Board in 1966, he was succeeded in the cabinet post by Clarence A. Gaines. Still another Negro high in the City Hall ranks during the Locher administration was Bertram Gardner, executive director of the Community Relations Board.

On the larger city scene, Cleveland's leading Negroes included George Anthony Moore, associate director of the National Council of Christians and Jews in Cleveland; Merle A. McCurdy, United States Attorney; Charles W. White, judge in the Cuyahoga County Court of Appeals; State Representative Carl B. Stokes, who came close to being elected mayor in the fall of 1966; Clayborne George, attorney and chairman of the Cleveland Civil Service Commission, and his wife, Zelma George, singer-actress who was an alternate delegate to the United Nations in the Eisenhower administration; Common Pleas Judge Perry B. Jackson; Dr. Middleton Lambright, prominent surgeon and physician who was the first Negro to serve as president of the Cleveland Academy of Medicine; Municipal Judge Theodore Williams and Municipal Judge Paul White; George Elie, president of the Elie Wrecking Company, a nationwide operation, and Ludie Couch, president of the Couch Sausage Company; Emmett Cooper and William Boyd, members of the Cleveland Board of Education.

No matter what avenue you use to approach Cleveland, eventually you reach the inescapable conclusion that the influence of the New England founding fathers, their descendants and their followers, re-

mains the most powerful single force in Cleveland's development to
this day. The city's ancestral lineage and background is everywhere
apparent—in the rather staid architecture of the office buildings and
institutions and in the charming styles that predominate in the residential
neighborhoods; in the ultraconservative business life of the community,
the anonymity of the ruling establishment, and the city government's
lack of aggressiveness. Cleveland, in the large and real areas of
personality and mores, remains a colony of Connecticut to this day.

Perhaps the heritage of New England is manifest most noticeably
in the attractive residential areas of the city and its suburbs. Here is
Cleveland at its very best. Other American cities have more impressive
central cities, newer and higher skyscrapers, bigger and wider freeways,
but no other city lives better at home. The remarkable side-phenome-
non here is that the good life is widespread. The neighborhoods of
beautiful homes are not concentrated in any single section, but may
be found within any given set of compass points. No matter which
direction you travel, you will encounter such residential beauty as to
give you pause—some, in the more affluent quarters, overwhelming in
their grandeur. Cleveland is heavily partial to the single home with a
full sweep of green lawn, flower borders, and thick clusters of heavily
leafed trees. There are many areas where apartment buildings rule, and
it is true that they are becoming more numerous, but only in recent
years has the city seen the development of high-rise apartments on a
major scale, such as the complex of luxury towers which has sprung
up along the western lakeshore, where Cleveland and Lakewood meet.
The "Gold Coast" district there is the prototype for similar developments
along the eastern shoreline, especially in Euclid and in Bratenahl. Those
tall apartment buildings, like the thirty-story Winton Place in Lakewood,
are spreading the skyline of the city and giving it a new nighttime
glitter and more of the urban look that Cleveland, for all its metropolitan size, has lacked until now. Indeed, one of the clichés to be
heard from the lips of discontented citizens is that Cleveland is "the
biggest small town in the country." They do not say it kindly, but
fretfully. Yet it is a paradoxical fact that Cleveland also is one of
the most sophisticated of cities at the cultural level, in its high residential standards, in its social and political innovations.

The Chamber of Commerce has been doing its level, confusing best
to try to straighten out—or at least explain—the many contradictions
that present themselves to the casual tourist and old-time resident alike
in the old Forest City, but theirs is a losing battle. Some things simply
are not to be explained. Anyway, it smacks of a defensive posture even
to try. The Chamber should go on the aggressive and attack this
image business in a forthright way by stressing the positive.

It is, for example, a positive fact that right in the heart of Cleveland there is a real, honest-to-goodness salt mine in full operation.

It is also an indisputable fact that the salt mine is situated on a piece of acreage known as Whiskey Island.

Either one of those facts is guaranteed to put any city ahead in the national image derby, but how many large American cities, other than Cleveland, can boast of both?

Motorists approaching the center of the city on the west side shoreway have a clear view of the salt mine's superstructures to the north. This International Salt Company operation is on the banks of the Cuyahoga River, near the river's old mouth, long filled in. The present mouth of the Cuyahoga, a short distance to the east, is a man-made shortcut. The salt has been under Cleveland a long time—millions of years. It was there even before the Ice Age brought the glaciers. It is part of the vast Salina formation that underlies several states at depths ranging from eight hundred feet to more than a mile. It extends under Lake Erie, from the lower peninsula of Michigan to Cleveland and east, past Ashtabula and into Pennsylvania and New York. It also extends south, under Ohio, to West Virginia.

The Whiskey Island mine was begun in the late 1950s and became operative in 1962. It reaches down some eighteen hundred feet and then laterals out under Lake Erie to tap a treasure-house of salt—International estimates the fifty-one-hundred-acre reserve it is working under agreement with the State of Ohio contains some one hundred million tons of high-quality rock salt.

Clevelanders haven't quite made up their minds whether to be proud of their very own salt mine or not. As everybody knows, salt mines themselves don't have a very good image, although the International people insist they really are very nice places. The temperature down there, under Cleveland, is about seventy-five degrees the year round and the air is very tangy.

"A salt mine's a pretty healthful place to work," one International spokesman said. "No respiratory trouble. The salt helps clean you out."

Perhaps, fifty or a hundred years hence, when the company has extracted its hundred million tons of salt, the city can rent the underground caverns out as a spa, or vacation center. Then all Clevelanders will have to do to escape the whistling winter winds off Lake Erie and subzero temperatures is simply drop down the old shaft a mere eighteen hundred feet and frolic around in a subtropical seventy-five-degree climate.

Incidentally, Whiskey Island really isn't an island, and there isn't any whiskey there; not that anybody is admitting, anyway. It won its colorful name in the founding days of the town when it was the site of a distillery. It is a picturesque piece of real estate in its own rough-hewn, cluttered way. As the rock salt is mined and brought to the surface, it is piled in towering conical stacks on the banks of the meandering old river, and the romantic eye can see in them snow-covered miniatures of Mount Fuji. They glitter in the bright sunlight, and sometimes their salty beauty is enhanced by a distinct turquoise cast.

Contrastingly, there are other man-made mountains nearby; some of yellow sand for industrial use, and russet red peaks of iron ore carried to Cleveland from the Mesabi Range in Minnesota or the Steep Rock Mines in Canada in the long lake freighters for the steel mills. The low-slung boats, peculiar to the Great Lakes in their general conformation and size—some of them are longer than seven hundred feet—move in ponderous procession into Cleveland Harbor during the sailing season. Some make their way, unbelievably, into the crooked Cuyahoga and corkscrew their way to the steel mills upriver. Others veer to the western end of the breakwater-protected harbor, there to be relieved of their ore by the Hulett unloaders that crouch like giant grasshoppers along that part of the lakefront, just north of the salt mine.

It's like an industrial carnival at night when the dipping unloaders, outlined in electric lights, bob for the ore deep in the hold of the carriers, then sail it high overhead to the inland stockpile on an illuminated crane. There's a rhythm and beauty to the scene that has its own appreciative audience among the motorists flying along the lakefront shoreway, the sitters on the grassy slopes of Edgewater Park, and the residents of such near West Side streets as Tillman Avenue and Herman Avenue, which overlook the old riverfront and lake harbor. But not everybody views the scene for its beauty. Some savvy onlookers form their own conclusions as to the health of the industrial economy through close surveillance of the iron mountains on Cleveland's lakefront. The rate of growth and shrinkage in the ore piles can be a reliable indicator of the appetite of the steel industry, and Cleveland's prosperity is closely linked with the well-being of steel, for this is the leading ore-receiving port in the world and one of the nation's leading steel manufacturing centers—the headquarters city, in fact, of the giant Republic Steel Company.

Steel is an essential, integral part of the Cleveland image. It has left its mark on the landscape, it is part of the skyline, and its influence is felt in the everyday life of the city. Cleveland, in turn, has exerted a considerable influence on steel. Back in the 1840s, two Cleveland scientists, Dr. J. Lang Cassels, a chemist, and Colonel Charles Whittlesey, geologist, made an exploratory trip into the wilds of Michigan's Upper Peninsula to scout persistent Chippewa Indian tales of mountains made of iron. Frontiersmen also had contributed to the legends of the area with reports that their compasses behaved in wildly erratic manner in the area. The expedition by Dr. Cassels and Colonel Whittlesey into the region around Negaunee, Michigan, was fruitful. They returned to Cleveland with data on the rich iron ore deposit which existed there, and in a public lecture on the trip, given in the Apollo Theater in 1846, Colonel Whittlesey described the possibilities of the situation in such glowing terms that a number of Cleveland businessmen were moved to action. The city became the heart of the Great Lakes ore mining and shipping industry, and remains so to this day.

The presence of the steel industry, as well as the deep reserve of mechanical ingenuity usually to be found in an industrial, manufacturing city, helped Cleveland at the turn of the century to make a strong bid for the role of automobile capital of the world. It lost to Detroit, as everybody knows, but only after a gallant battle.

Cleveland held the leading position as an automobile manufacturing city in the earliest years of the horseless carriage—from 1896 until 1904. It remained an important center of production until 1932. In those turbulent three decades, some eighty different makes of cars were produced in Cleveland, beginning with the Winton and ending with the Hupmobile. Alexander Winton built the first car in September 1896. It was an experimental two-seat carriage that would do ten miles an hour. The following year he drove one of his cars a mile in one minute, forty-eight seconds to highlight the Memorial Day celebration in Cleveland.

On March 24, 1898, a Pennsylvania mining engineer, Robert Allison, visited Winton's small shop on East 45th Street, between Perkins and Hough avenues, looked at the four cars under construction, and selected the one he liked best. He paid Winton one thousand dollars cash for the car, and the manufacturer agreed to deliver it to him at his home in Port Carbon, Pennsylvania, the following week. It was a simple transaction but historically important as one of the first sales of an American-made gasoline-powered automobile, and the vehicle rightfully holds a place in the Smithsonian Institution.

Winton sold twenty-five cars in that year of 1898, and the following year he drew nationwide attention when, under the sponsorship of the *Plain Dealer*, he attempted to drive one of his automobiles to New York City in less than fifty hours' running time. Riding with him on the trip was a *Plain Dealer* reporter, Charles B. Shanks, who had promoted the distance test. He later left the newspaper to become sales manager of Winton's company. The automobile pioneer carried with him a letter to be delivered to the mayor of New York, Robert A. Van Wyck, from the mayor of Cleveland, John H. Farley, The letter said:

"The City of Cleveland sends greetings to the executive of the nation's metropolis upon the occasion of the first long distance auto-

mobile trip ever made on this continent. New York and Cleveland
have long been connected by water and by rail, and now they are
joined by the horseless carriage route."

Winton arrived in New York after forty-seven hours and thirty-four
minutes. The mileage charted was 707.4 and Winton's ledger showed
an expenditure of one dollar for the gasoline consumed by his car.
Gasoline was something of a waste product in those days, and the
six gallons he purchased to begin his trip cost him only one cent a
gallon. Even more remarkable was that his hydrocarbon engine achieved
some forty miles to the gallon and he needed only fifteen gallons for
the long trip. It shouldn't be necessary to point out that this phenomenal
performance was over the worst of roads, but the fact helps to under-
line the wonder of it all.

A Cleveland automobile historian, J. Richard Wager, relates a story
that tells how the Winton company confronted and defeated a disgruntled motorist of 1903. The story also indicates that, however much
cars have changed, the drivers remain very much the same.

"Winton was the largest exclusive auto maker in the nation in 1903
and Cleveland was the leading auto manufacturing city in America,"
wrote Wager. "Besides the Winton, the Stearns, White, Peerless, the
Gaeth, Hoffman, Ottokar, Russell, General and Marr were made here.

"About that time in Detroit a disgruntled Winton owner rode through
the streets in his car pulled by a team of horses. Signs declared: 'This
is the only way you can drive a Winton.'

"The Winton salesman was quick to counter the attack. He followed
the man around the city in a gleaming new Winton pulling a farm wagon
in which was hauled a donkey. The sign said: 'This is the only animal
that can't drive a Winton!'"

In time other names joined the growing list of automobiles manufactured in Cleveland. They included the Jordan, the Stearns-Knight,
the Templar, the Rollin, the Chandler, the Cleveland, and the Hupmobile, not to mention the leading electric cars of the time, the Baker
Electric and the Rauch & Lang Electric. The two later merged and
turned out the Baker-Raulang electrics until 1918.

Cleveland admitted defeat as an automobile manufacturing center in
1932, when the last Hupmobile came off the line, but it continued as
the leading supplier of auto parts. After World War II, the industry
began to return to Cleveland, joining the city's huge Fisher Body
plant which had continued to supply the Detroit assembly lines. Ford,
Chevrolet, and Chrysler all have built new factories in the metropolitan Cleveland area and are among the city's most important employers.
The automobile is still part of the Cleveland image.

Perhaps this is what makes identifying Cleveland clearly such a
troublesome matter; the image is made up of too many slivers and

fragmented parts. It has a little bit of everything, and in some instance a whole lot of something, but it is not what you would accurately describe as a monolithic institution. Cleveland, in fact, is not any kind of an institution. It is a collection of very interesting people who have come together from all parts of the globe to engage in a very interesting enterprise—the building of a new society in a new city in a new land. Only through patient, sympathetic analysis is it to be understood, but it is less difficult to appreciate.

A man from New Jersey—a very fair-minded type—recently gave Cleveland a thirty-day trial and testified that it made a new man out of him. Not only did the wind off the lake put a rubescent glow in his cheeks, but the variable temperatures generally gave a new spring to his step. It is not terribly uncommon for the mercury to rise or fall thirty to forty degrees in a matter of hours, the kind of development guaranteed to quicken anybody's pace. They have a saying around town that if you don't like the Cleveland weather, simply stick around for an hour or two—it will change.

Meteorologists assigned to the Greater Cleveland post by the United States Weather Bureau ride into town, fresh-faced and eager to battle the elements, the little weather vanes attached to their beanies whirling excitedly every which way. They can hardly wait to take up the challenge of predicting, scientifically, what kind of weather Cleveland will have from day to day. Usually it is only a matter of months— sometimes only days—before the vagaries of the climate, with all the eccentricities of performance that the slope of the terrain and the influence of Lake Erie can encourage, turn these happy, chattering young meteorologists into mature, gray-faced, and thoughtful men.

The way the Cleveland image has developed, unfortunately, it presents to the outside world the picture of a rather grim-faced city on the edge of the Arctic Circle; a city which has an amazingly large population, considering that survival every winter is a touch-and-go situation.

This simply is not a true picture, and it's partly the fault of geographers and itinerant journalists who insist on confusing Cleveland with Buffalo—probably because Buffalo Bill Cody once lived in Cleveland, as a boy, for about four years.

At any rate, the confusion of Cleveland's identity with that of Buffalo is only part of Cleveland's terrible winter image. A good deal of the blame must reside in the well-known tendency of Clevelanders to exaggerate the severity of their own winter, in interesting contrast with the way that Californians and Floridians try to suppress news about bad weather. Clevelanders apparently would rather be cast as heroes than sissies.

Local historians like to tell especially of the year 1816, which was even rougher than most Cleveland winters. It has been called "The Year without a Summer." The cold weather was not confined to Cleveland, but was felt generally through a large area of Ohio. An Urbana, Ohio, newspaper of the time claimed that it snowed every month of the entire year. This chilling information was amplified with the story of a local swain who started out with his sweetheart for a July 4 picnic. They never got a chance to open their big lunch hamper because en route to the picnic grove they were forced to turn back by a raging blizzard.

The year 1857 was another one worth remembering because it was said to have featured frost every month, even through the summertime. A Cleveland historian, C. A. Post, wrote, with a straight face:

"One old gentleman used to tell of coming home to Cleveland very early the morning of July 5th of that year after attending a ball at the Cataract House in Newburgh, and as he passed along the road he scraped from the top of the rail fence enough snow to make a snow-ball."

There is no way of telling, at this late date, precisely how truthful the tales of terrible winters may have been, but it doesn't really matter. Every city has good weather and every city has bad weather. Whichever a person will take it to be, good or bad, depends on his own attitude. It is possible to be bored to distraction by the monotony of blue skies and sunshine that cities less fortunate than Cleveland have to put up with every year. There is none of the pulse-pounding excitement of bounding out of bed each morning, as Clevelanders normally do, to see what fearful consignment of weather the new day has brought. It's part of the adventure of living in Cleveland, this uncertainty of the elements.

There is drama and excitement in really bad weather, in the driving snow and the lashing rain, the angry skies and the boiling lake. One of the most sensitive persons of our time, Helen Keller, said it in her own way when she was trapped in her room in the Statler Hotel in Cleveland by the great blizzard that struck the city in early November of 1913. It was one of the worst storms in Cleveland history. Twenty-one inches of snow were borne upon the area by winds that reached a velocity of seventy-nine miles an hour, and life in the community came to a standstill for most of a week. Even without sight or hearing, as she was, Miss Keller's impressions of the storm, as related to a reporter for the Cleveland *Press*, were vivid:

"I am stirred to the depth of my being by the storm, and my body, mind and soul are better for this great experience—the greatest of its kind in my life. Few times in my life has it been given me to feel sensations akin to those I have experienced as a captive of the blizzard in Cleveland during Sunday, Monday, and Tuesday.

"I knew it was storming before I was told. The rooms, the corridors, everywhere within the building, vibrated with the power of the storm without—when I knew it was snowing as it never had before in this part of the world, I wished to rush out and throw myself into the snow and ride upon the tempest. I raised my window, the gale blew upon me; as I was in evening dress the wind stung my chest, but I loved it. I put my hands in the snow on the window sill. It was softer than the softest down. I made a ball of it and pressed it to my cheek. I drank deep of its odor, for it has an odor soft and sweet as the daintiest perfume."

Helen Keller voiced, poetically, what a lot of Clevelanders feel. They grumble about the weather for the record, but most of them wouldn't want it any other way but the way it is.

Cleveland weather is capricious and it often is uncomfortably extreme, but whatever else it is, Cleveland weather is never dull. At its peak moments it is grandly dramatic, exciting, and beautiful. When one of those moments is at hand and the fresh gale out of the lake is pulling the whitecaps up from the water and rustling the city's forest of trees, it is possible to believe that this, after all, really is the best location in the nation.

XXV

A City of Culture

THE intermixture in Cleveland of the genteel strain of New England aristocracy with the nationalities of Central Europe gave the city a new brand of conservatism that is unmistakably evident in the proper way of life that prevails and the city's careful pace. But those two breeds, once a world apart, are close together on the common ground of an abiding devotion to culture. Their coalition in support of the arts has given Cleveland a cultural strength that is almost unique in America.

The fine arts, generally reserved as the side amusement of dilettantes in most metropolitan centers of the United States, are the subject of lively mass interest and civic concern in the big town on Lake Erie. When, for example, the Metropolitan Opera Company of New York comes to Cleveland in the springtime, as it has more or less regularly since 1899, it performs in the cavernous Public Auditorium before single audiences numbering more than eight thousand persons. There are nights when the Met outdraws the Indians playing a short distance away in the downtown Municipal Stadium.

Cleveland is the spa where the Metropolitan Opera Company traditionally comes to get well. The receipts taken in at the Public Hall box office, even during the lean Depression years, have proven a powerful nostrum, sufficient to eliminate the quaver in the throats of hungry tenors and to restore the flesh tone to the skin of the Met's front-office officials.

It is said, in what undoubtedly is an apocryphal story, that when some critics questioned the acoustics in the great auditorium, one of the opera representatives volunteered to test the hall's sound qualities at different points of vantage during a performance. When it was all over, he returned smilingly to the office and pronounced the acoustics to be astonishingly good.

"Why," he marveled, "I went into the far reaches of the balcony, just as far away from the stage as I could get and just as high as I could go; so far away, in fact, that the stage was almost out of sight, and so high up that occasional clouds drifting past obscured my vision entirely. Even so, the rustle of the money and the clinking of coins at the distant ticket windows came through just as clear as could be."

During the week of grand opera, Cleveland annually goes on a big culture binge. Special trains, planes, and buses converge on the city from all over Ohio, Pennsylvania, Indiana, and Michigan, and the music-lovers have a field day. So also, it goes without saying, does Society.

Cleveland is the quiet refuge of fantastically large fortunes whose custodians have been schooled in circumspect, conservative ways so that they are not immediately detectable when they walk the streets or visit public places. These people of wealth have attained a maximum degree of anonymity which is broken wide open during the grand opera season. Then the horseshoe circle in Public Hall comes alive with the glitter and glow of precious stones, the soft ripple of ermine and mink, the persistent rustle of satin and silk—all in combination providing rather a dazzling show in themselves.

In a less spectacular way, but more consistently, the social set is on view at Severance Hall, the stately Romanesque building in University Circle which houses the famous Cleveland Orchestra. The building, gift of John L. Severance, provides a suitably elegant setting for an orchestra which is acknowledged to be among the world's greatest. That reputation for musical excellence which the Cleveland Orchestra has built—especially under the leadership of conductor George Szell—was further enhanced in the summer of 1965 during a highly successful tour of the Soviet Union, and such critical music centers as Warsaw, Paris, Prague, and London.

The tour, sponsored by the American State Department, brought most of the European critics to their feet in appreciation of the great orchestra. They were virtually unanimous and almost giddy in their acclaim of the Clevelanders. Almost all of them seemed to be astonished that such a superb and sensitive musical instrument could emerge out of the materialistic society of America—especially from a city in the industrial heartland.

Typical of the stories recounting the triumphant tour was the following United Press International story of June 23, 1965:

CLEVELAND MUSICIANS FLY TO AMSTERDAM AFTER CAPTIVATING LONDON

By Michael Kraft

LONDON—(UPI)—The Cleveland Orchestra flew to Amsterdam from the captivated capital of Britain today for the last stop on its triumphant European tour.

"Another conquered capital" was happy George Szell's description of London after enthusiastic audiences and critics cheered the Cleveland Orchestra for its two concerts here.

The newspaper Guardian said today that "the technical excellence of the Cleveland Orchestra has been warmly and rightly praised by one and all. Last night's concert in the Royal Festival Hall confirmed these congratulatory impressions."

As they did after Monday night's concert, the critics praised Conductor Szell's approach.

The Financial Times, which carries extensive coverage of the arts, said, "The character of the orchestra is somehow that of Cleveland itself, the most cultivated of American cities."

High recognition, indeed, from a distant, respected arbiter of things cultural! When the *Financial Times* of London singles out Cleveland and unqualifiedly acknowledges it to be "the most cultivated of American cities," the distinction is not a minor one. It is entirely possible, furthermore, that this precious compliment even may be a statement of complete truth.

Singular evidence of the interest that Clevelanders have in the symphony orchestra was the way in which they welcomed home their conquering musicians at the end of that memorable 1965 tour. Air travelers passing through the Cleveland Hopkins International Airport on the night of June 26 must have been intrigued and puzzled by the civic uproar. Nearly six thousand persons filled the terminal. They carried banners, waved placards, blew horns, whirled rackety noise-makers, and capered joyously about as the Pan American World Airways jetliner taxied to the gate where floodlights, television cameras, reporters, and a welcoming civic delegation headed by Mayor Ralph Locher awaited.

Triumphant homecomings of this kind are not uncommon in America, but they usually are reserved for athletes, beauty queens, and champion baton twirlers.

An onlooker who identified himself as a resident of Bayonne, New Jersey, approached a reporter and wondered aloud over the airport rally.

"Is it possible," he asked, "that the Indians have clinched the American League pennant this early in the season?"

The reporter assured him that his wild speculation was far wide of the mark; that the enthusiastic Clevelanders were there to welcome home the city's orchestra.

The man from Bayonne did not readily believe the story.

"You have to be kidding," he said. "All this for a bunch of fiddlers?"

The Cleveland Orchestra traces its beginning to 1918. On December 11 of that year, Conductor Nikolai Sokoloff led a fifty-seven-man symphony in its first concert, held in Grays Armory on Bolivar Road and Prospect Avenue. It represented the second major attempt to found an orchestra in Cleveland. Earlier, in 1895, a pioneer group of forty musicians tried to gain a foothold in the community, and struggled manfully through two lackluster seasons before conceding defeat. The major force in the revival of the orchestra dream after World War I was Mrs. Adella Prentiss Hughes, a truly remarkable patroness of the arts in Cleveland.

The Russian-born Sokoloff continued as director of the Cleveland Orchestra until 1933, when he resigned to become national director of the federal government's Works Progress Administration (WPA) music project. The highlight of his Cleveland career undoubtedly came on the night of February 5, 1931, with the concert that officially opened the palatial Severance Hall at 11001 Euclid Avenue. Less than thirteen years after it was begun, the Cleveland Orchestra found itself with a permanent home of monumental dimensions, thanks to the generosity of John L. Severance, who provided the $2,500,000 for its construction.

Artur Rodzinski succeeded Sokoloff as director of the orchestra and remained in the post until 1943. Erich Leinsdorf then held the baton briefly, yielding it in 1946 to Szell, who was an immediate hit in Cleveland. He is generally credited with having raised the Cleveland Orchestra to its leading position in the world of music, and the people of the city like winners. The kind of loyalty and civic pride they demonstrate in a cultural institution is, as the man from Bayonne hinted, more commonly reserved for sports in American cities.

Make no mistake: Clevelanders are ferociously sports-minded. Their devotion to the baseball Indians and the football Browns is beyond question, as attendance records through the years attest. But their devotion and enthusiasm carries over into the arts, and sometimes so informally as to shake the artists. A prime example is to be found in an incident which occurred during a concert by the Cleveland Orchestra on the Mall during the Great Lakes Exposition of 1937. Guest conductor of the orchestra for this outdoor concert was the concert pianist, José Iturbi.

The concert was to be broadcast over the nationwide facilities of the Columbia Broadcasting System, and so it was carefully timed. At the precise moment, Iturbi raised his baton and the orchestra began to play. About two golden minutes later, Iturbi brought his stick down sharply and the great orchestra stopped, right in the middle of a line, so to speak. The announcer of the CBS outlet in Cleveland, WGAR, was a young man named Maurice Condon, and his powers of improvisation were put to the test while officials scurried about, desperately trying to find out why Iturbi had stopped conducting and had stalked off the band shell stage.

The maestro finally explained his precipitate action. While he had been leading the orchestra through the opening bars of its first number, he was horrified to observe any number of Cleveland music-lovers in the Mall audience gnawing away at hot dogs while they lolled in the sunshine and reveled in good music. They were, in fact, enjoying themselves just as they would at a baseball game or a football game, but Iturbi did not approve of the combination of good music and hot dogs. He would not conduct until the hot dog eaters made their choice between their stomachs and the aesthetic food he was trying to feed them. Mr. Iturbi did not understand his audience or he would have understood that these people were paying good music the highest possible compliment in their power. They had given the orchestra an informal parity with baseball and football.

This same fine appreciation, if not the same informality, is apportioned by Clevelanders in generous doses to all branches of the fine arts. Their support is reflected in the high quality of culture that prevails in the city. The Cleveland Museum of Art, for example, was only fifty years old in 1966; yet it held indisputable position as a treasure-house of art second in America only to New York's Metropolitan Museum.

The Art Museum is a pillared temple of neo-classic Georgia marble design whose classic lines are mirrored in the peaceful waters of Wade Park Lagoon, which separates it from Euclid Avenue. It is the rarest jewel in the famed University Circle area of the East Side. Like the Cleveland Orchestra, whose Severance Hall home is close by, the museum is almost wholly the product of an enlightened philanthropy. Thanks to the generosity of wealthy Cleveland families, it is one of the richest institutions of its kind anywhere. Its endowed wealth is estimated at around one hundred million dollars, and its annual income, from investments, is pegged close to three million dollars.

The fateful decade that represented the gestation period of the museum began in 1881. In that year, a well-to-do Clevelander named Hinman B. Hurlbut included in his will a bequest to be used in building a museum in the city. The following year, Jeptha Homer Wade died and left a beautiful, forested tract of land to the city for use as a park. It was accepted and named, appropriately, Wade Park. The will specified, however, that four acres of the land should be held in reserve for a civic use to be determined.

Jeptha H. Wade was a self-made man who had begun life as an artist. He detoured into a business career which was highlighted by his achievement in putting together the Western Union Telegraph Company. Ten years after his death, his grandson, also named Jeptha H. Wade, specified that the four-acre plot of land should be the site of an art museum.

In the intervening years of 1889 and 1890 two other wealthy Cleve-

landers, John Huntington and Horace Kelley, had died and left money
to be used for a museum. In 1913 all these bequests came together
to create the institution. The magnificent building was financed by the
John Huntington Art and Polytechnic Trust and the Horace Kelley Art
Foundation. The Hinman B. Hurlbut Fund was put aside as an endowment.

Even as the mighty museum was under construction, art-conscious
Clevelanders made important gifts to it. The first—a group of Italian
primitive paintings—came from Delia E. Holden, wife of the *Plain
Dealer* publisher and mining magnate, Liberty E. Holden. Shortly thereafter, Mr. and Mrs. John L. Severance contributed an outstanding collection of arms and armor, while Mr. Severance's sister, Mrs. Dudley P.
Allen, donated the eight large tapestries depicting the story of Dido
and Aeneas which decorate the famous armor court.

The new museum opened its doors on June 6, 1916. The story of its
first fifty years is one of continuous growth in wealth, prestige, and
popularity. While the original building stands unchanged, a new connecting building at its rear was built in 1957, more than doubling the
size of the early museum. Gifts from the leading families of the city
meanwhile continued to keep pace with the physical growth of the
institution. Among the prominent benefactors have been Mr. and Mrs.
Ralph Thrall King and Mr. and Mrs. Edward B. Greene. The most
spectacular of all the contributions to the modern museum, however,
were those from a grandnephew of the famous Senator Mark Hanna,
Leonard C. Hanna, Jr., who during his lifetime turned generous chunks
of the family's iron, coal, and shipping fortune over to a variety of
Cleveland institutions, principally Western Reserve University, University Hospitals, and the Museum of Art. He reached his philanthropic
heights in 1957 with his last bequest to the museum—an endowment of
some twenty million dollars plus his own private art collection whose
worth was estimated at $1,400,000.

This bequest by Leonard C. Hanna, Jr., in the words of the *Plain
Dealer* art critic, Miss Helen Borsick, provided "a fabulous new lease
on greatness for the museum just before it sprouted a new wing to
house its growing reputation and collections . . .

"In an amazingly short time, as museums go," wrote Miss Borsick,
"it has become one of the country's richest and best. Nowhere is there
to be found a place of greater educational interest, good taste, excellence
and beauty combined, dedicated to the finest expressions of the creativity of man."

The center of Cleveland's culture, University Circle, is a vaguely
defined area just beyond the busy East 105th Street and Euclid Avenue
uptown area. It has been called, with reason, "the American Parnassus."
Within its 488 acres of city land is probably the most intensive group-

ing of cultural institutions in the United States—some thirty-four centers of culture and learning. They include the Museum of Art, Severance Hall, the Cleveland Institute of Music, the Cleveland Institute of Art, the Fine Arts Garden, the Western Reserve Historical Society, the Museum of Natural Science, University Hospitals, and two great universities, Case Institute of Technology and Western Reserve University.

The value of University Circle's buildings has been placed in the area of one billion dollars, but that figure is continually being revised upward as development continues. A long-range plan, under way since 1960, calls for the expenditure of $175 million in the immediate future for further improvements calculated to make this entire area one of the nation's showplaces.

The cultural magnet in the heart of the Circle unquestionably is the existence there, side-by-side, of the two great universities—a situation that must be regarded as the happy product of circumstances and a rivalry that existed between two important Cleveland families many years ago.

Leonard Case, Jr., son of a pioneer Cleveland resident who had made a fortune in real estate, bequeathed property for the establishment and endowment of the Case School of Applied Science at the time of his death in 1880. Case felt there was a community need for an institution for the training of scientists, engineers, and other expert technicians. In that same year, another wealthy Clevelander, Amasa Stone, a railroad builder and industrialist, induced Western Reserve College in Hudson, twenty miles to the southeast, to move to Cleveland—to a site next door to the proposed Case School! Reserve had been a Hudson institution since 1826, but Stone's offer overpowered its loyalty to the little town. The lure was $500,000 from the industrialist—$150,000 to be used for the erection of college buildings and $350,000 more as a permanent endowment fund. The offer was contingent upon the fulfillment of three conditions: 1. that the college be removed to Cleveland; 2. that citizens of Cleveland provide suitable grounds for its campus, and 3. that the name should be changed to Adelbert College of Western Reserve University. (The new name was to memorialize the philanthropist's son, Adelbert Stone, who had died while a student at Yale University.)

Part of Western Reserve College already was in Cleveland. It was the Medical College on Erie Street (East 9th Street), which had shifted to Cleveland from Willoughby in 1843. One of the men instrumental in that move, interestingly, was Leonard Case, Sr., father of the man who founded Case School (now Case Institute of Technology).

Among the Clevelanders who chipped in to provide a site for Western

Reserve were Jeptha H. Wade, Captain Alva Bradley, a shipping and real estate tycoon, and Truman P. Handy, dean of Cleveland bankers. They bought the Holden property in what was then called the East End, directly adjacent to the Case site. It is said that this placement of Reserve, cheek by jowl with the technical institution, was no accident; that a sharp rivalry existed between the Case and Stone families and it, more than anything else, influenced Reserve's location. For whatever significance it may hold, the Amasa Stone Chapel on the W.R.U. campus has a tower which is adorned on three sides with some happy, frolicking cherubim and seraphim. The fourth side—that which faces the Case campus—is decorated, however, with a set of ferocious-looking, glaring, slavering gargoyles.

Once there was a spirited rivalry between these two neighboring institutions and their student bodies. It reached its peak in the annual football game, a rather one-sided series dominated by Reserve. Even that competitive fervor is dying as the two universities continue to expand and to coalesce as they grow. It is almost impossible, physically, to tell where Western Reserve ends and Case Tech begins. Their campuses have overlapped and meshed together. Clevelanders do not doubt but that in time the two institutions will merge to form one of the truly formidable universities of the nation. Talks leading toward that goal have been under way over the years and already have borne fruit. In late 1966, a special committee headed by Henry T. Heald, former president of the Ford Foundation, concluded that past collaboration of the two universities had yielded academically desirable results and recommended that the neighboring institutions federate under a single governing board of trustees, a single president, and a chancellor. The report urged that this change be effected before June 30, 1967.

The W.R.U. board of trustees and their counterparts at Case Tech voted to follow the recommendation in early January of 1967. President John S. Millis of Western Reserve earlier had asked that his name be removed from consideration for the presidency of the federated institutions, but said that he would be willing to serve in any other capacity. It was clearly indicated that the young (forty-six) president of Case Tech, Dr. Robert Morse, would be named president of Case Western Reserve University—the unlikely name suggested for the merged schools—and that Dr. Millis would become chancellor. The new university would have a combined enrollment of about 10,500 (W.R.U., 8700; Case Tech, 1800) and physical assets appraised at more than two hundred million dollars.

In the same cultural explosion of the 1880s that gave birth to Case and Western Reserve, the Cleveland Catholic Diocese and the Society of Jesus cooperated in the founding of St. Ignatius College on the near West Side, at West 30th Street and Carroll Avenue. The new institution opened its doors in 1886 with combined high school and college facilities. In May 1923 the name of St. Ignatius College was dropped in favor of Cleveland University, but this proved to be a short-lived substitution. Again, in September of the same year, the name was changed to John Carroll University in honor of the first Roman Catholic bishop in America. (The name of St. Ignatius was retained for the high school, however.) John Carroll remained a West Side institution until 1935, when it moved to a new campus at North Park and Miramar Drive in University Heights on the East Side.

The Jesuits' brief use of the name Cleveland University did not represent the first time the city's name had been incorporated into the name of an institution of higher learning. Nor was the suburb of University Heights the original user of that name. In 1850 another community called University Heights had been established on a promontory jutting out into the Cuyahoga River Valley immediately south and west of today's downtown area. It was given that name in anticipation of an institution called Cleveland University which was established there. Reverend Asa Mahan, who had been president of Oberlin College, was named president of the new university, and William Slade, later the governor of Vermont, served as secretary-treasurer.

Cleveland University struggled to win a foothold in the city for several years before it finally collapsed. University Heights then became known as Lincoln Heights before it eventually lost its identity as a separate entity and was swallowed by the expanding city. The old street names remain, and those such as Literary Avenue, Professor Street, College Avenue, and University Road are the cause of puzzlement among strangers driving through the old neighborhood today.

The name of Cleveland College was revived again in 1925 to identify a downtown college founded to promote higher education among adults. Newton D. Baker, former mayor and secretary of war, was one of the organizers of the institution which, while an independent corporation, affiliated itself with Western Reserve University. The experiment was a smashing success, eventually taking over the old Chamber of Commerce Building on Public Square and reaching a peak enrollment of nearly ten thousand students. After World War II, however, Western Reserve officials, for reasons of their own, decided to close the downtown college. Some of the faculty and student body were absorbed by the main campus.

The old name, done to death three times, refused to die. Cleveland State University came into being in 1965, created by the State of Ohio through the efforts principally of Governor James A. Rhodes. Genesis of the new university was Fenn College, a YMCA-sponsored institution that had its beginning as a night school in 1881.

It may be that the launching of this state university one day will be counted as one of the most significant happenings in Cleveland's modern history. The twenty-two-story skyscraper home of Fenn College at East 24th Street and Euclid Avenue and two smaller buildings of the college established the campus of the new state university in the heart of the city. The future development of Cleveland State inevitably will alter the face and character of the entire central city.

Officials anticipated an enrollment of some thirty thousand students at CSU within fifteen years, and their plans called for the expenditure of two hundred million dollars on a 135-acre campus between Euclid and Superior avenues. That area today is, in the main, a dreary sweep of old stores, shops, and other obsolete buildings. This lifeless, unattractive collection is to be cleared to make way for a grassy, forested campus setting for a complex of bright new university buildings. It is a prospect applauded by most Clevelanders, who foresee not only the elimination of one of the worst sections of blight in the downtown area, but also a transfusion of young blood calculated to give new life to the entire central area of the city.

The most common complaint against downtown urban renewal programs in most American cities has been that while the destruction of old streets and ramshackle neighborhoods beautifies, the renewal effort also tends to sterilize. It is all very well to replace eyesores with monumental buildings and splashing fountains, but these lifeless objects do not attract people downtown at night. Renewal too often has meant depopulation. Not even the construction of a few high-rise apartment buildings is enough to return life to the center of the renovated city.

Cleveland thinks it has found the best solution to the problem in the placement downtown of Cleveland State University and still another new institution of higher learning, Cuyahoga Community College. The latter, the first junior college in Ohio, was started in 1964 and found immediate acceptance of its two-year curriculum. Within two years, it had an enrollment of more than nine thousand students. CCC also will have its permanent campus downtown—a forty-acre campus at East 30th Street and Woodland Avenue, within the St. Vincent Urban Renewal Area, a former slum neighborhood. Initial construction plans called for $22.5 million worth of college buildings. (The junior college also has a 130-acre "branch" campus on the site of the former Crile Veterans' Hospital in suburban Parma and Parma Heights.)

All told, there will be approximately fifty thousand students enrolled in the CSU and CCC student bodies in downtown Cleveland by 1980. With so many young people downtown, there can't be any question where the action will be. Many of the students will be around-the-clock campus dwellers and with so many thousands of young persons living in the heart of the city, it is possible to predict major changes in the atmosphere, tempo, and appearance of the central area.

Culture has been a major enlivening factor in Cleveland. An outstanding example of how a single cultural activity can contribute substantially to a community's *joie de vivre* is provided by the internationally known Cleveland Play House, the nation's first professional resident theater.

The Play House got off to a faltering beginning in 1915 with the encouragement of a small group of theater-lovers who were at odds with the stereotyped productions of the day. Cleveland, however, was slow to accept an experimental theater and the organization seemed to be ready for the big deathbed scene at the end of 1920, when there was a sudden last-minute rescue that saved the day most dramatically. It was a reorganization that brought in Frederic McConnell of Pittsburgh as the full-time director with "a clear hand and a clear field." He was given two professional assistants, K. Elmo Lowe, associate director, and the late Max Eisenstat. McConnell stayed on the job for thirty-eight years and provided the Play House with his special guiding genius during its critically important formative period. He retired in 1958 to the post of consulting director and his long-time associate, K. Elmo Lowe, succeeded him as executive director.

During the interim years, the Cleveland Play House firmly established its reputation as one of the world's leading professional resident theaters and, probably more important, it securely won the affection and patronage of Clevelanders. Now it has a complex of facilities and a staff of seventy-five professional actors, directors, designers, and other such talents needed to keep its three theaters going. The Play House actually has two buildings to house those three theaters, shop facilities, dressing rooms, and administrative offices.

Mr. and Mrs. Francis E. Drury donated the land at 2040 East 86th Street where the main building of the Play House was built in 1927. It is a structure of Romanesque design and contains two theaters parallel to each other which share shop facilities, dressing rooms, and offices. The larger of the two theaters, named the Drury Theater, seats 530 persons. The companion theater, which accommodates 160 playgoers, was called the Brooks Theater after the first president of the Play House, Charles S. Brooks, one of the dreamers who made the Play House a reality.

During the middle 1940s, the Play House acquired a former church building on East 77th Street and Euclid, not far from its main building. The old church, an impressive structure, was converted into the large Euclid-77th Theater, which seats 560 persons and which represents a significant departure from conventional theater design. There is no proscenium arch, and the open, semicircular stage projects out into the high-banked, fan-shaped auditorium. Director McConnell conceived the general plan of the theater, and it was a successful innovation that brought him praise from expert observers. But McConnell was wise enough to know, as he once said, "It is the human structure that counts most."

"Daily at the Play House," he pointed out, "scores of paid actors, designers, directors, technicians and administrative personnel are busy on a strenuous program of performing and preparing a series of plays. In an average day there is a public performance in each of the three theaters; three other plays are in rehearsal and scenic preparation, and there is the usual quota of meetings, conferences, auditions, study, planning, script reading and research with—thrown in as a fillip—rumor and gossip, laughter and tears." Box office receipts (including season ticket sales) cover 90 per cent of the operating costs of this remarkable theater enterprise. The Play House Fund, consisting of contributions from interested Clevelanders, foundations, and other organizations, supplies the necessary financial aid for maintenance and operations.

The official stated policy of the Play House is "to leave show business as such to the commercial profit-making enterprises already set up for that purpose and to keep the routine entertainment piece to a minimum." In its brief history, the resident theater has presented the finest plays of all time; a list that by 1966 had totaled some eight hundred productions from the Greek classics to outstanding contemporary works.

Brooks Atkinson of the New York *Times* once wrote of the Cleveland Play House:

"Cleveland is lucky with its Play House, where the staff is not afraid of work, ideas or entertainment. A Gotham theatergoer may be pardoned for looking a little enviously at a working institution like the Cleveland Play House where the drama is continuously cultivated as an art."

Ben Hecht was another who had words of praise for the resident theater. "The Cleveland Play House," he said, "well may be the only future possible for the American theater. I'm sure that our next generation will see a hundred such animated drama centers as the Play House, and what a boon for tomorrow's playwrights and actors that would be!"

As eventful as the Play House's past has been, and as impressive its accomplishments, all appears to have been prologue to more dramatic developments ahead. Plans are under way for a new, larger Play House Center whose theaters and auxiliary facilities will be the most modern in the United States. It will be placed, most likely, in the downtown area—probably within the Cleveland State University area—to make it more accessible to playgoers from all sections of the city.

There it would be in proximity to the city's major legitimate theater, the Hanna Theater, and the cluster of motion picture theaters, night clubs, and restaurants in Playhouse Square on upper Euclid Avenue. The prospect of the move into the central city is one that pleases most Clevelanders mightily. They are personally concerned by such things. Clevelanders, as I mentioned previously, take their culture seriously.

XXVI

A New Face to the Future

ERIEVIEW has been the key word in Cleveland in the postwar renaissance that grew out of widespread public dissatisfaction with the city's downtown appearance, turned seedy by a long, tough depression and the deleterious effects of wartime austerity. By 1945, Tom Johnson's City on a Hill had slumped into a frowzy condition that aroused clamorous calls for action.

The answer, after a painfully long period of self-examination and debate, was the undertaking of the Erieview Project, said to be the most extensive, most ambitious urban renewal program in the United States; a program that gave the city a new downtown skyline by the mid-1960s and promised much more in the way of rehabilitation-in-depth of the central city.

Erieview was related, in its public nature and in its scope, to the earlier makeover of downtown by Mayor Johnson's Group Plan in the opening decades of the modern century. The Group Plan had been a large-scale municipal attack against the civic deterioration that had established cankerous slums in a large section downtown north of Superior Avenue, along St. Clair and Lakeside avenues and reaching from Ontario Street eastward, beyond East 9th Street. Some of the oldest homes and building blocks in the city crowded those shabby neighborhoods, and the total effect was that of a vast rookery in which lawlessness and disease were free to flourish.

While the young city pondered several plans of action, there were developments that helped to solve the problem. The federal, county, and municipal governments simultaneously reached the point of requiring new buildings, and all three planned to construct monumental structures in the baroque style of the day. But Clevelanders who visited the Columbian Exposition in Chicago in 1893 were taken by the outstanding architecture and arrangement of a collection of white buildings which were the inspiration of the famous architect, Daniel H. Burnham. They showed the French influence in maintaining equal height and a related design of their cornices, and they were grouped around the greensward of an open mall.

Cleveland enthusiastically adopted the Burnham Group Plan as its own. Burnham was chosen to promote the plan and to adapt it to the site of the downtown slum area in Cleveland. He was assisted by Arnold W. Brunner and John M. Carrere, leading Cleveland architects. The resulting redevelopment program which was undertaken by the Johnson administration, beginning in 1905, was the largest-scale example of city planning the United States had seen since Pierre Charles L'Enfant designed Washington, D.C., in 1791. The Group Plan cleared 101.4 acres of its man-made ugliness, trucked away the rubble, and built in its place one of the finest collection of public buildings in any city in the nation. This stately group was arranged around a forty-acre park called the Mall—an impressive, open plaza extending from Rockwell Avenue on the south to the very edge of the bluff overlooking the lakefront. This northernmost section of the Mall originally was to have been the site of the Union Terminal, but the Van Sweringens took the matter into their own hands and placed it on Public Square. In so doing, they probably rendered a favor to the city, which now has an open, unimpeded view of Lake Erie, the slips for the ocean craft that now crowd into Cleveland's harbor, the busy east-west shoreway, and the huge Municipal Stadium. All of these lakefront attractions, incidentally, were built on fill land which was created by the city to the north of the railroad tracks that grabbed the choice shoreline acreage during the nineteenth century.

The Mall was given a face-lifting and made more utilitarian at the same time in the early 1960s. The cavernous Public Auditorium, even with its great hall and underground exposition space, had been made semi-obsolete by large new halls in other cities; and in order to enlarge the city's convention center, that section of the Mall from St. Clair Avenue to Lakeside Avenue was excavated for construction of a fourteen-million-dollar underground hall and garage. The addition made the Cleveland facility the largest municipal exposition hall in the United States. It also opened the way to the beautification of the Mall itself. The same Leonard C. Hanna, Jr., who had given the bulk of the family fortune to the Art Museum also left a large amount of money in the hands of a group of trustees headed by Harold T. Clark with orders to dispose of the money in the most beneficial civic direction they might choose to follow. Clark and his associates decided to invest two million dollars to top the Mall with a block-long pool and ten splashing fountains. The redesigned Mall, completed in 1964, gave Cleveland one of the loveliest public parks of any city in the world; a spectacle of Metro-Goldwyn-Mayer dimensions by day or night, summer or winter. It is a setting especially appreciated by camera experts in search of a classic background, lunch-hour strollers, and the hundreds of thousands of persons who attend events in Public Hall. This is

Tom L. Johnson's Group Plan brought up to date; a magnificent mall provided at last with a jewel worthy of its setting.

Close by this outstanding achievement of planners of an earlier decade was a contrasting deterioration that embarrassed the city's pride. The area adjacent to Public Hall, from East 6th Street eastward, remained a sorry slum. And the gateway avenue to the city from the lakefront, East 9th Street, a broad avenue which begins at the water's edge and rises to the higher altitude of the triangular bluff on which the central city rests, was pocked with skid row saloons, empty storefronts, sagging buildings plastered with political signs, and doorways filled with empty bottles. Bleary-eyed castoffs moved tentatively and spraddle-legged through their wine-colored haze up and down the blighted street, and the air of defeat hung over everything. East 9th Street was a blemish that disfigured the most conspicuous part of downtown Cleveland; a strange lapse, considering the importance of the street in the city's plan of movement. Inexplicably, the people who planned Cleveland and the people who developed Cleveland refused to believe that anybody in the town ever would be so neurotic as to want to travel in a north-south direction at any time. Their inability to reckon with the unpredictability of future generations is what made East 9th Street strategically important because it is a no-nonsense street, running south from the lake through the heart of downtown. It is made to order for the modern-day eccentrics who like north-south movement. On the other hand, downtown is laid out with a profusion of wide, straight avenues running from east to west and back again.

So many north-south travelers wound up crashing into solid stone walls and walking through plate glass windows of the storefronts that Cleveland developed a distinctive group of arcades to carry the north-south pedestrian traffic safely through buildings barring their way. The most famous of these arcades is the building known simply as the Arcade, which in reality is two ten-story buildings, one on Euclid Avenue and the other on Superior Avenue, joined by a four-hundred-foot esplanade under a glass-domed roof. The Arcade in 1961 was placed on the federal government's list of historic American buildings.

Only two streets in the downtown area, East 9th and West 3rd, will take travelers to the waterfront, and of these two, only East 9th penetrates the southern part of downtown. West 3rd ends abruptly when it reaches Superior Avenue after a short, but gallant, uphill run of four city blocks.

One reason for the decayed condition of East 9th Street was the gradual decline over the years in the use of the downtown lakefront by shipping interests, prior to the rejuvenating effect of the St. Lawrence Seaway. The old paddle-wheel passenger boats that used to ply the Great Lakes, linking Cleveland with other inland ports, became obsolete and too costly to operate. They gradually were retired from service, and the pier at the foot of East 9th Street which once had accommodated such vessels as the *Seeandbee*, the *City of Cleveland*, the *City of Detroit*, the *City of Buffalo*, the *City of Erie*, and the *Goodtime*, became a lonely, little-used wharf. Except for fishermen and spooners, there was very little traffic on the lower part of East 9th and the street, not surprisingly, fell ill. Clevelanders winced whenever they looked its way, but there was no community urge to administer medication until the St. Lawrence Seaway in the 1950s restored the city to a position of importance once again as a port of general commerce, not just an iron ore receiving port.

Small ocean craft had been touching at Cleveland for close to a hundred years, thanks to the Welland Canal, but the Seaway opened the way to the larger ships and a more profitable maritime commerce. The picturesque long ore boats suddenly were joined by ships from all parts of the world. Their arrival in Cleveland not only provided an exciting new silhouette on Lake Erie's waters, but they also presented an urgent need for development of the neglected waterfront. Only eight berths were available for use by the oceangoing ships when the Seaway opened in 1959. Eight years later, the downtown port could accommodate twenty-one ships at a time. The pre-Seaway average of fifty-eight thousand tons a year handled by the Cleveland port had risen in 1965 to 531,000 tons, and the city was still expanding its facilities to meet the requirements of ships that suddenly were converging on Cleveland from all parts of the world.

The St. Lawrence Seaway did something more than simply create a world port out of Cleveland. It restored the waterfront as an important part of the city and, as a side effect, it introduced a picturesque new element to the downtown scene—throngs of sailors from foreign ships who gave the downtown streets a badly needed touch of romance. The revival of the lakefront turned the city's eyes to the dismaying sight of East 9th Street and all the other dilapidated neighborhoods along the eastern bluff of downtown, reaching all the way back to Superior Avenue and even deeper. This is the area that came to be identified as the target for urban renewal; the area that was called Erieview.

Erieview, launched in 1960 by Mayor Anthony J. Celebrezze, contemplated the rebuilding of some 163 acres—a task that involved the destruction of 237 substandard buildings, the erection of 4.7 million feet of new office space, and a boost in the number of downtown dwelling units from 1180 to 5500 or more. All this was to be done at an estimated cost of $280 million over a period of fifteen years. The designer of Erieview, Architect I. M. Pei of New York, presented his plans for the reconstruction project on November 22, 1960, and they were approved by the city's planning commission three days later— breathtaking speed in a city that likes to move with painful deliberation, and a tipoff to the civic enthusiasm engendered by the proposals to return Cleveland to the ranks of progressive American cities.

The bulldozers moved to the attack early in 1961. The buildings they toppled in the early stages of the renewal effort fell to the ground with hardly a protest from the people of the city and without any regrets—except, perhaps, the venerable old Central Armory on Lakeside Avenue. This ancient building, lacking only a drawbridge and moat to qualify as a setting for King Arthur, stood across from City Hall, and some of the more conservative members of the city administration dabbed at misty eyes to see it go. The medieval conservatism that has characterized so many Cleveland governments moved some onlookers to suggest that most of the mayors who have held office since 1935 would have been more at home with quarters in the armory styled for the Middle Ages than the relatively modern City Hall. But the old redoubt fell under Erieview's crunching forward movement without anybody stepping forward with an offer to man its walls and towers.

So many buildings had been toppled and cleared away by the middle 1960s that visitors to the city, lacking background information, invariably were startled by the scene of destruction. Some of them with a more humanitarian streak had to be restrained from summoning the Red Cross to the scene of obvious disaster. Even in its early stages, however, Erieview has given Cleveland a new skyline and a wholly new orientation toward the long-neglected lakefront. The first building in the urban renewal project was a forty-story dark-green skyscraper given the name of Erieview Tower. Even before the building, second tallest in the city, was completed at its East 9th Street and Lakeside Avenue site, it was a subject of controversy and heated discussion. Its forty stories of dark-green glass and darker-green vertical siding are unrelieved by any glitter or sparkle of adornment. But where some saw only gloom in this rectangular giant, there were enthusiasts who hailed it as a thing of subdued beauty. In direct contrast, the new thirty-two-story Federal Building, also of glass wall construction, stands opposite the Erieview Tower, on the other side of East 9th Street. This government skyscraper has stainless steel facing that gleams and flashes in the sunlight. A lot of pedestrian-taxpayers naturally wondered aloud what kind of metal was used, and federal spokesmen went to great pains to quash the story that it was solid silver.

At any rate, Cleveland is in upheaval in the 1960s and a new city gradually is emerging from the rubble of an exciting history. With sprawling educational institutions like Cleveland State University and

356 A NEW FACE TO THE FUTURE

Cuyahoga Community College becoming major installations in the downtown area, and urban renewal accelerating its pace, the familiar old
outline of the city will grow dimmer by the month. Someday, experts
predict, Cleveland will be the core of a megalopolis that is said to
be building along the axis extending from Detroit to Pittsburgh. It
even may turn out to be the Best Location in the Nation, who knows?
But even if it doesn't scale that lofty promotional peak, it still deserves
to go into the books as one of the most interesting locations you'll find
anywhere—and that, in the minds of the real experts, is the greater
distinction, by far.

INDEX

Greek people, 325
Green, James F., 223
Greenberg, Hank, 251, 280
Greenbriar Suite, 193
Greene, Edward B., 343
Greenwood, Don, 287
Griswold, Solomon, 12
Griswold, Sylvanus, 12
Gromyko, Andrei, 2
Group Plan of buildings, 184, 190, 351–53
Grove, The, 326
Groza, Lou ("The Toe"), 287, 289–90
Gruber's Restaurant, 251
Guardian Bank, 199
Guiteau, Charles J., 121
Gun, Anna, 13
Gun, Elijah, 13

Haas, Sammy, 209
Hale, Odell ("Bad News"), 275
Halket, James, 13
Hall, William B., 13
Halle Brothers department store, 253
Hamilton, James, 13
Hammond, Jane, 112
Hampton, Horton, 196
Hanchet, Luke, 13
Hancock, Winfield S., 121–22
Handy, Truman P., 44, 345
Hanna, Dan R., 146
Hanna, Howard M., 145
Hanna, Leonard, 226, 343, 352
Hanna, Marcus Alonzo (Mark), 64, 118–19, 123–24, 152, 154–66, 169, 171–72, 203, 246, 343
Hanna, Ruth, 203
Hanna, Garretson & Company, 154
Hanna Hash, 247
Hanna Theater, 119, 350
Harbach, Frederick, 44
Harbor Inn, 258
Harder, Mel, 275–76
Harding, Warren G., 246
Hard Luck Joe (race horse), 254–55
Harkness, Charles, 143
Harris, Thomas, 13
Harrison, Benjamin, 123
Harry Fagan's Beacon House, 258
Hart, William, 12
Harte, Bret, 117
Harvard Club, 233–35, 237
Hathaway, Asahel, 12
Hatton, A. R., 248
Havens, Munson, 19
Have Tux, Will Travel, 262
Hawkins, Lawrence J., 130
Hawley, Davis, 32, 268

Hayden, Warren S., 186
Hayes, Rutherford B., 122–23, 209
Heald, Henry T., 345
Health Museum, 308
Health and Welfare Department, 329
Hebebrand, Arthur, 233
Heigh-Ho Silver, 249
Henry, Frederick A., 248
Herald (Cleveland), 82, 93, 98
Herman Avenue, 332
Herrick, Myron T., 172
Hewitt, Isaac L., 116
Hewitt and Tuttle, 64, 154
Hickox, Abram, 37, 41, 52
Hickox, Milo H., 48
Higbee Company, 192
Hill Street, 191
Hilow, William ("Squeaky"), 249, 250–51
Hilton Hotel, 87
Hinman B. Hurlbut Fund, 343
Hippodrome Theater, 261
Hitchcock, Peter, 27, 42
Hobart, Garret, 158
Hockey, 266
Hodge, O. J., 41, 65
Hodge, Velorus, 41
Holbrook, Daniel, 12
Holden, Delia E., 343
Holden, Liberty E., 19, 123, 246, 343, 345
Hollenden Hotel, 207, 209, 223, 240, 246–48, 257, 259
Hollenden House (since 1963), 246
Holley, John Milton, 12, 16
Holmes, Charles G., 217–18
Holmes, Uriel, Jr., 12
Holmes County, 22
Home-rule policy, 234
Honest Yockim, 249–50
Honky-tonks, 257–58
Hook and Ladder No. 1, 122
Hoover, Cassie L., 131
Hoover, Ezekiel, 38
Hoover, Lydia, 130
Hope, Leslie Townes (Bob), 140, 261–62
Hopkins International Airport, 252, 318–19, 322, 340
Horace Kelley Art Foundation, 343
Horse racing, 145, 250, 253
Hostelries, 44, 120
Hostetler, Joseph C., 275
Hough Avenue, 328, 333
Housing, 328, 330, 354
Houston, Lin, 287
Howard, Nathaniel R., 205–8
Howe, Frederic C., 164, 167
Howe, Henry, 103–4

Kosciuszko Avenue, 238
Kovachy, Julius, 212
Kuryer, 327

Labor movement, 47, 239, 241, 243–44,
   304–5, 326, 328
Lackawanna Railroad, 200
Lady Hester, 146
Lady Prevost, 40
Lajoie, Napoleon, 268–70, 288
Lake County, 222, 233
Lake Erie, 1, 4, 7–8, 13, 16, 21, 40, 43,
   58, 61, 82, 94, 103, 114–15, 123,
   153, 198, 217–18, 252, 326, 331,
   338, 352, 354
Lake Erie, Battle of, 40–41, 81–82
Lake Erie Islands, 41
Lake Huron, 116
Lake Shore Bank, 308
Lake Shore Country Club, 69
Lakeside Avenue, 40, 109–10, 258, 351–
   52, 355
Lakeside Hospital, 199
Lake Street, 40
Lake Superior, 115–16, 216
Lake View Cemetery, 77, 123–24, 261
Lake Superior, 115–16, 216
Lake View Cemetery, 77, 123–24, 261
Lakewood, 184–86, 205, 326, 330
Lakewood Baptist Church, 298
Lamb, Joseph, 130–31
Lambright, Middleton, 329
Landis, James M., 242
Landis, Kenesaw Mountain, 70
Landon, Joseph, 7, 13, 21
Land speculators, 50, 164, 184
Lane, Frank, 282
Lanyon, Jimmy, 97
Laurence, 40
Lausche, Frank J., 240–43, 256, 322–23
Lavelli, Dante, 287
La Voz Hispana, 327
Law enforcement, 167, 202–4, 209, 230–
   32, 235–36, 239–40, 243
Leacock, Stephen, 90, 95
Leader (Cleveland), 93, 101, 106, 111,
   121, 173–74, 285
League Park, 268–69, 273–74, 276–77,
   279, 282
Lebanese people, 324
Lecture platform, 117–18, 259
Lee, Jimmy, 223
Lee Road, 181–82
Leinsdorf, Erich, 341
Lemon, Bob, 281
Lewis, Cliff, 287
Lewis, Franklin, 268
Lewis, Ron, 254
Lexington Avenue, 274

Lightning Spitter (Cleveland), 100
Lincoln, Abraham, 89–90, 95, 102, 120,
   122
Lincoln Heights, 346
Linndale, 328
Literary Avenue, 346
Lithuanian people, 326–27
Little Italy, 47
Locher, Ralph S., 329, 340
Lock, John, 13
Long, David, 31–32, 42, 46
Loomis, Luther, 12
Lopez, Al, 281–82
Lorain, 43, 165
Lorain Avenue, 285, 322, 325
Lorain Steel Company, 165
Lorain Street and Woodland Avenue
   Railway, 161
Lord, Samuel P., 12
Love, William, 12
Lowe, K. Elmo, 348
Luce, Henry R., 110–11
Ludlow, 328
Lunte, Harry, 272
Lupica, Charlie, 264–65
Lyman, William, 12

MacAndrew, Evaline, 240, 242
McBride, Arthur B. ("Mickey"), 285–91
McBride, Lucia, 238
McCafferty, Manus, 257
McCallister, Jack, 275
McCarrens, John S., 112–13
McConkie, C. C., 112
McConnell, Frederic, 348–49
McCormick, Medill, 203
McCurdy, Merle A., 329
McDougald, Gil, 281
McGaha, Mel, 282
McGuire, Jim, 270
McIntyre, Joseph, 13
Mack, Connie, 267–69
McKinley, William, 71, 83, 123, 131,
   155–59, 246
McKinney, Price, 217, 219, 222–23, 226
McKinney Steel Company, 222–23
McKisson, Mayor, 87
McMartin, Duncan R., 216
McMartin, Laura, 218–19
Madigan, Joseph V., 113
Magazine of Western History, 53
Mahan, Asa, 346
M. A. Hanna & Company, 155
Mails, Walter ("Duster"), 273
Main Street, 60
Main Street Bridge, 54, 79, 258
Malaria, 34
Mall, The, 80, 87, 190, 341–42, 352
Manry, Robert, 96